Transnational
West Virginia

West Virginia and Appalachia 1
A Series Edited by Ronald L. Lewis

Transnational West Virginia

Ethnic Communities and Economic Change, 1840–1940

**Edited by Ken Fones-Wolf
and Ronald L. Lewis**

West Virginia University Press
Morgantown 2002

West Virginia University Press, Morgantown 26506
© 2002 by West Virginia University Press

First paperbound edition published 2003 by West Virginia University Press
Printed in the United States of America

10 09 08 07 06 05 04   9 8 7 6 5 4 3 2

ISBN 0-937058-76-9 (paperback)

Library of Congress Cataloguing-in-Publication Data

Transnational West Virginia: Ethnic Communities and Economic Change, 1840-1940 /
    [edited] by Ken Fones-Wolf and Ronald L. Lewis.
    p. cm. — (West Virginia and Appalachia ; 1)
    1. I. Title. II. Fones-Wolf, Ken III. Lewis, Ronald L. IV. Series.
    IN PROCESS

Library of Congress Control Number: 2002108955

Cover design by Alcorn Publication Design
Cover Illustration: Courtesy of Library of Congress — LC–USZ62–113735
    *New York — Welcome to the Land of Freedom – An Ocean Steamer Passing the Statue of Liberty: Scene on the
    Steerage Deck*. Frank Leslie's Illustrated Newspaper, July 2, 1887.
Cover Photograph: Courtesy Jim Clark
Printed in USA by BookMasters

Contents

Section IV: Representations of Ethnic Work Communities

Epilogue: Leaving West Virginia

Tables, Charts, and Figures

Chapter 11

Introduction: Networks Large and Small

What is the meaning of the term "Transnational West Virginia"? Aside from a few brief weeks in the spring of 1861, the counties of what became West Virginia were part of only one nation. Significant numbers of its people, however, as the essays in this volume will make clear, drew upon networks, ideas, and cultures that stretched far beyond West Virginia's and even the nation's boundaries to forge and remake their identities. Furthermore, virtually all West Virginians experienced economic, social, and cultural processes that could hardly be contained within a single state's (or a single nation's) borders. Our goal in these essays is to explore the ways in which a few of these larger historical forces, particularly the migrations of people and the development of new economic systems, shaped the politics, culture, and society of one particular region over the course of a century.

The triumph of the "global economy" made economic historians early practitioners of a transnational approach to history. Markets transcended national and even continental boundaries from at least the fourteenth century, and new industrial technologies began to be transported (sometimes smuggled) across borders and oceans routinely by the eighteenth century. Ironically, however, early studies of West Virginia's economic development typically emphasized its physical and cultural isolation, usually as an explanation for the poverty of the mountain communities. Rugged topography prevented Appalachians from connecting to markets and modernizing forces, which resulted in "mental and cultural isolation, holding people in disadvantaged areas, resisting those changes that would bring them into contact with the outside world." Thus, the mountains of West Virginia created a culture of poverty.

Fortunately, subsequent work by historians focusing on the political economy of West Virginia (and Appalachia, more broadly) helped demolish the older stereotypes of an isolated culture of poverty that characterized much of the earlier scholarly work on the state and the region. Over the past thirty years historians have explored the economic transformation of the state within the context of larger narratives of the development of capitalism. In the 1970s and

1980s, such scholars as John Alexander Williams and Ronald Eller utilized an alternative model of internal colonialism to explain local poverty as a result of political, economic, and cultural domination by powerful corporations operating outside of the region. The ownership of land and mineral rights by outsiders doomed the state's economic development.

Other scholars followed the internal colonial model with one that emphasized dependency theory adapted from Immanuel Wallerstein's world systems approach. Utilized by such scholars as Paul Salstrom, David Walls, and Richard Simon, this theory explains the "global spread of modern capitalism in which core and periphery regions develop collaterally within the same institutional structure." Core and periphery regions do not develop equally, however. Periphery regions, like West Virginia, are dependent upon core regions and cannot overcome barriers to development that existed at the onset of industrialization. As applied to West Virginia, this model explains the state's backwardness through its lack of capital and human resources and its inability to generate internal investment that could keep profits in the state. West Virginia's economic development, which relied heavily on the extraction of natural resources, thus was subservient to core commercial and manufacturing centers such as Philadelphia, New York, and Pittsburgh.

Whatever economic model scholars have used, it is clear that West Virginians have been entangled in a web of economic forces and relationships that transcended its political boundaries. Large national and multinational corporations have controlled resources and exerted influence over decisions that disadvantaged local businesses, institutions, and people relative to those of other areas. Typically, representatives of these powerful corporations have attempted to dominate political decision-making as well, obtaining favorable rulings on land and tax policies that have left the state dependent upon factors beyond its control. Attempting to blend insights from all of these approaches, Dwight Billings and Kathleen Blee have suggested that "[c]apitalist markets, state coercion, and cultural strategies worked together to set and keep" the neighboring state of Kentucky on the road to rural poverty.

The century of West Virginia's history we are exploring in these essays was a time of dramatic economic transformation. This is not to suggest that before the extension of the Baltimore & Ohio Railroad (completed to Wheeling in 1852), there was no economic dynamism. Salt-making in the Kanawha Valley, iron-making in the upper Monongahela Valley, and livestock raising all provided opportunities for entrepreneurs to acquire wealth beyond their needs. But economic development temporarily bypassed much of the state with its forbidding terrain and its transportation problems. Not until the post-Civil War railroad boom connected the rich natural resources of the region to manufacturing centers did West Virginia become a major field for capital investment. Then, between 1880 and 1930, the state's economy and landscape was transformed by successive waves of resource extraction, starting with its hardwood forests and proceeding through oil, natural gas, and especially coal.

In many studies, resource extraction has become synonymous with the state's capitalist transformation, and with good reason. In 1920, there were nearly as many coal miners in the state as there were employees of all manufacturing industries combined. By 1930, despite the onset of a depression that slashed employment in coal, mineral extraction accounted for 19.3 percent of West Virginia's workforce, just slightly less than agriculture (20.7 percent) and all of manufacturing and mechanical pursuits (23.4 percent). The impact of this transformation was truly phenomenal; West Virginia produced about 4.9 million tons of coal in 1887 but over 89 million tons in 1917. Equally important, coal brought prominent investors into the state; J. P. Morgan, John D. Rockefeller, and E. H. Harriman were just some of the powerful corporate executives who "competed and connived to build the roads that would carry West Virginia coal." Most of the state's leading politicians also had ties to the industry.

Coal is at the center of the larger context of economic change transforming West Virginia, but the story neither began nor ended there. Inexpensive fuel and improved transportation spurred change in local communities prior to the Civil War, and they opened up other economic opportunities well into the twentieth century. All of these changes resulted in demands for labor that brought massive numbers of migrants through the state. These migrants were a part of an international labor migration triggered by the ascendancy of transnational industrial capitalist economies. It is important that we not reduce these migrants to mere bystanders. Instead, the essays in this volume focus on the movements of people through and within the state largely in response to economic transformation. It is the transnational connections of those people that most concern us in these essays.

Like economic history, immigration and ethnic history has a venerable tradition of employing transnational perspectives, even if the term is of relatively recent vintage. Early practitioners of immigration history traced their lineages to three distinct schools of scholarship, according to Rudolph J. Vecoli, perhaps the most prominent contemporary historian of immigration. On the one hand, pioneering researchers like Frank Thistlethwaite and Marcus Lee Hansen were academic descendants of Frederick Jackson Turner. This school practiced "grass roots history" and coined the phrase "history from the bottom up" in the 1920s. Hansen, for example, prepared to learn five different languages in order to write his magisterial history of the Atlantic migration to the United States. Old World backgrounds of the immigrants were integral to their migrations, at first within national and continental borders, and eventually back and forth across oceans in response to international labor markets. Another school explored the transformation of traditional peasants into modern individuals, utilizing the insights of the Chicago School of Sociology. W. I. Thomas and Forian Znaniecki, for example, studied the social construction of the Polish ethnic community and "cultural adaptations within the city's ethnic enclaves." The final source of this rich sub-field of scholarship owed much to cultural anthropology. In particular, Vecoli cites the insights of pioneering interdisciplinary scholar Caroline Ware who wrote in 1940: "In the still unexplored history of the non-dominant cultural groups of the industrial cities lies the story of an emerging industrial culture that represents the dynamic cultural frontier of modern America."

The best of the recent work on immigration history has returned to the insights of these pioneers in the field. According to David Montgomery, their work focuses "on the transnational networks fashioned by kinsfolk and neighbors that have escorted migrants to their destinations and nurtured a vast array of fraternal organizations, parishes, gymnastic clubs, newspapers, shops, and commemorations." But much of that work relied on urban venues to situate these networks and develop the institutions and artifacts of an ethnic identity. The industrial transformation of West Virginia took place in a predominantly rural setting. As late as 1910 less than 20 percent of the state's population lived in urban areas. Nor did the immigrants of the state ever soar to the high percentages that characterized the populations of cities like Chicago, or factory towns like Lawrence, Massachusetts; never did the foreign-born portion of West Virginians surpass 5 percent, and in 1920 immigrants and their American-born children comprised only one-tenth of the total.

Why then should we study the transnational character of an area where the vast majority of its people were rooted in an indigenous culture? As the essays in this volume will make clear, our response emphasizes two important reasons for *Transnational West Virginia*. First, despite the rural and overwhelmingly native-born nature of the state's people, labor migrants were critical to the economic transformation of the state and the region. For perhaps the most graphic example, during the critical years of the industrialization of McDowell County in southern West Virginia, the African American population grew from 1/10 of 1 percent to over 30 percent. And the contributions of labor migrants began early—immigrants were critical in the construction of the B&O Railroad in the antebellum era—and continued for a century. Virtually every effort to reshape the political economy of the state involved pockets of migrants. Efforts to develop farming in the new state brought German and Swiss immigrants; railroad construction utilized African American and Irish laborers; the coal industry relied on a judicious mixture of southern and eastern European immigrants, supervisory personnel from Great Britain, and blacks escaping the racism of the South. Industries and services that built upon the dynamism of resource extraction also owed much to labor migrants. The pre-Civil War industrialization of Wheeling brought so many immigrants that native-born observers lumped them all together. Manufacturing industries that took advantage of cheap fuel rates in the twentieth century had to import workers with the necessary skills, and coal communities depended upon outsiders with the skills to organize far-flung commercial networks.

In sum, it was the skills and the labor of these migrants that made modern West Virginia. Even in a state and a region that we think of as off the beaten path of major labor migrations, the non-dominant groups that Caroline Ware wrote about contributed to the emerging industrial culture. Although never surpassing 7 percent of the state's population, blacks comprised about one-fifth of the state's coal miners. Germans made up over one-third workers in Wheeling, the most crucial industrial center of the new state of West Virginia in 1863, while southern and eastern Europeans represented one-third of the workforce in the nation's richest coal seam in Monongalia County. Even small numbers of French and Belgian craftsmen were instrumental in making West Virginia one of the leading glass-producing states in the country. Thus, these essays add to a critical re-evaluation of the development of the Mountain State, one that links the history of West Virginia to an international capitalism which spawned the great labor migrations of the late nineteenth and early twentieth centuries.

A second reason behind this collection of essays is to shift the focus away from West Virginia and to explore the "importance of solidarities and processes" that structured the movements of a variety of nationalities. Because we root this in one particular area, this gives us the opportunities to examine "the cultural adaptations within" a state's ethnic enclaves as well as the "changing social relationships between them" as they struggled to come to grips with new meanings of modernity and citizenship. Earlier scholarship has done this for cities, but rarely have historians tried to apply these insights to a rural industrial setting. Moreover, because West Virginia attracted old immigrants, new immigrants, and African American migrants, the collection of these essays enables some comparisons that investigate the importance of race, not only for blacks but also for those "inbetween peoples" who were not clearly in either group in the minds of the older, established residents of the state.

These essays help to reveal the multiple identities of labor migrants that were also both larger and smaller than the nation. Railroad workers in the undeveloped terrain of Preston County identified themselves as Corkonians or Fardowns, not Irish or Irish American, when trying to maintain control over precious jobs, but the Italian migrants of the Kanawha Valley thought of themselves as members of an international syndicalist working class. Meanwhile, Jews and Belgians moved into booming areas through well developed occupational networks that facilitated commercial opportunities for one group and the preservation of craft legacies for the other. As migrant groups transplanted old solidarities in new environments, they interacted with state authorities who • had their own agendas. Swiss farmers arrived at the beckoning of both well-meaning and deceitful immigration commissioners only to find their investments complicated by an archaic system of land titles. Forty years later, the state hoped to attract British immigrant coal miners but was stymied by both federal law and unions. Meanwhile, employers enlarged their labor pool through the use of padrones who skirted laws and ethics to supply southern and eastern European workers. Finally, labor migrants sought citizenship in a new country in settings that often proved hostile. Germans who had experienced the democratic upheavals of 1848 brought their republican ideals to a state in the midst of a titanic struggle over slavery; Greek, Slavic, Hungarian, and Italian coal miners sought freedom and economic opportunity during the post-World War I environment of repressive Americanization and economic collapse; African Americans gravitated to the hope of greater political and economic freedom at a time when coal companies were demonstrating increased control over the lives of their workers.

Transnational West Virginia, then, seeks to contribute to broadening the history of the state by telling some of the stories of the non-dominant cultural groups and to an immigration and ethnic historiography by applying the insights developed in urban settings to a rural industrializing region. The essays will help place West Virginia and Appalachia more firmly in the transnational themes of capitalist transformation and labor migrations, but will also explore some of the more important recent themes of immigration history—the continuity of internal and international migrations, the chains and networks that facilitated movement, the importance of labor markets and market niches, transnational solidarities, and state policies—in one particular setting. We should also admit to some help in this endeavor, particularly the important influence of *Goldenseal*, the magazine of traditional life in West Virginia, which has published some wonderful stories reflecting on the ethnic diversity within the state. Since the 1970s, the magazine has featured articles on Italian, Hungarian, Greek, Spanish, and French (among other) immigrants who collectively helped to create modern West Virginia. The essays in this volume build upon those exciting cultural tales.

The structure of the volume groups the essays around certain themes. The first two essays explore the roots of economic change and the accompanying labor migrations in pre-Civil War western Virginia. Matthew Mason writes about the important lingering provincial identities among Irish railroad laborers who were building the B&O Railroad. Immigrants from Ireland already had twenty years of experience as construction workers on internal improvement projects—first canals and subsequently railroads—in the United States, but famine conditions in Ireland changed the dynamics of emigration. With tens of thousands of impoverished Irish arriving in America, railroad laborers sought jobs that offered steady work for immigrants from their own towns and counties. Connaught men, Corkonians, or Fardown/Longford men relied on local solidarities to monopolize labor crews, albeit local solidarities transplanted in a new nation.

Ken Fones-Wolf examines two successive waves of German immigration and the impact that events in Europe had on Wheeling in the crucial decades before the Civil War. The first wave resulted primarily from a stagnant economy and booming population growth in the 1830s. German immigrants established a thriving community of artisans and small businessmen in an increasingly important center of Ohio Valley commercial and industrial activity. They also made peace with the dominant political culture of a slave state. Then a second wave began in the wake of the 1848 democratic revolutions in Europe. This wave changed the politics of Wheeling by bringing immigrants inspired by visions of new citizenship in the American republic, visions that did not so easily coexist with slavery. In the 1850s, this new German community helped give form and substance to antislavery politics that would eventually lead to the new state of West Virginia.

The second group of essays deals with communities that filled special economic niches in the state's economic development. One of the first items on the new state's agenda was the recruitment of immigrants to buy lands and develop a broader tax base for the fledgling government. In 1864, West Virginia appointed an immigration commissioner to promote the state's rich resources and inexpensive land. Although the position was never adequately funded, the commissioner did have success in attracting several hundred Swiss immigrants who overcame remote locations, competing land claims, and unscrupulous promoters to establish enduring communities. Elizabeth Cometti's engaging tale of Helvetia, which involved research in Switzerland and the United States, was originally published in the 1960s, testifying to an early interest in transnational history.

Deborah Weiner has produced a fascinating study of a much overlooked community in Appalachia, eastern European Jews. Typically studied in the context of particular occupational concentrations in large cities, West Virginia's Jews filled important middlemen roles in the boomtown atmosphere of coal towns. Weiner traces their mercantile talents to their "outsider" role in Russia and Poland. Jews were thus not part of the transnational labor migrations, although they were intricately tied to the economic transformation of the region nonetheless. Although they left Europe as a result of political persecution, they transplanted their culture where opportunities presented themselves.

The success of the coal, oil, and particularly gas industries stimulated other types of opportunities as well. Natural gas development in West Virginia occurred at a critical moment in the mechanization of the window-glass industry. Craft workers faced the potential replacement of their skills and the loss of their autonomy in the huge, new factories being built in Pennsylvania, Ohio, and Indiana. In response, many French and Belgian craftsmen pooled their resources and drew upon the cooperative cultures of their homelands to open factories and continue traditional craft forms of production in the Mountain State. For a generation, Ken Fones-Wolf demonstrates, Belgian window-glass artisans sustained transnational craft communities in places like Clarksburg and Salem, communities connected by technologies, markets, unions, politics, and even war with towns in the Charleroi basin of Belgium.

The third group of essays focuses on migrant communities in the coalfields. While this is one of the more familiar topics in West Virginia history, these essays highlight the important racial and ethnic dynamics that contributed to the state's development. Joe W. Trotter Jr. places the arrival of African Americans in southern West Virginia in the context of a much larger northward migration. Indeed, African Americans routinely moved several times within the South before venturing beyond, and even then kept ties that enabled them to return south when jobs vanished. This migration resulted both from the racism and the boll weevils that pushed African Americans northward and from the attractions of good-paying jobs and political opportunities that drew them into the orbit of modern capitalism. Like southern and eastern European peasants, African American migrations were steps in a proletarianization process that was creating the multiracial American working class.

Frederick Barkey and William Klaus explore the experiences of Italian immigrants in the coalfields. Barkey emphasizes the relations with other groups of miners already present. Mine owners recruited Italians to serve as strikebreakers, with the idea of enabling operators to break the grip that the United Mine Workers had in southern West Virginia. Operators even used unscrupulous padrones to enmesh the Calabrians and Sicilians, who were desperately in need of steady work, in a terribly exploitative system of peonage. But mine owners were unaware of the traditions of spontaneous revolts and labor activism that Italians transplanted in their new home. Ultimately, the 'Talys' of Boomer utilized their connections with internationalist, syndicalist ideas to infuse a new militancy into the struggles of the UMW and to develop a local class solidarity that transcended ethnic divisions. On the other hand, Klaus, who examines

Italians in the north-central West Virginia coalfields, is concerned with a different dynamic, one that treats divisions within the Italian communities rather than solidarities across communities. In the Fairmont area, the date of arrival as well as one's place in the geographic and occupational structures emerging in the area shaped tendencies toward accommodation or conflict. Reinforcing those tendencies was the Catholic Church, which had a much greater presence in Fairmont than in the small surrounding towns. Thus whether an Italian paraded through the streets of Fairmont on Columbus Day or behind a red flag in a strike demonstration depended upon solidarities both larger and smaller than the nation.

The fourth group of essays steps back from the migrant communities and explores the representation of these non-dominant groups in the minds of more established West Virginians. Anne Knowles uses the novella of Rebecca Harding Davis, *Life in the Iron Mills*, to demonstrate just how far removed even sympathetic observers were from the realities of life in ethnic working-class communities. Davis's story, seen by literary scholars as one of the first examples of "realist" fiction, poorly interpreted the lives of Welsh ironworkers. Not only did Davis not have a clear sense of the variety of immigrant cultures she was witnessing, but also she imposed her own values about the mind-numbing nature of blue-collar work onto highly skilled workers who took great pride in their craft and often exhibited a quite sophisticated appreciation of literature and education.

Kenneth Bailey returns to the issue of state agents recruiting immigrant labor for West Virginia's development nearly a half-century after the efforts documented by Elizabeth Cometti. By the early twentieth century state officials wanted labor for the coal mines, but detested the sorts of workers that the mining companies were attracting. Instead of African Americans and the new southern and eastern European immigrants, the state immigration commissioner hoped to attract a "better sort" of coal miner, those from England, Scotland, and Wales. These efforts, however, conflicted with national immigration policy as well as with the interests of the United Mine Workers. Although the union could use federal agencies to block state officials from fulfilling their goals of attracting desirable immigrants, it was ultimately powerless to stem the flow of labor migrants recruited through less savory channels.

By the 1920s, many Americans had developed strong ideas about immigrant communities and their tendency to disturb the dominant social patterns, especially in those areas where large numbers of newcomers challenged the established religious and political institutions or made demands upon local resources. One such area, studied by Ronald Lewis, was Scott's Run in Monongalia County where rich coal seams were readily accessible. There, local groups hoped to balance the constant demand for labor with the community's concerns by Americanizing the immigrants. In one guise Americanization could be quite repressive, demanding social, cultural, and political conformity and enforcing its demands through vigilante groups like the Ku Klux Klan. But Americanization also had a benevolent face, one that sought to narrow the chasm separating struggling immigrants from their hosts. Emerging alongside the Klan were humanitarian educational programs, settlement houses, and reformers who would eventually bring Eleanor Roosevelt to "the Run."

The volume concludes with an essay that suggests the more recent history of the role of labor migrations in West Virginia. Susan Johnson looks at the early years of a more dominant twentieth-century pattern, the out-migration of the state's population. For the past three-quarters of a century, the Mountain State's population has either stagnated or declined. The transnational economic forces that attracted labor migrants began to shift in ways that left West Virginia's economy in a shambles. Long-time residents began to look elsewhere for job opportunities even before the First World War. One of the destinations was Akron, center of an expanding industry that required large numbers of workers capable of performing hard, heavy labor. So many mountaineers went to Akron that the city was nicknamed the capital of West Virginia. But like the labor migrants who maintained networks larger and smaller than the boundaries of states or nations, the migrants to Akron kept ties to their homes, and brought experiences, attitudes, and cultures that transformed the rubber city.

Thus, these essays provide an overview of the impact of international capitalism on the social, cultural, and political history of West Virginia. Shaping that history in critical ways were the immigrants and migrants who brought new skills, political ideas, forms of solidarity, and most importantly their labor to the state. The meaning of the phrase "transnational West Virginia" for us, then, tries to capture both those larger economic forces and the movement of peoples across boundaries, and their centrality in understanding the state. This collection is only a starting point. Among those left out are the migrant laborers who work harvesting fruit in the eastern panhandle as well as the large numbers of female migrants who appear only at the edges. Many groups have received only a modest mention. Greeks, Hungarians, Spaniards, Finns, and Poles, for example, all deserve to have their stories added to this picture, so there is much work yet to be done. Likewise, the more recent labor migrations out of West Virginia and of new groups of Latinos and Asians into the state will certainly demand their place. We hope this volume is a catalyst for such work.

The Editors

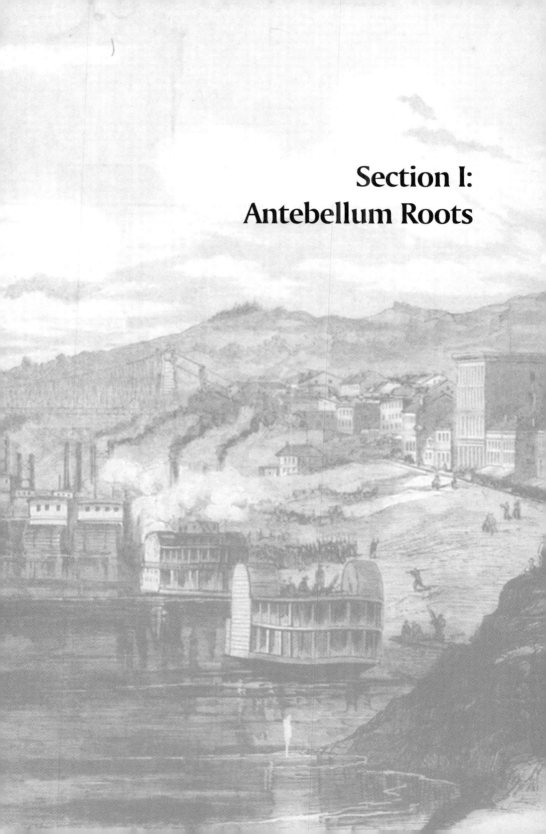

Section I:
Antebellum Roots

"Closing the B&O Line at Rosby's Rock, Christmas Eve, 1852." From Edward Hungerford,
The Story of the Baltimore & Ohio Railroad, 1827-1927 *(New York: G. P. Putnam's Sons,*
1928), 256.

Paddy vs. Paddy: Labor Unrest and Provincial Identities along the Baltimore and Ohio Railroad, 1849-1851

Matthew Mason

In the late 1840s, the Baltimore and Ohio Railroad neared its objective, the Ohio River town of Wheeling. As the workmen under the employ of subcontractors laid track in western Maryland and Virginia, B & O executives and well-wishers looked with anticipation for the completion of this pioneering long-distance railroad. Yet more than the challenging topography of Appalachia threatened to delay the project's fruition. For between 1849 and 1851, labor violence plagued the B & O. The Irish construction workers, also known as trackmen, fought each other ferociously for control of the work.

While railroad construction work was not in demand among native-born Americans, Irishmen placed a high value on it. They had experienced drastic economic insecurity in their homeland for decades. The trackmen who had left Ireland in the wake of the sufferings of the Great Famine were different in degree, but not in kind, from earlier nineteenth-century immigrants; they had all fled a troubled economy which could promise them no consistent support. Regular employment was thus a valuable novelty in the lives of these immigrants, and they were prepared to retain it by any means available.

The trackmen's battles with each other were also part of a struggle to assert their wills against those of their employers, who brought all their power and influence to bear to keep the work going. The company was determined to break the grip of those laborers who would monopolize the work on a particular part of the line, for the B & O was not about to be dictated to by Irish immigrants.[1]

The riots revealed more than the trackmen's willingness to resist their employers, however. They also exhibited the workers' identities. Although the rioters' ultimate object was to resist the policies of their employers, their violence was directed towards their fellow Irishmen. Thus they did not organize themselves along the lines of class in its usual sense. Ireland had a long history of bitter sectarian strife, but in this wave of unrest along the B & O both the attackers and the attacked were Catholics who combined themselves not by class or religion, but by allegiance to their respective home provinces or counties in Ireland. Generations of labor migration within Ireland and Great Britain had forged rival provincial or county identities. Such rivalries had often turned violent in Ireland, as locals formed secret societies to forcibly protest the hiring of workers from another county or province, who typically drove down wages. B & O trackmen found such traditional identities and methods useful in organizing themselves in America. Historians have not widely recognized these identifications, as they have generally stressed the ethnic solidarity of Irish immigrants, forged in the face of American discrimination. Yet these trackmen drew on their Old World experiences and loyalties, rather than an identity constructed in the New World.

For their part, the Marylanders and Virginians along the railroad's path were not well attuned to the subtleties in the rioters' self-identifications. Some, especially newspaper editors, treated them all as Irishmen and applied the requisite stereotypes to them as a whole. Most of the surrounding populace cared less about Irish provinces or control of the line than about the threat to their peace and safety. They therefore sought to suppress what they saw as Irish turbulence, and in the process joined with editors in attaching their own identifications on the rioters. Yet in 1851 the trackmen on the B & O continued to fight each other under labels drawn from their particular parts of the Emerald Isle.

On October 19, 1849, a newspaper editor described foreboding among the citizens of the western Maryland town of Cumberland. By that date the main construction activity on the B & O was just west of Cumberland. He wrote:

> Some fear has been felt in this region lest we should have . . . a repetition of the scenes that occurred in June last on the Central Rail Road in Pennsylvania. The Connaught men at that time were driven from the Pennsylvania work by the Fair-Downs, the latter having swept the line for many miles. The party defeated there are now, for the most part, scattered along the line of the Baltimore and Ohio Rail Road west of this place. Being strong in numbers they have, it is said, indicated a disposition to exclude their opponents from the service of the Company. . . . Of course many scenes of violence may be looked for. Some of them have already occurred which have never been reported.[2]

This article proved prescient. It effectively described the bulk of the conflicts which would ensue over nearly the next two years between Cumberland, Maryland, and Wheeling, Virginia, as factions hailing from certain Irish locales fought for exclusive control of the work.

November 17, 1849, inaugurated this series of riots. On that day, about three hundred trackmen calling themselves Connaught men attempted to drive other workers away from the excavation of the Kingwood Tunnel in Preston County, Virginia. They began "by tearing down and burning shanties, molesting several Americans, compelling them to leave off their work." They also assailed "another party of Irish, (Corkonians and Fardowns) and drove them from their work, threatening their lives, and in many cases accompanying their threats with severe blows." The county sheriff and a posse of about two hundred men marched through a snowstorm to apprehend the ringleaders. The contractors quickly fired the rioters.[3]

The winter of 1850-1851 witnessed more riots, at least one of which was a resumption of the Connaught men's attempt to forcibly secure a monopoly of construction work on certain sections of the B & O. The first large-scale violence occurred west of Cumberland on November 30, 1850.[4] A correspondent of the *Cumberland Alleganian* reported that "it was an attack made by the Connaught men against all others, whether German, Irish or English—they having determined to monopolize the whole work to themselves."[5] A volunteer company, raised by a B & O engineer, stopped the violence for Saturday.

> Thwarted thus in their general operations, a party of about 50 Connaught men made an attack on Monday night on the shantee at Section 43, where a number of Germans were at work. Meeting with resistance, the Irish procured firearms, and breaking open the door of the shantee, fired at the Germans, wounding some eight of them, one man very dangerously; they afterwards set fire to the shantee and burned it with all its contents.

The volunteer force from Cumberland returned, restoring peace and arresting twenty-five of the ringleaders.[6]

The Connaught men's determination "to monopolize the whole work to themselves" clearly motivated these attacks. Although many of the victims hailed from parts of Ireland outside the province of Connaught (some of whom were probably famine immigrants[7]), this was more than a simple party feud among the Irish. The rioters failed in this attempt at monopoly, however, as management responded sharply to this challenge to their control over employment on the line: by December 13, 1850, the Connaught men had been "discharged from the 1st Division of the Road."[8]

The cause of violence was not so evident in reports of an incident west of Cumberland in March 1851. A western Virginia paper reported that "a murderous assault was made upon six or eight men while asleep in a shanty . . . by a party of Irish, numbering, it is said, some 25 or 30." The aggressors, armed with guns, had driven their quarry to the loft of the shanty. Unsuccessful in their attempt to burn the structure down, "they then promised to forebear any further assault provided the assailed would vacate the shanty and leave the work. Relying upon this promise, the latter came out and the assailants immediately attacked them with guns, pistols, clubs and stones, and beat them in the most brutal and savage manner."[9] The report did not specify the composition of the opposing parties or the motive for the attack. The sheriff and constables of Allegany County "succeeded in arresting seven persons supposed to be implicated in the affair,"[10] and in May, the Allegany County Court convicted seven Irishmen—presumably the instigators of the March atrocities—of "assault with intent to murder."[11] Although it appears that the aggressors were Irish, and that they insisted that their rivals "leave the work," expelling six or eight men would probably not have created a monopoly for the attackers. Still, the assault may have been a first step in that direction.

The motive to riot is also difficult to discern in two final incidents reported on the B & O's path to the Ohio. A Wheeling sheet printed word of "a somewhat serious riot" thirty-six miles from that city in May 1851, relating that "the rioters have possession of the road." Once again the company called on the local militia to quell the uprising.[12] On July 9, 1851, about seventy Fardowns attacked the Connaught men who were sleeping in the company town of Greigsville, Virginia, near the Kingwood Tunnel. "Every shanty on the section was attacked," read one report, "and all who did not effect their escape, were more or less beaten; and twenty more seriously injured."[13] The fact that the assailants went after "every shanty on the section" seems to indicate that they wanted to drive all the Connaught men from the area, but some question can be entertained as to whether they seriously considered seventy men a force sufficient to accomplish this object.

These incidents demonstrated that the laborers' attachments to Irish provinces or counties played enough of a role in their lives that they were willing to fight under their respective banners. The B & O workers were not unusual in this regard. Irish laborers on several internal improvements throughout America fought along lines of Irish locality, after having built their shanties in groups according to nativity.[14] One historian, who collected information on riots in the United States, encountered so many regional feuds among Irish immigrant laborers that a typical note reads: "Usual row. Local differences at home." Yet his record demonstrates that "differences at home" were not the only reason they fought. At least two of the frays he documented, one in New York and one in Massachusetts, involved one party seeking to drive another from a railroad.[15] In these instances, as in many along the B & O, "local differences at home" often formed the identities under which men fought for employment on public works in America.

Parochial labor feuds were nothing new to Irish laborers. They were frequent phenomena among seasonal migrants within Ireland and to England, many of whom later emigrated to America. Migrants from one region often undercut the wages of workers in the area into which they moved, creating great hostility between laborers of the respective regions. Differences of language or dialect may have been a divisive force as well.[16]

At least some of the trackmen's attachments apparently were not local in the purest sense, but rather provincial. There were on the B & O three main factions: the Connaught men, the Corkonians, and the Fardowns/Longford men.[17] The Connaught men declared their allegiance not to a county but to their northwestern Irish province. It is unclear whether the other factions' loyalties lay with county or province. County Cork was the largest and most populous of Ireland's thirty-two counties,[18] so men from all over Munster may have chosen a name which recognized the Corkonians' prominence at home and/or among the migrant group. Emigrants from Leinster may have fought under the banner of County Longford simply because it was a leading county for out-migration and may also have formed a large proportion of that province's emigrants; over 20 percent of the county's population left during the years of the Great Famine.[19] The latter two monikers may have represented a truly local attachment to these counties, but it seems unlikely that all Corkonians were from Cork, or that all the Longford men or Fardowns were from Longford. Still, these localities may have provided the vast majority of each respective group.

Were these provincial and county loyalties products of the American scene, constructed by the immigrants in order to deal more effectively with the new situation? Or were they pre-existing affiliations which instigators of riots tapped to protect their group's place on the railroad line? The trackmen settled along the line in provincial groupings, suggesting that they brought their loyalties to the railroad.

Evidence from migration within nineteenth-century Ireland confirms the idea that these attachments had their origins in Ireland. Migrant laborers within Ireland stirred up strong hostility among the inhabitants of their area of destination. Hence, if a laborer was from a neighboring county, the animosity developed for workers from that county, whereas migration between provinces would stir up provincial rivalry. This process had its positive function as well, helping to create not only hatred but loyalty to one's county or province, as the case may be. Ruth-Ann Harris, author of a recent study of Irish labor migration, found that most migration within Ireland was short-distance, or movement from one county to another neighboring county within the same province. The Corkonians and Longford men may have brought the product of this type of migration with them to North American public works: local, county loyalties. At any rate, they drew their group names from such previous loyalties. Yet the inhabitants of the deeply impoverished province of Connaught were much more likely to seek work in other provinces. This propensity, together with general prejudice against the denizens of this least Anglicized and modernized section of Ireland, meant that migrant Connaught harvesters encountered the greatest hostility of all.[20] Hence, the Connaught men were the most likely candidates to assume a provincial, as opposed to a county-level, identity. That these patterns were followed in the naming of factions in the New World suggests that the organization of violence along the B & O took advantage of, rather than created, these factions.

The workers' strategy of monopolizing sections of the line grew out of both their experiences in the Eastern Hemisphere and the condition of employment along North America's internal improvements. Labor migrants to England had been on the receiving end of attempts to dominate a trade. Englishmen, who bitterly resented outside competition, attacked Irish migrants who attempted to work in certain occupations, including railway construction. Irish emigrants in England, in turn, sought to exclude other groups from certain trades.[21]

It would be natural to assume that it would take prejudice and necessity to force Irish immigrants into railroad construction. Trackmen's work was arduous and dangerous, and death from accident, exposure, and disease was frightfully high among them.[22] Though many Irish spokesmen held out hopes that work on internal improvements would be a springboard to land ownership, most of the immigrants who entered this line of work "journeyed from job to job on public works, and had fixed on them the name of 'strollers.'"[23] Furthermore, performing rough, unskilled labor carried a social stigma in much of the United States.[24] Yet far from fighting to get out of such an occupation, certain groups of B & O construction workers fought to establish and protect a monopoly over their respective parts of the line.

Railroad construction was worth fighting for because it offered a blessing of great worth to an Irish immigrant of the laboring class if he could help ensure his group's dominance on the line: relatively steady employment. In the years after the Napoleonic Wars, demand for Irish agricultural exports declined, and the existence of the common day laborer in many areas of Ireland became increasingly precarious. His life was marked by pitifully low wages and a woeful irregularity of work.[25] Wages were low on America's internal improvements as well, and his work days could be reduced by bad weather, bad health, or other forms of bad luck. Especially if he had a family, he barely made ends meet when the work was regular, and the 1840s were a time of decreasing regularity of employment on North American public works.[26] He might rescue a degree of certainty out of this very contingent situation if his faction could monopolize the precious work on part of the B & O line.

Historians have largely neglected the importance of such factionalism for Irish-American identity in the nineteenth century. Although territorial loyalties and feuds were a part of the nineteenth-century Irish experience, historical orthodoxy holds that Irish migrants rather quickly discarded their provincialism, uniting as Irishmen and Irishwomen in the face of discrimination abroad.

"The effects of migration," one typical scholar asserts, "reduced regionalism. The Tipperary countryman who would not tolerate his fellow countryman from Connacht [sic] was forced when he worked alongside him in England to accept their common nationality. Irish nationalism was thus forged out of experiences such as this."[27] Students of Irish immigrants in America have argued that they banded together to resist assimilation, pursuing a strategy of ethnic solidarity. Indeed, the common wisdom is that the American exiles "became more Irish than the Irish who stayed at home."[28]

This description does not fit the Irish trackmen of the B & O. To be sure, the experience of these men and their families who lived with them was not typical of Irish immigrants. They lived and worked in relative isolation, laying track largely in the countryside and associating mostly with men in their own line of work, as did railroad men of all occupations.[29] Most of the B & O trackmen had sold their labor to construction contractors soon after arriving in New York or Baltimore, and Irish exiles on American public works were generally new arrivals, not far removed from the influences of their native land. Although the internal improvement laborers' situation was unique, it is significant that they pursued a strategy of regional, not ethnic, solidarity. *These* Irish were not yet "more Irish than the Irish who stayed home" in terms of identity. Nor did they do that which is often portrayed as the only alternative to a new Irish nationalism—assimilate quickly to American culture. They identified with—and against—each other in a way not usually acknowledged by historians of their compatriots.[30]

On only one occasion did the trackmen demonstrate the kind of cohesiveness attributed to Irish Americans. This was a strike in March 1850, in which it was reported that the construction workers halted work "with great unanimity upon almost every Section under contract." "The unanimity," asserted one writer, "proves that it had been maturely premeditated."[31] Further evidence of coordination came from another railroad. "The men on the entire line of the Central Rail Road in Pennsylvania stopped work on the 1st of March, with a demand for higher wages," wrote a worried observer.

> We have not heard from the Central Road in Virginia, but we should not be surprised if there was concert of action among the laborers on the public works throughout the United States, in reference to this subject. It is a well known fact that they employ confidential agents, through whom they communicate, secretly, with operatives engaged on another section, or even in another state. The order comes, and *it must be obeyed*, or else there is a riot, and the mandate is thus carried out perforce....This is a common history of such transactions.[32]

Such speculations surely exaggerated the extent of the 1850 strike; if it truly had spread "throughout the United States," it would have drawn a great deal of attention from contemporaries and historians. But the report points to the relatively widespread nature of the strike, and to the existence among track-men of a network which certainly resembles later union organizations. This network was at least a brief attempt to communicate the objectives and en-force the chosen means of its leaders in a rough form of collective bargaining with the respective railroads. It may represent an instance of inter-factional cooperation in the place of the usual conflict; perhaps they were willing to let a rising tide of wages lift all boats so long as their vessels were securely anchored to their respective sections of the line.

The strike also demonstrated another Old World continuity, for the strik-ing workmen apparently drew on the secret societies which have long been common amongst Catholics in Ireland. One writer has maintained that secret societies "represent a permanent feature of Irish life."[33] Their main objectives have traditionally lain in the realm of economic questions such as land owner-ship. They have often scored successes related to labor issues—so many that an early twentieth-century English observer earlier described them in the ag-gregate as a "vast trades union for the protection of the Irish peasantry."[34] Nineteenth-century secret societies were most often organized by "labourers or very poor tenants"[35]—in other words, people of the very social strata from which the B & O trackmen came.

The actions of the Ribbonmen, the name under which many secret orders flourished in the Irish countryside during the years the B & O was being built, seem the clearest antecedent for certain practices among B & O construction workers. The Ribbonmen's activities "were almost invariably concerned with a specific issue—a particular eviction, a rise in rents, a protest against the em-ployment of labourers from another county."[36] The B & O riots of 1849-1851 strongly resembled the Ribbonmen's use of violence as "a protest against the employment of labourers from another county." Historian Peter Way has shown that secret societies of Irish laborers were in continuous existence along the nearby Chesapeake and Ohio Canal.[37] George Potter has argued that Irish se-cret societies traveled intact across the Atlantic to public works, growing to be large organizations with headquarters in New York. He may have exaggerated the geographical extent and coordination of the societies, but they do seem to have flourished on the soil traversed by Irishmen building North America's in-ternal improvements. The secret society that seems to have been behind the March 1850 strike achieved inter-factional cooperation, an aberration in the provincial factions' usual relations.

Although the construction workers worked to some degree in isolation in sparsely populated western Maryland and Virginia, they did interact with sev-eral neighboring communities. This was true mostly in relation to their riots, however. The trackmen's turbulence thus tended to confirm the stereotypes native-born Americans held of Irishmen. Thus the relations between the itinerant laborers and the locals gave the latter occasion to lump the former together under a pejorative collective identity.

In the late 1840s and early 1850s, the newspapers of western Virginia and Maryland articulated a harshly negative image of Irishmen. Their editors found room for several anecdotes featuring incredibly stupid Irish characters. These specimens were not so much uneducated as they were dimwitted.[38] The papers of Charlestown, Virginia, regaled their readers with a tale of a young Irish swindler,[39] and one of "a blundering son of Erin, who, with the peculiar tact of his countrymen, was eternally getting into hot water."[40] A revealing article from 1850 described "A Real Irishman":

> An Irishman builds him a turf stye, gets his fuel from the bogs, digs his patch of potatoes, and then lives upon them in idleness: like a true savage, he does not think it worth while to work that he may better himself. . . . Their love of "fun" eternally engages them in mischievous combinations, which are eternally baffled by their own blessed instinct of blundering.[41]

Beyond such stories, these papers perpetuated local traditions based on experiences with the pugnacious Irishman, and were quick to report any more recent skirmishes. In March 1850, a Hagerstown sheet marked "the 28th anniversary of the battle of Funkstown, which it will be remembered by our older citizens, was fought between the Irish working upon the Turnpike and the citizens of that town." Predictably, "a 'Paddy' was the cause of the feud."[42] In contemporary news, Irishmen assaulted at least two citizens of Cumberland, and brought their factional rivalries to the streets of that town.[43] The representations of the Irish in these newspapers emphasized the nature rather than nurture of "Paddy." Irishmen were a racialized and homogenous "Other," with barbarism and blundering as inherited national instincts.

The press coverage of the strikes echoed this negative general image. Only one sympathetic editorial response to the B & O trackmen in their struggles with their employers appeared between 1849 and 1851. In its coverage of the March 1850 strike, the *Cumberland Civilian*, while not exactly supporting the strikers, sympathized with their inability to accept the low wages and high food prices dealt them by the contractors. The editor decried such treatment, which kept the workers "merely at the *living point*."[44] Most editors, however, regarded the Irish as savages, and explained their violence accordingly. During the Kingwood Tunnel riot, one indicated, there were "deeds of violence committed, which will probably never be judicially investigated, as these people, like the Indians, generally carry off their slain."[45]

On the whole, the local inhabitants joined the editors in reprobating those whom they called Irishmen, and feared the consequences to them of their violent dispositions. Expressions of compassion from the B & O trackmen's neighbors were not unheard of. For instance, farmers along the line helped to feed some of the strikers of March 1850.[46] Significantly, however, the farmers' sympathy with their grievances was not impaired by fear of the trackmen attacking them. If there was violence in connection with the strike, it was aimed at the strikers' fellow laborers and did not threaten these farmers. This was to be the only occasion on which the locals supported the laborers.

The B & O's Appalachian neighbors, alarmed for their safety, consistently lent their support to the railroad management in its drive to control its laborers. Time and again they sent their militia or volunteers out to the scene of violence, at the company's behest and to protect their communities. Yet this ad hoc system of law enforcement proved inadequate to the task.[47]

In 1849, the company moved to remedy this situation, much to the delight of the inhabitants of the railroad's frontier. In response to the November riot at the Kingwood Tunnel, the contractors in the area, at the suggestion of B & O official Benjamin H. Latrobe Jr., "hired 25 men at $1.25 per day, armed with muskets and bayonets, to travel the line and quell any disturbances." The contractors clothed them with "authority to arrest persons engaged in riotous acts, dead or alive."[48] This police force was probably the first in railroad history.[49]

At the commencement of the March 1850 strike, however, the police force was nowhere to be found. Though the force was originally "designed to be permanent during the continuance of the work,"[50] the contractors had not been sufficiently prompt in paying the volunteers' wages, and the policemen disbanded.[51] The strikers' attempts to enforce solidarity brought the police back rather quickly. A couple of weeks into the walkout, several workers went back to work, "but were persuaded or compelled to suspend operations by the laborers who were still standing out."[52] Some men working in the shafts of the tunnel, Latrobe reported, "were threatened and even shot at by the malcontents," and the armed police were reinstated to stand guard; otherwise, they "must have been compelled to suspend their labor." In light of these events, Latrobe proposed to Thomas Swann, the company's president, that the company join with the contractors to keep the police force in constant operation. "The authorities of the county," he assured Swann, "confer all the requisite civil and military powers upon the persons employed in the police service, so that all their official acts will be under the shield of the law—and will be sustained by the citizens who enjoy the protection which the measure will afford them, and which they can obtain in no other way."[53] Here was telling evidence of western Virginians' support of and utter reliance on the private police force to keep the peace while railroad construction progressed nearby.

Latrobe's subsequent missives described the success of the private constabulary. In 1850, he related that it had "preserved good order, . . . as far as its range extended."[54] Public constabularies and militia had to help put down the riots of March and May 1851. Still, Latrobe was triumphant in August 1851. "The hands here are disposed to be turbulent," he regretted to say, "but the police employed keep order. I may take occasion to say that this system of an armed police force, has been adopted upon the Pennsylvania rail road and with results as satisfactory as upon this line. Indeed it is admitted to be indispensable."[55] As late as December 1852, when the line was nearly complete to Wheeling, the armed guards played an active role in keeping the peace on the line.[56] The company had at once rendered its labor force more tractable and reassured the neighboring populace. In their reciprocal efforts to eliminate the railroad violence they had acted upon the Irishmen as a unit.

But if the native Americans they dealt with tended to lump them together, so long as the Connaught men or Corkonians needed the rough labor of building America's nineteenth-century infrastructure, they would organize themselves in provincial rather than national or even class terms. To be sure, the kind of intra-ethnic strife the B & O trackmen engaged in served in time as the seedbed of not only class but ethnic identity, and class and ethnicity have long served as overlapping identities for Americans.[57] Yet as late as 1851, the hills of western Maryland and Virginia hosted trackmen who identified themselves not as Irish but as men hailing from particular provinces in Ireland.

NOTES

1. The 1849-1851 riots were the second series of such battles on the B & O. Between 1829 and 1834 the line was the scene of recurring labor unrest, most of it surrounding similar issues of control of the work. For a fuller history see Matthew E. Mason, "'The Hands Here Are Disposed to Be Turbulent': Unrest among the Irish Trackmen of the Baltimore and Ohio Railroad, 1829-1851," *Labor History* 39 (Aug.1998): 253-72. For a general history of the construction of the B & O, see James D. Dilts, *The Great Road: The Building of the Baltimore and Ohio, the Nation's First Railroad, 1828-1853* (Stanford, Calif.: Stanford University Press, 1993).

2. *Cumberland [Md.] Civilian*, 19 Oct. 1849.

3. *Fellowsville [Va.] Democrat*, cited in *Cumberland [Md.] Alleganian*, 24 Nov. 1849. See also *Cumberland Civilian*, 16 and 23 Nov. 1849.

4. *Cumberland Civilian*, 25 Oct. 1850, included a report from a Uniontown, Pennsylvania, paper of "rumors of a terrible riot, with immense loss of life, among the laborers" at the Kingwood Tunnel. The folks at the *Civilian*, however, were "inclined to believe the rumor is without foundation," and printed no further mention of such a riot.

5. *Cumberland Alleganian*, 7 Dec. 1850.

6. *Cumberland Civilian*, 6 Dec. 1850.

7. B & O Chief Engineer Benjamin H. Latrobe Jr., reviewing these difficulties, wrote of how "2,500 men were brought from New York in the winter of 1850-51, and distributed among the several contracts as far West as Cheat River, 75 miles from Cumberland; and although every proper inducement was offered to retain them, more than half soon dispersed." He attributed their delinquency in part to the factional strife of the Irish, and since the November 30-December 2, 1850 riot was apparently the only major strife in the winter of 1850-51, the famine immigrants must have been among its victims. *Twenty-seventh Annual Report of the Baltimore and Ohio Railroad* (Baltimore: John Murphy and Co., 1853), appendix, 5-7. See also Dilts, *The Great Road*, 359-60.

8. *Cumberland Civilian*, 15 Mar. 1850.

9. *Banner* (Fairmount, Va.), cited in *Cumberland Alleganian*, 29 Mar. 1851.

10. *Cumberland Alleganian*, 29 Mar. 1851.

11. Ibid., 24 May 1851.

12. Ibid., 10 May 1851.

13. Ibid., 19 July 1851.

14. *Niles' Weekly Register* (Baltimore) 45 (1834): 366, 382, 399; 46 (15 Mar. 1834): 35; 60 (5 June 1841): 224. See also Benjamin H. Latrobe Jr., Journals, 27 Jan. 1834, Box 5, MS 1638, Mrs. Gamble Latrobe Collection, Maryland Historical Society, Baltimore; Peter Way, *Common Labour: Workers and the Digging of North American Canals, 1780-1860* (New York: Cambridge University Press, 1993), 193-8. Andrew Leary O'Brien's account of his brief stint as a canaller in Pennsylvania, read with caution on account of his class bias, provides a vivid picture of the ongoing and often senseless violence of these rival factions (Annette McDonald Suarez, ed.,

The Journal of Andrew Leary O'Brien [Athens: University of Georgia Press, 1946], 30-2).

15. David Maydole Matteson Papers, Manuscript Division, Library of Congress, Washington, D.C., Boxes 2-4, quotation in Box 4.

16. See Ruth-Ann M. Harris, *The Nearest Place That Wasn't Ireland: Early Nineteenth-Century Irish Labor Migration* (Ames: University of Iowa Press, 1994), xiii-xv, 91-2, 98-9. O'Brien ascribed the divisions in part to Northerners' resentment of a perceived lack of valor in the Irish Revolution of 1798 on the part of the militia of County Kerry (*The Journal of Andrew Leary O'Brien*, 30).17.   Both historian George W. Potter (*To The Golden Door: The Story of the Irish in Ireland and America* [Boston: Little, Brown, & Co., 1960], 342) and contemporary O'Brien (*The Journal of Andrew Leary O'Brien*, 30) indicate only two factions, conflating the Fardowns and Connaught men into one Northern faction set against the Corkonians; but on the B & O, Connaught men fought Fardowns as well as Corkonians and vice versa, as in the Nov. 1849 and July 1851 riots.

18. James S. Donnelly Jr., *The Land and the People of Nineteenth-Century Cork: The Rural Economy and the Land Question* (London and Boston: Routledge and Kegan Paul, 1975), 2.

19. Ibid., 125. Potter indicates that the moniker "Fardown" has been attached to inhabitants of Ireland's northern counties since the ninth century, when the northern city of Armagh, "which was 'far down' from the rest of the country," was the center of learning on the isle. It seems to have had reference to the low elevation of the northern countryside (*To the Golden Door*, 328n; see also *The Journal of Andrew Leary O'Brien*, 30).

20. Harris, *The Nearest Place That Wasn't Ireland*, 75-100, quotation on 92.

21. Ibid., 157, 159.

22. Contemporaries estimated that one of every four builders of American railroads died of work-related causes; that their mortality rate was three times higher than that of men in other walks of life; and that more Irishmen died working railroads than on emigrant ships (Potter, *To the Golden Door*, 340).

23. Ibid., 317.

24. Peter Way describes how Irish dominance of canal work led to a stereotype, similar to that which assumed that people of African descent were better suited for labor in hot weather, which assumed "that the Irish were more suited to strenuous work than their Anglo peers" (*Common Labour*, 90). Ira Berlin and Herbert G. Gutman have demonstrated that Irish immigrants to the Southern United States were highly concentrated in unskilled trades, which "identified the Irish with the slave, [while] native-born Southern whites insulated themselves from such imputations" ("Natives and Immigrants, Free Men and Slaves: Urban Workingmen in the Antebellum American South," *American Historical Review* 88 [December 1983]: 1175-1200, quotation on 1187). Any dispute over how "Southern" the route of the Baltimore and Ohio Railroad is or was would be endless, but the track does lie below the Mason-Dixon Line. More significantly, it is certain that the Irish trackmen were "identified with the slave," for they

worked directly with bondsmen, at least at first, and the work required no special skill (see Mason, "'The Hands Here,'" 254, 260).

25. Donnelly, *The Land and the People of Nineteenth-Century Cork*, 19-22; Harris, *The Nearest Place that Wasn't Ireland*, 45-6.

26. Way, *Common Labour*, 115-22, 238-9.

27. Harris, *The Nearest Place That Wasn't Ireland*, 192.

28. Milton M. Gordon, *Assimilation in American Life: The Role of Race, Religion, and National Origins* (New York: Oxford University Press, 1964), 134-6; Kerby A. Miller, *Emigrants and Exiles: Ireland and the Irish Exodus to North America* (New York: Oxford University Press, 1985), esp. 237-8; Ronald Takaki, *A Different Mirror: A History of Multicultural America* (Boston: Little, Brown, and Co., 1993), 9; D. George Boyce, *Nineteenth-Century Ireland: The Search for Stability* (Savage, Md.: Barnes and Noble, 1991), 139 (quotation).

29. Walter Licht, *Working for the Railroad: The Organization of Work in the Nineteenth Century* (Princeton, N.J.: Princeton University Press, 1983), 231-6.

30. Peter Way, however, does recognize that region was more important than "Irishness" for the canallers he studied (*Common Labour*, 193-8). George Potter hit the mark when he wrote about the persistence of these factions, which he called secret societies, as "a separate episode" in the history of the Irish in America, yet a significant one (*To The Golden Door*, 336).

31. *Cumberland Civilian*, 8 Mar. 1850. See also *Cumberland Alleganian*, 9 Mar. 1850.

32. *Cumberland Civilian*, 15 Mar. 1850.

33. T. Desmond Williams, ed., *Secret Societies in Ireland* (Dublin: Gill and MacMillan Limited, 1973), 6.

34. Ibid., 8, 26-8, 71, quotation on 8.

35. Boyce, *Nineteenth-Century Ireland*, 25.

36. Williams, *Secret Societies in Ireland*, 31.

37. Way, *Common Labour*, 214-28, quotation on 214.

38. *Cumberland Civilian*, 7 Dec. 1849; *Shepherdstown [Va.] Register*, 5 and 26 Mar. 1850.

39. *Spirit of Jefferson*, 25 Apr. 1848.

40. *Virginia Free Press*, 24 May 1849. This paper also printed a story describing two dimwitted Irishmen under the headline, "MORE PADDYISM" (14 Mar. 1850), and a piece presenting a caricature of "An Irishman's Speech" (13 Dec. 1850).

41. *Shepherdstown Register*, 26 Feb. 1850.

42. *Hagerstown [Md.] Herald of Freedom*, 20 Mar. 1850.

43. *Cumberland Civilian*, 2 and 23 Nov. 1849; 20 Sept. 1850.

44. Ibid., 15 Mar. 1850.

45. Ibid., 16 Nov. 1849.

46. Ibid., 8 Mar. 1850.

47. Indeed, the history of the riots on the B & O revealed the truth of Michael Feldberg's observation that a common feature of Jacksonian America was "the inability of public officials to prevent or suppress riots before they required the intervention of military troops." There were no real police forces as we know them today in antebellum America, leading to a reliance on unreliable volunteers

or the militia. See *The Turbulent Era: Riot and Disorder in Jacksonian America* (New York: Oxford University Press, 1980), 27-8, 108-12, quotation on 27.

48. *Fellowsville Democrat*, cited in *Cumberland Alleganian*, 24 Nov. 1849. See also Latrobe to Thomas Swann, 11 Dec. 1849, in "Reports, B&O Rr. Co." Letter Copybook, B & O Railroad Museum, Baltimore.

49. Walter Licht dates railroad police vaguely from "at least 1855," with no mention of the force in question (*Working for the Railroad*, 122). There was some precedent from canals. As early as 1830, the C & O Canal vainly petitioned Maryland's state government to establish a police force for them, and C & O contractors saw canal police as the solution to their troubles with secret societies and labor unrest later in that decade. Canada's Board of Works employed a police force along its country's canals in the early 1840s, but they were not very effective (Way, *Common Labour*, 196, 212, 225-27, 249-50, 253, 260-1). Nor were they private police, so the B & O may still be the first internal improvement to employ its own force.

50. Latrobe to Swann, 11 Dec. 1849, "Reports, B&O Rr. Co."

51. Latrobe to Swann, 8 Apr. 1850, ibid.

52. *Cumberland Alleganian*, 16 Mar. 1850.

53. Latrobe to Swann, 8 Apr. 1850, "Reports, B&O Rr. Co."

54. *Twenty-Fourth Annual Report of the Baltimore and Ohio Railroad* (Baltimore: John Murphy and Co., 1850), 51.

55. Latrobe to Fielding Lucas, 12 Aug. 1851, "Reports, B&O Rr. Co." "The hands" on internal improvements did not share Latrobe's affection for private police, in part because the policemen's wages came out of the construction laborers' pay (Potter, *To the Golden Door*, 339-40).

56. Dilts, *The Great Road*, 360.

57. See David A. Gerber, *The Making of an American Pluralism: Buffalo, New York, 1825-1860* (Urbana and Chicago: University of Illinois Press, 1989), 113-20, for an excellent discussion of how ethnicity emerged from the very process of intra-ethnic conflict. For another valuable example from the literature on the interaction of class and ethnicity in America, see David Montgomery, "The Shuttle and the Cross: Weavers and Artisans in the Kensington Riots of 1844," *Journal of Social History* 5 (1972): 411-46.

"Wheeling, Virginia, Showing the Suspension Bridge and Embarkation of the German Rifles, Captain Plankey, 1861." Sketch by J. A. Faris, from the Oglebay Mansion Museum Institute, Wheeling, W.Va.

Caught between Revolutions:
Wheeling Germans in the Civil War Era

Ken Fones-Wolf

On the evening of October 11, 1860, a troop of mostly German "Wide Awakes" paraded their support for Abraham Lincoln in the north end of Wheeling. At Colonel Thoburn's house, the German Company C of the Wide Awakes received a wreath for its valiant support of Republicanism. As the demonstration worked its way through the streets, opponents of the "Black Republicans" responded by throwing stones at the rear of the line. Moving further up Main Street near the First Ward Hose house, the paraders found one intersection blocked. When they stopped to remove the barriers, a group of "ruffians" hurled stones and bottles while others pored in behind the Wide Awakes to set the trap. With no help in sight, the Wide Awakes decided to fight back, wading into the mobs on both sides using torches as their weapons and eventually dispersing their tormentors. Three more times, the parade ranks broke to fight off attacks, before speedily reforming their parade and returning to safer quarters. Approvingly, the Wheeling *Intelligencer* praised the Wide Awakes who "stood their ground like men who know their right."[1]

Reading the *Intelligencer* in the fall of 1860 might lead one to believe that the vast majority of Germans in the city were strong supporters of Lincoln in the upcoming presidential contest. After all, many Americans felt that Germans, especially those who lived in urban areas, were hostile to slavery.[2] Moreover, the German Wide-Awakes had already earned plaudits from their counterparts as far away as Pittsburgh "for their independent manliness in being Republicans in a Slave State" and for standing up to "dastardly scoundrels" who threw stones at Republican gatherings.[3] However, Germans probably also comprised a significant portion of the "ruffians" who cornered the Wide Awakes on the evening of October 11. The first ward of Wheeling was one of the most German wards in the city, and key leaders of the Douglas Democrats were north end Germans. The Wide Awakes, in contrast, came mostly from the south end of Wheeling or from Ritchietown, just beyond the city limits.[4]

The fighting between these two groups of Germans was more than a turf war. Instead, this division helps provide insight into the remaking of the German-American community in Wheeling in the middle of the nineteenth century.

This remaking owed a great deal to the revolutions of 1848 that shook Europe, and particularly many German states. In the aftermath of failed uprisings emigration greatly accelerated, sending a flood of newcomers to such burgeoning midwestern urban centers as Cincinnati, St. Louis, and Detroit.[5] This influx helped change the social, economic, and political makeup of those cities. Likewise, German immigrants changed Wheeling's landscape during the 1850s in ways that would collide with the growing sectional conflict threatening to divide the United States. Thus, Wheeling's Germans were caught between two revolutions, one that drove them from their homelands and one that would draw them into the streets in 1860, into a brutal Civil War, and eventually into the new state of West Virginia.

The story of Wheeling's Germans contributes to our understanding of this critical era on several levels. First, it explores the political behavior of urban Germans in a slave state, offering an example for comparison with work done on German politics in free states. Second, it suggests some insights into the complex mix of factors that divided this ethnic community and contributed to the inconsistent voting patterns historians have long noted. Third, it highlights the important contributions Germans made in keeping the border regions attached to the Union, greatly facilitating the eventual triumph of the North in the Civil War.[6] Wheeling's Germans helped make the city a haven of pro-Union sentiment that ultimately resulted in the creation of West Virginia. Finally, this story highlights the important trans-national character of German-American politics, a politics shaped by events in Germany and America.

Wheeling in 1850

In 1850, Wheeling was a bustling industrial town with a population of 11,435 and a diversified economy. With iron, nail, glass, and textile factories leading the way, it ranked third in all of Virginia in manufacturing, employing nearly two thousand persons.[7] Benefiting first from the National Road, Wheeling early staked its claim to preeminence in northwest Virginia. Although already far behind Pittsburgh in population and industrial development, the designation of Wheeling as the terminus of the Baltimore and Ohio Railroad (B&O) positioned it to renew that urban rivalry. The erection of a suspension bridge across the river in 1849 threatened to make Wheeling the hub of Ohio River commerce, and evoked a frantic legal battle with Pittsburgh and Pennsylvania that reached the United States Supreme Court in 1852.[8]

Wheeling occupied an unusual place in the explosive sectional politics characterizing the 1850s. North of the Mason-Dixon Line in an area with a minimal attachment to slavery, the city resembled its midwestern counterparts more than its sister cities in Virginia. Most noticeably, Wheeling had few African Americans (less than 1 percent), while free blacks and slaves made up between 20 and 40 percent of the male industrial workforce of Richmond, Lynchburg, and Petersburg. In contrast, 86 percent of Wheeling's 1850 household heads were born outside of Virginia, including many in the North, and more than half of its voting-age males in 1860 were either immigrants or their sons. Comparable ratios for Lynchburg and Petersburg would have ranged between one in four and one in six.[9] Although smaller than Petersburg, Wheeling had a greater portion of its adult male population involved in manufacturing. Moreover, Wheeling industry relied to a far lesser degree on agricultural products or the trappings of a slave economy than Richmond, Lynchburg, or Petersburg did.[10]

In politics, however, Virginia's cities shared similar Whig inclinations in the early 1850s. The Whig program of expanded internal improvements and banks as well as higher protective tariffs appealed to urban manufacturing interests present in Wheeling and other Old Dominion urban centers. Although careful to distance themselves from the antislavery elements of Northern Whigs, party spokesmen in Wheeling continually praised the American Plan of Henry Clay and sought greater state support for the transportation and capital resources necessary to enable the city to compete with Pittsburgh. In most of these endeavors, Tidewater agrarians frustrated the Wheeling business interests.[11] Between the 1820s and the 1850s, these differences fostered sectional tensions within the state of Virginia. Westerners resented the political dominance of the Tidewater region and the state government's neglect of the needs of the trans-Allegheny region. By a vote of 643 to 3, Wheeling citizens overwhelmingly rejected the Virginia Constitution of 1830 that kept in place a representation system giving eastern counties a decided advantage in the state legislature. Westerners also resented state tax policies that fell heavily on their internal improvements and lightly on the assets of Tidewater slaveholders. Two decades later, trans-Allegheny counties made some gains in the convention bill that finally passed in 1850, but the mixed basis of white population and property still gave the eastern counties a seventy-six to fifty-nine advantage in delegates to the state legislature.[12]

Despite frustrations, Wheeling's business leaders gained important benefits from the state government. When Pennsylvania won a Supreme Court decision against the Wheeling suspension bridge on the grounds that it inhibited river commerce and could thus be regulated by Congress, Virginia's congressional delegation successfully lobbied for an act protecting the bridge as a part of the post road and requiring boats "not to interfere with the elevation and construction of said bridge."[13] Virginia also assisted Wheeling by requiring the B&O Railroad to create its terminus at that city, even if the legislature's intent was to prevent the B&O from intruding into Richmond's commerce. For southern business interests hoping to tap the trade of Ohio and the Midwest, this designation promised much. At the opening of the B&O, Wheeling leaders paid homage to its place in sectional politics; L. W. Gosnell toasted the railroad that brought forth the twin sisters of Baltimore and Wheeling. He added that soon "the West will marry one and the South the other, and join together, in bands of steel, their future destiny."[14] Finally, the state government blocked the right-of-way of a competing railroad line through the northern panhandle of Virginia, a development that aided Wheeling at the expense of Pittsburgh.[15] Thus, in terms of politics, Wheeling developed something of a split personality. In local and state elections, the city generally gave support to Whig candidates, but in the 1850s it voted for a Democrat to represent the district in Congress. Wheeling political and business leaders relied on Virginia's power to protect local commercial interests. The growing presence of Germans in Wheeling only added to this complexity.

Germans were among the early European-stock settlers who arrived in the Wheeling area in the eighteenth century. By the 1830s, they mixed with large numbers of Scots Irish immigrants and northern migrants to help make the trans-Allegheny portion of Virginia much more diverse economically and ethnically more cosmopolitan.[16] Over the ensuing twenty years the German ratio would increase as a result of conditions in Europe. Through the mid 1840s the German economy experienced little of the dynamism that characterized the British and, to a lesser extent, the American economies. Especially in Germany's western and southwestern regions, which provided the bulk of the emigrants, an "agrarian and small-scale manufacturing economy existed with a framework of social and political institutions that seemed at least archaic" if not worse, according to historian Bruce Levine. Landed aristocrats, semifeudal obligations, craft guilds, and authoritarian state mechanisms constrained political and social change, while an explosive population growth constricted economic opportunity and drove down wages and standards of living.[17] Particularly in places like Baden, Wuerttemberg, Hesse, and Bavaria, urban handicraft workers felt the squeeze of overcrowded labor markets and looked for avenues of escape. This social group provided the bulk of the German immigrants who ultimately settled in the northern panhandle of Virginia.[18]

By 1850 Germans comprised Wheeling's principal ethnic community. Especially in the more industrial sections—the First Ward in the north end and the Fifth Ward in the south—recent German immigrants and their children accounted for about one-third of the households. Overall, about two of every nine Wheelingites resided in a German immigrant home.[19] They occupied a distinctly plebeian social stratum, reflecting their European backgrounds.

Almost half (49.3 percent) of German males were craftsmen—butchers, tailors, shoemakers, leatherworkers, carpenters, coopers, and others. However, this encompassed wide variations; sweated trades like tailoring or shoemaking paid far less than more elite crafts such as making cabinets or coaches. Somewhere in between were building trades workers—the carpenters, plasterers, and masons who made up between a fifth and a quarter of the craftsmen. Another third of German men were laborers, many who had skills but were not able to obtain a skilled job, and 3.5 percent were miners. Already, there was a small core of merchants and manufacturers, epitomized best by the Stifels, who left Wuerttemberg in the 1830s to establish a calico print works in Wheeling. Finally, about one-ninth of the Germans were small proprietors—operators of saloons, coffee houses, hotels, bakeries, butcher shops, and other small businesses. Some, like baker Gottlieb Bayha, who arrived in Wheeling in 1834, became quite prominent.[20]

Although they comprised a significant and stable plebeian group that began to achieve some prosperity, Germans played only a small role in politics before 1850. For example, there were no German-born constables, school commissioners, or other city officials before 1849. In large part, the property restrictions on suffrage in the Virginia Constitution prevented the middling sorts from exerting any formal role in government until 1851.[21] Informally, Germans did contribute; immigrant journalist Herrmann Schuricht claimed that Germans demonstrated against the state's unequal systems of taxation and representation that so distressed the western portions of Virginia. Principally, however, Germans concentrated on establishing their presence in the city's public culture and civic spaces. They originated or dominated many of the orchestras, brass bands, singing societies, fraternal orders, fire companies, and churches that constituted Wheeling's public life. They also formed a Benevolent Association; they obtained nearly half of the city's licenses for saloons and coffee houses; and they operated many of the halls that hosted concerts, balls, and other events.[22] While these activities seem commonplace, for people from a more autocratic social order, this civic culture represented a tremendous step toward ideals of "social freedom and independent existence."[23]

German Revolution and Wheeling Germans

Events in Germany helped reshape Wheeling's public culture after 1850. A revolutionary movement swept Europe in 1848-49, involving thousands of Germans in those areas where economic and political conditions had already triggered massive emigration. The revolutions galvanized a broad cross section of the German middle and working classes, generating a movement for reform of the archaic elements of the old order and the establishment of a government "on a broad democratic basis." Skilled craftsmen flocked to a revolution that represented hopes for increased civil liberties, economic opportunities, and political participation. Craft societies in the centers of emigration (Baden, Wuerttemberg, Hesse, and Bavaria) organized strikes and mobilized demonstrations to press their demands. When the revolution was finally crushed, German ports sent half a million people to an America that many immigrants pictured as "a new world, a free world, a world of great ideas and purposes," according to Carl Schurz.[24] Not all of these newcomers had been active participants in the revolutions, but many had been touched by the promise of republicanism, greater freedom, and economic opportunity.

The immigrants of the early 1850s changed the landscape of Wheeling. Their arrival coincided with changes in the city, especially residential development and the expansion of the iron, leather, and glass industries in the Fifth Ward and in Ritchietown, just south of the city boundary. This heavily industrial section received most of the incoming Germans who gave it a political character strongly influenced by the events in Europe. The north end, in contrast, was home to the more settled and prospering elements of the German community. Indeed, by 1860, nearly 60 percent of the Germans living in the north end of the city had arrived before 1848; on the south side, only about one in three had been in the United States when the revolutions erupted. The coincidence of German immigration and the expansion of these neighborhoods meant that immigrants dominated the south end polity by the end of the 1850s (see table 2.1). Moreover, many of the post-1848 immigrants who influenced local politics arrived with knowledge of the opportunities present in Wheeling, attesting to the transnational character of this German community. For example, William Coleman sailed from Havre and landed in Philadelphia in the spring of 1854; within a week he was in Wheeling where he remained. John Boeshar arrived in New York on May 12, 1848, and in Wheeling on May 18; Charles Robeck was in Baltimore on November 16, 1854, and in Wheeling before the end of the month. All applied for citizenship in Wheeling soon after their arrival.[25]

The recent flood of German immigrants did not appear to change significantly the ethnic group's social position in the city. In general, Germans occupied an occupational position between the Irish at the bottom and the American-born or those born in England, Scotland, and Wales. For instance, slightly more than one in five Germans occupied the upper rungs of the occupational ladder by 1860, while more than one-third of American-born and just under a quarter of those born in Great Britain had attained a similar status. Meanwhile, just over a third of German men were in the bottom categories compared to less than one-seventh of American- born men. The Irish were clearly the most

Table 2.1
Wheeling's Voting-Age Males, 1860,
by Poll Location and Ethnic Group[26]

Poll	Germans	Irish	Other For.	American	Number
1st Ward	34.9%	13.5%	1.5%	50.0%	458
Court House	21.3	12.0	5.9	60.8	933
4th Ward	28.3	19.9	11.2	40.6	643
5th Ward	34.9	16.1	7.1	42.0	921
Ritchietown	52.6	6.1	12.7	28.7	544
City Average	32.8%	13.8%	7.7%	45.7%	3499

disadvantaged group; although one in seven achieved an upper-status occupation, over half remained laborers or service workers.[27]

The aggregate picture for Germans, however, masks the important changes created by the post-1850 immigrants, reflected in the differences between the north and south ends of the city. By 1860, nearly 8 percent of German males in the north end had moved into the elite categories of merchant and manufacturer, and more than a quarter were in the upper occupational categories. South end Germans were far more heavily represented in trades and less skilled industrial jobs (see table 2.2). This mix of class and ethnicity periodically flared in labor unrest that affected the south end disproportionately. For example, German workers helped shut down the iron mills in December 1853 and participated in strikes of B&O Railroad workers in December 1855. They also made up the bulk of the rebellious iron molders who established a cooperative following a dispute with employers.[28]

In politics, the impact of the events in Europe flashed rather quickly in Wheeling. Local Germans created a stir in the Old Dominion in September of 1852 when they hosted a "Congress of German Revolutionists" which supported the famed Hungarian revolutionary leader Louis Kossuth. Although the gathering was so small that it could convene around a single table, the Congress garnered a great deal of attention and issued grandiose proclamations. In a slave state that had only recently broadened its suffrage, this small gathering of Germans raised eyebrows with its statement "that democracy is a principle for which there is no local, but only a universal triumph, a principle which knows neither an Old World nor a New. The world is its sphere, the human family its aim."[30] The impact of such statements took on added significance because

Table 2.2
Occupational Structure of Wheeling's Germans, by Residence[29]

Wards	Elite	Mid. Class	Skilled	Unskilled	Number in Sample
1-4	7.7%	17.9%	44.9%	29.6%	274
5, S. Wheel.	2.6%	9.5%	42.2%	45.8%	273

the Congress included three Wheeling Germans and led to public awareness of such organizations as the "Wheeling League of Freemen (Freie Gemeinde)" and a branch of the Turnverein. In the minds of many, both groups had links to revolutionary movements in Europe, and their radical principles "frightened the slaveholders and church-goers" of Virginia.[31]

During the next two years, Germans figured in a number of local social and political issues that became entangled with nativist sentiments, but typically in ways that cut across the German community. For example, temperance and anti-saloon agitation in 1853-54 united the majority of Germans in oppostion to temperance legislation, but members of the south-end German Methodist Church disagreed with many of their countrymen.[32] Likewise, in May 1853, Germans divided over an intense debate involving schools. The city had only recently implemented a public school system, but many leading Germans were Catholic and sent their children to Catholic schools. Wheeling Protestants worried that Catholics were secretly trying to undermine support for the public schools, and their fears quickly spilled over into a general anti-Catholic sentiment. While the Whig party led this, some leading German Democrats, like *Virginische Staats-Zeitung* editor John Buersner, also weighed in against the Catholics.[33] This anti-Catholic sentiment exploded within the German community between December 1853 and January 1854, sparked by the visit of the papal nuncio, Gaetano Bedini. Following the example of radical German Freethinkers and Turners in Cincinnati, Wheeling's radicals posted handbills throughout the city and gathered to disturb proceedings at the city's cathedral. Their handbills and posters harkened to the revolutionary republican spirit of 1848 in Europe, emphasizing "No Priests, No Kings, No Popery."[34]

Although some Wheeling Germans opposed slavery, community leaders worked to diminish any threat to the dominant social order. For example, in anticipation of the impending Kansas-Nebraska Act that potentially opened new territories to slavery through "popular sovereignty," a group of antislavery activists invaded Wheeling in March 1854 looking for recruits to colonize Nebraska on a "free state" basis. Less than a week later, a group of prominent

Germans organized a mass meeting to protest the antislavery activists. The editor of the *Virginische Staats-Zeitung* spoke on the connection between abolitionism and the local temperance agitation that had targeted Germans. The meeting resolved to "stand by Virginia" in defense of principles and against Northern "fanatics."[35] In a city where every local newspaper blamed sectional tensions on abolitionist agitators, few Germans raised their voice in opposition in 1854. Noteworthy here was the support from leading German manufacturers in the city, men like Jacob Berger, John Hoffman, and William Miller who had entered the business elite in the 1850s and had benefited from the state's role in the B&O controversies. Importantly, they were also Catholics, a group denigrated by northern Whigs and abolitionists. At a time when sectionalism was intensifying, their stalwart support for the Democratic party and the South trumped nativist sentiments in the city.[36]

In general, the nativists in Wheeling had little staying power. In contrast to the Know-Nothing movement in places like Louisville and Cincinnati, the party in Wheeling engaged in very few actions against the Germans. In addition, the substantial German (and especially German Catholic) presence in the city, particularly among the business elite, made local politicians reluctant to attack them. Occasional discussions of raising the bar against immigrant voters typically met only lukewarm support.[37] Thus, despite the early dramatic appearances of German radicalism in September 1852 and January 1854, post-1848 Germans appeared to have only a marginal impact on politics in the city through 1855. In the presidential contest of 1852, most of the city voted for Zachary Scott against Franklin Pierce, demonstrating the predominant local Whig sentiment. A year later, every ward in the city voted heavily for the local Democrat in the state senate race; the primary issue was his opposition to granting the right-of-way to a panhandle railroad that would connect Ohio to Pittsburgh. But in 1855, the city returned to its Whiggish traditions on state economic issues and voted for local successors to the Whig party for Congress and governor by fairly consistent margins, even in immigrant-dominated wards.[38]

German leaders in Wheeling also diminished anti-immigrant sentiment through their participation in patriotic commemorations and public events. Typically, Germans celebrated American Independence Day "in an enthusiastic manner," participating in parades and hosting lavish picnics with beer and cigars. George Washington's birthday was another popular occasion for Germans to demonstrate their allegiance to a heroic Virginia icon. Equally important was the part played by Germans in civic celebrations. Their bands routinely accompanied the annual fire company parades every September and provided most of the music for the dedication of the new Customs House. In February 1855,

Germans formed their own militia company, the German Rifle Company, which emphasized their attachment to the state. The German Riflemen frequently put on martial displays or filled the ranks of periodic parades and worked closely with the older local militia company, the Virginia Fencibles.[39]

Germans were also valuable contributors to Wheeling's social calendar. By the mid-1850s, the balls and concerts of the Maennerchor, the leading German singing society, were major local events. These performances included a concert that alternated orchestra selections, choral pieces, and special vocalists and ensembles, interspersed with comic selections. After the concert, there was dancing, concluding with a midnight supper or buffet. The Maennerchor's concerts and balls occurred around New Year's Day and every May and October, but other groups offered scaled-down entertainments, especially in the smaller German public halls in the south end.[40] Likewise, the German Turnverein, despite its radical heritage, held popular athletic competitions that usually culminated with a ball and a dinner. The popularity of the Turnverein's events soon spurred competing groups, the Wheeling Gymnastic Association and a branch of the Young Men's Christian Association, but neither had the Turnverein's following.[41]

In a variety of religious and voluntary organizations, Germans demonstrated their civic consciousness as well as pride in their cultural heritage. The 1850s witnessed a surge of church building. Germans built a Reformed church, a Methodist church, St. James Evangelical Lutheran Church and St. Alphonsus Catholic Church to complement the Lutheran, Reformed, and Methodist churches already in existence. Germans also established their own lodges of the Odd Fellows (the William Tell Lodge) and the Red Men, fraternal orders that had large followings in Wheeling, as well as their own unique contribution, the Haru Gari order.[42] With special pride they pointed to such activities as the German Christian Aid Society, established out of the German Methodist church, and the German Beneficial Society, organizations designed to demonstrate a republican concern for the community's well being. Indeed, in 1856 when residents of Wheeling began lobbying the state legislature for a House of Refuge to reform juvenile offenders, the *Intelligencer* traced the origins of this movement to Germany.[43]

All of these German contributions to the civic culture of Wheeling diminished, but did not completely eliminate, anti-immigrant sentiments. On occasion, the predominately German "Guards" Fire Company from South Wheeling tangled with the "Old Reds" of the First Ward or with the "Young America" company from Wheeling Island. Likewise, individuals or small groups of Germans and Irish might clash during a Christmastime celebration or at a picnic. But Germans generally bristled at any hints that they were not good citizens.

In April 1855 they met at the courthouse to protest comments made in the nativist *Times and Gazette*, which Julius Ballenberg called "a malicious misrepresentation, [and an] insult to foreign born citizens" which had the "tendency to incite riot and discord among our citizens."[44]

Sectionalism and German Politics

The presidential election of 1856 for the first time hinted at the divisions within Wheeling's German community created by the post-1848 immigrants. Throughout 1856, the Wheeling newspapers reported constantly on events in Kansas where "free state" forces battled pro-slavery groups in a bloody conflict. Meanwhile, former Whigs wrung their hands at the demise of any alternative to the unabashed pro-southern agrarianism of the Democratic party in Virginia; the owners of the Whig-sympathizing *Daily Intelligencer* were so discouraged by political prospects that they sold the paper.[45] The Democratic paper, the *Argus*, gleeful at the disarray in the ranks of the American party did worry that the "Black Republicans" who nominated John C. Fremont for president posed a dangerous threat. In fact, a Virginia delegate to the Fremont convention had been arrested upon his return to Wheeling.[46] Even though Democratic candidate James Buchanan swept to an easy victory in the city, the number of voters in the heavily German Fifth Ward doubled, representing the first time that many of the post-1848 German immigrants were eligible to vote. Even more troubling, Fremont received 5 percent of the votes in the Fifth Ward and 6 percent in Ritchietown while no other ward surpassed 1 percent. These were not large numbers, but given the intimidation against Republicans in Virginia and the lack of a secret ballot, they represented a budding challenge to slavery.[47]

The unsettled nature of Wheeling politics resumed its split personality the following year. In May 1857, Democrat Sherrard Clemens easily won the Congressional seat. However, in races for the state senate and house of delegates, candidates from the Distribution party (mostly ex-Whigs) won all three races. In each race, the two most heavily German wards, the First and the Fifth, were diametrically opposed—the Fifth was most advantageous for the Distribution candidates and the First was the most stalwart Democratic ward.[48] What these election results confirm is the dilemma facing an industrial city in a slave state; while in state politics Wheeling citizens could promote an alternative voice, in national politics state leaders expected them to elect Democrats loyal to the sectional interests of Virginia and the South. Germans opposed to slavery had little room to maneuver outside that paradigm; no local newspaper supported anti-slavery politics and leaders of the German community seemed submissive to the "slave power."[49]

Slowly, in 1857 anti-southern voices began to emerge, helped by the anti-slavery conscience of the new *Intelligencer* editor, Archibald Campbell. As early as October 1856, he reminded Wheeling Germans that their countrymen in cities like St. Louis and Pittsburgh were defecting to the Republican party. Then, during campaigning in the spring of 1857, Campbell criticized the Democratic paper's obsession with slaves, "Black Republicanism," and the chivalry of Virginia, and began contesting the version of events in Kansas supplied by the *Argus*.[50] On the Fourth of July, the *Intelligencer* called for greater tolerance in local politics, claiming that free speech and a free press "should be the essence of our patriotism." Of special interest to Campbell was the Fourth of July celebration of the Germans in Elm Grove. There, Lewis Stifel Jr., son of a German manufacturer who would become prominent in the local Republican party, offered extemporaneous remarks. According to Campbell, "Every heart was deeply influenced by the patriotic and noble words as they heartily flowed from the mouth of the young speaker." Less than two weeks later when the Turnverein, of which young Stifel was a member, gathered to celebrate its anniversary, "a melee occurred between some Americans and Germans."[51] It is impossible to know if the two events were related, but the *Intelligencer* had focused attention on the Germans in ways that might have drawn the ire of proslavery sympathizers.

The behavior of southern slaveholders on the national scene in 1857 and 1858 further eroded the support of south end Germans for the status quo. The Dred Scott decision enabling slaveholders to take their slaves into free states and the attempt to recognize the pro-slavery Lecompton Constitution for Kansas led many people to believe that the Southern Democrats had become the aggressors in the sectional conflict. As a result, the Democratic party was losing popular support in the North, a situation made worse when proslavery party leaders worked to undermine their most charismatic free-state politician, Stephen A. Douglas, because he failed to support the pro-slavery Lecompton Constitution. Wheeling Germans increasingly looked to the example offered by their countrymen to the west and the east—in Ohio and Pennsylvania—and began to desert the party of the "slave power."[52]

The mayoral elections of 1858 and 1859 made it obvious just how divided the city was becoming. Democrats nominated James W. Paxton, a banker from the Third Ward, while the opposition chose James Tanner, a physician and pharmacist who operated an office in the south end. Paxton won all three northern wards with over 56 percent of the votes, but lost the election because the Fourth and Fifth Wards gave 71 percent of their votes to Tanner in a heavy turnout. Shortly after the election, the *Argus* accused the *Intelligencer* of promoting "the evil genius of abolitionism" among a "few narrow contracted Yankees."[53] Another year widened the breach. The 1859 mayoral election pitted two men with

Whig credentials, glass manufacturer Thomas Sweeney from the north end and south-end sawmill owner Andrew Wilson. One key difference was that the public associated Sweeney with pro-southern radicalism. Interestingly, Sweeney won in the north and center wards with 66.5 percent of the vote, but came up short because Wilson won 71 percent on the south side, almost 79 percent in the Fifth Ward.[54]

These elections highlighted divisions in the city's German community. The German weekly, *Virginische Staats-Zeitung*, which spoke principally for the more entrenched Germans in the First, Second, and Third Wards, supported the Democratic party. This German community had a greater proportion of Catholics and felt more at home with the Democratic party's emphasis on personal liberty and its opposition to nativism. These wards were also home to the majority of those Germans who had risen into the local business elite, many of whom felt a loyalty to the state of Virginia.[55] In contrast, the more recent immigrants in the Fifth Ward and Ritchietown began to see greater advantages in the party opposing the Democrats. Especially important was the issue of the public lands. Pro-southern Democrats opposed opening western lands to homesteading, preferring that slaveholders be allowed to acquire property there. Republicans favored populating the new territories with free, white labor, promoting homesteading both to benefit the working class and to soothe northern racists who hoped to keep blacks out of the region.[56] In January 1858, German citizens held a public meeting to lobby for a homestead act and against the monopolizing of public lands by slaveholders. Meanwhile, the *Intelligencer* made it acceptable to oppose the slave power, claiming that the predominant sentiment in the panhandle region was unionist and antislavery, but not abolitionist. Campbell provided an alternative for antislavery Germans; he praised the "intelligent and industrious" immigrants in Wheeling while chastizing the anti-commercial "spirit of the old cavaliers" which hampered merchants, manufacturers, and workers for the benefit of the large plantations.[57]

By the spring of 1859, both parties openly courted the important German vote that represented nearly one-third of the city's electorate. This enabled a significant number of Germans to play a more public role in local politics for the first time. The *Intelligencer* predicted that, because the "instinct of the Teutonic mind is toward individual liberty," Germans would become the "most important influence" for free soil. Editor Archibald Campbell also praised the "ultra-democratic" tendencies of the group and remarked how important the German working class was to the Republican party. Indeed, over half (54.9 percent) of the Republican activists in the city were workers, and nearly 40 percent were foreign born.[58] At the same time, Wheeling's most prominent Germans clung to the Democratic party. Shortly after the 1859 mayoral election, Democrats gathered to send delegates to the upcoming state party convention. Among the list of men who played key parts in the drama were Jacob Berger, Sebastian Lutz, John and Peter Zoeckler, and Jacob Zimmer, some of the wealthiest Germans in the city. Thirteen of the fifteen participants came from the north side; none were from either the Fifth Ward or South Wheeling. Twelve of the twenty-two for whom information is available were Catholic.[59]

These divisions became evident and more contentious in the spring and summer of 1859. In the May contest for the Congressional seat from northwestern Virginia, the popular incumbent Democrat, Sherrard Clemens, ran against the former Whig, now Republican judge, Ralph Berkshire. Clemens won the city by carrying the First, Second, and Third Wards with nearly 59 percent of the vote, but he lost both the Fifth Ward and Ritchietown. The *Intelligencer* gave the German element in the southern end of Wheeling credit for Berkshire's impressive showing. Just six weeks later, numerous incidents of fighting between Americans and Germans punctuated mixed gatherings to celebrate the Fourth of July. But the skirmishes were not limited to immigrants and non-immigrants; that fall police arrested several notable German Democrats for fisticuffs involving other Germans.[60] Clearly the political stakes were rising.

The political differences separating the two German enclaves (north side and south side) widened during the political campaign of 1860, but both groups staked a claim to American nationalism. German Democrats, hoping to combine their nationalist sentiments with support for the dominant Virginia party, formed a solid group of Douglas supporters. On the other side, *Intelligencer* editor Archibald Campbell sought to unite the Republicans "under the banner of Union and conservatism, and place our opponents under the opposite of secession and anarchy," particularly appealing to the interests of workingmen.[61] Germans in the more plebeian south end openly supported Republicans, raising a "Lincoln/Hamlin pole" near the La Belle Rolling Mills and forming a company of "Wide Awakes."[62] Thus, Germans were conspicuous in two (the northern Democratic and Republican) of the four political camps in the race. Jacob Berger, William Klinkler, and John Buersner represented the Douglas men at the state Democratic convention, but Lincoln rallies typically included German bands and banners with German slogans ("Unsere Einsige Wahl" or "Ehret Freie Arbeit, Freier Boden"), and retired to Naegle's Hall. Leaders of the Wide Awakes included Fred Naegle, John Ensinger, and John Oesterling.[63]

A profile of German Democratic and Republican leaders provides useful insights and helps explain the factors dividing the German community. Newspapers identified forty-two Germans who played prominent roles in the Democratic party and twenty-nine influential Republicans. Occupationally, the two groups were similar: 41 percent of the Democrats and 45 percent of the Republicans were artisans or factory workers. The majority of both groups were merchants, manufacturers, professionals, proprietors, or white-collar employees, but nearly one- fourth of the Democrats compared to only 7 percent of the Republicans were in the top merchant/manufacturer group. Relative wealth bears out this observation. Republican leaders' average wealth was $2,096; for Democrats it was $5,014. Six Democrats owned more than $10,000 in property; no Republicans were that wealthy. Moreover, 38 percent of the Republicans owned property valued at less than $100; only 17 percent of the Democrats were so poor. Much of this can be explained by the length of time in the United States. Although the average age of the Democrats was forty compared to about thirty-five for the Republican leaders, nearly two-thirds of the Democrats had arrived before 1848; less that one-third of the Republicans had been Americans that long. Leaders of the two parties were also residentially segregated: 61.9 percent of the Democrats lived on the north side, while just 20.7 percent of the Republicans resided there. Finally, religion made a significant difference; of those for whom religion could be determined, 55 percent of the Democrats but only 25 percent of the Republicans were Catholics.[64] In short, the local Republicans were rooted in the more plebeian German communities of the Fifth Ward and Ritchietown among men and women who had experienced the European Revolutions of 1848.

German Republicans brought some of that same spirit of public rebellion to the Lincoln campaign. The South Wheeling Wide Awakes procured uniforms and torches, and began military-like drills, accompanied by their own glee club. They participated in numerous local parades and demonstrations, but also helped pro-Lincoln rallies in Pennsylvania and Ohio. Indeed, as the German Wide Awakes boarded a steamer to take them to Pittsburgh, "dastardly scoundrels" pelted them with stones. A week later their countrymen from Pittsburgh rewarded them with a wreath for their courage and "manliness." Special workingmen's meetings "struck terror or at least mortification into the hearts of secessionists," and resulted in Lincoln victories in straw polls at several South Wheeling factories. Of course, the most aggressive Republicans took their marches and torchlight processions to the pro-Democratic northern end of the city, where Wide Awakes wielded torches against hostile mobs.[65]

The work of the German Wide Awakes paid off on election day. Not even Virginia's "slave power" could sap the pro-Union sentiments of Wheeling's Germans. In the First Ward, that translated into votes for Douglas, as more prominent Germans refused to break with the Democratic party but also rejected the proslavery Breckinridge Democracy. In the Fifth Ward and Ritchietown, however, Lincoln was the top vote-getter in the four-way race; this despite the fact that former Whig leaders like Chester Hubbard threw their support to Bell and the American party. In the showdown between support for the Union versus the interests of slavery, the most heavily German polling places (Wards 1, 5, and Ritchietown) chose the Union, defying a state torn between Breckinridge and Bell. In fact, many felt a growing confidence in their ability to be *antislavery*. The Republican party applauded "the Bully Fifth Ward" and the "Independent Republic of Ritchietown," acknowledging the influence of these plebeian German communities.[66]

Germans and West Virginia's Revolution

The "revolutionary" task of northwestern Virginia's Germans was, as yet, far from complete. Lincoln's victory brought immediate repercussions upon Wheeling. State Democratic officials moved quickly to increase their control of its trans-Appalachian region. They fired *Virginische Staats-Zeitung* editor John Buersner from the post office for supporting Douglas rather than Breckinridge, and state banks suspended specie payments in the region, greatly disturbing monetary affairs. Finally, as expected, Democratic governor John Letcher called for a convention to consider secession.[67] This last measure required that counties choose delegates in a special February 1861 election. Four candidates— John H. Pendleton, Thomas Sweeney, Chester Hubbard, and Sherrard Clemens— announced for the two positions from Ohio County. Pendleton, Sweeney, and Hubbard were Whigs, Clemens a Democrat. Party, however, had little bearing on the vote. The consensus of belief was that Pendleton "probably" and Sweeney possibly would vote for secession. On the other side, Hubbard was a pro-Union, old-line Whig and Clemens, although a Democrat, had begun voting with the Republicans in Congress. Wheeling Republicans boosted Hubbard and Clemens, despite the fact that neither was a party member, and they singled out working-men for special attention. In a blatant appeal to Germans who had lived through the Revolution of 1848, a meeting of workers noted, "the world's hope of freedom is centered in America, to which we with becoming and patriotic pride, have, for over three-quarters of a century, looked to as the asylum of the oppressed." Secession, to the plebeian Germans in South Wheeling, was a rejection of that revolutionary spirit.[68] In parades and demonstrations and on election day, these Germans sent a pro-Union message (see table 2.3).

The outbreak of war following the firing on Fort Sumter in April 1861 would, for a time, unify the Germans of Wheeling, and help them contribute to yet another revolution, the creation of West Virginia. Within days of the outbreak of war, Germans began forming Union military companies and drilling in South Wheeling. The German Riflemen, which included Democrats August Rolf, John Salade, and Louis Franzheim among its officers, volunteered for service.

Table 2.3
1861 Vote for Secession Convention Delegates[69]

Candidate	1st Ward	2d-3d Ward	4th Ward	5th Ward	Ritchietown
Pendleton	195	311	203	42	17
Sweeney	373	460	266	82	27
Hubbard	222	454	339	507	392
Clemens	167	357	402	475	386

Democratic leader Jacob Berger joined with Republican Louis Stifel to represent Germans in a local convention to oppose secession. When the Democratic *Virginische Staats-Zeitung* printed Lincoln's call for volunteers to suppress the rebellion, recruiters were "soon overrun by applications from a large number of Germans."[70] Wheeling overwhelmingly opposed Virginia's secession, and the names of the eighty men who voted to secede were published in a broadside entitled "Traitors in Wheeling." Only three of the eighty were Germans. In the Fifth Ward, the iron works of John H. Pendleton, a secession sympathizer, burned to the ground under suspicious circumstances.[71]

Over the next year, Wheeling became a stronghold of Union support and hosted the conventions of trans-Appalachian Virginians that would eventually create West Virginia. The *Intelligencer* was the premier newspaper in support of separation from Virginia, and the presence of the Union Army made the city a haven for antislavery politics that would become a part of the state constitution. Germans united in the Union party and raised companies of recruits both for the Union Army and for a Home Guard militia. In fact, Battery A of the First Virginia Light Artillery and Company C of the Fifth Virginia Cavalry were entirely German units, raised largely in Wheeling. The south end of town also returned the largest pluralities for the new state movement, coinciding with a greater German presence in city government. Ritchietown, for instance, elected a majority of Germans to local offices.[72]

The war years, however, taught both the Union Army and the local Republican party some sobering lessons about the independence of Wheeling Germans. They had gravitated to the Union cause because it represented certain ideals that they held dear, but they also expected the army and the Republican party to treat everyone fairly and respect personal liberty. Once mobilized politically, Wheeling Germans continued to assert the interests of their group in ways that challenged the Union Army and the Republican party. Indeed, less than a month after enlisting, members of Edward Plankey's Second Regiment, Virginia militia rebelled against the army's orders. Plankey, a carpenter from the Fifth Ward, had been a leader of the German Riflemen in the city for several years. When the *Staats-Zeitung* solicited volunteers, his militia group volunteered. When ordered into the field, however, about a dozen refused to go "on account of having no equipments." The army then imprisoned the rebels on Wheeling Island, forcing them to sleep on the bare ground, providing limited food, and denying them water for drinking and washing. Only after the *Staats-Zeitung* formally complained were the prisoners released and given a dishonorable discharge.[73]

Local Republican officials charged with managing the war effort likewise ran afoul of the German community. In May, they threatened to shut down the Democratic newspaper, the *Daily Union*, which instead sold its interests. During the summer, city authorities began rounding up men suspected of pro-secession sympathies, including a few Germans, and the city council began arresting tavern owners who sold liquor to soldiers. The latter actions fell heavily upon Germans and involved substantial fines.[74] Germans directed much of their anger at Thomas Hornbrook, a prominent businessman serving as the state armorer of the provisional government. Hornbrook arrested William Kryter, a leading German Democrat, and confiscated a large number of his store's guns. Hornbrook also provoked a strike of the mostly German coal miners that winter when he arbitrarily raised the price of black powder, essential to the miners. Even the local court recognized that Hornbrook's services "have been altogether gratuitous." Many shared the beliefs of former Whig Chester Hubbard, who wrote to his son that the Republican party was putting party above patriotism, "thus dampening the ardor of some of our best men."[75]

Germans retaliated against what they perceived as unjust treatment. Kryter successfully sued Hornbrook in court for the unwarranted seizure of his weapons, and George Franzheim pressed the city council to reduce fines for those charged with selling liquor to soldiers. Twice, in 1862, German boys from the southern end of town defended their group by taking on Americans from the center of town in melees.[76] Even some of the patriotic German men who volunteered for military service began to have doubts. Louis Myers wrote to Archibald Campbell to call attention to the way his unit had been "shamefully mistreated" by the army. Despite recognition as "a gallant, efficient and popular officer," Gus Rolf resigned his commission from the company formed by the German Riflemen in September 1862, and Captain Edward Plankey turned over leadership of his company in March of 1863. One man in the city wrote his brother that many of the south-end workers, who had been stalwart Republicans at the start of the war, were thinking of heading to Canada when rumors of a military draft circulated in August 1862.[77]

Despite their commitment to the Union, new divisions opened in the German community. Lincoln's Emancipation Proclamation cooled the ardor of some, but more troubling to most Germans was the heavy-handed treatment of anyone who raised objections to government policies. During 1862 and 1863, Democrats raised questions about the Confiscation Act, conscription policies, and proposals for the nationalization of the banking system. Particularly galling to many in West Virginia who believed in the Republic's guarantee of government by the people was the insistence by federal officials that West Virginia's new state constitution include an anti-slavery amendment.[78] Republicans also angered many Germans through their treatment of coal miners, stogie makers, and brewery workers. Germans made up the majority of these trades, and they all struck for wage increases in 1863 to match a rising cost of living. The workers received little support from either local officials or their employers, many of whom were noted Republicans.[79]

In March 1863, some key Germans helped revive the Democratic party. Men like John Hoffman (a partner of Jacob Berger), George Franzheim, John Zoeckler, and Conrad Stroble counseled Germans who cared about liberty to refuse to vote for the state constitution. They also accused Republicans of padding election returns with fraudulent soldier votes and of intimidating Democrats with soldiers and violence. In May and October 1863, elections under the new city charter and state government passed with lopsided victories for the Union party, but Democrats claimed that the Republican party could not win an election without buying votes or threatening violence.[80] Democrats turned to sensational reporting about Republican promises made to blacks and stories about the "despotism" of the federal government, hoping to attract the votes of immigrants and workers. They expected some benefits from upcoming elections in 1864 under a new system using the secret ballot, asserting that "the secret ballot is the freeman's weapon—it is the laboring man's protection."[81]

Elections in 1864 did not quite meet the Democrats' expectations, but they demonstrated some erosion of German support for the Republicans. The January mayoral election signalled the revival of the Democrats as the party's candidate garnered nearly two-thirds of the votes in the First and Second Wards. An expanding population in the south end caused the city to create two wards out of the old Fifth, but both the Fifth and Sixth Wards gave almost 61 percent of its votes to the Union party.[82] In the ensuing six months, Democratic newspapers stepped up their attacks on the "Radical" Republicans and began making blatantly racist appeals to the fears of wage earners, with some success. Pro-Democratic sentiment grew to such an extent in the summer of 1864 that Union officials banned publication of the *Daily Register*, a Democratic paper, and put its editors in jail. *Register* editor Lewis Baker was also the proprietor of the only German weekly operating in the city, *Der Arbeiter Freund*. To many liberty-loving Germans it appeared that the Republicans had gone too far. Democrats hoped to exploit that advantage by including Jacob Berger on its county ticket and recruiting such leading Germans as John Bayha, John Pfarr, and George Franzheim to play important roles in party demonstrations and parades.[83]

The presidential election in November demonstrated that Democrats were regaining parts of the German community. Democrat George McClellan won the First and Second Wards, where prominent Germans had clung to the party in 1860. Interestingly, McClellan also won the Fifth Ward, previously a strong-hold of pro-Republican Germans. What had changed? Perhaps some Germans, as well as Irish and American-born workers responded to the Democratic scare tactics as well as to what often appeared as an overly aggressive Republican administration. Equally important, however, was the fact that in 1859 the German Catholics had built their church in this ward. By 1864, many of the Catholics who formerly worshipped and lived in the north end may have found it easier to relocate in the Fifth Ward, a place where industrial jobs were far more plentiful. The fact that Lincoln won 61 percent of the votes in the Sixth Ward and 57 percent in Ritchietown (by then called South Wheeling) suggests that religion had a significant role in winning the German Fifth Ward for the Democratic party.[84]

Whatever the party, Germans by 1864 exerted a considerable presence in Wheeling politics. The part they played in the sectional drama unfolding in 1860 and in the statehood movement between 1861 and 1863 meant that they could no longer be ignored for positions in government. Ironically, given their pre-war role, as they began to win public office in the post-Civil War years, most won through the Democratic party. In 1864-65, six Germans served on the city council; all were Democrats. In South Wheeling, where Germans made up over half the polity, they dominated local government offices. But there, Germans split loyalty between the Republicans and the Democrats. However, a new German immigration would reshape the city in the 1870s and 1880s, altering the status, culture, and political power of Wheeling's dominant ethnic community, and reinforcing the transnational character of ethnicity.

Conclusion

Events in Germany helped reshape Wheeling twice in those crucial decades preceding the Civil War. Economic stagnation and archaic social and political institutions sent a wave of immigrants looking for economic opportunity, which the city provided. By the late 1840s, Germans had established themselves in the commercial and industrial life of the city. Like other groups involved in commerce, they chafed against proslavery politics that constrained the impact of the market economy. At the same time, some of these Germans benefited from the political clout of Virginia's "slave power." Then, in 1848, revolutions in Europe would bring a new wave of German immigrants, many of whom brought hopes for involvement in a more democratic and more egalitarian society where they might experience both political and economic opportunities. Many of these immigrants, during the political crisis of the 1850s, occupied a more plebeian world of small stores, artisan shops, and wage labor. They experienced the constraints of the slave society with fewer of the benefits. In Wheeling, these two groups were residentially segregated; the first lived principally in the north end, the second was concentrated in the south.

The story of these two groups caught between the impact of a revolution in Europe and one that shook the United States with even greater force a decade later, provides a number of insights on the history of this era. First, it suggests the barriers that German immigrants confronted in a slave state. Certainly, those who were opposed to slavery operated in a political culture without many options. Pro-northern sentiments confronted a hostility that muted voices that might have earlier supported Free-Soilism, a position that ultimately proved attractive to the Germans in the south end of Wheeling. Second, as has been demonstrated in other studies of immigrant political behavior in the 1850s, the city's Germans were not a united group. Religion and economic status, in particular, divided the community's Democrats and Republicans. While they might unite when attacked, Catholic and wealthier Germans found a comfortable home in the Democratic party; more plebeian and Protestant Germans gravitated toward the Republicans. This finding supports the work of many earlier scholars, but carries the story forward a bit to explore just how the Civil War impacted that political behavior.

Finally, we might flip this story around and ask what insights the Civil War era might provide about the Germans of West Virginia. In that critical time, Wheeling's German community demonstrated the transnational character of ethnic groups. They implanted much of their culture and many of their institutions in their new home, but maintained critical attachments to their homeland. The post-1848 immigrants who would change the city's politics came directly to Wheeling because they had familial or local ties there and because those friends and family members wrote home about opportunities. In saloons, coffee houses, and singing societies or at gymnastic exhibitions, concerts, and picnics, recent arrivals made new connections and let established Germans know about events at home. At the same time newer Germans enjoyed the freedoms and joys of Fourth of July picnics or parades on Washington's birthday. New social and political ideas thus traveled back and forth across the Atlantic but also interacted with political events in both places. In Wheeling, the integration of new arrivals did not lead to harmony, but mixed with the city's unique location in the sectional politics of the 1850s to create deep divisions within the German community.

NOTES

The author would like to thank the West Virginia Humanities Council for a fellowship in support of this project. I would also like to thank Kenneth Noe, Kenneth Martis, and Bruce Levine for reading and commenting on earlier drafts of this article. They were excellent critics; unfortunately, I must accept the blame for whatever inadequacies remain.

1. Wheeling *Daily Intelligencer*, 12 Oct. 1860, 3; 13 Oct., 3.
2. The most complete recent work on Germans and the coming of the Civil War is Bruce Levine, *The Spirit of 1848: German Immigrants, Labor Conflict, and the Coming of the Civil War* (Urbana: University of Illinois Press, 1992). Of course, there has been a long debate in the historical literature over whether Germans supported Lincoln. An excellent sampling of this literature is contained in Frederick C. Luebke, ed., *Ethnic Voters and the Election of Lincoln* (Lincoln: University. of Nebraska Press, 1971).
3. *Daily Intelligencer*, 5 Oct. 1860, 3; 26 Sept. 1860, 3.
4. Among the leading Douglas Democrats in the north end were John Zoeckler, John Pfarr, William Kryter, and William Klinkler. See *Intelligencer*, 2 Aug. 1860, 3. For the formation of the German Wide Awakes in South Wheeling, see *Daily Intelligencer*, 8 Sept. 1860, 3.
5. See David Ward, *Cities and Immigrants: A Geography of Change in Nineteenth-Century America* (New York: Oxford University Press, 1971), 62-3; Jon Teaford, *Cities of the Heartland: The Rise and Fall of the Industrial Midwest* (Bloomington: Indiana University Press, 1993), chap. 1.
6. William Freehling's recent work suggests just how important the defection of this slave-state region was to the eventual triumph of the Union Army. See Freehling, *The South vs. The South: How Anti-Confederate Southerners Shaped the Course of the Civil War* (New York: Oxford University Press, 2001), esp. chaps. 4-5. For studies that emphasize how divided the mountain South was generally, see John Inscoe, *Mountain Masters: Slavery, and the Sectional Crisis in Western North Carolina* (Knoxville: University of Tennessee Press, 1989). For a view of the Wheeling area more specifically, see Kenneth W. Noe, "'Deadened Color and Colder Horror': Rebecca Harding Davis and the Myth of Unionist Appalachia," in *Confronting Appalachian Stereotypes: Back Talk from an American Region,* ed. Dwight Billings, Gurney Norman, and Katherine Ledford (Lexington: University Press of Kentucky, 1999), 67-84.
7. J. D. B. DeBow, *Statistical View of the United States . . .a Compendium of the Seventh Census* (Washington, D.C., A. O. P. Nicholson, 1854), 195, 326-31.
8. L. Diane Barnes, "Urban Rivalry in the Upper Ohio Valley: Wheeling and Pittsburgh in the Nineteenth Century," *Pennsylvania Magazine of History and Biography* 123 (July 1999): 222-5; Elizabeth Brand Monroe, *The Wheeling Bridge Case: Its Significance in American Law and Technology* (Boston: Northeastern University Press, 1992), 32-6.

9. Wheeling figures were compiled from DeBow, *Statistical View*, 326-31; Robert Simmons, "Wheeling and Its Hinterland: An Egalitarian Society?" (Ph.D. diss., West Virginia University, 1990), 174; and from a count of 3,499 voting-age males in the Manuscript Census schedules, *Eighth Census of the United States, 1860*, for Ohio County, available on microfilm in the West Virginia and Regional History Collection, West Virginia University (hereafter cited as 1860 manuscript census schedules, WVRHC). Figures for Lynchburg and Petersburg are from L. Diane Barnes, "Hammer and Hand in the Old South: Artisan Workers in Petersburg, Virginia, 1820-1860," (Ph.D. diss., West Virginia University, 2000), 170. Richmond's numbers are derived from Werner Steger, "'United to Support, but Not Combined to Injure': Free Workers and Immigrants in Richmond, Virginia, during the Era of Sectionalism, 1847-1865," (Ph.D. diss., George Washington University, 1999), 127-133.

10. Barnes, "Hammer and Hand," chap. 1; Steven Elliott Tripp, *Yankee Town, Southern City: Race and Class Relations in Civil War Lynchburg* (New York: New York University Press, 1997), chap. 1; Steger, "United to Support," 130.

11. Robert L. Morris, "The Wheeling *Daily Intelligencer* and the Civil War," (Ph.D. diss., West Virginia University, 1964), 23-4; Barnes, "Urban Rivalry in the Upper Ohio Valley," pp. 222-3.

12. Richard Orr Curry, *A House Divided: A Study of Statehood Politics and the Copperhead Movement in West Virginia* (Pittsburgh: University of Pittsburgh Press, 1964), chap. 2; Morris, "The Wheeling *Daily Intelligencer* and the Civil War," 13; Charles Henry Ambler, *Sectionalism in Virginia from 1776 to 1861* (New York: Russell & Russell, 1964), 259-61.

13. Monroe, *Wheeling Bridge Case*, 145-6; Barnes, "Urban Rivalry in the Upper Ohio Valley," 225. Also, see James G. Dilts, *The Great Road: The Building of the Baltimore and Ohio, The Nation's First Railroad, 1828-1853* (Stanford: Stanford University Press, 1993).

14. William Prescott Smith, *A History and Description of the Baltimore and Ohio Railroad* (Baltimore: J. Murphy & Co., 1853), 186. On the battle over the terminus of the B&O, see Curry, *A House Divided*, 23; and Ambler, *Sectionalism in Virginia*, 241-2. For an outstanding discussion of the role of railroads and sectional politics in southwestern Virginia, see Kenneth W. Noe, *Southwest Virginia's Railroad: Modernization and the Sectional Crisis* (Urbana: University of Illinois Press, 1994).

15. On the effort of Wheeling interests to block the panhandle right-of-way, see *Daily Intelligencer*, 7 May 1853, 2; 13 Aug. 1853, 2.

16. Herrmann Schuricht, *History of the German Element in Virginia*, 2 vols. (Baltimore: Genealogical Publishing Co., 1977), vol. 2, 108-9; William G. Shade, *Democratizing the Old Dominion: Virginia and the Second Party System, 1824-1861* (Charlottesville: University Press of Virginia, 1996), 47; Charles A. Wingerter, *History of Greater Wheeling and Vicinity* (Chicago: Lewis Publishing Co., 1912), 48-9.

17. Levine, *Spirit of 1848*, 15-27.

18. These four locations were four of the top five points of origin for Virginia

Germans. See U.S. Bureau of the Census, Eighth, *Population of the United States in 1860* (Washington, D.C.: GPO, 1864), 520; Guenter Moltmann, "The Pattern of German Emigration to the United States in the Nineteenth Century," in *America and the Germans: An Assessment of a Three-Hundred-Year History*, ed. Frank Trommler and Joseph McVeigh (Philadelphia: University of Pennsylvania Press, 1985), 17-21; Levine, *Spirit of 1848*, 27-34.

19. This percentage would be far higher if it included all who had German surnames. These numbers were compiled from the Manuscript Census schedules, *Seventh Census of the U.S. 1850*, Ohio County, Virginia, WVRHC; and from Simmons, "Wheeling and the Hinterland," 174-5.

20. This profile is drawn from 714 German-born men in the 1850 manuscript census schedules for Ohio County, Virginia. Information on Stifel and Bayha comes from profiles supplied in Gibson Lamb Cranmer, *History of Wheeling City and Ohio County, West Virginia, and Representative Citizens* (Chicago: Biographical Publishing Co., 1902), 622, 683.

21. *Ohio County (WV) Index, Volume 1: Index to the County Court Order Books, 1777-1881*, compiled by Kenneth Fischer Craft Jr. (n.p.: Heritage Books, Inc., 1997), 37, 51, 183; Shade, *Democratizing the Old Dominion*, 50-54.

22. Schuricht, *History of the German Element*, vol. 2, 110; J. H. Newton, G. G. Nichols, and A. G. Sprankle, *History of the Pan-Handle: Being Historical Collections of the Counties of Ohio, Brook, Marshall, and Hancock, West Virginia* (Wheeling: J. A. Caldwell, 1879), 194-6, 228-9; *William's Wheeling Directory, City Guide, and Business Mirror* (Wheeling: John H. Thompson, 1856), 40, 42; *Ohio County (WV) Index*, vol. 1, pp. 116-7. This corresponds to the large German community in Richmond, described quite well in Gregg D. Kimball, *American City, Southern Place: A Cultural History of Antebellum Richmond* (Athens: University of Georgia Press, 2000), 52-54.

23. The phrase is Stephan Born's, quoted in Bruce Levine, *Spirit of 1848*, 35. I also wish to thank Katherine Aaslestad for helping me contextualize the significance of this public culture for German immigrants.

24. Levine, *Spirit of 1848*, chap. 2; Carl J. Friedrich, "The European Background," in *The Forty-Eighters: Political Refugees of the German Revolution of 1848*, ed. A. E. Zucker (New York: Columbia University Press, 1950), 3-25 (quote from Carl Schurz on 16-7). For the importance of the United States in the imagination of Germans in the 1840s, see Hartmut Keil, "German Working-Class Immigration and the Social Democratic Tradition of Germany," in *German Workers' Culture in the United States 1850 to 1920*, ed. Hartmut Keil (Washington, D.C.: Smithsonian Institution Press, 1988), 2-3.

25. This information comes from "Alien Declarations," in the Ohio County Court Records, Reel 158, in WVRHC. Kimball, in *American City, Southern Place*, 53-4, found that Germans in Richmond were less interested in naturalization.

26. Tabulated from the 1860 manuscript census schedules, WVRHC.

27. The occupational structure of Wheeling, by ethnic group (percentages), tabulated from the 1860 manuscript census schedules. The occupational categories used

were as follows: Upper—merchant, manufacturer, proprietor, white collar, and professional; Middle—artisans and factory craftsmen (skilled glass and iron workers); Lower—miners, laborers, and service jobs.

Group	Upper	Middle	Lower	Number
American	33.4	53.2	13.4	605
British	24.0	46.4	29.6	125
German	20.7	43.4	35.9	546
Irish	15.5	30.2	54.3	212

28. *Daily Intelligencer*, 29 Dec. 1853, 3; 8 Dec. 1855, 3; John R. Commons, David J. Saposs, Edward B. Mittelman, Henry E. Hoagland, John B. Andrews, Selig Perlman, Dan D. Lescohier, Elizbeth Brandeis, and Philip Taft, *History of Labour in the United States*, Vol. 1 (New York: Augustus M. Kelley, 1966), 569.

29. Samples were compiled from the 1860 manuscript census schedules, WVRHC.

30. *Daily Intelligencer*, 22 Sept. 1852, 3; Schuricht, *History of the German Element*, vol. 2, 34; Klaus Wust, *The Virginia Germans* (Charlottesville: University Press of Virginia, 1969), 210.

31. *Daily Intelligencer*, 23 Sept. 1852, 3; 21 Oct. 1852, 3; Schuricht, *History of the German Element*, vol. 2, 34. On the importance of the Turners, see Augustus J. Prahl, "The Turner," in *The Forty-Eighters*, ed. Zucker, 79-110.

32. *Daily Intelligencer*, 5 May 1853, 3; 12 Sept. 1853, 3; 14 Sept. 1853, 3; 25 Mar. 1854, 2.

33. *Daily Intelligencer*, 26 May 1853, 3; 16 June 1853, 2; Wingerter, *History of Greater Wheeling*, 453-5.

34. *Daily Intelligencer*, 30 Dec. 1853, 3; 9 Jan. 1854, 2; 10 Jan. 1854, 3. See also Levine, *Spirit of 1848*, 188-91.

35. *Daily Intelligencer*, 17 Mar., 3, 21 Mar., 2, 24 Mar., 2-3, and 25 Mar., 2, all 1854.

36. The list of prominent Germans attached to the Democrats included Gottlieb Bayha, Jacob Berger, John Hoffman, Christian Hess, William Miller, and John Pfarr, among others. Berger was perhaps the key. John Ingham notes that the Wheeling iron and steel elite was more open and fluid than its counterparts in other cities; even Catholics were accepted into the group. John N. Ingham, *The Iron Barons: A Social Analysis of an American Urban Elite, 1874-1965* (Westport, Conn.: Greenwood Press, 1978), 69-78.

37. Anti-German riots in Louisville and Cincinnati received considerable coverage in the Wheeling *Daily Intelligencer*; see 27 Sept. 1854, 3, 6 Apr. 1854, 3; 9 Aug. 1855, 3. For German mobilization against efforts to restrict voting, see *Daily Intelligencer*, 6 Feb. 1855; 28 Apr. 1855, 3; and for the German support for the Know-Nothings, 1 June 1855, 2; 4 June 1855, 2. About 35% of the German households in Wheeling were Catholic. See John M. Lenhart, *History of St. Alphonsus Church* (Wheeling, St. Alphonsus Church, 1956), 34. Also, see Levine, *Spirit of 1848*, chap. 7. Steger, in "United to Support," 166-7, notes that the anti-abolitionism of Germans in Richmond also diminished the appeal of nativism in that city.

38. *Daily Intelligencer*, 4 Nov. 1852, 3; 27 May 1853, 3; 29 May 1855, 2. These party votes carried no antislavery implications, as neither party broke with the proslavery sentiments of Virgina; see Henry T. Shanks, *The Secession Movement in Virginia, 1847-1861* (New York: AMS Press, 1971), 48-51.

39. *Daily Intelligencer*, 4 July 1853, 2; 6 July 1855, 3; 23 Feb. 1860, 3; 25 Sept. 1854, 3; 23 Feb. 1855, 3; 15 May 1855, 3; *Wheeling Argus*, 19 Sept. 1856, 3.

40. Edward C. Wolf, "Wheeling's German Singing Societies," *West Virginia History* 42 (fall-winter 1980-81): 1-56. Throughout the United States, Germans gained respect from Americans for their musical societies, even in the face of nativism. For one example, see the letter from Martin Weitz to his father, July 29, 1855, reproduced in *News from the Land of Freedom: German Immigrants Write Home*, ed. Walter D. Kamphoefner, Wolfgang Helbich, and Ulrike Sommer (Ithaca: Cornell University Press, 1991), 345-6.

41. *Daily Intelligencer*, 1 Nov. 1854, 3; 17 July 1857, 3; *William's Wheeling Directory*, 1856, 42.

42. Wingerter, *History of Greater Wheeling*, 494-504; *William's Wheeling Directory*, 1856, 40-1.

43. *Daily Intelligencer*, 5 Jan. 1856, 2; 6 June 1854, 3; Newton, *History of the Pan-Handle*, 229.

44. Robert L. Plummer and William C. Handlan, *A History of Fire Fighting in Wheeling* (Wheeling?, n.p., 1925), 50; *Daily Intelligencer*, 4 Dec. 1855, 3; 28 Apr. 1855, 3.

45. *Daily Intelligencer*, 9 Oct. 1856, 2.

46. *Daily Argus*, 19 Sept. 1856, 1; *Daily Intelligencer*, 9 Oct. 1856, 2.

47. *Daily Intelligencer*, 27 Nov. 1856, 3; 5 Nov. 1856, 3; *Daily Argus*, 19 Sept. 1856, 1-2.

48. *Daily Intelligencer*, 27 Jan. 1857, 3; 29 May 1857, 3; 1 June 1857, 3.

49. Leonard Richards's fascinating new book, *The Slave Power: The Free North and Southern Domination, 1780-1860* (Baton Rouge: Louisiana State University Press, 2000), highlights the pressures that proslavery interests in the Democratic party were able to bring to bear to keep the South united; see esp., chap. 8. For a more pronounced German submission to the "slave power" in Richmond, see Steger, "United to Support," 166-7.

50. *Daily Intelligencer*, 28 Oct. 1856, 2; 13 Apr. 1857, 2; 8 July 1857, 2.

51. *Daily Intelligencer*, 7 July 1857, 2; 18 July 1857, 3.

52. Richards, *The Slave Power*, 202-8, wonderfully captures the extremes to which the Democratic party was willing to go to push the Lecompton Constitution, and the political toll it took. For the Germans in Cincinnati and Cleveland, see Levine, *Spirit of 1848*, 252; for Pittsburgh, see Michael F. Holt, *Forging a Majority: The Formation of the Republican Party in Pittsburgh, 1848-1860* (New Haven: Yale University Press, 1969).

53. *Daily Intelligencer*, 26 Jan. 1858, 3; 29 Jan. 1858, 2.

54. *Daily Intelligencer*, 26 Jan. 1859.

55. Five of the six members of the publishing committee of the paper hailed from the north and center sections of the city, *Virginische Staats-Zeitung*, 26 Mar. 1859.

Likewise, the wealthiest Germans in Wheeling—Peter Beck, Jacob Berger, G. W. Franzheim, Christian Hess, Sebastian Lutz, William Miller, Jacob Zimmer, John Pfarr, and Lewis Stifel, all lived in either the north or center sections of the city or on the island. Wealth and residence were determined from the 1860 manuscript census schedules, WVRHC. Suggestions about the heavier Catholic concentration in the north end are based upon marriages in the Catholic church reported in the Ohio County Court records. I was able to link 50 marriages (1846-56) between German Catholics to names in city directories and the census manuscripts; 54% of the Catholics lived in the north end, 24% in the center of Wheeling, and only 22% in the south end. Ohio County Court Records, Reel 86, Ohio County Marriages, WVRHC.

56. Eric Foner, *Free Soil, Free Labor, Free Men: The Ideology of the Republican Party before the Civil War* (New York: Oxford University Press, 1970), chaps. 7-8; Bruce Levine, *Half Slave and Half Free: The Roots of Civil War* (New York: Hill & Wang, 1992), chap. 9.

57. *Daily Intelligencer*, 8 Jan. 1858, 2; 1 Feb. 1858, 2; 5 Feb. 1858, 2; 10 Feb. 1858, 2. This, of course, also fed into the older trans-Appalachian hostility to the Tidewater planters; see Curry, *House Divided*, chap. 2; and Ambler, *Sectionalism in Virginia*, chap. 10.

58. *Daily Intelligencer*, 22 Jan. 1859, 1; 19 May 1859, 2; 13 June 1859, 3. For a profile of the Wheeling Republican party, see Simmons, "Wheeling and the Hinterland," 155-6.

59. *Daily Intelligencer*, 16 Feb. 1859, 3. Information on the leaders came from the 1860 manuscript census schedules; the biographical sketches can be found in Cramner, *History of Wheeling City*.

60. *Daily Intelligencer*, 27 May 1859, 3; 6 July 1859, 3; 5 Sept. 1859, 2; 20 Oct. 1859, 3. The prominent German Democrats arrested by the police were Charles Zoeckler and William Klinkler.

61. J. E. Jacobs to Archibald Campbell, 10 Jan. 1860, in Archibald Campbell Papers, WVRHC; *Daily Intelligencer*, 2 Aug. 1860, 3; 6 Aug. 1860, 3.

62. *Daily Intelligencer*, 6 Aug. 1860, 3; 21-27 Aug. 1860,3.

63. *Daily Intelligencer*, 13 Aug. 1860, 3; 8 Sept. 1860, 3; 14 Sept. 1860, 2; 15 Sept. 1860, 3.

64. This profile relies on names listed in the Wheeling newspapers between 1859 and 1863, and compares those names with information from the 1860 manuscript census schedules, WVRHC. See also n. 55 (above) for information concerning Catholics.

65. *Daily Intelligencer*, 5 Sept. 1860, 3; 8 Sept. 1860, 3; 17 Sept. 1860, 3; 26 Sept. 1860, 3; 5 Oct. 1860, 3; 13 Oct. 1860, 3; Jacobs to Campbell, 10 Jan. 1860, Campbell Papers.

66. *Daily Intelligencer*, 7 Nov. 1860, 2; Chester D. Hubbard to Will Hubbard, 8 Oct. 1860, 7 Nov. 1860, in Hubbard Family Papers, WVRHC; Clippings, undated, in the Campbell Papers.

67. *Daily Intelligencer*, 10 Nov. 1860, 3; Chester D. Hubbard to Will Hubbard, 10 Nov. 1860, 25 Nov. 1860, and 3 Jan. 1861, all in Hubbard Family Papers.

68. Chester Hubbard to Will Hubbard, 16 Feb. 1861, Hubbard Family Papers; Sherrard Clemens to Alexander Campbell, 23 Jan. 1861, Campbell Papers; *Daily Intelligencer*, 7 Jan. 1861, 3; 14 Jan. 1861, 2; Wheeling *Daily Union*, 2 Feb. 1861, 2; 4 Feb. 1861, 2; 6 Feb. 1861, 2.

69. *Daily Intelligencer*, 5 Feb. 1861.

70. *Daily Union*, 6 May 1861, 3; 7 May 1861, 2; *Daily Intelligencer*, 16 Apr. 1861, 3; 25 Apr. 1861, 3; 20 May 1861, 3.

71. *Daily Intelligencer*, 25 May 1861, 3; "Traitors in Wheeling," (ca. May 1861) in Campbell Papers; *Daily Union*, 7 May 1861, 3.

72. *Daily Intelligencer*, 31 Jan. 1861, 3; 24 May 1861, 3; 25 Oct. 1861, 1; *Annual Report of the Adjutant General of the State of West Virginia for the Year Ending December 31, 1865* (Wheeling: John Frew, 1866), 394-6, 405.

73. *Daily Intelligencer*, 12 July 1861, 3; 17 July 1861, 3; *Annual Report of the Adjutant General of the State of West Virginia for the Year Ending December 31, 1864* (Wheeling: John F. McDermott, 1865), 604.

74. *Daily Intelligencer*, 14 May 1861, 2; 18 July 1861, 3; 31 Aug. 1861, 3; 24 Oct. 1861, 3.

75. Wheeling *Daily Register*, 23 Sept. 1863, 3; *Daily Intelligencer*, 25 Dec. 1861, 3; Chester Hubbard to Will Hubbard, 20 Sept. 1861, in Hubbard Family Papers.

76. *Daily Register*, 23 Sept. 1863, 3; *Daily Intelligencer*, 13 Nov. 1861, 3; 28 Mar. 1862, 3; 7 July 1862, 3.

76. Louis A. Myers to *Daily Intelligencer*, 24 Jan. 1862, in Campbell Papers; *Adjutant General's Report, 1864*, 602-3; *Daily Intelligencer*, 16 Sept. 1862, 3; Dana Hubbard to Will Hubbard, 13 Aug. 1862, Hubbard Family Papers.

78. *Daily Intelligencer*, 11 Feb. 1862, 3; 5 Aug. 1862, 2; *Daily Press*, 26 Jan. 1863, 3; Curry, *House Divided*, 94-8.

79. For labor actions, see *Daily Intelligencer*, 2 Dec. 1862, 2; *Daily Register*, 23 Sept. 1863, 2; 6 Oct. 1863, 3; 24 Oct. 1863, 3; *Daily Press*, 28 Jan. 1863, 3.

80. *Daily Press*, 7 Feb. 1863, 2; 9 Mar. 1863, 2; *Daily Register*, 24 Oct. 1863, 3; 25 Oct. 1863, 3; *Daily Intelligencer*, 30 May 1863, 3; 23 Oct. 1863, 2-3.

81. *Daily Register*, 13 Oct. 1863, 1; 5 Nov. 1863, 3; 20 Nov. 1863, 3; 12 Jan. 1864, 1; 25 Jan. 1864, 2.

82. *Daily Register*, 25 Jan. 1864, 2; 27 Jan. 1864, 2; *Daily Intelligencer*, 26 Jan. 1862, 2.

83. *Daily Register*, 22 Sept. 1864, 2; 23 Sept. 1864, 2; 4 Oct. 1864, 3; 18 Oct. 1864, 2; 21 Oct. 1864, 2.

84. *Daily Intelligencer*, 1 Nov. 1864, 3; 9 Nov. 1864, 3; *Daily Register*, 21 Oct. 1864, 2; 4 Nov. 1864, 3; 9 Nov. 1864, 3. On the dedication of St. Alphonsus Church, see John Lenhart, *History of St. Alphonsus Church* (Wheeling: n.p., 1956), 34.

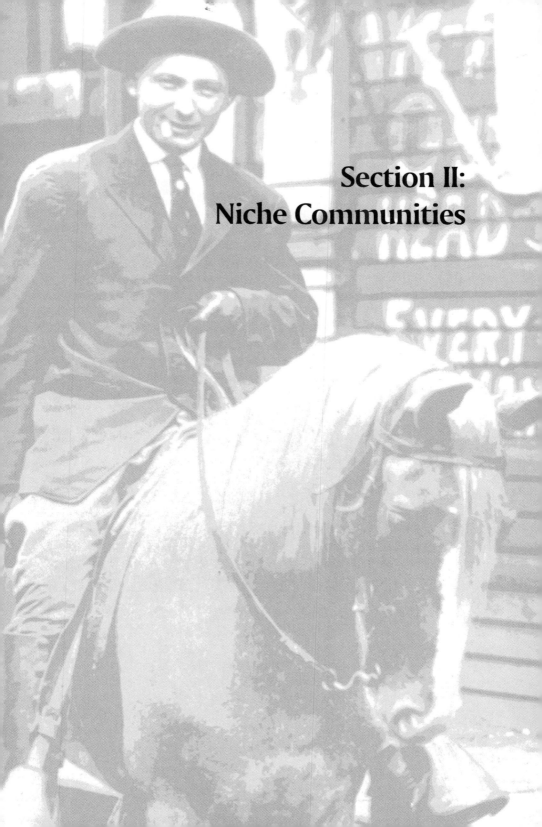

Section II:
Niche Communities

"Helvetia Brass Band." West Virginia and Regional History Collection, West Virginia University Libraries, Morgantown, W.Va.

Swiss Immigration to West Virginia 1864-1884: A Case Study

Elizabeth Cometti

Swiss immigration to the United States reached its peak in 1882-1883, the same years that witnessed the crest of the great migratory flow from Germany, the Scandinavian countries, and the Netherlands. The largest number of Swiss immigrants came from the German cantons of Schaffhausen, Glarus, Basel-Stadt, and Bern; hence those who took part in the modest exodus from Switzerland conformed to the essentially Teutonic character of the majority of the partici- pants in the second great stage of nineteenth-century migration.[1] The Swiss preferred to locate in the Middle West, but they also established important settlements in the Middle Atlantic States and in the South, as well as in Califor- nia.[2] In the southern states the number of Swiss immigrants increased after the Civil War, partly as a result of the persistent though often poorly organized efforts of those states to increase their immigrant population.[3] The efforts of West Virginia to attract immigrants followed the usual disorganized methods, and her experiences with Swiss immigration, particularly in the two decades following the war, illustrate a characteristic conflict of interests: on the one hand, the people of the state anxious to advance its prosperity; on the other, a legislature reluctant to provide funds and a few unscrupulous agents eager to appropriate whatever they could.

In West Virginia, Swiss immigration was a focal point for much of the immigration controversy, and the problems which arose there provide the basis for a case study which should throw light on the general immigration problems of the post-Civil War period. Swiss immigrants were generally esteemed in West Virginia, as they were throughout America. The American consuls in Switzer- land reported that the Swiss were a moral, ingenious, and industrious people, fortunate, in comparison with other Europeans, in their social, political, and economic backgrounds. Land ownership was widely diffused and a compulsory school system reduced illiteracy to a minimum. There was, to be sure, "some pinching" among the industrious poor, but little actual distress and scarcely any pauperism. Nor was there any of the labor unrest evident in other parts of

Source: The Mississippi Valley Historical Review 47 (June 1960): 66-87

51

Europe and in the United States. Emigration was stimulated more by the cheap, fertile lands, high wages, and superior opportunities in America than by the poverty, overpopulation, and technological dislocations in Switzerland.[4]

"The German ... emigrates when he can," it was said, "the Switzer only when he must."[5] Until the last third of the nineteenth century it was not unusual for the cantonal and communal governments to subsidize the emigration of indigent and, occasionally, of undesirable Swiss. Emigration was also stimulated by reports, written sometimes at the instigation of agents to facilitate their *commerce d' âmes*, and by material help from relatives and friends, who had preceded the prospective emigrant to America. But prosperity for one did not guarantee it for all, and by 1871 Swiss consuls in the United States were urging their government to discourage the emigration of paupers and of the unfit. The laissez-faire policy of some cantons and the lax enforcement of regulations in others, however, nullified local attempts to screen and protect emigrants.[6] The most powerful deterrent to precarious migration was the post-Civil War immigration policy of the United States, which denied admission to undesirable elements, including potential public charges, and to contract labor.[7]

The agent's role in Swiss emigration is evident in the per capita ratio of agencies to emigrants in the various Swiss cantons. The canton of Vaud, for example, with five sub-agents in a population of 238,730, had an annual emigration of one per cent, or a total of 957 emigrants from 1882 to 1885; Basel-Stadt, on the other hand, with twelve sub-agents in a population of 65,101, had an annual emigration of slightly more than 7.5 per cent, or a total of 1,976 during the same period.[8] In promoting emigration, however, the agents, whether American or Swiss, all too often cheated and deceived their clients and spread fantastic reports about conditions in the New World, where everyone, including the Indian, was reputed to be the friendliest of mortals.[9]

Many of the guidebooks on the United States which the Swiss and other Europeans saw were translated and printed at the expense and in the interest of land associations, railroad companies, and state immigration bureaus; therefore, in spite of the publisher's claim to impartiality, they were sectional in scope and not objective[10] In their eagerness to fill westbound immigrant trains and coaches, railroad companies gave large per capita commissions to steamship lines and immigration agents and diverted passengers from competitors. "All the officers connected with Castle Garden," it was reported, were "in the pay of some road or other and the Company that bids the highest will get the most immigrants."[11] This fierce competition at least brought some advantages to the immigrant, usually the victim of agents, hotel runners, ticket scalpers, and other irresponsible elements encountered in travel.[12] The railroads offered him such inducements as daily immigrant trains, special connections for the

West, special rates, improved accommodations, "colonist-sleepers," free baggage allowances, and reception centers at destination points, where cheap lands were available from the railroads, government, and land companies.[13]

Railroad companies and land associations found it advantageous to collaborate with state immigration agencies, hoping by this nexus to inspire confidence in the companies' activities and lift them "from the lower level of private enterprise for mere profit to the higher plane of public service."[14] Jacob Ottenheimer, for example, the promoter of a Swiss-German settlement in Kentucky, relied on the office of the State Geological Survey and Bureau of Immigration for a cheap source of advertising. Nor was it unusual for an agent to represent both a railroad or a land company and a state immigration bureau, with the company paying his expenses. In co-operating with private enterprise, the state director of immigration ran the risk, however, of being accused of partiality and of discriminating against parts of the state in the distribution of immigrants.[15]

The interplay of these essential forces in post-Civil War migration appeared in Swiss immigration to West Virginia. Even before the Civil War ended, this new state, born of that war, took steps to encourage immigration to the state. An act for this purpose, passed on March 3, 1864, authorized the governor to appoint a "commissioner of emigration," who was charged to enter into correspondence with "the principal sources of emigration" in Germany, Austria, Switzerland, Sweden, and Great Britain, and to publicize West Virginia's advantages. In executing his duties, the commissioner was to co-operate with the United States immigration officials, consulates, and commercial agencies, as well as with private and official emigrant and transportation societies in the European countries, and to secure the services of "intelligent and obliging correspondents" at emigration centers. The governor, in turn, was authorized to make arrangements with port authorities at Baltimore and with the Baltimore and Ohio Railroad for the guidance of foreigners to West Virginia, provided this service could be had at no additional expense.[16]

Joseph H. Diss Debar, appointed as the state's "commissioner of emigration," was well qualified for this post. A native of Alsace, where his father had been superintendent of the estates of the great Prince Cardinal de Rohan, Debar had received an excellent education in France, and had become a proficient linguist. He had sailed for the United States in 1842 on the same vessel that brought Charles Dickens to this country. While on shipboard, the young Alsatian, who was a skillful amateur artist, painted a small likeness of the famous Englishman. Four years later Debar moved to western Virginia as the agent of a large land company with holdings in Doddridge County.[17] In the secession crisis, Debar supported the Union and the movement for statehood in West

Virginia. In 1864 he was elected a representative in the state legislature and later that year was appointed commissioner of immigration.[18]

When Debar took office as commissioner, West Virginia had a population of around four hundred thousand, four per cent of which had migrated from Germany, Switzerland, Great Britain, Belgium, and the Scandinavian countries.[19] The settlement of the state, begun in 1731, had been fitful and uneven, interrupted by conflict and obstructed by formidable hills. A century later, the Potomac, Kanawha, Monongahela, and Ohio valleys had lost their frontier character, but the areas drained by the headwaters of these streams still challenged the pioneering spirit. Land was cheap. In the yet unexploited southern coal fields it was worth from fifty to seventy-five cents an acre; large tracts of timbered land at the head of the Cheat and Greenbrier rivers sold for between one and two and a half dollars per acre; and improved bottom land in the Tygart Valley cost only twenty to fifty dollars per acre. Coal, salt, and other mineral resources promised to be virtually inexhaustible. The climate, according to the guidebooks, was salubrious and the landscape spectacularly green. Railway facilities were still quite inadequate except in the northern part of the state, but the Covington and Ohio, a parent of the Chesapeake and Ohio, was pushing westward through the Kanawha Valley, and other lines were in various stages of planning. Despite many seasons of wear and tear, the ante-bellum turnpikes were still usable, and the streams which had served the pioneers, and the Indians before them, still found their way to the sea.[20]

Against these impressive assets, West Virginia had to admit certain liabilities. Among the worst of these was the prevailing disorder in the state's land records. Debar warned immigrants that "land suits should always be avoided in West Virginia, even at a sacrifice, by parties not in possession of a full purse, superhuman patience, and a long lease of life."[21] Not by coincidence were the principal advertisers in Debar's *West Virginia Handbook and Immigrant's Guide* lawyers specializing in Virginia and West Virginia land titles; immigrants, especially those with little or no knowledge of the English language, were the most likely dupes of unscrupulous land agents.

The "Southern antecedents" of West Virginia also repelled many foreigners, as did some unflattering reports about the natives, of whom 15 per cent were illiterate. The state was thus at a disadvantage in a period in which governments and railroads were beckoning immigrants farther west with generous offers of land. For many immigrants West Virginia had a reputation - not wholly deserved - of being "a rough, mountainous section, *exhausted by slave labor*, sparsely settled by an ignorant and un-enterprising people, and with land titles of an unsettled and dangerous character."[22]

A further difficulty stemmed from the failure of the state immigration act of 1864 to provide for financing the office of the commissioner, other than to stipulate that if he should visit the sources of emigration in Europe his expenses were to be "defrayed by subscriptions on the part of private individuals, associations or corporations having as one of their objects the encouragement of emigration."[23] It looked, indeed, as if the penny-pinching legislature intended that land speculators with a stake in immigration should pay the bill for promoting it.

Undismayed by the perplexities of his new office, Debar succeeded in publishing a small pamphlet in English and German, three thousand copies of which he circulated in the United States and abroad, and he appointed as general agent for southern Germany and Switzerland an official of the Interior Department of Württemberg.[24] But aside from a free pass issued by the Baltimore and Ohio Railroad, Debar received little encouragement from either private quarters or from the state legislature in his promotional work. Although both he and the governor made repeated recommendations for an immigration service which would attract small farmers, capital, and skilled labor to West Virginia,[25] no effective legislative action was taken, and during his seven years in office, from 1864 to 1871, the total disbursements in his favor came to only $4,824.44. The fruits of this outlay were correspondingly meager: just two colonies in "embryo," as Debar reported to the governor.[26] "Seven years, the Mountain [Debar] has laboured," scoffed a free-lance immigration agent in 1871, but "not a mouse" had the Commissioner produced.[27]

This criticism was altogether undeserved. In addition to the chilly indifference of the legislature to his proposals, Debar was at a disadvantage in competing for immigrants at Castle Garden, New York's debarkation center, where the officers in charge were receiving per capita commissions for directing passengers westward. Since the Baltimore and Ohio did not grant allowances for tickets sold at Castle Garden, the authorities there discouraged traffic to West Virginia on that line in favor of the Pennsylvania Central line to Pittsburgh, justifying this favoritism on the ground that it was cheaper – the difference was only $1.50 according to Debar – to go by the Pittsburgh than by the Baltimore route. The Baltimore and Ohio was finally compelled to reduce its immigrant fare by nearly one half to meet the competition of the Pennsylvania line to the Ohio River "over which so many emigrants originally bound" for West Virginia had "been let astray."[28]

Debar also encountered problems at the sources of emigration. "With few exceptions," he reported, "the recruiting of emigrants is everywhere looked upon with disfavor and jealousy, and even prohibited by law under heavy penalties. Even the license of forwarding agent, or transportation broker, is only granted to persons of respectable standing, under heavy bond and security, and immediately withdrawn upon conviction of *solicitation to emigration*." Officials, such as Debar, were merely "tolerated" to furnish information about their country, and then only to prospective emigrants who presumably had decided on their destination.[29]

The longer Debar remained in office, the more he was convinced that few people would be attracted to West Virginia unless the state reformed its land laws, improved its transportation facilities, and provided more complete information on the resources of the state. To attain this last objective, he advocated a geological survey of the state. But West Virginia was not yet ready for this undertaking, nor was it willing to support an adequate publicity program. Inquiries concerning handbooks, maps, and geological surveys regularly arrived at the office of the governor, frequently from correspondents who could promote immigration, but it was seldom possible to furnish in full the information requested. Debar thought that government and private interests should cooperate in promoting immigration, the former by organizing a state board of immigration and county societies, the latter, by selling land with perfect titles, on easy terms, and at prices "not only fair but below market rates." This financial sacrifice, he believed, would speedily be offset by an increment in land values resulting from the influx of settlers.[30]

Debar favored group migration, in nuclei of twenty or thirty culturally homogeneous families, organized for their mutual protection and benefit. The settlers should have cultural facilities and should manage their farms as they wished.[31] One of his last official appeals was in behalf of his former countrymen in Alsace and Lorraine after the Franco-Prussian War. Something should have been done in West Virginia, he said, to aid the victims of that conflict. A public collection would have attracted favorable attention to the state, which needed the technical skill of the spirited and intelligent inhabitants of the ceded provinces. He chided West Virginians on their failure to recognize the advantages which would accrue to the state, but his efforts again were unsuccessful.[32] His service as commissioner was terminated in 1871, when a Democratic administration came into office and the state board of public works, acting under authority given by a new immigration law, appointed Dr. Daniel Mayer, and, later, the Reverend James Richards, to succeed him. The official achievements of these two commissioners were as inconsequential as their combined expenditures of less than one thousand dollars in eight years.[33]

During Debar's service as commissioner he had shown a preference, in accordance with the immigration act of 1864, for immigrants from northern Europe, including Switzerland. To the Swiss, in turn, the Mountain State, with its clear brooks, forested slopes, and excellent climate, seemed to offer enough similarities to their homeland to be especially attractive; and by 1869 the first steps had been taken toward the establishment of Swiss settlements in the state. In that year some of the members of a Swiss *Gruetli Verein* in Brooklyn, impressed by the glowing accounts brought to them by a compatriot who had been in the eastern part of the state as a surveyor, decided to migrate to Randoph County. There they purchased land in lots of one hundred acres. Some months later, however, the success of their venture was seriously threatened when a court decision voided their titles. In order to retain their property the immigrants had to pay for it a second time, and it seems probable that only the tactfulness with which the legal owners refrained from pressing a hard bargain prevented the disillusioned Swiss from abandoning both the project and any further interest in West Virginia.[34]

The little settlement, nostalgically named Helvetia, grew slowly. Four years after its founding it had only slightly over two hundred inhabitants, mostly of Swiss origin, but including, also, a small contingent of German immigrants. The staple crops were potatoes and grain; there were two schools and two sawmills; and by 1875 the inevitable brass band and mutual aid society – *Schweizer-Kranken-Unterstützung-Verein* – had been organized. By 1880 new colonies had been established at Alpena and West Huttonsville in Randolph County, while the neighboring counties of Fayette, Kanawha, and Webster, south and west of Randolph, had also attracted a few Swiss who founded Cotton Hill, Kendalia, and New St. Gallen.[35]

Although land in Randolph County was of excellent quality and contained rich coal deposits, the Swiss consul general thought that its price, two dollars per acre, was too high considering the poor transportation facilities of the county. Ownership of land was highly concentrated; one man owned or controlled more than half of the land in the county. The landowners preferred to sell directly to the settlers, whom they cautioned not to buy from self-appointed agents at the risk of acquiring fraudulent titles.[36] The advice was sound, for the dealings of some agents then at work were crippling the efforts of the state to attract the Swiss and other immigrants.

Since the German-speaking immigrants had need of an interpreter in their business dealings with the West Virginians, they unfortunately welcomed the arrival in Randolph County of Carl Emmanuel Lutz, a compatriot who had been living in the United States for many years. Taking his Swiss origin at its exceptionally high face value, the settlers of Helvetia did not investigate Lutz's past until his conduct began to belie the Swiss reputation for integrity.[37] This man, they later learned when he was denounced by one of his victims as "a miserable crook, defrauder, and liar," was a member of a good Bernese family and had been an employee of the Swiss government until he was sentenced to a five-year prison term in 1839. Leaving Switzerland some time later, Lutz came to Jeffersonville, New York, where he borrowed money from his trusting fellow countrymen and swindled several people. Lawsuits followed, even one with his son. Jumping bail following an adverse court decision, he went to Scranton, Pennsylvania, and eventually to West Virginia.[38]

In West Virginia, Lutz was to become a principal figure in shaping the course of Swiss immigration, and one of those who did most to undo the efforts which Debar and others had made to present a favorable image of the state to emigrants. Attired in a fresh suit of "sheep's clothing," he opened an office in Randolph County, ostensibly for the purpose of helping the settlers. Since those who had land for sale did not give him a commission for his services, he levied a dollar per acre from the buyers. If the latter paid in installments, Lutz kept the money until the last payment had been made, at which time he gave the total amount received to the seller and the deed to the buyer. The danger in this arrangement was that the owner could sell the land to someone else while the first purchaser was paying for it. Lutz himself was accused not only of reselling and giving titles for land that had already been sold, but also of tampering with blueprints, and of buying land on credit, reselling it, and never paying the original owners. Although this strange "protector" soon became persona non grata in Helvetia, he established promising connections with some leading citizens of the area. Consequently, instead of leaving Randolph County following his unlamented departure from Helvetia, he boldly transferred to Alpena.[39]

His most significant work was now to begin. In 1879 the West Virginia legislature, heretofore extremely apathetic toward immigration, was stirred into action by petitions from prominent residents of Randolph, Harrison, Lewis, and Barbour counties in support of a petition from Lutz praying for an appropriation of money for the purpose of encouraging immigration from Switzerland. In March the legislature passed an act cut to his order. It directed the governor to commission Lutz as state immigration agent, and specified that he should hold this position "until changed by the Legislature or removed by the Governor for any act detrimental to the interests of the state." The agent was required "to use all proper means to induce Swiss and other immigration" to West Virginia and to furnish information on the state, without "any partiality or misrepresentation … relative to the various sections and interests of the state."[40]

Late that summer Lutz issued an unusual communication to his "countrymen in Switzerland" which gave anything but an impartial account of West Virginia. The new commissioner stated that while he was prepared to give information on all the counties of the state, for the moment he would "only talk to some extent about Randolph County, and principally about Dry Fork District in said county." He invited immigrants to this region but limited his invitation to those having good health, intelligence, industry, willingness to endure hardships during the first five years, and possession "of about two hundred dollars after their arrival here." Dry Fork District, he told them, had many assets to recommend it – no hail nor hurricanes, communication by roads with the outside world, land "not too stony nor steep," "no animals or insects to fear," and "perfect titles to land." The soil was excellent, timber was varied and abundant, and nature was, in short, at her superb best. Wild land cost only from three to five dollars per acre. West Virginians "were a clever and accommodating people." Alpena, the progressive new Swiss colony, was connected with the outside world by a wagon road and postoffice. A sawmill had been built and a school would soon be ready. Provisions were cheap. A good cow could be bought for twenty-five dollars, a horse for sixty dollars, and a sheep for two dollars. Those interested in coming to this garden spot of Dry Fork should communicate with Otto Stoer, at Basel, who would instruct them "how to find Alpina by the nearest route."[41]

But the close of this communication was even more unusual. It showed that some report of Lutz's activities had already reached Switzerland, for he followed his description of the charms of Dry Fork with a strident defense of his own reputation: "All who are inclined to believe [that] the West Virginia Legislature and the Governor of the State had entrusted the interests of the State and the immigrants into the hands of a rogue, as it was stated lately in a newspaper out in Switzerland, by a set of low, mean and selfish characters, settled at Helvetia, in this county, and warning people not to come here, of course such parties are not expected to be seen in our colony, Alpina. The said black spirits in human bodies are already sued before our higher court, and also a pamphlet is this moment under print, which will describe and mark what kind of beings the said characters are."[42]

In West Virginia, the Swiss Aid Society for Illness, to whose members Lutz was referring, had indeed been active in frustrating the plans of their former protector. The Society had informed the Swiss authorities that Lutz's agents, Otto Stoer of Basel and John Rudolph Strasser of Bern, had flooded the Swiss newspapers with false reports, as a result of which several families had been induced to go to Alpena, in reality "an isolated region in the Allegheny Mountains." Lutz, the Helvetians had written, was a finished scoundrel. [43]

The police department of Bern could not immediately investigate the activities of Strasser because he was in West Virginia during the summer of 1879. But the Basel police lost no time in summoning Otto Stoer. He testified that in arranging emigration to West Virginia he was acting in good faith, confident that settlers were bound to make good in that region. Contrary to the accusation, he had not published false statements; all he had done was to invite prospective emigrants to come to him for information, after which he had forwarded their names to Lutz, who was, he said, a man of good reputation. What better recommendation could Lutz have than his appointment as sole immigration agent of West Virginia? Stoer denied receiving a per capita payment for the settlers he directed to Alpena, but he did admit receiving a commission of five per cent for selling land to them. The charges of the Helvetia Aid Society were utterly groundless, he insisted, and stemmed from jealousy of the rival colony of Alpena, which was not isolated, as was charged, because mail arrived there twice a week.[44]

Much of Stoer's testimony was substantiated by Ulrich Bieri, an immigrant to Alpena, in a deposition prepared for the Bernese authorities. Indeed, Bieri was so convinced that any industrious man could make a good living in West Virginia that he had returned to Bern to take his large family to the new state. Alpena, he said, was laid out for eighty houses, some of which were still under construction. Prospective builders received a half-acre of land without cost and paid three dollars an acre for what they bought. Bieri denied that all settlers in Helvetia were hostile to Lutz, a very respectable man who had been helpful to the immigrants.[45]

The police record of John R. Strasser, who testified on August 31, showed that he was no novice in matters of immigration; indeed, he had been twice punished for violations of immigration laws.[46] In his testimony Strasser, like Stoer, accused the Helvetia Aid Society of misrepresentations prompted by hate and revenge. The signers of the Society's report, he said, were even then under bail following their arrest for libel. It was Helvetia that was virtually inaccessible, and not Alpena, which was only eighteen miles from the county seat (Beverly). On the recent Fourth of July one hundred and fifty visitors had come to Alpena and not one of them had been lost or had encountered trouble finding the settlement.[47]

In view of the conflict in evidence the Swiss authorities acted with caution. While no legal action was taken against the agents, the Federal Council stopped their activities and published a statement in the *Federal Gazette (Bundesblatt)* advising against emigration to Alpena, as the colony was located "in a remote region and for a considerable distance almost entirely deprived of the means of communication," and warning that "the greatest caution" should be used in acquiring land in the colony.[48]

While the hearings were going on in Switzerland, Lutz was continuing his dubious promotional schemes. In May, 1879, he wrote to Governor Henry M. Mathews of West Virginia about a plan of the Swiss government to locate "a complex of about 100,000 acres of wild lands" suitable for Swiss immigrants. Tennessee, he warned, was trying to attract the prospective settlers, but he was convinced that if West Virginia would take proper steps it would be favored, especially since the Governor's home county of Greenbrier had the kind of land that the Swiss wanted. He cautioned Mathews not to write to the Swiss consul in Washington, because that official had an interest in a colony in Grundy County, Tennessee, and therefore was not impartial; he should communicate, instead, with Captain John B. Isler, in care of the Swiss consulate. "I give to you the above hints," Lutz added significantly, "and leave it now to your Excellency to make use of it if you choose to do so."[49]

Lutz's primary object in writing this letter is not altogether clear; but six weeks later C. J. P. Cresap, an attorney in Randolph County, sent to the Governor's private secretary a request from Lutz for funds to enable "Strasser the Agent of Lutz from Switzerland ... to spend a month in traveling over the State." Whatever might be left "after paying Strasser's expenses," Cresap explained, "will be spent in Europe advertising & Strasser desires to take it with him."[50] When the Helvtia Aid Society learned of this request, its spokesman immediately forwarded the information to the Swiss Federal Council as fresh proof that Strasser and Lutz were indeed trafficking in human beings.[51]

By the fall of 1879 the uproar against Lutz was subsiding in Helvetia, but in Alpena new charges were being made. Swiss immigrants there wrote to Governor Mathews accusing Lutz of (1) using improper means and promises to attract immigrants to Alpena, (2) borrowing money from them under false pretenses, (3) taking commissions for interpreting and for making purchases of land and chattels for the settlers, (4) threatening to sue the settlers for organizing into a protective association, and (5) compelling some settlers to sign a petition in his favor. The complainants warned the Governor that if these activities were permitted to continue, not only the welfare of the new colony, but also the reputation of West Virginia would be undermined. Instead of using his office to aid newcomers, they said, Commissioner Lutz was using it to victimize them.[52]

Mathews, after some delay, entrusted the investigation of these charges to Joseph J. Woods, a member of the state senate, who met with both complainants and accused and with Lutz's real estate associates, Elihu Hutton and Cresap.[53] On the basis of the hearings and written evidence submitted by the defendant, Woods decided that "none of the charges made in the petition can be substantially sustained." Nor did he believe that there were "any other matters aside from those specified in the petition wherein Mr. Lutz has acted in an improper manner, or in a manner contrary to his duties as Commissioner of Immigration." If the settlers had not found homes on their arrival, as had been promised them, that was the fault of the construction company, not of Lutz. Lutz had borrowed money from some of the immigrants, but only for the purpose of helping newcomers; when Lutz was repaid, he would discharge his own obligations. The readiness of Woods to accept the testimony of Lutz and his witnesses did not extend to his accusers. The complainants, Woods reported to the Governor, had expected too much in Alpena, where they were compelled to perform pioneer labor, for which they had no inclination. In time they would become satisfied with their new surroundings.[54]

If the charges from Alpena did not lead to conviction of Lutz for improper conduct as commissioner of immigration, it did free that community from his "fangs." Still further embarrassed by the loss of over six thousand acres of land on account of delinquent taxes, he quickly transferred his activities to new hunting grounds in nearby West Huttonsville. Here a community was being established as a prospective Swiss settlement under the aegis of the West Huttonsville Land and Immigration Company, an organization in which Lutz had a guiding interest. The Company sent an agent to Switzerland and within a few months he had conducted more than thirty immigrants to West Huttonsville. The town was laid out in eighty half-acre lots, some of which were given to actual settlers or were sold for residence or business sites. Lutz shrewdly donated several lots to a group of influential West Virginians. The promoters of West Huttonsville promised the public that they would "handle only such property as had good title,"their "object being to establish a safe and reliable Agency," so that persons dealing with them might make "safe investments with no risk of buying 'WILD-CAT TITLES.'"[55]

The anti-Lutz faction in Alpena hastened, out of "purely humane interest," to report this new venture to John Hitz, the Swiss consul general in Washington. The consul was told that the West Huttonsville Land Company actually intended to make the immigrants pay the traveling expenses of the agent by increasing the price of the land sold to them; and he was urged to take the necessary steps to prevent the defrauding of prospective immigrants. Hitz decided, however, not to take any official action against Lutz or the company; but he promised to watch the developments at West Huttonsville and to interfere if necessary, even though Lutz's business associate, Elihu Hutton, had denied the charges of fraud. Privately, Hitz deplored that a fine state like West Virginia "so inviting to foreign emigrants should in the matter of immigration have been so unfortunate as to select a person to represent it, so sadly deficient in essential qualifications for the trust as Mr. Lutz has proved himself to be."[56]

Lutz continued to style himself state immigration agent and to submit reports to the governors for several years after the expenditure of the single appropriation of five hundred dollars, for which he gave only the vaguest accounting. He took credit for bringing a total of 725 settlers to Helvetia, Alpena, and West Huttonsville, and said that he had even paid from his own pocket some of the expenses involved in their immigration. More Swiss would have come, he assured Governor Mathews, but for the groundless warning against Alpena issued by the Federal Council of Switzerland and the slanderous propaganda of railroad agents who had induced twelve Swiss families originally bound for West Huttonsville to continue westward. "If our authorities do not adopt measures to counteract this kind of underhand business," he warned the Governor, "we will see our money go to build up other States." Among the proposals offered at this time by Lutz for improving the immigration service in West Virginia was one in which he especially urged that the state acquire about fifty thousand acres of wild land to be sold at the lowest price possible, and that it extend credit to needy families for the first three years following their arrival, after which they would be required to make annual payments on the principal and interest. As an alternate plan, he proposed that the state empower the immigration agent, or some other person, to select fifty thousand acres of unimproved land, one tenth of which would be given to poor families and the remainder sold to immigrants of means at slightly increased price. Only land suitable for immigrant Swiss farmers should be considered.[57]

Although no action was taken on these proposals, Lutz continued to send recommendations and requests to the legislature and to Governor Mathews and his successor. To support one of his plans he asked for five thousand dollars, although two thousand, he concluded, would be "better than nothing at all."[58] The legislature, he later charged, was remiss in failing to give him the necessary support, and he had been obliged to ask his agents in Switzerland not to send any more immigrants. Nowhere outside of West Virginia, he complained, was there an agent "without Salary, without appropriations nor any other encouragement to work with." He finally reduced his request "to the most modest sum of $500-$1000 per year," and left the matter of his salary to the judgment of the legislature; but the legislature would not grant him even this modest sum.[59]

The state was in need of a more wholesome immigration administration and a more effective immigration policy than Lutz could offer, and in his message to the legislature on January 12, 1881, Governor Mathews, who had sometimes supported him, advocated major changes in the program. The Governor explained that although West Virginia was "especially inviting to the Swiss and the inhabitants of the mountainous portion of Germany," some "persons unfriendly" to the state had published articles in the Swiss press which "grossly misrepresented the resources, laws, and condition of society of the State." A few promoters of Swiss colonization, particularly Emanuel D. Ludwig, had done much, however, to counteract this unfavorable publicity; and three scientists who had visited West Virginia in the interest of the "Swiss Commerce and Colonization Society" were expected to submit a good report on the state. He asked the legislature to repeal the existing "crude and imperfect" immigration laws in favor of an enactment providing for an efficient immigration service, adequately financed. He also advocated the publication of a handbook on the state's resources to replace the nearly exhausted edition hastily prepared for the Centennial Exposition.[60]

In response to the Governor's recommendations, the senate, a few days later, appointed a committee to study past immigration measures and to recommend new legislation. The report of this committee, prefaced by the customary complimentary comments on natural resources, bluntly stated that all past efforts to promote immigration had been "desultory and without system." Records in the auditor's office showed that sums totaling $6,408.71 had been spent for this purpose, yet nothing could be found to show how the money was expended or what number of immigrants had been "induced to settle in this State" through the instrumentality of immigration agents. None of them had made any reports, so far as the Committee could find, "except E. C. Lutz [*sic*] by which it appears that some seven hundred and fifty-five were located in Randolph County, but only a part of that number during the time of his term of office." Apparently the committee had not seen Debar's reports, nor had it found any statistics showing the number of immigrants residing in West Virginia.

From testimony taken during the study the committee concluded that "one of the greatest impediments to immigration into this State was the lack of a proper organized Bureau of Immigration and Agriculture and also the reputed defectiveness of ... land title." Immigration agents for other states had "industriously circulated pamphlets and circulars through many countries of Europe, as well as various parts of the United States, disparaging the titles of ... lands [in West Virginia], and warning emigrants of the danger of purchasing homes in this State, by reason thereof." Two other causes of failure, the committee believed, were the superior immigration service of other states and the well-organized and successful efforts of the railroads and other common carriers to induce immigrants to go farther west. The committee had no doubt that "a well devised system of immigration would be highly promotive" in bringing "good, substantial settlers" to the state, where they could buy land with perfect titles for as little as one to five dollars per acre. If West Virginia continued "to pursue the loose and unsystematized policy of former years," the report concluded, "the State had better entirely abandon all efforts at immigration."[61] Following the reading of this report, a member of the committee introduced a comprehensive bill to provide the much-recommended improved immigration service; but this bill was tabled at its second reading,[62] and the promotion of immigration ceased to be a matter of legislative concern in West Virginia.

The conditions which controlled immigration were changing in 1881 and 1882. In Europe, the Swiss and other governments, alarmed by the malpractices of emigration agents and carriers, adopted legislation to regulate their activities and to stop the dissemination of misleading propaganda about conditions in the

New World. Doubtless the problems which arose in West Virginia had some bearing on Switzerland's taking a lead in legislating for the protection of her emigrants. [63]

The changing economy of West Virginia was also affecting the state's immigration needs. Until the 1880's West Virginia, essentially an agricultural state with vast tracts of unimproved lands, was seeking to attract farmers with some capital. The best recruiting grounds for such people were the countries of northern and western Europe. Then came the spectacular development of the southern coal fields in the wake of the Chesapeake and Ohio and the Norfolk and Western railroads. The mushrooming coal companies along these routes needed cheap, unskilled brawn to exploit the newly opened mines. It mattered not whether these laborers had any capital, for the mining communities and everything in them, from the monotonous rows of shacks to the smoking coke ovens, were owned by the employers. These new captains of industry found a plentiful supply of labor in the swelling stream of immigrants from southern and eastern Europe and of southern Negroes. No agents were needed to bring these people, hungry for work, to West Virginia; a soiled card from a friend, a word heard at a railroad station, a rumor sufficed.

The census reports of the last three decades of the nineteenth century indicate the changing character of foreign immigration to West Virginia and to other parts of the United States. In 1880 the national origins of the four leading elements in the foreign-born population of West Virginia, which totaled 18,265, were British (9,503), German (7,029), Swiss (810), and Canadian (255). Ten years later the German element led with 7,292, followed by the British with 2,700, the Italian with 632, and the Swiss with 610, in a total foreign-born population of 18,883. In 1900 the number of foreign-born inhabitants in West Virginia had increased to 22,451. Of these, 6,537 had come from Germany, 2,921 from Italy, 1,025 form Austria, and 810 from Hungary. The Swiss, with 696, had been relegated to sixth place. Even in Randolph County they accounted for only 27 per cent of the foreign-born population.[64] But the isolated, stunted little communities of Helvetia and Alpena continued to display the unmistakable stamp of their Swiss origin far into the twentieth century.

NOTES

1. Oscar Handlin, *Immigration as a Factor in American History* (Englewood Cliffs, N. J., 1959), 16; Ludwig Karrer, *L' Émigration Suisse et la Loi Federale sur les Operations des Agences d'Émigration* (Berne, 1887), 139. The author gratefully acknowledges the kindness of Dr. Leonhard Haas, Director of the Bundesarchiv, Bern, and of Sister M. Alacoque Funkeler and Dr. Walter Perl for their assistance in translating.

2. Under the sponsorship of associations or individuals, many of the Swiss established colonies in which they frequently perpetuated the names, the economy, and the customs of their homeland. See Guy S. Métraux, "Social and Cultural Aspects of Swiss Immigration into the United States in the Nineteenth Century" (Ph.D. dissertation, Yale University, 1949), 22-27, 53-54, 66-73, 106-38; Karreer, *L'Émigration Suisse*, 5-6, 24-29, 35-37.

3. See Bert J. Loewenberg, "Efforts of the South to Encourage Immigration, 1865-1900," *South Atlantic Quarterly* (Durham), XXXIII (October, 1934), 363-85. For typical local attempts to encourage immigration, *Proceedings of the State Immigration Convention, Held under the Auspices of the Virginia Agricultural and Mechanical Society ..., Richmond, Virginia, October 16-17, 1894* (Richmond, 1894); Jeán Dell'Orto, *Immigration et Colonisation en Louisiane* (New Orleans, 1877).

4. "Emigration and Immigration: Reports of the Consular Officers of the United States, " *House Exec. Docs.*, 49 Cong., 2 Sess., No. 157 (Serial 2483), 332-51. Only one small group of emigrants, converts to Mormonism, left Switzerland for religious reasons during this period. *Ibid.*, 341-42, 351; Karrer, *L'Émigration Suisse*, 151-52, 191.

5. *House Exec. Docs.*, 49 Cong., 2 Sess., No. 157, p. 350.

6. Karrer, *L'Émigration Suisse*, 15-41, 99-105; Métraux, "Swiss Immigration," 54-55. As early as 1855 the canton of Ticino forbade all communal subsidies for emigration and all contracts obligating the emigrant to personal service in return for the cost of transportation.

7. Edith Abbott, *Immigration: Select Documents and Case Records* (Chicago, 1924), 181-88. The problems of Swiss emigration were greatly reduced as a result of the Swiss Federal Laws of December 24, 1880, and of March 22, 1888, for controlling the operation of emigration agencies, which specifically enjoined the migration of aged, sick, infirm, or destitute persons, as well as minors. Karrer, *L'Émigration Suisse*, 114-20; James D. Whelpley, *The Problem of the Immigrant* (London, 1905), 179-206.

8. Karrer, *L'Émigration Suisse,* 139-40.

9. *Ibid.*, 38, 181-84; *House Exec. Docs.*, 49 Cong., 2 Sess., No. 157, pp. 337-38.

10. For examples of such publications, see *California: Issued by the Immigrant Association of California* (San Francisco, 1882); C. E. Williams, *Yuba and Sutter Counties, California: Their Resources, Advantages, and Opportunities* (San Francisco, 1887); *Emigrant's Guide to Western, Central, Eastern, and Southern Texas* (Houston, 1874). More objective than these was Evan R. Jones, *The Emigrants' Friend: Containing*

Information and Advice for Persons Intending to Emigrate to the United States (London, 1880). See also James B. Hedges, "The Colonization Work of the Northern Pacific Railroad," *Mississippi Valley Historical Review* (Cedar Rapids), XIII (December, 1926), 315-16; Hedges, "Promotion of Immigration to the Pacific Northwest by the Railroads," *ibid.*, XV (September, 1928), 186, 201; Loewenberg, "Efforts of the South to Encourage Immigration," *South Atlantic Quarterly*, XXXIII (October, 1934), 375-76.

11. Quoted in Hedges, "Colonization Work of the Northern Pacific," *Mississippi Valley Historical Review*, XIII (December, 1926), 338.

12. *Ibid.*, 318; Karrer, *L'Émigration Suisse*, 18; "Immigrant Passenger Business," *Railway Age* (Chicago), XIII (November 16, 1888), 730-31.

13. *Second Annual Report of the Great Northern Railway Company, Fiscal Year Ending June 30th. 1891*, p.16; "Emigration Agent," *S P Bulletin, Texas and Louisiana Lines* (May, 1958), 22-25; Hedges, "Colonization Work of the Northern Pacific," *Mississippi Valley Historical Review*, XIII (December, 1926), 320-21, 337; Loewenberg, "Efforts of the South to Encourage Immigration," *South Atlantic Quarterly*, XXXIII (October, 1934), 376-77; St. Louis *Republican*, April 23, 1880; New York *Daily Tribune*, January 8, April 17, 1868.

14. Hedges, "Colonization Work of the Northern Pacific," *Mississippi Valley Historical Review*, XIII (December, 1926), 341-42.

15. A. E. Bigge, "Ottenheim, Kentucky: A Planned Settlement," *Filson Club History Quarterly* (Louisville), XXX (October, 1956), 299-314.

16. *Acts of the Legislature of West Virginia, at Its Second Session Commencing January 19, 1864* (Wheeling, 1864), 29-31.

17. Boyd B. Stutler, "Joseph H. Diss Debar - Prophet, Colonizer," *West Virginia Review* (Charleston), IX (December, 1931), 154-56; Roberta S. Turney, "The Encouragement of Immigration in West Virginia, 1863-1871," *West Virginia History* (Charleston), XII (October, 1950), 46-60. Debar's portrait of Dickens is now in the West Virginia State Museum.

18. West Virginia Legis., *House Journal*, 2 Sess. (1864), 13. A contested election had been decided against him by the House in 1863. *Ibid.*, 1 Sess. (1863), 23, 120, 122, 127, 134-35. Although Debar is remembered chiefly in West Virginia as the designer of the state seal, he was also a champion of education, internal improvements, a geological survey, and a liberal immigration policy. See *First Biennial Report of the Department of Archives and History of the State of West Virginia* (Charleston, 1906), 80-87; and "Report of the Committee on Seals," West Virginia Legis., *House Journal*, 1 Sess. (1863), 1-2.

19. Joseph H. Diss Debar, *The West Virginia Hand Book and Immigrant's Guide* (Parkersburg, 1870), 31.

20. *Ibid.*, 172, 185; Phil Conley (ed.), *The West Virginia Encyclopedia* (Charleston, 1929), 729-32; Charles H. Ambler, *A History of Transportation in the Ohio Valley* (Glendale, 1932).

21. Debar, *West Virginia Hand Book*, 170.

22. Joseph H. Diss Debar, *Sixth Annual Report of the Commissioner of Immigration of ... West Virginia ... 1869* (Wheeling, 1870), 11; Debar, *Seventh Annual Report of the Commissioner of Immigration of ... West Virginia ... 1870* (Wheeling, 1871), 5; Daniel Mayer, *Eight Annual Report of the Commissioner of Immigration of ... West Virginia* (Charleston, 1872), 3.
23. West Virginia Legis., *Acts*, 2 Sess. (1864), 30.
24. Debar, *Sixth Annual Report*, 4. When the supply of pamphlets was exhausted, Debar had others printed and distributed, together with additional publicity material.
25. Debar, *Sixth Annual Report* ; West Virginia Legis., *House Journal*, 3 Sess. (1865), 14; West Virginia Legis., *Senate Journal*, 6 Sess. (1868), 22; *ibid.*, 9 Sess. (1871), 20-21; *Biennial Message of Gov. Henry M. Mathews to the Legislature of West Virginia, Session of 1881* (Wheeling, 1881), 18-23.
26. West Virginia Legis., *Senate Journal,* 16 Sess. (1881), 238; Debar, *Sixth Annual Report,* 17.
27. W. F. Gray to John J. Jacob, March 18, 21, 1871, Jacob Papers (Library, West Virginia Department of Archives and History), Box XXIII, No. 64.
28. Joseph H. Diss Debar, *Annual Report of the Commissioner of Immigration, 1867,* 6; Turney, "Encouragement of Immigration," *West Virginia History,* XII (October, 1950), 53-56.
29. Debar, *Sixth Annual Report,* 10; Karrer, *L'Émigration Suisse,* 99-105.
30. On the need for a geological survey, see West Virginia Legis., *Senate Journal,* 15 Sess. (1879), 32-33.
31. Debar, *Sixth Annual Report,* 16-24; *Seventh Annual Report,* 5.
32. Parkersburg *Daily Times,* March 3, 15, 17, 1871.
33. Turney, "Encouragement of Immigration," *West Virginia History,* XII (October, 1950), 59-60; West Virginia Legis., *Senate Journal,* 16 Sess. (1881), 238; Mayer, *Eighth Annual Report,* 3-4.
34. Eugene Daetwyler, Annie Teuscher, and E. Metzner, *The Story of the Helvetia Community* (Morgantown, W.Va., n.d.), 3-6; Nettie Vass Davis, "Helvetia - West Virginia's Swiss Village," *West Virginia Review,* XII (December, 1934), 80-81.
35. Swiss Consulate General, Washington, "Administrative Report," 1875 (Bundesarchiv, Bern), 101-112; "Projected Colony, Immigration in West Virginia, 1879," EVD - BIGA - Immigration, 1848-1934 (Bundesarchiv), Box 18, folio 2; John Schatzman to Henry M. Mathews, February 28, 1881, Emanuel D. Ludwig to Mathews, September 26, 1879, May 22, 1880, Henry M. Mathews Papers (Library, West Virginia Department of Archives and History), Box XXXVI (b), Nos. 287, 214.
36. Swiss Consulate, "Report," 1875.
37. Daetwyler *et al., Helvetia Community,* 5-6.
38. August Vogel to the Federal Council, March 24, 1879, and Ed. van Bergen to Vogel, April 28, 1879, "Projected Colony Alpina: Randolph County, West Virginia," EVD - BIGA - Immigration, 1848-1934, Box 18.
39. Swiss Consulate, "Report," 1875. The conduct of Otto Brunner in Bernstadt, Kentucky, was somewhat similar to that of Lutz. Métraux, "Swiss Immigration," 138-47.

40. West Virginia Legis., *House Journal*, 15 Sess. (1879), 217, 292-93.

41. The spelling of the name of this community has changed from "Alpina" or "Alpine" to "Alpena." Hamill Kenny, *West Virginia Place Names* (Piedmont, W. Va., 1945), 77-78. Otto Stoer of Basel had twenty-seven sub-agents in 1882 and 1883, twenty-five in 1884, and twenty-four in 1885. Karrer, *L'Émigration Suisse*, 122.

42. "Report ... State Agent on Immigration," West Virginia Legis., *House Journal*, 16 Sess. (1881), 1-3.

43. August Vogel to Federal Council, March 24, 1879, "Projected Colony Alpina," Immigration, 1848-1934, Box 18.

44. A. von Werdt to Director of Justice and Police Department, Bern, August 4, 1879; Werdt to the Government of the Canton of Basel (endorsed by Department of Commerce and Agriculture, August 7, 1879); Report, Police Department, Canton of Basel, August 9, 1879, "Projected Colony Alpina," Immigration, 1848-1934, Box 18.

45. Deposition of Ulrich Bieri, August 25, 1879, *ibid.*

46. Reports, Police Department, Bern, February 12, 17, 1879, *ibid.* Strasser had also been exiled for theft and disturbing the peace and was regarded as a man of unfriendly and rebellious disposition toward his family and neighbors.

47. John R. Strasser, Report for Federal Council, August 31, 1879, *ibid.* See Clara M. Preysz, "The Swiss Settlement at Alpena, W. Va.," Randolph County Historical Society, *Magazine of History and Biography* (Elkins, W. Va.), No. 9 (1937), 33-37.

48. President of the Council of the Canton of Basel to Swiss Department of Commerce and Agriculture, August 13, 1879; Department of Commerce and Agriculture to Federal Council, September 3, 1879; Council of the Canton of Bern to Department of Commerce and Agriculture, September 10, 1879; Excerpt from the Protocol of the eighty-first meeting of the Swiss Federal Council, September 10, 1879, "Projected Colony Alpina," Immigration, 1848-1934, Box 18. See, also, Emigration to the Colony "Alpina," Department of Commerce and Agriculture, September 10, 1879, translation, Mathews Papers, Box XLIV (b), "Miscellaneous."

49. Lutz to Mathews, May 28, 1879, Mathews Papers, Box XXXVI (b), No. 217. On Grundy County, Tennessee, see Karrer, *L'Émigration Suisse*, 25-29.

50. C. J. P. Cresap to Randolph Stalnaker, July 7, 1879, Mathews Papers, Box XXXVI (a), No. 68. See also George W. Atkinson and Alvaro F. Gibbens, *Prominent Men of West Virginia* (Wheeling, 1890), 67, 527-28, and Hu Maxwell, *History of Randolph County* (Morgantown, 1898), 233.

51. August Vogel to Federal Council, July 11, 1879, "Projected Colony Alpina," Immigration, 1848-1934, Box 18.

52. R. Agricola to Mathews, October 15, 1879, "Report ... State Agent on Immigration," West Virginia Legis., *House Journal*, 16 Sess. (1881), 3-4.

53. Atkinson and Gibbens, *Prominent Men of West Virginia*, 80, 707.

54. "Report ... State Agent on Immigration," West Virginia Legis., *House Journal*, 16 Sess. (1881), 3-4; State of West Virginia to Joseph J. Woods, July, 1880, Mathews Papers, Box XLIV (b). Compare with the report of the investigation

commission to the Swiss consul concerning Grundy County, Tennessee. Karrer, *L'Émigration Suisse, 25-29.*

55. Beverly (W. Va.) *Randolph Enterprise*, November 13, 27, 1879; January 1, 8, 15, May 20, June 3, 1880.
56. Agricola to John Hitz, December 23, 1879 (copy); Hitz to [?], January 22, 1880 (copy), "Projected Colony Alpina," Immigration, 1848-1934, Box 18. See, also, Emanuel D. Ludwig to Mathews, May 22, 1880, Mathews Papers, Box XXXVI (b), No. 214; and Hitz to Ludwig, May 15, 1880, *ibid.*, Box XXXVI (a), No. 151.
57. Lutz to Mathews, n.d., "Report ... State Agent on Immigration," West Virginia Legis., *House Journal*, 16 Sess. (1881), 10-13.
58. *Reports of the State Immigration Agent, Trustees of Berkeley Springs* (Wheeling, 1882), 3-5.
59. Lutz to Governor Jacob B. Jackson, December, 1884, Jackson Papers (Library, West Virginia Department of Archives and History), Box XLVI, No. 295.
60. Mathews, *Biennial Message*, 1881, pp. 21-22; Métraux, "Swiss Immigration," 139-40.
61. West Virginia Legis., *Senate Journal*, 16 Sess. (1881), 236-39.
62. *Ibid.*, 240, 245, 576 [i.e., 276].
63. Métraux, "Swiss Immigration," 101-102.
64. United States Census Office, *Tenth Census* (1880), Vol. I, *Population* (Washington, 1883), 492-95, 534; *Eleventh Census* (1890), Vol. I, *Population* (Washington, 1895), 608-609, 307; *Twelfth Census* (1900), Vol. I, *Population* (Washington, 1901), clxxiii-clxxiv, 793.

"Dave Scott, Jewish Peddler in the Southern West Virginia Coalfields."
Photo courtesy Goldenseal *magazine, W.Va. Division of Culture and History*

From Shtetl to Coalfield:
The Migration of East European Jews to Southern West Virginia

Deborah R. Weiner

In 1898, fifteen-year-old David Skot ran away from home. He left tiny Kolk, "a town of poverty" in the Ukraine, for a land where, he had been told, "the streets were paved with gold." He landed in Baltimore, where a cousin briefly took him in. But life in his new home was not what he had expected. Shortly after his arrival, the newly re-named David Scott left the city in search of better opportunities.[1]

David Scott was an early participant in a movement that would bring more than two million East European Jews to America's shores in the late nineteenth and early twentieth centuries. Sana Moscovitch Pickus joined the immigration movement at the other end of its time span. She arrived in Baltimore in 1921, accompanied by her newly-wed daughter and son-in-law, to unite with her three sons already established in America. Her husband, Mendel, had died in 1909 "in his birthplace, the 'ancestral' home of the Pickus family, that is, in the town of Uzda, province of Minsk, Russia." The Pickus family had been grain dealers, an occupation particularly hard hit by changes in the Russian Empire's economy at the turn of the century. A pious woman, Sana Pickus brought with her two prayer books with Yiddish commentary and a two-volume set of the *Tsenah Urenah*, a Yiddish translation of the Hebrew Bible designed for the common folk.[2]

The immigration sagas of Scott and the Pickuses adhere closely to the first half of the archetypal success story of East European Jewish migration to America enshrined in family narratives and history books: shtetl origins and old country tribulations, early poverty in the new land, hard work and determination, family cohesion, the piety of the elders. The second half of the story will depart from the conventional narrative, which usually unfolds entirely within the confines of America's major metropolitan areas, from gritty ethnic neighborhood to middle-class suburb. Instead, Scott's search for economic advancement will lead him to the coalfields of southern West Virginia, where he will become a leading merchant in the town of Welch. Sana Pickus will join her sons in Beckley, West Virginia, and attend her first American high holiday services in a Presbyterian church that the town's Jewish community borrowed or rented for the occasion of her arrival.[3]

Although atypical, Scott and the Pickuses were hardly unique. A significant minority of Jewish immigrants from eastern Europe ventured beyond major U.S. cities to settle in towns and rural areas throughout the country. Enough of them found their way to the coalfields of southern West Virginia to form several small yet vital Jewish communities. By the early 1920s, Jews had established congregations in Keystone, Kimball, Welch, Williamson, Logan, Beckley, and the regional hub of Bluefield.[4]

To understand why some Jewish immigrants migrated to the coalfields, it is necessary to consider who they were and where they started from. This seemingly common-sense observation has only recently become the standard view of historians of American immigration, who previously gave slight attention to the pre-migration backgrounds of their subjects. In the new formulation, immigrants' old country experience combined with the situation they encountered in America to shape their lives here; rather than being "uprooted" from their past, they are now seen as having "transplanted" themselves by adapting their old ways to their new environment.[5] The life experiences, skills, networks, and culture that coalfield Jews brought from their place of origin had a substantial impact on the communities they developed in southern West Virginia. For the vast majority, that place of origin can be traced to the Russian and Austro-Hungarian Empires of eastern Europe.

A Brief History of the Jews in Eastern Europe

By the late nineteenth century eastern Europe had long been home to the world's largest Jewish population. Jews had entered the region in substantial numbers starting in the thirteenth century. As a dispersed and mostly landless minority, they had developed skills and networks in commercial pursuits. Welcomed by the rulers of Poland, Hungary, and Rumania, they found a niche as traders and artisans in an agricultural feudal economy. The Polish gentry in particular, which eventually controlled the vast territory stretching from Poland to Lithuania, White Russia, and the Ukraine, found Jews to be most suited to serve as the economic link between noble and serf, as well as between the rural economy and the evolving international cash economy. Not only did Jews have far-reaching connections and experience in trade, they had one other invaluable attribute: as a low-status religious minority, they would be unable to mount a challenge to the gentry's hegemony, as the small Christian merchant class or the lower nobility might, if given the opportunity. As Poland grew and flourished from the fourteenth to seventeenth centuries—largely because of its increasing prominence as supplier of grain to European and eastern markets—so did its Jewish communities, whose members filled all levels of commerce, from financiers, exporters, and estate managers to the much more numerous petty traders, tavern and innkeepers, teamsters, and artisans living in small towns and villages throughout the countryside. Like other ethnic groups within the greater Polish state, Jews enjoyed communal autonomy within their small towns (known as shtetls), enabling them to form their own communities and develop a way of life grounded in the precepts and rituals of Judaism.[6]

The Jewish population served as a classic "entrepreneurial minority," or "middleman minority," terms coined by sociologists and historians to describe a worldwide phenomenon: in many agricultural societies, religious and/or ethnic minorities have occupied the economic position, or "status gap," between ruling elite and majority peasant population, performing necessary distributive and managerial functions yet never losing their standing as outsiders. The Chinese in Southeast Asia and Indians in colonial Africa represent two other prominent examples. In all these cases, ethnic minorities have negotiated the terrain between indigenous, largely non-cash, rural economies and local to distant markets, serving as "intermediaries between the ruling elite and the masses, . . . between the producers and the consumers." While mixing on a daily basis with members of the majority population, they have remained separate by virtue of their own decision to preserve their cultural heritage as well as by their social status as, literally, "out-castes" often despised for their otherness. Their economic position has often enabled many of their number to achieve material success yet without the political power often associated with such success.[7]

As societies have moved from feudalistic to capitalistic forms of economic organization, the activities traditionally carried out by middleman minorities have positioned some of their members to play an important role in capital investment, market expansion, and economic innovation. Ruling elites have found their presence useful not only for the services they have provided but because such minorities could not develop into a bourgeoisie strong enough to challenge the power structure—and also, as a highly visible "other" involved in commercial activities, they have proven ideal scapegoats to blame for the disruptions caused by economic transformation. This is not completely the result of hypocritical calculation: in traditional, rural societies undergoing a transition to capitalism, members of the majority population, including elites, often come to see middleman minorities as the embodiment of capitalist enterprise, capitalist values, and capitalist excesses. Misgivings about socioeconomic change are projected onto them, and they become considered as a problematic element within the population. As a result, they have frequently become the focus of hostility and retribution by those who have suffered materially or socially in the transition to capitalism.[8]

While the middleman minority concept offers an intriguing cross-cultural perspective on ethnic relations within an evolving world system of capitalist expansion, when applied too broadly it ignores differences among as well as complexities within the societies to which it has been applied. Even the Jews of eastern Europe, seen by most scholars as the quintessential middleman minority, do not conform entirely to the theory. For one thing, the Polish lands of the medieval and early modern period contained numerous ethnic groups; Jews were far from being the only minority. Historians identify Poland's heterogeneity as significant in allowing Polish Jewry to flourish; as Gershon Hundert observes, "the status of Jews was most favorable in states of multiple nationality in which they were less conspicuous." Nevertheless, most of these ethnic groups inhabited their own distinct geographical locations, with Jewish communities dispersed among them. As a result Jews were often the only prominent local minority surrounded by a majority population that was itself a minority group within the multi-ethnic Polish state.[9]

Some historians point out that the concept of "otherness" is often taken too far in the middleman minority literature. Jack Kugelmass stresses the intimacy of Jews and peasants in the Polish countryside, contending that economic interdependence and close proximity resulted in "an exchange of language and folklore that goes well beyond the apparent yet deceptive dissimilarity of religion, language, and social status." The authors of the ethnographic study *Life Is with People* document this cultural exchange between Jews and the Lithuanian, Ukrainian, Russian, and Polish peasants with whom they interacted, highlighting shared superstitions, health care and child rearing practices, and even certain economic behaviors (such as a propensity to bargain). The marketplace served as their main point of contact and symbolized "the interdependence, the reciprocity, the ambivalence that exist(ed) between Jew and Gentile." Daily economic intercourse bred familiarity between Jews and peasants, and this familiarity, combined with deep social, cultural, and religious disparities, led Kugelmass to use the paradoxical term "native aliens" to describe the Jews of eastern Europe.[10]

Noting the longstanding, largely peaceful coexistence of Jews and peasants, Hillel Kieval suggests that even though their differences may have fostered an ongoing degree of mutual suspicion and misunderstanding, "outbreaks of anti-Jewish hostility may represent not the natural outcome of traditional entrepreneur-client relations but a significant disruption of conventional patterns." Such outbreaks began to increase as Eastern Europe moved into the modern era. In the mid-seventeenth century, Poland entered a long period of economic decline that ultimately would contribute to its complete destruction as an independent political entity. As conditions worsened, blame fell on the most visible representatives of the commercial economy, the Jews—though they too suffered in the general economic malaise. Throughout modern history, scapegoating of Jews has proved to be a complex phenomenon that draws power not only from economic relationships and conditions but also from ancient religious myths and aversions that come to the fore during times of trouble, often incited by the Christian church establishment or by people who stand to benefit directly from anti-Semitism, such as politicians and economic competitors. These factors merged throughout the eighteenth century, and by the time neighboring states moved to carve up the former great power, Poland was widely perceived to suffer from a "Jewish problem."[11]

Most of Polish Jewry suddenly became Russian Jewry when the Russian Empire took over Lithuania, White Russia, most of the Ukraine, and much of Poland itself during the partitions of the Polish lands from the 1770s to 1790s. Prussia and the Austro-Hungarian Empire nabbed the western and southern portions of the Polish state. The new Prussian Poland contained a significant number of Jews, whose history eventually would merge with that of Central European Jewry. Austria-Hungary inherited a large Jewish population in the area of southeastern Poland known as Galicia. Conditions there kept Galician Jews tied to East European Jewry; yet, since Jews already lived in other parts of the empire, they did not represent a particularly unusual or foreign element to the Hapsburg rulers.[12]

The Russian Empire, however, went from having virtually no Jews to having the largest Jewish population in the world. Because of the longstanding enmity of the Russian Orthodox church, Jews had been generally banned from Russia since medieval times and the small number who did live there had been expelled early in the eighteenth century. With the acquisition of Polish lands, Russian rulers found themselves faced with the task of integrating a variety of entirely new ethnic groups into their empire, yet the Jews, both because of their perceived culpability in Poland's decline as well as the animosity of the Russian Orthodox church, constituted a special case. The tsarist regime embarked on a contradictory two-pronged approach to its new Jewish population: assimilation to submerge Jews into the larger society and segregation to protect vulnerable groups—peasants subject to "Jewish exploitation" and tradesmen subject to Jewish competition—from their perceived evil influence.[13]

Russia's Jewish policy through the nineteenth century shifted between those two poles in response to political and economic developments, displaying a marked inconsistency which lent a deep instability to Jewish life. The most significant segregation measure occurred almost immediately: creation of the Jewish Pale of Settlement, which confined Jewish residency to the western parts of the empire they already inhabited, preventing them from moving to the

Russian interior—although the boundaries of the Pale altered somewhat and later exceptions were made for the very wealthy, highly skilled, or professional.[14] Assimilation measures took forms both cruel and benign, the most infamous being the attempt to forcibly convert Jewish army recruits to Christianity after conscripting them as young children. This program prompted a dread of conscription that lasted long after it was abolished (in any case, military service remained something Jews feared and avoided because of the abuse Jewish recruits encountered and the near-impossibility of following religious rituals while in the army). Jews were encouraged to attend Russian schools (to promote assimilation) and then subjected to restrictive quotas (to protect other students from Jewish competition); suddenly expelled from residency in certain areas and then sometimes allowed to move back; urged to engage in "productive" activities such as agriculture yet limited by myriad and shifting prohibitions on landownership; denied access to certain occupations yet blamed for concentrating in the areas of the economy that remained open to them.[15]

Meanwhile, eastern Europe's transition from feudalism to capitalism caused economic dislocation and social disruption which intensified in the late nineteenth century for Jews and non-Jews alike. Growing competition from distant markets crippled small-scale agriculture and enterprise while encouraging the consolidation of land and commerce. An agricultural crisis developed as population growth outstripped the land's ability to sustain its inhabitants. Peasants, petty traders, and artisans displaced from the countryside began to seek work in urban and industrial areas, but the emerging industrial sector did not develop quickly enough to absorb them. While a minority of the region's inhabitants benefited from new opportunities which began to open up, the more common outcome for all ethnic groups was impoverishment caused by the obliteration of their traditional role in the economy.[16]

As economic modernization spread through eastern Europe, vast numbers of Jews—small-scale traders and skilled workers—lost their livelihood. The construction of railroads, for example, threw thousands of teamsters (a traditionally Jewish occupation) out of work. It also introduced foreign grain imports and changed the way local agricultural products were marketed, thus destroying the role of grain dealers such as the Pickuses. Chronic unemployment resulted, even as the Jewish workforce turned away from commerce and toward manufacturing. In the Pale, market forces and government policy combined to promote a dramatic occupational shift. In 1818 some 86 percent of the Jewish workforce engaged in commerce, while by 1897 only 32 percent worked in commerce and 38 percent worked in manufacturing (skilled and unskilled).[17]

The transition to capitalism did not occur evenly throughout the region, however. It took place in fits and starts, with some areas undergoing rapid change as others became economic backwaters. As late as the turn of the twentieth century, for example, Jews in much of the Lithuanian countryside continued to perform virtually all non-farming functions in a primitive agricultural economy, serving as tailors, shoemakers, carpenters, blacksmiths, wheelwrights, raftsmen, teamsters, peddlers, millers, and estate lessees. Most lived in shtetls and worked in the surrounding countryside, while peasant villages often contained one or two Jewish families as well. Jews and peasants alike barely eked out a living. Yet even this meager existence was threatened by increasingly-enforced legal restrictions against Jewish residency in the countryside.[18]

While Jews throughout eastern Europe faced erratic and often dire economic conditions, the situation in the Russian Empire became especially unbearable. Anti-Jewish violence rose as Jews found themselves blamed for the mounting social and economic crisis. The pogroms of 1881 to 1882, which destroyed life and property in over two hundred communities mostly in the Ukraine, caused material distress for the immediate victims and psychological distress for the entire Jewish population. The tsarist regime concluded that the Jews had themselves provoked the riots and reacted with the oppressive May Laws of 1882, which ushered in an era of heightened anti-Jewish legislation. These laws prohibited Jews from purchasing real estate, led to more frequent expulsions from the countryside, and made it extremely difficult for them to own land or engage in certain trades. Forbidden to leave the Pale, Jews from the countryside crowded into the region's larger towns and cities, where there was not enough work to go around. Discrimination in some industrial sectors (particularly heavy industry) and a general dearth of capital caused them to gravitate to the low-capital, labor intensive clothing industry, where they filled all ranks and suffered from intense competition. Meanwhile, their status as an officially-despised group led to further harassment, from low-level, routine abuse to a devastating outbreak of pogroms between 1903 and 1906.[19]

Suffering from economic devastation and in the midst of a social transformation which had loosened the bonds of community and tradition, Russian Jews proved highly receptive to the drastic solutions which emerged in the wake of violence and repression. Many people flocked to political movements such as socialism, communism, and Zionism. But for the masses of Jews who increasingly saw no economic or social future for themselves in Russia, the answer seemed more obvious: departure.[20]

Although the pogroms and May Laws served as a potent catalyst for the emigration movement that gathered steam in the 1880s, the economic disruptions caused by modernization must be considered the underlying cause. Jews began to leave Russia in modest yet significant numbers well before the pogroms. As early as 1869 a Hebrew-language newspaper declared that "the reasons for this emigration are the shrinking possibilities of gaining a livelihood and the fear of military service." Moreover, Russian Jews were far from alone in their desire to leave their native land—across Europe, economic transformation with its accompanying social and political turmoil spread from west to east, leaving great migrations in its wake. Wrenching changes in the German states had sparked a massive movement to America in the mid-nineteenth century which included some two hundred thousand German Jews who would pave the way for their eastern coreligionists. The late nineteenth and early twentieth centuries saw millions of southern and eastern Europeans migrate to growing industrial centers in their own and neighboring countries as well as overseas.[21]

Migration from Austria-Hungary to America almost tripled in the single year between 1879 and 1880, ushering in a thirty-year period that would bring more than three million residents of that multi-national empire to the United States. Among them were Jews from Galicia and Hungary. The Hapsburg empire had abolished most legal restrictions against Jews in the mid-nineteenth century and they had begun to integrate into the empire's political, economic, and social life, though they still faced some popular hostility and official discrimination. According to historian Raphael Mahler, "Jewish emigration from Galicia was entirely motivated by poverty . . . that caused mass emigration of both Jews and non-Jews." In Hungary, reported the U.S. Immigration Commission of 1911, "The backward state of industrial development, . . . generally impoverished resources, . . . and the growth of a population which the land can not support" led to widespread emigration. The report merely listed Jews among Austria-Hungary's many migrating ethnic groups, but devoted a special section to Jews in the Russian Empire, noting that governmental restrictions and popular violence, along with terrible economic conditions, gave them "double cause for emigration." In fact, Jews in the Russian Empire emigrated in much larger percentages than either the Jews of Austria-Hungary or other ethnic groups emigrating from Russia, indicating that legal liabilities, persecutions, and pogroms provided an additional and powerful motivating force.[22]

Emigration was a complex phenomenon influenced by many factors. As historian Simon Kuznets points out, the pattern of European migration to America followed a similar course among all ethnic groups of the period: first a trickle, then a moderate flow, then an explosive rise. He attributes this, in part, to the decreasing costs of migration, as shipping rates lowered and, most important, as early migrants provided information and financial assistance to family members and others who followed in their footsteps. For many young men—both Jews and non-Jews—the looming prospect of conscription into the Russian army provided the most immediate stimulus to departure.

Meanwhile, the "pull" of America combined with the "push" of local conditions; according to historian Stephen Berk, "knowledge of the free, dynamic, wealthy nation burgeoning overseas was penetrating into the nooks and crannies of the Pale." While rumor may have overstated the opportunities and lifestyle available to newly-arrived immigrants, the Jewish press and earlier emigrants provided much credible information on the booming U.S. economy, not to mention America's tradition of religious tolerance and legal rights. Debates raged among Jews about whether Palestine or America should be their destination, but the difficulties of reaching and settling in the Holy Land, then controlled by the less-than-receptive rulers of the Ottoman Empire, dictated that only the most ideologically committed would end up there. Millions of ordinary people fixed their sights on the "Goldeneh Medinah," America.[23]

The East European Legacy and Central Appalachian Jews

The East European Jews who migrated to the United States emerged from a traditional way of life developed over centuries yet tempered by the modernizing trends of the late 1800s. A close-knit family- and communally-based culture continued to exert a powerful hold over the bulk of the population. Despite widespread urbanization most people were not too far removed from their shtetl origins while many clung tenuously to their rural niche. The tenets of Orthodox Judaism still permeated Jewish life, though the very fact of mass emigration showed that the influence of religion was not quite as dominant as it once had been. Rabbis had warned against America, calling it a heathen land where Jews turned away from their heritage; these admonitions gradually lost force as more and more people made the decision to leave. Although the most pious Jews remained least likely to emigrate, the majority of those who ventured across the ocean, representing a large cross section of Jewish society, considered themselves to be observant Jews, and they brought their traditional practices with them.[24]

The Jewish immigrants who arrived in Central Appalachia shared in the eastern European legacy. They came from throughout the region, from the Russian Pale, Galicia, Hungary, and Rumania.[25] Their hometowns were buffeted by the social currents sweeping through eastern Europe, where the forces of modernity and traditionalism vied for the hearts and minds of ordinary Jews. The Totz, Foreman, and Bank families, related through marriage before emigration, hailed from Raseiniai, Lithuania, a medium-sized town and one of the centers of the Haskalah (Jewish Enlightenment), a movement that promoted the modernization of European Jewry. Israel Noah Spector and his brothers, on the other hand, came from the Ukrainian city of Nezhin, a center of the ultra-religious Hasidic movement, to which his family probably belonged since he was named for famed Hasidic leader (and Nezhin resident) Israel Noah Schneerson. Evidently their differences were not unreconcilable since the Totzes and Spectors intermarried in the United States; Foremans, Spectors, Banks, and Totzes lived in several small towns in southern West Virginia and eastern Kentucky. The three Starer brothers, Dave, Moe, and Abe, came to Pocahontas, Virginia, and Kimball, West Virginia, from the small Galician town of Zablotów, another Hasidic stronghold, while the small town of Bolechów, "a cradle of the Jewish Enlightenment movement in eastern Galicia," was the starting point for future Matewan, West Virginia, tailor Abe Scherer. The four Seligman brothers grew up in the Lithuanian hamlet of Ylakiai as sons of a Hebrew *maskil* (adherent of the Haskalah) who raised them to be fine scholars. A rabbi who served briefly in the coalfields remarked of these Northfork, West Virginia, merchants that "It was a revelation to me to find Jewish laymen in an obscure coal town who could read and understand modern Hebrew."[26]

Central Appalachian Jews hailed from eastern Europe's largest cities as well as the small towns and villages of the countryside. Budapest sisters Charlotte, Pauline, and Gizella Wilczek married three friends from much smaller Hungarian towns who brought them to Logan. From the Latvian port city of Libau came the three Michaelson brothers, Sol, Max, and Ted, tailors who eventually plied their trade in the tiny coal town of Davy, West Virginia. Chaim Brownstein started out in the Jewish agricultural colony of Marculesti in Bessarabia and ended up in an unincorporated hamlet in Logan County. Mary Schwachter fled an impoverished farm—and a "religious fanatic" husband—in the mountainous Transylvanian region of Austria-Hungary, taking two sons with her. She lived for a time in Pocahontas, Virginia, and her son Harry eventually became a prosperous merchant in Williamson. The Lopinsky family, prominent throughout the southern West Virginia coalfields as well as in the state capital of Charleston, originated in the small town of Jonava, located in the forests of Lithuania where the timber industry held sway.[27]

Amidst this diversity, some patterns can be discerned which suggest that the unusual decision to move to the coalfields may have been influenced, at least in part, by the particular old country origins of Central Appalachian Jews. The following discussion is based on data from 710 East-European-born Jews living in the coalfields between 1880 and 1930, identified primarily through census records, naturalization records, and interviews with descendants. These sources provided varying levels of information; while the former state citizenship of 705 people could be determined (i.e., Russian Empire, Austria-Hungary, Rumania, Germany, etc.), more precise information was not available for most. Three hundred fifty-seven could be identified only as originating in the Russian Empire, leaving 348 whose regional origins could be more closely ascertained (i.e., Lithuania, White Russia, Hungary, Russian Poland, Galicia, etc.). Of those 348, the birthplaces of 122 could be determined with a fair degree of certainty.[28]

Based on those birthplaces, it appears that, on the whole, Jews who settled in small coalfield towns tended to come from more rural backgrounds than the general East European Jewish population. By 1897, almost half of the Jews in the Russian Pale lived in incorporated cities.[29] The majority of Jewish immigrants to the coalfields, on the other hand, originated in the shtetls and villages of eastern Europe. Of the coalfield immigrants whose birthplaces were ascertained, almost 60 percent came from towns of less than five thousand inhabitants (including towns and villages so small that population figures were not listed in standard sources). More than 70 percent came from towns of less than ten thousand inhabitants.

These figures tend to support the theory, advanced by many historians, that immigrants sought out locales in the United States with similar characteristics to the places they left behind, where conditions would be somewhat familiar and where they would be able to draw on past experiences and previously-acquired skills to earn a livelihood. Ewa Morawska, for example, notes that Jewish immigrants to Johnstown, Pennsylvania, were more likely to have a background in rural petty trade than the general Jewish migration stream from eastern Europe, in which skilled workers were highly over-represented. In *The Business of Jews in Louisiana*, Elliott Ashkenazi points out that the French-speaking Louisiana countryside attracted Jewish immigrants from rural, French-speaking Alsace-Lorraine who wanted to continue to pursue economic activities that were increasingly difficult to carry out in the old country. Thus the act of immigration, seemingly a radical step, had its conservative impulse, as immigrants sought environments that would allow them to continue to do what they could no longer do in their homeland because of deteriorating economic or social conditions.[30]

Broad geographic trends are also apparent in the origins of coalfield Jews. More than 72 percent came from the Russian Empire, with 16 percent from Austria-Hungary and 3 percent from Rumania. (Seven percent were from Western or Central Europe, primarily Germany.) Though Jews migrated to the coalfields from all over Eastern Europe, Lithuania and Hungary provided a disproportionate share. Of the 348 immigrants whose regional origins were determined, eighty-four came from Lithuania and seventy-four came from Hungary, the two together accounting for 45 percent of those with known regional origins. Significantly, the two groups were not only the largest Jewish groups in the coalfields, they were also the earliest (along with some German Jews), accounting for 53 percent of those of known regional origin who arrived before 1900.

Since Poland and the Ukraine had much larger Jewish populations than Lithuania or Hungary, the over-representation of Lithuanians and Hungarians in the coalfields appears striking. Three factors account for their disproportionate presence: the over-representation of those two groups in the earlier stages of general Jewish migration from eastern Europe to the United States; the probability that early Jewish migrants to America were more likely to move away from U.S. port cities than later migrants; and the impact of chain migration. [31]

Austro-Hungarian Jews made their greatest impact on the East European Jewish migration stream between 1881 and 1902; they contributed 20 to 26 percent annually of Jewish immigrants to the United States during that period, while between 1903 and 1914 they contributed only 15 to 16 percent. (These figures apply primarily to Hungary and Galicia, where most of the Hapsburg empire's Jews emigrated from.) Meanwhile, Lithuanian Jews emigrated in greater proportions than other Russian Jews in the early years because economic conditions in Lithuania were the worst in the Pale. Because of the "economic stagnation and almost total absence of industry" in the region's small commercial centers, stated a 1907 study, "These little towns supply a large number of the Jewish emigrants to the United States."[32]

The over-representation of Lithuanian Jews in the eastern European migration stream diminished after the savage pogroms that struck southwest Russia in the first decade of the new century sparked movement from that region. Yet by the time of the pogroms of 1903 to 1906, most of the foreign-born Jews who lived (or would eventually live) in the coalfields had already come to America. An analysis of the 456 East European Jewish immigrants whose date of immigration was available reveals that most coalfield Jews arrived in this country during the earlier stages of Jewish migration to the United States. By 1903, fully 60 percent of East European-born coalfield Jews had arrived in America (though not necessarily the coalfields), while only one-third of all East European Jewish immigrants to the United States had arrived. The bulk of Jewish immigrants to America came between 1903 and 1924, some 1.6 million people, or two-thirds of the total who came during the great migration of 1881 to 1924. In contrast, only 40 percent of East European-born coalfield Jews arrived in America after 1902. It is not surprising, therefore, that the coalfield Jewish population was weighted toward those regional groups that had a large presence early in the migration stream.[33]

The relatively early immigration of coalfield Jews compared to the general East European Jewish immigrant population supports the hypothesis of American Jewish historians that earlier East European Jewish immigrants were more likely to move away from their first homes in U.S. port cities than later arrivals. It is unclear why these earlier arrivals may have been more likely to quit their first American homes; perhaps economic opportunities in large cities (especially New York) increased for later immigrants—or opportunities in the U.S. hinterland were more prevalent earlier in the period than they were later.[34]

The pervasive phenomenon of chain migration provides the best explanation of trends related to the origins of Central Appalachian Jews. Historians have documented how great migrations have been heavily influenced by kin-based networks, and Jewish migrants to the coalfields offer no exception. Most Jews came to the coalfields not as isolated individuals, but as parts of families whose members arrived together or, more commonly, in succession, with early settlers encouraging their relatives to join them either directly from Europe or from their first homes in the United States. These settlers may well have had a predilection for small town life because of their roots in the East European countryside—and the circumstances they encountered in the United States also helped lead them to the coalfields, as will be seen. Yet the concentrations from certain eastern European locales evident among coalfield Jews are largely the result of migration chains, with other factors playing a secondary role.[35]

Journey to America

While Jews who ended up in Central Appalachia may have differed in some respects from the general Jewish migration stream, they shared in all the reasons for quitting the old country. Their stories reveal the same lack of economic opportunity, fear of conscription, and oppression that caused millions to emigrate. While economic motivations were paramount, other factors also pertained. Bernard Silverman was born in Kishinev in 1902; his family arrived in the United States in 1904, not long after the infamous Kishinev pogrom. When the tsar's troops came to eighteen-year-old Louis Fink's corner of the Ukraine in pursuit of new recruits, he fled to the nearest port. Both ended up in Beckley. Some young people were motivated by adventure as much as anything else; when thirteen-year-old Joseph Lopinsky could not convince his fairly well-to-do parents to leave Lithuania, he "appropriated to himself money enough to pay his way and ran off for America." At Hamburg he wrote them that he was about to sail to the United States.[36]

Yet for most—even those who benefited from the money and advice of relatives already ensconced in America—the journey out of eastern Europe was not so easily undertaken. The story of James Pickus is perhaps more typical. Although he managed to acquire a foreign passport which would enable him to join his brothers in Beckley, he postponed his travel when his mother's home in Minsk province was struck by fire. After helping her recover, he found that his visa had expired. Unable to get it renewed, he had to be smuggled across the border. Such illegal border crossings were rampant, since permanent emigration from the Russian Empire was forbidden by law and foreign passports for temporary travel were expensive and difficult to obtain. Russian passport laws were notoriously inconsistent and contradictory, their enforcement even more so. The U.S. Immigration Commission concluded in 1911 that "Russian law makes it very difficult for a Russian subject to leave his native land in a lawful manner." Potential emigrants suffered lengthy bureaucratic delays and reversals. They often had to resort to bribing officials and/or border guards, obtaining false passports, or crossing the border secretly in the dead of night. An entire industry—mostly Jewish-operated—developed to assist people to leave, from the agents of European steamship companies to the smugglers who illegally conveyed people across the border. These individuals and organizations ranged from the merely unscrupulous to the downright criminal, and with no governmental regulation of their activities, they found myriad opportunities to cheat and exploit the would-be emigrants. While local governmental officials avidly pursued the profits to be made from illegal emigration, the upper levels of the Russian government chose to look the other way as Jews and other non-desirable ethnic groups (Poles, especially) streamed for the borders.[37]

In Austria-Hungary emigration was not forbidden and borders were easily crossed, while governmental regulation was nonexistent until 1903. Nevertheless, all eastern European emigrants faced the hazards of fraud, theft, and other forms of abuse and exploitation as they journeyed from their homes to European port cities and across the ocean. One historian has described the entire emigration process as "arduous . . . (often) inhumane and barbaric." While Russia and Hungary had their own ports at Libau, Odessa, and Fiume, most travelers carried steamship tickets of companies based in the German ports of Hamburg and Bremen. Travel through Germany was strictly regulated by the authorities, with prison-like conditions for those in transit. German officials set up control stations on the Russian and Austrian borders to examine the emigrants and those who posed a potential public health problem were turned back. The steamship companies performed similar physical examinations once the travelers reached their embarkation points. Since American law required that the companies pay for the return voyage of emigrants debarred from the United States for health reasons, they were quick to reject those who might not pass inspection by U.S. officials. (These European inspections had much to do with the low rate of deportation from Ellis Island and other U.S. points of debarkation.)[38]

Once safely on the boat, passengers in the low-paying steerage section had to endure intensely cramped quarters. James Pickus's son Manuel vividly recalls his father's description: "They were stuffed in like pickles in a jar." Such overcrowding bred highly unsanitary conditions. With near-inedible food, mistreatment by crew members, and seasickness added to the mix, steerage travelers spent the ten- to sixteen-day voyage in varying degrees of misery.[39]

Nevertheless, because steamships had completely replaced sailing ships by the 1880s, the transatlantic journey was cheaper, safer, and faster than ever before. While socioeconomic push and pull factors may have motivated millions of people throughout Europe to quit the old country, this technological advancement in shipping enabled the great migrations of 1880 to 1924 to become a reality. For laborers who had already become accustomed to seasonal migration within Europe as a result of the continent's economic transformation, America simply became another destination where job opportunities could feasibly be pursued. The United States also became more attainable for those who desired a more permanent relocation. As historian Walter Nugent wryly points out, "Families could migrate and expect to arrive intact." Both types of migration, temporary and permanent, occurred during the period.[40]

Because of the particular social and legal liabilities they suffered under in the Russian Empire as well as rising anti-semitism throughout eastern Europe, Jews showed a greater inclination toward permanent settlement in the United States than all other groups who came during the era, with the exception of the Irish. Though single males were over-represented among Jews as they were among virtually all ethnic groups, Jewish immigration tended to be a family undertaking. Females made up 44 percent of all Jewish immigrants to America between 1899 and 1914, compared to 30 percent of non-Jewish immigrants; children under fourteen made up a quarter of Jewish immigrants, while they made up only 11 percent of non-Jewish immigrants. And Jews were far less likely to return to Europe than non-Jews. Although historian Jonathan Sarna has exploded the commonly-accepted "myth of no return" by reporting that the Jewish return migration rate exceeded 20 percent between 1881 and 1900, this was well below the 35 to 50 percent return migration rates of non-Jewish ethnic groups from eastern Europe. Moreover, the Jewish return rate tumbled to 6 to 7 percent after 1900 with no corresponding drop for other groups—a good indication of how Jews viewed their chances for a decent life in Russia.[41]

Although Jews migrated as families, breadwinners often came over first, with other family members following once their fares had been earned for them in America. Many coalfield Jews followed this pattern as well. The Pickus brothers offer an example of young men who brought elderly parents and sisters over; census records show that they were not alone in doing so. And not all trailblazers were male—Mary Schwachter, unable to pay for the journey to America for herself and her two boys, deposited them in Budapest where thirteen-year-old Harry became an apprentice department store clerk. She went on to the United States with her sister, and three years later sent steamship tickets to her sons. By then the future Williamson businessman had become an active member of the Hungarian Socialist Youth (an avocation he probably did not pursue in Mingo County). The resourceful teenager had a better voyage than most: while his brother remained confined to his bunk with seasickness, Harry and a "slight, dark Rumanian girl" spent the evenings dancing to music provided by some fellow steerage passengers, while onlookers from the upper decks tossed coins down to the entertainers. He made a net profit of $7.30 on the journey.[42]

Encountering the American Reality

Harry Schwachter may have demonstrated more entrepreneurial spirit than the average steerage passenger (or at least, superior dancing abilities), but everyone who landed in America during the 1881 to 1924 immigration wave would need a certain amount of resourcefulness to find his or her way in the dynamic U.S. economy. The varying premigration skills, networks, and resources that immigrants brought from Europe would interact with the circumstances they encountered here to determine their position in the economy, their adaptation to America, even the geographic distribution of their particular ethnic group. Most new immigrants chose to settle in the growing industrial cities of the Northeast and Midwest, where opportunities for employment were plentiful—though rapid mechanization meant that jobs were increasingly unskilled and low paying. Skilled or unskilled, most immigrants relied on ethnic and kin-based networks to ease their way into the job market and to guide them to various parts of the country. These networks became the basis of the ethnic neighborhoods and institutions of urban America, and proved invaluable to the immigrants' adjustment to American life.[43]

The late nineteenth century saw industrial capitalism hit its stride in the United States. It was an era marked by increasing use of mass production methods, expansion of markets, business growth and consolidation, and industrial labor shortages. Several factors helped East European Jews find their place in this booming economy. Perhaps most important, many arrived with skills that could be readily transferred. Almost two-thirds of the Russian Jewish immigrant workforce consisted of those who had been skilled workers in the old country and of those, over half had been employed in the clothing industry. In fact, some 30 percent of all Russian Jewish workers who came to America between 1899 and 1914 were tailors or seamstresses. Jewish immigrants found ready opportunity in the garment industry, which not only was undergoing rapid expansion, but was already largely dominated by German Jews, who proved receptive to employing their newly-arrived coreligionists. Although economic, social, and cultural tensions between America's German- and East European-based Jewish communities would become legendary, the existence of a small but well-established American Jewish population aided in the adaptation of East European Jewish immigrants by providing employment and social services, as well as by advocating for public policies favorable to immigrants.[44]

Like the eastern Europeans, most German Jewish immigrants had been petty traders and artisans in the old country as a result of similar, centuries-old socioeconomic forces.[45] Their arrival in America in the mid-nineteenth century had coincided with the birth of the ready-to-wear clothing industry. German Jewish immigrants with experience in trade but limited financial resources entered into all facets of the new industry, which required only a small capital investment and, moreover, was "dominated by no business aristocracy and responsive to new ideas." Those most recently arrived from Europe found opportunity "in the one profession universally open to them: peddling." Dispersing throughout rural America, peddlers helped increase the market for ready-made clothing while enabling themselves to get started in business. German Jews achieved rapid economic mobility and by the time the Eastern Europeans arrived, they had emerged as a fairly established and acculturated American Jewish community.[46]

Timing, the opportunities offered by the American economy, and premigration skills were just some of the elements that influenced the economic destiny of East European Jews. Other factors were perhaps more intangible. Some historians contend that the permanent nature of the Jewish migration gave Jews greater motivation to try to improve their circumstances than immigrants who saw their time in America as temporary. In his comparative study of Italian and Jewish immigrants in New York City, Thomas Kessner concludes that the combination of premigration skills and permanent orientation enabled Jews to "land higher on the status ladder than Italians" and achieve greater economic mobility. Moreover, even though most Jews arrived as skilled workers, they came from families and communities rooted in trade and commerce, and were thus more prepared than other immigrant groups to make their way in an American environment that rewarded market values and enterprising behavior. As Kessner put it, "The 'middlemen of Europe' brought more entrepreneurial savvy and 'middle class' values." Ironically, the very commercial traits for which Jews were denounced in eastern Europe would be considered commendable—and prove advantageous—in their new home.[47]

The garment industry provided a solid base for launching Jewish economic life in the United States. The vast numbers of East European Jewish immigrants soon dwarfed the existing American Jewish population, and eastern Europeans gradually took over leadership of the industry from the German Jews. Meanwhile, Jewish immigrant neighborhoods enabled the flourishing of an internal ethnic-based economy, and many Jews managed to avoid employment in the garment industry by instead providing a variety of goods and services to their fellow immigrants.[48]

Unfortunately, the propitious timing of mass migration did not mean that the immigrants—Jewish or otherwise—would avoid hardship and suffering in their new homes. Most of them experienced American industrial capitalism as cruel and unforgiving. Where immigrants found opportunities to work, employers found vast opportunities to exploit. Workers faced harsh and dangerous conditions, meager pay, and long hours especially in the unskilled sector of the economy. The spread of mechanization and mass production techniques in the garment industry caused this sector to constantly expand, with a corresponding drop in the fortunes of Jewish immigrants. It did not help that their employers were also Jewish. As writer Irving Howe put it, "The relations between German and East European Jews in the garment industry during the eighties and nineties were often those of class enemies," and once eastern Europeans took over the upper levels of the industry, Jewish bosses continued to "hire greenhorns whom they could exploit with familial rapacity." Those who tried to escape the sweatshops and factories by becoming pushcart peddlers or opening small shops confronted fierce competition from like-minded fellow immigrants in overpopulated urban neighborhoods. Despite the existence of a vibrant ethnic economy, says Howe, "The majority of Jewish immigrants . . . could not hope to escape the traumas of proletarianization."[49]

Overcrowding, inferior housing, and poor sanitation encouraged disease and a variety of social ills in immigrant neighborhoods throughout urban America. Conflict within and among different immigrant groups proved unavoidable in a situation where people from a variety of cultures lived together in crowded and poverty-stricken conditions. Meanwhile, old stock Americans, shocked by the changing face of the urban landscape, displayed increasingly nativist tendencies, with anti-Semitism as a highly visible component. The Jews' concentration in certain economic sectors was not entirely the result of their premigration background, since they faced discrimination in some industries. For example, a study of Jewish wage earners in Pittsburgh noted "rabid anti-Semitism which existed at the mills and the mines, both among the workers imported from Eastern Europe and among the employers." Jewish workers therefore clustered in the city's garment industry and its cigar-making industry, another traditionally Jewish occupation extending back to the old country.[50]

Jewish immigrants responded to the realities of American life with a variety of strategies to ensure their economic and spiritual survival, improve their working and living conditions, and, if possible, advance up the economic ladder. By relying on Jewish networks in largely Jewish economic arenas, they avoided discrimination while assisting relatives and friends to get ahead. Like most immigrant groups, they continued the old country practice of involving husbands, wives, and children in work toward family subsistence. They also drew on their experiences in the old country to forge a dynamic labor movement that fought for—and often won—higher pay and better working conditions. Mutual aid associations, often based on hometown origins, provided everything from burial services to insurance to small loans to sociability.[51]

While some Jewish immigrants managed to overcome the difficulties of their situation and achieve a measure of success, many others simply learned to lower their immediate expectations to focus on daily survival. Instead they transferred their goals and dreams onto their children. Indeed, while most in the immigrant generation experienced only a "slow improvement" in their condition during their lifetime, economic mobility would occur among the second generation, inheritors of the drives and ambitions (often felt as burdens) of their elders. In the meantime, immigrant Jews created a vibrant urban culture that helped them sustain their lives: a blend of family togetherness, religious observance, labor movement culture, street life, and, most of all, *Yiddishkeit*.[52]

A small but significant minority of Jewish immigrants devised yet another solution to the adverse conditions and excessive competition of the big cities: they left. Because census statistics do not reveal religious affiliation, their numbers are difficult to determine. But some historians estimate that as many as 30 percent of East European Jews chose to settle outside of major metropolitan areas, opting instead for the nation's smaller cities and towns. As noted earlier, this course of action may have appealed to immigrants who originated in the less populous shtetls and villages of Eastern Europe. Yet, whether they sought to duplicate their rural old-country role or whether they simply felt restricted by circumstances in the large cities, their primary motivation was economic.[53]

East European Jews who migrated away from large cities sought possibilities for self-employment that proved elusive in places such as New York City, despite the undeniable opportunities of the urban industrial economy. Less populated locales offered a different type of economic potential: in the nation's principal urban centers at the turn of the century, 60 percent of Jews worked in manufacturing, while in small cities and towns, 70 percent were employed in trade and service. Through the same kinds of ethnic networks that brought the immigrants to metropolitan areas across the United States, some Jewish immigrants learned about opportunities in less obvious places. Like the German Jews of the mid-nineteenth century, eastern Europeans who migrated to smaller cities and towns often got their start as peddlers and then opened retail establishments. Their economic profile, therefore, more closely resembled their German Jewish predecessors than their big city relatives.[54] However, this route taken by some East European Jews has long been obscured in both popular and scholarly writing on American Jewry, as the overwhelming focus has been on the urban Jewish experience and most particularly on the Jews of New York City. Historians of small Jewish communities have protested the stereotypical profile of American Jewry which contrasts German-based small Jewish communities with big-city East European Jews. They note that eastern European migration chains bolstered existing small-town German-Jewish settlements while also creating hundreds of new communities, thus becoming a critical demographic element in small-town Jewry and providing a counterpoint to the urban experience of the majority of East European Jews in America.[55]

Among those struggling to earn a living in New York City was Joseph Lopinsky, who, having run away from his comfortable Lithuanian home, landed in New York in 1884 "without a dollar, without language and without a known friend." He tried to survive on low-paying factory work before deciding to strike out for more promising territory. Years later, his cousin Sam Abrams would suffer the failure of his small notions store in Brooklyn. Faced with the prospect of starting from scratch, Abrams contacted his Lopinsky cousins in southern West Virginia. After arriving from Hungary in 1900, Rudolph Eiland found poorly-paid work in a New York City cigar factory. In Cincinnati, Isadore and Lizzie Weiner also clung to cigar factory jobs in order to support their young family in the 1910s. While most future coalfield residents first obtained less-than-sustaining work in the Jewish-oriented industries of major cities, still others found jobs wherever they could. Soon after landing in Baltimore in 1898, David Scott hitchhiked to Washington, D.C., where he worked cleaning a theater and as a Western Union messenger boy. He slept at the theater at night, or at the Salvation Army. Sam Polon also landed in Baltimore, where "he got such jobs as he could pick up, painted N&W cars, and did odd jobs such as loading drays, etc."[56]

Baltimore's large Jewish community supplied many future coalfield residents, such as Annie Wasserkrug, daughter of struggling immigrants, who left school in the sixth grade to work "in the needle trade." She married tailor Louis Fink, who eventually opened a small grocery store near the Baltimore & Ohio Railroad terminus. They managed to scrape together enough money to seek out a better opportunity. According to their son, "Salesmen who used to call . . . told (Louis Fink) about West Virginia and the black diamonds. He became fascinated with that."[57]

These stories typify the experience of Jewish immigrants who eventually settled in southern West Virginia. The majority landed in New York City, though a substantial minority arrived at the port of Baltimore. Unless they already had connections in the coalfields, they generally lived and worked for some years in the immigrant enclaves of those two cities before deciding to venture out.

Some came to the United States as children and spent their youth in Baltimore or New York, migrating to the coalfields as young adults. Interviews with the descendants of coalfield Jewish immigrants reveal that the desire for self-employment drove many of them to leave their first American homes. As more than one interviewee put it, their "dream" was to own a store, rather than work for somebody else. Dissatisfied with their life chances in the big city, they had reason to believe that opportunity for success would be greater in a seemingly unlikely place: the steep mountains of Central Appalachia.[58]

Into the Coalfields: The Role of Networks

Jacob Epstein probably never set foot in the southern West Virginia coalfields, yet he may have been the single individual most responsible for the creation of Jewish communities there. A Lithuanian Jew who arrived in America in 1879 at age fifteen, Epstein started out peddling in Pennsylvania, northern West Virginia, and western Maryland. Two years later he settled in Baltimore where he proceeded to build one of the city's largest wholesale firms, the Baltimore Bargain House. According to his biographer, "From the outset Jacob Epstein set out to do a jobbing business with the peddlers who played such an important part in those days in bringing needed wares, and entertaining stories, to rural housewives. . . . Trusting the peddlers, he was willing to sell to a number of them on credit, which was unobtainable from most of the larger wholesale houses. As a result, his business prospered from the very beginning."[59]

But Epstein did not rely only on farm women for a customer base. He kept up with regional developments, and when other young Jewish immigrants came to the Baltimore Bargain House looking for a start in business, he outfitted them with goods and dispatched many of them to peddle in the lumber and coal settlements which had begun to sprout up along the newly-built rail lines to the west and south of Baltimore. Epstein apparently took somewhat of a paternal interest in his peddlers; not only did he extend them goods on credit—which they needed since they had no cash—he also offered them advice on all manner of topics (to maintain their health on the road, he urged them to "eat prunes"). The solid relationship that developed between the Baltimore Bargain House and its retailer clients lasted for decades, as peddlers became small shopkeepers and successful merchants in small towns in Central Appalachia and throughout the South. Their business helped the Baltimore Bargain House become "one of the four largest wholesale houses in the United States" by 1900 (according to the firm's literature), and enabled Epstein to become a prominent philanthropist, a major supporter of such institutions as Johns Hopkins University and the Baltimore Museum of Art.[60]

Epstein sent his peddlers out on the very same rail lines that were just beginning to haul the treasures of the mountains off to distant markets. This two-way traffic has not received much detailed exploration in historical accounts of Central Appalachia, which focus on the exporting of resources from the region but rarely on the importing of goods into it. Many studies do point out that, as the agricultural economy gave way to an industrial economy, the population became increasingly less self-sufficient, requiring outside imports to furnish the necessities—not to mention the comforts—of life. Ronald Lewis notes that industrialization brought the "commercialization of the countryside," with a "wage earning population now dependent on others to produce their subsistence." Thus a ready and expanding retail market was created, comprised of a growing population of workers and their families.[61]

But who were the people who arrived to respond to this entrepreneurial opportunity, and how did they find their way to it? Without an examination of this group, discussions of coalfield development are incomplete. The exporting may have been carried out by the coal industry under the auspices of absentee corporate landowners, but, with the notable exception of company stores, the importing was carried out by an entirely different set of people: people who had their own commercial networks and were linked to different kinds of markets. Certainly not all—or even most—merchants in the coalfields were Jewish. But Jews did emerge as a significant minority in many southern West Virginia towns. In their role as traders, they played an important part in bringing the products of American consumer culture into the mountains and tying the region to national markets.[62]

It was their link to the Baltimore Bargain House that brought many of the earliest Jewish entrepreneurs to the coalfields. Some descendants later recalled that the wholesaler directed their fathers and grandfathers to the region even as the railroads were under construction. As one man put it, the peddlers would disembark "where the railroad ended" and immediately begin to trudge up the hillsides with their packs. According to his son, Wolf Bank "chose to pick up some things from the Baltimore Bargain House and start peddling" a few years after his arrival in America from his native Lithuania. His brother Harry did the same, and the two arrived in McDowell County, West Virginia, by the mid-1890s, shortly after the Norfolk & Western pushed through the area. Fellow Lithuanian-Jewish peddler Jacob Shore entered the county around the same time, also with a pack filled with Baltimore Bargain House goods. Others who had peddled the wholesaler's products in Pennsylvania, Maryland, and northern West Virginia learned about opportunities in the southern coalfields through their connection with the firm. Having saved up some money, they immediately opened stores upon arriving in the region. Jacob Berman peddled in Maryland, and "when he had a little capital ahead, then he went to Keystone and opened up his little clothing store," according to his son. After peddling in the northern part of the state, the Pickus brothers, Louis and Nathan, established stores in Beckley in 1911 just as the town was beginning to emerge as a southern West Virginia coalfield center.[63]

Other Jewish wholesalers also realized that the coalfields offered a potentially lucrative new market, though Jacob Epstein certainly was the most significant. Because of his influence, Baltimore would remain the dominant urban connection for Jews in the Pocahontas and New River coalfields. Peddlers and merchants in the Williamson-Thacker and Logan coalfields, however, were likely to be outfitted by suppliers in Cincinnati—the western terminus of the N&W and a national "center of German-Jewish clothing enterprise."[64]

Members of Jewish networks helped to link the countryside to urban markets by drawing on their own community's resources as well as their knowledge of developments occurring in the larger economic sphere around them. A steady supply of young, recently-arrived immigrants in search of opportunity enabled more established Jewish business owners to expand their customer base into new and promising territory. Certainly the primary incentive of businessmen such as Baltimore's Jacob Epstein was a desire to increase their own business. Yet another motivation also pertained, rooted in the Hebrew concept of *tzedekah*, the communal obligation to help others. By enabling a young man get a start in life, they were performing a *mitzvah* (often loosely translated as "good deed," the term literally means "commandment"—an act of righteousness commanded by God). That their good deed furthered their own business goals and strengthened the economic condition of the Jewish community as a whole provided confirmation of the intertwining of communal and individual good. In his study of German-Jewish immigrants, Avraham Barkai corroborates this dual motivation in his discussion of how a typical young peddler might get his start: "Already-settled earlier immigrants, relatives or not, were eager to take a risk and provide him with a few dollars' worth of merchandise on credit, not only because they had the good intention of helping him on his way, but also out of self-interest, to expand their own market." [65]

Peddling was not the only path from urban obscurity to small-town merchantry. Many Jewish newcomers to the coalfields managed to skip that laborious step (or had accomplished it before they came to the region). In fact, while many descendants of coalfield Jewish immigrants have a peddling tale to tell of one of their ancestors, the actual number of Jewish peddlers in the region appears to have been surprisingly small. An analysis of Jewish occupations uncovered only twenty-eight peddlers out of a sample of more than eight hundred Jews who worked in the Central Appalachian coalfields from the 1870s to the

1950s. (Undoubtedly there were many more peddlers that did not show up in the sources investigated.) This does not mean that their prominence in Jewish family lore is undeserved. As founders of the Jewish communities that arose, their influence extended far beyond their numbers. Not only did they establish their own (often quite large) families, they were responsible for bringing numerous relatives and friends to the region through the process of chain migration. Later newcomers would get their start not as peddlers, but as clerks in stores owned by former peddlers. The historical literature on small-town American Jewry validates the conspicuous presence of peddlers in the memories of later generations: the occupation provided the basis for small-town Jewish communities throughout the nation.[66]

Nevertheless, peddlers and the migration chains that arose from their initial forays into the region were not the only way Jewish networks drew people to the coalfields. Within predominantly Jewish industries in Baltimore, Cincinnati, even as far away as New York City, rumors of the economic potential of the coalfields were evidently rampant. One coalfield resident described how his uncle Ike Levinson, a toiler in Baltimore's clothing industry, heard "in the trade, through rumors" that "there was a good opportunity for small merchants" in the region. Looking for the chance to work for himself, he arrived in Welch around 1906 and opened a small clothing store. Later he sent for his sister and brother-in-law to join him. Cincinnati cigar factory worker Isadore Weiner learned of an opportunity to own a store in Charleston, on the edge of the coalfields. That opportunity fell through, but while in the Charleston train station he heard the announcement, "next train to Logan," and saw a stream of people moving toward the platform. When he was informed that Logan was a booming coal town, he decided to board the train with them. Within a year, he too had his own clothing store.[67]

Some Jewish wholesale houses employed drummers—traveling salesmen—who crisscrossed the land, selling their employers' wares to small-town shopkeepers. "Those drummers were regular grapevines," asserted one Jewish man who grew up in the coalfields. Everywhere they went, as well as when they returned to their home bases, they brought information about the places they had visited: not only the climate for small business, but specific job openings as well. For Louis Fink, the drummers' tales about the "black diamonds" of West Virginia led him to close his Baltimore grocery store and open a Beckley clothing shop. David Scott came to southern West Virginia around 1904 after hearing from a drummer that a Jewish "horse trader" in Wilcoe needed a helper. (The "horse trader" was Jake Shore, who by then owned more than one coalfield enterprise.) Louis Schuchat of Baltimore also learned about a coalfield job from a Jewish drummer—but in his case, the job was bookkeeper for a coal company in Northfork, West Virginia, a rare instance of Jewish networks leading to employment in a non-Jewish milieu. Schuchat did not stay a coal company employee for very long, however. He eventually went to work as bookkeeper for a saloon (probably Jewish-owned) before opening his own saloon.[68]

In their search for the right opportunity, many pioneer Jewish coalfield settlers followed a circuitous route, leaving numerous jobs and locales in their wake. David Scott learned about the Wilcoe job while clerking for a Jewish merchant in High Point, North Carolina, where he landed after his experience as a theater cleaner and messenger in Washington, D.C., and a stint as a North Carolina farm worker. Joe Lopinsky left his factory job in New York for Hartford, Connecticut, then made stops in Maryland, North Carolina, and Ohio before opening the Famous Clothing Store in Charleston, West Virginia, which became a "leading clothing store of the city." He and his partner (and brother-in-law) Ben Hurvitz then branched out into the coalfields, first in Fayette and then McDowell County. Unlike the other Jewish migrants to small coalfield towns, they had already established themselves as successful businessmen before their arrival.[69]

Harry Schwachter perhaps wins the prize for most jobs before finding his niche in Williamson. After arriving in Baltimore, he joined his mother in Ohio, where the following occurred. In Newark he worked first in a glassworks, then as a grocery store clerk, a clothing store clerk, and a court interpreter. He then clerked in clothing stores in Cincinnati and Hamilton. Finally he saved enough money to open his own store in Coke-Otto, Ohio, which promptly failed, at which point he signed on as a laborer in a Hamilton paper mill. After again saving some money, he purchased a dilapidated small theater in New Richmond, but could not make a go of it. His second business failure led him to work in his mother's saloon in Cincinnati and then briefly as a furniture maker before he saw a want ad in a Cincinnati newspaper: a Jewish merchant in Williamson needed a clerk. When he arrived in Williamson in 1909, he was all of twenty years old, and had lived in America less than four years.[70]

Settlers who arrived in the coalfields through Jewish business networks— whether peddlers or those drawn by rumors and job openings—encouraged many more to follow in their footsteps. This chain migration went on for several decades, causing a constant infusion of "fresh blood" that allowed Jewish coalfield communities to grow. Some relatives arrived straight from Europe. These "greenhorns" faced a bewildering journey into the mountains. James Pickus, who had had a hard enough time getting out of Russia, continued his misadventures in America as he traveled to his brothers Louis and Nathan in Beckley. He disembarked at Ellis Island, where an official pinned a tag on him indicating his destination. He nevertheless missed his train connection in Washington, D.C. Undaunted yet hungry, he ducked into the train station restaurant, where he "saw his first fried eggs, his first white bread, and his first black man": the waiter. To his astonishment, the waiter directed the obviously confused foreigner to the Travelers Aid office—in Yiddish. Pickus eventually made it to Beckley unscathed.[71]

Other members of the migration chains, like their pioneering relatives before them, came to the coalfields from their homes in large American cities. Louis Koslow, seeking a job to support his wife and baby daughter, journeyed from New York City to Kimball around 1915 to work in the tailoring business owned by his brothers-in-law. He left his little family behind, but they joined him a year later after a severe polio epidemic struck the city. Around the turn of the century, Harry Abel came from Baltimore as a teenager to work for his uncle, Ben Hurvitz, in Fayette County. Years later he opened his own store in the Fayette County town of Mount Hope. When he became ill in the early 1920s, his brother-in-law Thomas Sopher left a job in a Baltimore cigar shop to help him run the store; Sopher stayed on to open one of his own. Isadore Gorsetman arrived during the Depression from Cleveland, where the economic situation was especially bleak because the steel companies "wouldn't hire Jews." He joined his brother-in-law in Charleston in 1935 and immediately headed into the coalfields, where he peddled household goods from his car.[72]

Clearly, the "push" of adverse conditions in the big cities combined with the "pull" of coalfield opportunities to stimulate Jewish migration to the region. Push factors were primarily economic. Migrants arrived in search of a job or, more ambitiously, a chance to become a small business owner, after having found these goals elusive in their previous locales. Other circumstances also came into play, including the difficult living conditions of urban ethnic neighborhoods. Pull factors often included an already-established relative but in all cases revolved around a newly-developing industrial economy that offered an opportunity for Jews to fill an economic niche providing retail services to a growing population. The coal industry (and the railroads that developed first, to pave the way for coal exploitation) attracted Jews to the region, but they came through their own networks and would remain a part of those networks, causing them to interact with the coal economy in their own special way.

The intertwining of family connections, access to resources from within the Jewish community, and cultural predilections based on an occupational history that extended back for generations, exerted a strong pull on Jews in their new environment and drew them to the consumer goods sector of the economy rather than to the region's dominant preoccupation, extractive industry. Paradoxically, precisely these factors caused Jewish entrepreneurs to bear more than a passing resemblance to the hard-bitten early coal operators chronicled by coalfield historians such as Ken Sullivan, Ron Eller, Howard B. Lee, and Jerry

Bruce Thomas: in both cases, immigrants with little capital but great determination to succeed drew on their previously-acquired skills, family backgrounds, and cultural resources to build businesses in the region. These parallels are worth pointing out, although the dramatically different nature of the two types of businesses, consumer goods and coal, makes it difficult to carry the comparison very far. For immigrant Jewish entrepreneurs, the characteristically-Jewish interpretation of the American Dream revolved not simply around gaining economic success or owning a piece of land or other such standard formulations, but rather around achieving self-employment, and more specifically, owning and successfully operating a store. This somewhat modest goal would sometimes lead to considerable wealth, but often to long hours of work and ongoing struggle.[73]

The wholesalers, rumors of economic opportunity, and migration chains that brought Jews to the coalfields clearly demonstrate that the process was far from random. The mythic story of the peddler-turned-shopkeeper, that he decided to settle in a certain town because "that's where the horse died," has little basis in fact, at least in this particular region. Not only did Jews enter into the broad territory of the southern coalfields for concrete reasons, but their settlement patterns within the region would also follow a distinct logic. Two factors in particular determined where Jewish communities would arise: the timing of migration in relation to local developments and opportunities, and the railroad connections that led from U.S. cities to specific places within the coalfields. Ultimately, Jews coalesced in the budding commercial centers, where they joined other immigrants from around the globe.

Ironically, the region attracted Jews and other immigrants because it was undergoing the same sort of transformation as the land they had escaped: transition from a rural, locally-based economy to an industrial capitalist economy fully linked with national and international markets. In other words, the "town of poverty" in the Ukraine that David Scott fled had more in common with the "streets paved with gold" in the United States than he ever would have suspected. But, whereas the socioeconomic changes occurring in eastern Europe bode ill for most of the Jewish population, the changes taking place in the mountains of southern West Virginia would provide many Jewish immigrants and their children with the opportunity they sought.

NOTES

1.   Isadore Scott, phone interview by author, 14 December 1997.
2.   Gerald Sorin, *A Time for Building: The Third Migration, 1880-1920*, Volume 3 of *The Jewish People in America*, ed. H. L. Feingold (Baltimore: Johns Hopkins University Press, 1992), 42; Abraham I. Shinedling and Manuel Pickus, *History of the Beckley Jewish Community* (Beckley, W.Va.: Biggs-Johnston-Withrow, 1955), 41 (quote); Manuel Pickus, interview by author, Charleston, W. Va., 18 May 1998; I.M. Rubinow, "Economic Condition of the Jews in Russia," *Bulletin of the Bureau of Labor* 72 (September 1907): 487-583; Joseph P. Schultz, "The 'Ze'enah U'Re'enah': Torah for the Folk," *Judaism* 36 (Winter 1987): 84-96.
3.   Shinedling and Pickus, *History of the Beckley Jewish Community*, 81-2.
4.   Keystone's B'nai Israel congregation was founded in the 1890s and disbanded in the early 1950s. Bluefield's Ahavath Sholom began around 1904 and is still in existence. Beth Jacob of Kimball lasted from the 1910s to the 1930s. Welch's Congregation Emanuel, Williamson's B'nai Israel, and Logan's B'nai El all started in the 1910s. The Welch and Logan congregations lasted into the 1980s while the Williamson congregation continues to this day. Beckley's still-extant Beth El originated in the early 1920s. Abraham Shinedling, *West Virginia Jewry: Origins and History, 1850-1958* (Philadelphia: Maurice Jacobs, Inc., 1963).
5.   Oscar Handlin's groundbreaking work *The Uprooted: The Epic Story of the Great Migrations That Made the American People* (Boston: Little, Brown and Company, 1951) insisted on the centrality of immigration to the American experience and made immigration history a key part of American historiography. Handlin did not ignore the immigrants' old-country roots. However, his focus on the traumas of American immigrant life led him to oversimplify their premigration background and to conclude that immigrants had to make a sharp break with their past. *The Uprooted* was the standard in the field until the recent wave of scholarship which started in the late 1960s. Scholars now tend to stress the continuities between immigrants' old-country and new-world experience. John Bodnar synthesized the new paradigm in *The Transplanted: A History of Immigrants in Urban America* (Bloomington: Indiana University Press, 1985).
6.   Gershon David Hundert, "Some Basic Characteristics of the Jewish Experience in Poland," in *From Shtetl to Socialism: Studies from Polin*, ed. A. Polonsky (Washington, D.C.: Littman Library of Jewish Civilization, 1993); Hillel Levine, *Economic Origins of Anti-Semitism: Poland and Its Jews in the Early Modern Period* (New Haven: Yale University Press, 1991); Nachum Gross, ed., *Economic History of the Jews* (New York: Schocken, 1975); Bernard Weinryb, *The Jews of Poland: A Social and Economic History of the Jewish Community in Poland from 1100 to 1800* (Philadelphia: Jewish Publication Society of America, 1973); Marc Zborowski and Elisabeth Herzog, *Life Is with People: The Jewish Little-Town of Eastern Europe* (New York: International Universities Press, 1952); "Hungary," *Encyclopaedia Judaica* (New York: MacMillan 1971), s.v. "Hungary," "Rumania." *Encyclopaedia Judaica* 14, 386-415.

7. For a good introduction to the middleman minority concept, see Walter P. Zenner, *Minorities in the Middle: A Cross-Cultural Analysis* (Albany: SUNY Press, 1991). Quote is from Zenner, xii.

8. Key works on the topic of middleman minorities are: Howard Becker, *Man in Reciprocity* (New York: Praeger, 1956); Irwin D. Rinder, "Social Relations in the Status Gap," *Social Problems* 6, no. 3 (winter 1958): 253-60; Edna Bonacich, "A Theory of Middleman Minorities," *American Sociological Review* 38 (October 1973): 583-94; Jack Kugelmass, "Native Aliens: The Jews of Poland as a Middleman Minority" (Ph.D. diss., New School for Social Research, 1980); Daniel Chirot and Anthony Reid, eds., *Essential Outsiders: Chinese and Jews in the Modern Transformation of Southeast Asia and Central Europe* (Seattle: University of Washington Press, 1997).

This topic has proved quite controversial. A major point of contention goes back to the cultural versus economic/structural debate which has long raged in discussions about ethnicity. In other words, is there something in the culture of these groups that predisposes them to take on the middleman role, or does it develop out of the socioeconomic context in which they find themselves (or a complex mixture of the two)? For discussions of the debates surrounding middleman minority theory, see Zenner, *Minorities in the Middle*, and three essays in the Chirot and Reid volume: Daniel Chirot, "Conflicting Identities and the Dangers of Communalism," 3-32; Anthony Reid, "Entrepreneurial Minorities, Nationalism, and the State," 33-71; Hillel Kieval, "Middleman Minorities and Blood," 208-33.

9. Hundert, "Some Basic Characteristics of the Jewish Experience in Poland," 20-23; Weinryb, *The Jews of Poland*.

10. Kugelmass, "Native Aliens," 39-40; Zborowski and Herzog, *Life Is with People* (quote, 67), Aleksander Hertz, *The Jews in Polish Culture* (Evanston, Ill.: Northwestern University Press, 1988), esp. 79-83.

11. Kieval, "Middleman Minorities and Blood," 215 (quote), 220; Levine, *Economic Origins of Anti-Semitism*, 140-60; Hertz, *The Jews in Polish Culture*, 185-206; Zenner, *Minorities in the Middle*, 46-60; Steven Beller, "'Pride and Prejudice' or 'Sense and Sensibility?' How Reasonable Was Anti-Semitism in Vienna, 1880-1939," in *Essential Outsiders*, ed. Chirot and Reid, 99-123.

12. William W. Hagen, *Germans, Poles, and Jews: The Nationality Conflict in the Prussian East, 1772-1914* (Chicago: University of Chicago Press, 1980); Raphael Mahler, "The Economic Background of Jewish Emigration from Galicia to the United States," in *East European Jews in Two Worlds: Studies from the YIVO Annual*, ed. D. Dash Moore (Evanston, Ill.: YIVO and Northwestern University Press, 1990), 125-37.

13. Salo W. Baron, *The Russian Jew under Tsar and Soviets* (New York: MacMillan Publishing Company, 1976), 8-10, 18; John Doyle Klier, *Russia Gathers Her Jews: The Origins of the "Jewish Question" in Russia, 1772-1825* (DeKalb, Ill.: Northern

Illinois University Press, 1986); Isaac Levitats, *The Jewish Community in Russia, 1844-1917* (Jerusalem: Posner & Sons, 1981), 2; Hans Rogger, *Jewish Policies and Right-Wing Politics in Imperial Russia* (Berkeley: University of California Press, 1986).

14. At first, limiting Jews to the Pale did not constitute a particularly onerous constraint. Russia was still a feudal society where political and civil rights did not exist. Jews were one of many different castes, each subject to certain restrictions and each granted certain privileges. Later in the nineteenth century, after the liberation of the serfs and the gradual (though never completed) extension of rights to the general population, Jews continued to suffer legal liabilities and in fact such discriminatory laws increased, thus officially designating them as an inferior group. Klier, *Russia Gathers Her Jews*, 73-6, 140, 143; Rubinow, "Economic Condition of the Jews in Russia," 488-97. At the time of the 1897 Russian Census, Jews made up 9 to 15 percent of the population in the five main regions of the Pale: Poland, Lithuania, White Russia, Southwestern Russia (Ukraine), and Southern (New) Russia. The Pale was home to almost five million Jews, accounting for 98 percent of the Empire's Jewish population. Rubinow, "Economic Condition of the Jews in Russia," 491, 521.

15. Michael Stanislawski, *Tsar Nicholas I and the Jews: The Transformation of Jewish Society in Russia, 1825-1855* (Philadelphia: Jewish Publication Society of America, 1983); Baron, *The Russian Jew under Tsar and Soviets*; Rogger, *Jewish Policies and Right-Wing Politics in Imperial Russia*; Stephen M. Berk, *Year of Crisis, Year of Hope: Russian Jewry and the Pogroms of 1881-1882* (Westport, Conn.: Greenwood Press, 1985); Simon Kuznets, "Immigration of Russian Jews to the United States: Background and Structure," in *Perspectives in American History* 9, ed. D. Fleming and B. Bailyn (Cambridge: Harvard University Press, 1975), 35-124.

16. Marc Raeff, *Understanding Imperial Russia: State and Society in the Old Regime* (New York: Columbia University Press, 1984), 180-91, 210-5; Mahler, "The Economic Background of Jewish Emigration from Galicia to the United States"; Baron, *The Russian Jew under Tsar and Soviets*, 94; Kuznets, "Immigration of Russian Jews to the United States," 53-79; Rubinow, "Economic Condition of the Jews in Russia," 487-583. Rubinow's detailed look at the economy of the Pale around the turn of the century is based on an 1898 investigation conducted by the St. Petersburg-based Jewish Colonization Society, which published a two-volume report in 1905 entitled "Sbornik Materialov ob Economicheskom Polozhenii Evreev v Rossii" ("Collection of Materials in Regard to the Economic Condition of the Jews in Russia").

Historian Marc Raeff notes that the Russian government aggravated the agricultural situation by limiting the mobility of peasants until the turn of the century (180-1). In general, the Russian Empire's policy of promoting economic modernization without allowing the population the freedoms necessary to mitigate its harsh effects or fully benefit from its new opportunities contributed greatly to the empire's economic and social crisis of the late nineteenth and early twentieth century. See also Peter Waldron, *The End of Imperial Russia, 1855-1917* (New York: St. Martin's Press, 1997).

17. Rubinow, "Economic Condition of the Jews in Russia," 532-5, 557-62; Mahler, "The Economic Background of Jewish Emigration from Galicia to the United States," 125-37; Baron, *The Russian Jew under Tsar and Soviets*, 82-98; Berk, *Year of Crisis, Year of Hope*, 24. Statistics are from Kuznets, "Immigration of Russian Jews to the United States," 77, and Rubinow, 500. In 1897, in addition to commerce and manufacturing, 19 percent of the Jewish population worked in "personal service," which included the hotel, restaurant, and saloon industries. Five percent were professionals, 3 percent worked in transportation, and 3 percent followed agricultural pursuits.

18. Hirsh Abramovitch, "Rural Jewish Occupations in Lithuania," *YIVO Annual of Jewish Social Science* (1947-1948): 205-21; Rubinow, "Economic Condition of the Jews in Russia," 535.

19. Rogger, *Jewish Policies and Right-Wing Politics in Imperial Russia*; Berk, *Year of Crisis, Year of Hope*, 35-55, 73, 180-1; John D. Klier and Shlomo Lambroza, eds., *Pogroms: Anti-Jewish Violence in Modern Russian History* (New York: Cambridge University Press, 1992), 46-51, 143, 328. For a catalogue of anti-Jewish legislation during the era, see Bernard K. Johnpoll, "Why They Left: Russian-Jewish Mass Migration and the Repressive Laws, 1881-1917," *American Jewish Archives* 47 (Spring-summer 1995): 17-54. On the economic impact of pogroms and the tsarist regime's Jewish policies see U.S. Immigration Commission, *Emigration Conditions in Europe, Reports of the Immigration Commission, Volume 12* (Washington, D.C.: GPO, 1911), 272, 276-80; Kuznets, "Immigration of Russian Jews to the United States," 60-79, 86-93; Rubinow, "Economic Condition of the Jews in Russia," 492-7, 583; Baron, *The Russian Jew under Tsar and Soviets*, 84-95; Berk, 38. On the psychological impact of pogroms, see Berk, 36, 101-4, and Baron, 45. On the 1903 to 1906 pogroms, see especially Klier and Lambroza, 191-289.

20. Berk, *Year of Crisis, Year of Hope*, 103-4; Baron, *The Russian Jew under Tsar and Soviets*, 132-55.

21. Mark Wischnitzer, *To Dwell in Safety: The Story of Jewish Migration since 1800* (Philadelphia: Jewish Publication Society of America), 28 (quote); Baron, *The Russian Jew under Tsar and Soviets*, 70. On the late nineteenth to early twentieth century mass migration movements in Europe, see Walter Nugent, *Crossings: The Great Transatlantic Migrations, 1870-1914* (Bloomington: Indiana University Press, 1992). On the emigration of Jews from the German lands, see Avraham Barkai, *Branching Out: German-Jewish Migration to the United States, 1820-1914* (New York: Holmes & Meier, 1994).

22. U.S. Immigration Commission, *Emigration Conditions in Europe*, 351-2, 361, 272 (quotes); Mahler, "The Economic Background of Jewish Emigration from Galicia to the United States," 125; *Encyclopaedia Judaica*, s.v. "Hungary." See Kuznets, "Immigration of Russian Jews to the United States," and Nugent, *Crossings*, for a comparative analysis of Jewish and non-Jewish emigration from Europe.

According to Kuznets (39), the Russian Empire supplied around 76 percent of Jewish immigrants to America between 1881 and 1914 while Austria-Hungary supplied 19 percent, even though they contained around 69 percent and 27 percent, respectively, of eastern Europe's Jewish population (the remainder was Rumanian) (*Encyclopaedia Judaica*, s.v. "Population." An average of 1.36 percent of the Russian Empire's Jewish population migrated to America each year between 1899 and 1914, compared to annual immigration rates of .4 to .5 percent for the Empire's Poles, Lithuanians, Finns, and Germans. These figures indicate that almost 22 percent of the Jewish population emigrated from Russia during that period, compared to between 6 and 8 percent for the other ethnic groups (Kuznets, 51). It must be noted that *migration* rates for non-Jews in the Russian Empire were considerably higher than their *emigration* rates; they were more likely than Jews to relocate to other parts of the empire. Russian Jews migrated to America at a higher rate than any other European group except the Irish (49-52).

23. Kuznets, "Immigration of Russian Jews to the United States," 83-5, 119; Rubinow, "Economic Condition of the Jews in Russia," 492, 495, 571; Berk, *Year of Crisis, Year of Hope*, 121; Baron, *The Russian Jew under Tsar and Soviets*, 67; Annual Reports of the Lomza Provincial Governor, 1907-1912, file no. 6513, Chancellory of the Warsaw Governor-General Collection (Kancelaria General-Gubernatora Warszawskiego), Main Archive of Old Documents(Archiwum Główne Akt Dawnych), Warsaw, Poland (translation courtesy of Robert Blobaum).

24. Baron, *The Russian Jew under Tsar and Soviets*; Zborowski and Herzog, *Life Is with People*; Levitats, *The Jewish Community in Russia, 1844-1917*; Abramovitch, "Rural Jewish Occupations in Lithuania"; Mahler, "The Economic Background of Jewish Emigration from Galicia to the United States," 137; Irving Howe, *World of Our Fathers* (New York: Harcourt Brace Jovanovich, 1976), 27; Moses Kligsberg, "Jewish Immigrants in Business: A Sociological Study," *American Jewish Historical Quarterly* 56 (March 1967): 283-318.

25. Several sources were used to determine the European origins of coalfield Jews. U.S. Manuscript Census records of 1900, 1910, and 1920 contained data on the nationality of the immigrants. They were examined for the following counties: Bell and Harlan in Kentucky; Tazewell and Wise in Virginia; Fayette, Logan, McDowell, Mingo, and Raleigh in West Virginia. Naturalization records in the county courthouses of the five West Virginia counties provided more detailed information, such as birthplace and point of embarkation. Several local history books also offered data on immigrant origins: Shinedling and Pickus, *History of the Beckley Jewish Community*; Rose Marino, *Welch and Its People* (Marceline, Mo.: Walsworth Press, 1985); Bell County Historical Society, *Bell County, Kentucky, History* (Paducah: Turner Publishing Co., 1994); Jack M. Jones, *Early Coal Mining in Pocahontas, Virginia* (Lynchburg, Va.: Jack M. Jones, 1983). In addition, interviews with descendants of Jewish immigrants revealed the European roots of some coalfield Jews.

In the following discussion of eastern European towns, "small town" refers to towns with a population of less than five thousand; "medium-sized" describes a population of five to ten thousand; "city" refers incorporated localities with populations, generally, above ten thousand. For population figures and descriptions of the towns, the following sources were consulted: *Encyclopaedia Judaica*; Chester Cohen, *Shtetl Finder Gazetteer: Jewish Communities in the Nineteenth and Twentieth Centuries* (Bowie, Md.: Heritage Books, 1989); Nancy Schoenburg and Stuart Schoenburg, *Lithuanian Jewish Communities* (New York: Garland Publishing, Inc., 1991); *Rand-McNally Indexed Atlas of the World, Volume 2: Foreign Countries* (Chicago: Rand, McNally & Company, 1905).
Several difficulties confront the researcher hunting for details regarding immigrant origins. Courthouse naturalization books contain information given by often-uneducated immigrants to local clerks who were unfamiliar with eastern European geography, not to mention spelling. Moreover, many eastern European towns have multiple spellings, based on the different languages used in their particular region. Quite often, they also have similar, or even identical, spellings to other towns in eastern Europe. While these problems cannot be completely overcome, an attempt was made to compensate by cross-checking and using multiple sources to reconstruct individual origins.

26. "Bolekhov," *Encyclopaedia Judaica* E.J, S.V. "Bolekhov" (first quote); Shinedling, *West Virginia Jewry*, 1103 (second quote).[27] Marilou S. Sniderman, *Diamond in the Rough: A Biography of Harry Schwachter on the Occasion of his Diamond Jubilee* (n.p.: 1963), 7 (quote).

28. See note 25.

29. Rubinow, "Economic Condition of the Jews in Russia," 494.

30. Ewa Morawska, *Insecure Prosperity: Small-Town Jews in Industrial America, 1890-1940* (Princeton: Princeton University Press, 1996), 30-46; Elliott Ashkenazi, *The Business of Jews in Louisiana, 1840-1875* (Tuscaloosa: University of Alabama Press, 1988), 3-4, 8; Ellen Eisenberg, "Argentine and American Jewry: A Case for Contrasting Immigrant Origins," *American Jewish Archives* 47 (spring-summer 1995): 1-16.

31. Rubinow, "Economic Condition of the Jews in Russia," 491.

32. Kuznets, "Immigration of Russian Jews to the United States," 39; Abramovitch, "Rural Jewish Occupations in Lithuania"; Rubinow, "Economic Condition of Russian Jews," 495 (quote), 502.

33. Kuznets, "Immigration of Russian Jews to the United States," 39, 47, 119.

34. Gertrude Dubrovsky, review of *Jewish Farmers in the Catskills*, by Abraham D. Lavender and Clarence B. Steinberg, *American Jewish Archives* 48, no. 1 (spring-summer 1996): 97-102. According to Dubrovsky, U.S. census statistics from 1890 show that at that time, up to two-thirds of Russian Jewish immigrants may have settled outside of the Northeast. This is a far higher percentage than after the turn of the century. However, the numbers are uncertain and the implications unclear, she notes. "It is this movement, the out-migration of Jews from the

cities, that has not been studied. . . . Where they went and what they did for how long are difficult questions to answer" (97-8).

35. Bodnar, *The Transplanted*, 57-62; Nugent, *Crossings*, 153. In *Insecure Prosperity*, Ewa Morawska notes similar clusterings in Johnstown of immigrants from the same extended families or eastern European towns (29). For an account of how chain migration influenced the early European-American settlement of Appalachia, see Ralph Mann, "Mountain Settlement: Appalachian and National Modes of Migration," *Journal of Appalachian Studies* 2 (fall 1996): 337-45. Census records, naturalization records, city directories, interviews, and local history books provided the chief sources of evidence for Jewish chain migration to the coalfields.

36. Jerome Paul David, "Jewish Consciousness in the Small Town: A Sociological Study of Jewish Identification" (master's thesis, Hebrew Union College, 1974), 3; Ira Sopher, interview by author, Beckley, W. Va., 13 October 1996; Sidney Fink, interview by author, Beckley, W. Va., 12 October 1996; Abraham I. Shinedling, "Memoir of Bernard Silverman," Biographies File, American Jewish Archives, Cincinnati, Ohio; "Col. Jos. M. Lopinsky," *McDowell Recorder*, 12 December 1913; "Taps Are Sounded for Col. J. M. Lopinsky," *McDowell Recorder*, 30 January 1914.

37. Pickus, interview; U.S. Immigration Commission, *Emigration Conditions in Europe*, 254-6, quote 257; Annual Reports of the Lomza Provincial Governor, 1907-1912; Pamela S. Nadell, "The Journey to America by Steam: The Jews of Eastern Europe in Transition," *American Jewish History* 71 (1981-1982): 269-84, esp. 269-271; Wischnitzer, *To Dwell in Safety*, 52.

38. U.S. Immigration Commission, *Emigration Conditions in Europe*, 357-60; Nadell, "The Journey to America by Steam," 269 (quote); Zosa Szajkowski, "Sufferings of Jewish Emigrants to America in Transit through Germany," *Jewish Social Studies* (winter/spring 1977): 105-16; Wischnitzer, *To Dwell in Safety*. Of the eighty-two coalfield Jews whose ports of embarkation were ascertained, twenty-five arrived in the U.S. from Bremen, twenty-one from Hamburg, ten from Libau, six from Antwerp and Liverpool, four from Rotterdam, and one or two from Main, Fiume, Taurogen, Cherbourg, Havre, Southampton, and Glasgow (Declaration of Intention books and Petition for Naturalization books, Fayette, Logan, McDowell, Mingo, Raleigh Counties, W. Va.).

39. Pickus, interview; Nadell, "The Journey to America by Steam."

40. Nugent, *Crossings,* 31-7, quote 36.

41. Kuznets, "Immigration of Russian Jews to the United States," 96, 98; Nugent, *Crossings*, 94, 160; Jonathan Sarna, "The Myth of No Return: Jewish Return Migration to Eastern Europe, 1881-1914," *American Jewish History* 71 (March 1981): 259-69; Ewa Morawska, "Return Migrations: Theoretical and Research Agenda," in *A Century of European Migrations, 1830 to 1930: Comparative Perspectives*, ed. R. Vecoli (Urbana: University of Illinois Press, 1991): 277-92; Mark Wyman, *Round-Trip to America: The Immigrants Return to Europe, 1880-1930* (Ithaca, N.Y.: Cornell University Press, 1993).
Return migration rates refer to the ratio of outgoing to incoming migrants.

From 1908 to 1923, return migration rates ranged from around 90 percent for Serbs to 60 percent for southern Italians to 5 percent for Jews (Wyman, 11). The Irish had the second lowest return migration rate during that period, 11 percent. Irish migration patterns tended to diverge from those of other ethnic groups. On Irish migration, see Nugent, 49-54, 160, and Hasia Diner, *Erin's Daughters in America: Irish Immigrant Women in the Nineteenth Century* (Baltimore: Johns Hopkins University Press, 1983).

42. Sniderman, *Diamond in the Rough*, 9-17 (quote, 15).

43. Caroline Golab, *Immigrant Destinations* (Philadelphia: Temple University Press, 1977), 5-6; Bodnar, *The Transplanted*, 57-65; Thomas Kessner, *The Golden Door: Italian and Jewish Mobility in New York City, 1880-1915* (New York: Oxford University Press), 8-10.

44. Bodnar, *The Transplanted*, xviii-xix; Kuznets, "Immigration of Russian Jews to the United States," 102, 109, 110; Howe, *World of Our Fathers*, 82,155; Kessner, *The Golden Door*, 62-8; Sorin, *A Time for Building*, 61-2, 67-8, 162-5.

45. Characterizing all Jews who came to America between 1820 and 1880 as "German" is somewhat of a simplification. Although the majority arrived from the German states, others came from the French Alsace, Hapsburg-controlled Bohemia and Moravia, and Prussian Poland. See Jacob Katz, *Out of the Ghetto: The Social Background of Jewish Emancipation, 1770-1870* (Cambridge: Harvard University Press, 1973); Hasia Diner, *A Time for Gathering: The Second Migration, 1820-1880*, Volume 2 of *The Jewish People in America*, ed. H. L. Feingold (Baltimore: Johns Hopkins University Press, 1992), 1-35; Barkai, *Branching Out*, 1-5, 15-34.

46. Lee Friedman, *Jewish Pioneers and Patriots* (New York: MacMillan Co., 1943), 19 (first quote); Priscilla Fishman, ed., *The Jews of the United States* (New York: New York Times Book Co., 1973), 19 (second quote); Barkai, *Branching Out*, esp. 44-9; Diner, *A Time for Gathering*, 60-85.

47. Kessner, *The Golden Door*, 68, 111. See also Moses Kligsberg, "Jewish Immigrants in Business," 283-318; Morawska, *Insecure Prosperity*, 23-6.

48. Sorin, *A Time for Building*, 74-78; Howe, *World of Our Fathers*, 139, 163.

49. Howe, *World of Our Fathers*, 76-84, 154-9, quotes 82, 80; Kessner, *The Golden Door*, 69; Sorin, *A Time for Building*, 74-6.

50. Howe, *World of Our Fathers*, 87-90, 96-101, 148-54; Sorin, *A Time for Building*, 70-3; John Higham, *Strangers in the Land: Patterns of American Nativism, 1860-1925* (New Brunswick, N.J.: Rutgers University Press, 1955), 92-5, 160, 278; David Gerber, ed., *Anti-Semitism in American History* (Urbana: University of Illinois Press, 1987); Ida Cohen Selevan, "Jewish Wage Earners in Pittsburgh, 1890-1930," *American Jewish Historical Quarterly* 65 (March 1976): 272-85, quote 272.

51. Bodnar, *The Transplanted*, 57-116; Sorin, *A Time for Building*, 75-86, 92-8; 109-35; Charlotte Baum, Paula Hyman, and Sonya Michel, *The Jewish Woman in America* (New York: Dial, 1976); Judith E. Smith, *Family Connections: A History of Italian and Jewish Immigrant Lives in Providence, Rhode Island, 1900-1940* (Albany: SUNY Press, 1985), 29-34, 47; Howe, *World of Our Fathers*, 129-35, 287-359; Daniel Soyer,

"Between Two Worlds: The Jewish *Landsmanshaftn* and Immigrant Identity," *American Jewish History* 76 (September 1986): 5-24.

52. Sorin, *A Time for Building*, 69-70, 99-108; Howe, *World of Our Fathers*, 208-24, 417-551. Irving Howe on *Yiddishkeit*: "*Yiddishkeit* refers to that phase of Jewish history during the past two centuries which is marked by the prevalence of Yiddish as the language of the east European Jews and by the growth among them of a culture resting mainly on that language. The culture of *Yiddishkeit* is no longer strictly that of traditional Orthodoxy, yet it retains strong ties to the religious past. It takes on an increasingly secular character yet is by no means confined to the secularist. . . . It refers to a way of life, a shared experience, which goes beyond opinion or ideology" (*World of Our Fathers*, 16).

53. Joel Perlmann, "Beyond New York: The Occupations of Russian Jewish Immigrants in Providence, R.I., and Other Small Jewish Communities, 1900-1915," *American Jewish History* 72 (March 1983): 370.

54. Morawska, *Insecure Prosperity*, 32, 36-7; Lee Shai Weissbach, "East European Immigrants and the Image of Jews in the Small-Town South," *American Jewish History* 85 (September 1997): 241-242, 250; Perlmann, "Beyond New York"; Steven Hertzberg, *Strangers within the Gate City: The Jews of Atlanta, 1845-1915* (Philadelphia: Jewish Publication Society of America, 1978), 103; Hal Rothman, " 'Same Horse, New Wagon': Tradition and Assimilation among the Jews of Wichita, 1865-1930," *Great Plains Quarterly* 15 (spring 1995): 83-104.

55. Weissbach, "East European Immigrants and the Image of Jews in the Small-Town South"; Marc Raphael, "Beyond New York," in *Jews of the American West*, ed. M. Rischin and J. Livingston (Detroit: Wayne State University Press, 1991): 52-65; Perlmann, "Beyond New York," 369-71. Southern and western Jewish historians have taken the lead in recounting the experience of smaller and non-metropolitan East European Jewish communities in America. See, for example, Hertzberg, *Strangers within the Gate City*; Rothman, "Same Horse, New Wagon"; Moses Rischin and John Livingston, eds., *Jews of the American West* (Detroit: Wayne State University Press, 1991); two articles by Norton Stern in the *Western States Jewish Historical Quarterly*, "The Jewish Community of a Nevada Mining Town" (October 1982, 48-78) and "The Major Role of Polish Jews in the Pioneer West" (July 1976, 326-44); Louis Schmier, "'We Were All Part of a Lost Generation': Jewish Religious Life in a Rural Southern Town, 1900-1940," in *Cultural Perspectives on the American South, Vol. 5*, ed. C.R. Wilson (New York: Gordon & Breach, 1991); Leonard Rogoff, "Synagogue and Jewish Church: A Congregational History of North Carolina," *Southern Jewish History* 1 (1998): 43-81.

56. "Col. Jos. M. Lopinsky," 1; Jean Abrams Wein, interview by author, Beckley, W. Va., 13 October 1996; Edward Eiland, interview by author and Maryanne Reed, Logan, W. Va., 28 May 1996; Sam and Harvey Weiner, interview with author, Logan, W. Va., 8 November 1996; Scott, interview; "Sam Polan Goes to School," *McDowell Recorder*, 7 November 1913.

57. Fink, interview.

58. Naturalization records, census data, and city directories all help to pinpoint the previous American homes of coalfield Jews and the length of time spent in those locales. Naturalization records also reveal debarkation points. Of one hundred records examined, sixty-five immigrants arrived at the port of New York and twenty-five arrived at the port of Baltimore. Sam and Harvey Weiner, interview; Pickus, interview; Bernard Gottlieb, interview by author, Clarksburg, W. Va., 5 November 1996; Fink, interview; Eiland, interview.

59. Lester S. Levy, *Jacob Epstein* (Baltimore: Maran Press, 1978), 15. Eli Evans, in his *The Provincials: A Personal History of Jews in the South* (New York: Simon & Schuster, 1997), 81, states that his peddler grandfather in North Carolina "ordered his assortment from the Baltimore Bargain House like all the peddlers."

60. Gail Bank, phone interview by author, 28 September and 4 October 1998 (first quote); Kenneth Bank, interview by author, Baltimore, 6 November 1998; Sylvan and Elaine Bank, phone interview by author, 4 March 1998; Reva Totz Hecker, interview by author, Baltimore, 5 November 1998; Pickus, interview; Betty Schuchat Gottlieb, interview by author, Parkersburg, W.Va., 18 December 1997; Shinedling, *West Virginia Jewry*, 1013; Levy, *Jacob Epstein*; Baltimore Bargain House postcard, Baltimore Bargain House collection, Jewish Museum of Maryland, Baltimore (second quote). The Baltimore Bargain House crops up in numerous accounts of small-town American Jewish life. In addition to Evans above, two examples include: "Jewish Heritage of the Winchester [Va.] Community," Winchester, Va., Folder, Small Collections, American Jewish Archives, Cincinnati; Wendy Lowe Besmann, *A Separate Circle: Jewish Life in Knoxville, Tennessee* (Knoxville: University of Tennessee Press, 2001), 31.

61. Ronald L. Lewis, *Transforming the Appalachian Countryside: Railroads, Deforestation, and Social Change in West Virginia, 1880-1920* (Chapel Hill: University of North Carolina Press, 1998), 185.

62. Although the coal industry certainly dominated the economic development of Central Appalachia, an examination of the people involved in importing goods into the mountains is necessary to gain a full and balanced understanding of the region's history. Lewis Atherton has made a similar point about historical depictions of the American frontier, which typically neglect the role of the merchant: "If the story of the frontier is to be told solely in terms of occupations like those of the cowboy and the farmer, the process of transforming the raw settlements into modern specialized communities will remain incompletely understood." *The Frontier Merchant in Mid-America* (Columbia: University of Missouri Press, 1971), 14. It should be noted that Jews were not the only group to play a predominantly mercantile role in the coalfield economy. Syrian and Lebanese immigrants also arrived in the region through their own networks, started out as peddlers and soon became merchants and important members of the town-based middle class. See Yvonne Snyder Farley, "To Keep Their Faith Strong: The Raleigh Orthodox Community," and "One of the Faithful: Asaff Rahall, Church Founder," *Goldenseal* 18, no. 2 (summer 1992): 43-53.

63. Pickus, interview; Ken Bank, interview; Gail Bank, interview; Sylvan Bank, interview; Harry Berman, interview by John C. Hennen Jr., Williamson, W.Va., 15 and 28 June 1989, Matewan Oral History Project, Matewan Development Center, Matewan, W.Va.

64. Sniderman, *Diamond in the Rough*; Sam and Harvey Weiner, interview; Barkai, *Branching Out*, 116.

65. Barkai, *Branching Out*, 46. According to Maimonides, the highest form of *tzedekah* consisted of helping someone to gain the capacity to help themselves. On how concepts of *tzedekah* and the performance of *mitzvot* translated into Jewish business practice, see Morawska, *Insecure Prosperity*, 20-1, 58-61.

66. A variety of sources was used to construct a database that contains more than two thousand Jewish men, women, and children who lived in the coalfields from the 1870s through the 1950s. Information on occupation was gathered for more than eight hundred of these residents. Sources included: manuscript census schedules of 1900, 1910, and 1920 for Bell and Harlan Counties, Ky.; Fayette, Logan, McDowell, Mingo, and Raleigh Counties, W.Va.; Tazewell and Wise Counties, Va. Also used were city directories for Pocahontas, Va., 1904, 1910, and 1915; Logan, W.Va., 1927; Beckley, W.Va., 1932 and 1940; Williamson, W.Va., 1952. Records of Jewish congregations in Logan, Welch, and Williamson, W.Va., provided data, as did personal interviews. Local history books such as Shinedling's *West Virginia Jewry* and Shinedling and Pickus's *The History of the Beckley Jewish Community*, as well as general local histories of McDowell and Logan Counties, W.Va.; and Welch, W.Va., were consulted. Peddlers were probably undercounted more than other workers in such sources because of their transience. On peddlers as founders of American Jewish communities, see, for example, Diner, *A Time for Gathering*, 68-9; Evans, *The Provincials*; Sorin, *A Time for Building*, 3-5, 153-7.

67. Bernard Gottlieb, interview; Sam and Harvey Weiner, interview.

68. Scott, interview; Fink, interview; Betty Schuchat Gottlieb, interview; McDowell County Manuscript Census, 1910.

69. Irving Alexander, "Wilcoe: People of a Coal Town" and "Jewish Merchants in the Coalfields," *Goldenseal* 16 (spring 1990): 28-35; Scott, interview; "Col. Jos. M. Lopinsky."

70. Sniderman, *Diamond in the Rough*.

71. Pickus, interview. Census records as well as virtually all the interviews conducted with Jews who grew up in the coalfields confirm the critical impact of chain migration.

72. Milton Koslow, interview by author, Charleston, W.Va., 13 May 1998; Sopher, interview; Shinedling and Pickus, *The History of the Beckley Jewish Community*; Isadore Gorsetman, interview author, Charleston, W.Va., 13 May 1998. Gorsetman's experience of discrimination in the steel industry finds scholarly confirmation in Selevan's study, "Jewish Wage Earners in Pittsburgh, 1890-1930."

73. Jerry Bruce Thomas, "Coal Country: The Rise of the Southern Smokeless Coal Industry and Its Effect on Area Development, 1872-1910" (Ph.D. diss., University of North Carolina, 1970), 83-8; Charles Kenneth Sullivan, "Coal Men and Coal Towns: Development of the Smokeless Coalfields of Southern West Virginia, 1873-1923" (Ph.D. diss., University of Pittsburgh, 1979); Ronald D Eller, *Miners, Millhands, and Mountaineers: Industrialization of the Appalachian South, 1880-1930* (Knoxville: University of Tennessee Press, 1982); Howard B. Lee, *Bloodletting in Appalachia* (Morgantown: West Virginia University Press, 1969).

*"Belgian Workers at the Modern Window Glass Co., Salem, West Virginia, ca. 1915
Courtesy of Clara A. McCann, Clarksburg, W.Va. (granddaughter of Edgar Quinaut)*

Craft, Ethnicity, and Identity: Belgian Glassworkers in West Virginia, 1898-1940

Ken Fones-Wolf

Visitors to the small West Virginia town of Salem in the fall of 1914 probably would have expressed surprise at the flavor of the social events they found there. If their stay was long enough, the Salem Concert Band, comprised largely of glassworkers, would have treated them to several concerts; they might have attended a variety of plays staged by actors speaking French, and they could have witnessed several parades. Undoubtedly, they would have noted the bustle on the street generated by men, women, and children raising over three thousand dollars for war relief as well as the storefronts exhibiting both American and Belgian flags. The people of Salem were not merely anxious citizens anticipating American involvement in World War I, however. These activities reflected the very personal motives of a growing segment of Salem, the Belgian immigrant glassworking community on the east end of town. A number of glassworker families had visited their birthplace that summer and were trapped in Belgium by the outbreak of war. Demonstrating their concern, nearly everyone in Salem pitched in, ignoring the fact that these immigrants supported the Socialist party and comprised the major political opposition in the town. For the next fifteen months, local people worked to successfully reunite families separated by the European conflict.[1]

This episode, apart from its value as a human-interest story about a community pulling together to confront their neighbors' hardships, reveals a number of things about the Belgian immigrant community. First, it suggests that the immigrant glassworkers maintained strong ties with their homeland, partly through travel back and forth, but also by transplanting aspects of Belgian culture in their new home. Second, these glassworkers were relatively well-paid industrial workers, able to travel to Europe in the summer when the cooperatively owned factory shut down the furnaces. Third, this immigrant community had a well-defined sociopolitical vision, shaped by their experiences in the Belgian workers movement and by the traditions of their craft. For them, politics meant not only voting the Socialist ticket but also establishing cooperative factories and stores.

All of these insights would have been true in the fall of 1914, but such snapshots do not tell the entire story. Just little more than a decade later, the

Socialist party would no longer be a force in local politics; the cooperative factories had either closed or become privately owned; and many of the Belgians were moving to the mechanized factories operated by the Libbey-Owens-Ford Company and the Pittsburgh Plate Glass Company.[2] Nevertheless, the immigrant glassworkers maintained important links to their country of origin and to the traditions of their trade. Indeed, the culture and politics of Belgian glassworkers continued to exert an influence on the industrial communities of north-central West Virginia well into the twentieth century.

This essay examines the Belgian glassworker communities that emerged around the turn of the century in Clarksburg and Salem, West Virginia. It seeks to understand the identity of these glassworkers by exploring the transnational character of markets, technologies, corporate initiatives, and labor activism in the window-glass industry. The story of the Belgian immigrants in West Virginia has an added benefit. Much of the literature on immigration in the early twentieth century focuses on the "new immigration" and those occupying the bottom rungs of the American working class.[3] Emphasizing southern and eastern Europeans who entered mining and mass-production factories neglects the smaller numbers of skilled immigrants who continued to come to America. The Belgian glassworkers who came to West Virginia between 1898 and 1920 were skilled craftsmen essential to the production process of an expanding industry. They moved to new communities and occupied the upper rungs of the working-class job market. Such immigrants contributed to working-class formation in ways decidedly different from the bulk of southern and eastern Europeans.[4] The rise and decline of this privileged position was also critical in shaping the identity of these Belgian communities.

A Transnational Network of Craftsmen

The reunion of Edgar Quinaut's family in December 1915 was noteworthy in the town of Salem only because the context of the war made emigration more difficult. In fact, during the previous decade many Belgian and French families in north-central West Virginia endured equally long periods separated by the Atlantic Ocean. Skilled workers in the window-glass industry were a highly mobile group, attempting to regulate a craft labor market to their advantage. The principal instrument that workers used for that regulation was the Knights of Labor. By 1880, skilled glassworkers in the United States established Local Assembly (LA) 300 of the Knights to unite the blowers, gatherers, flatteners, and cutters who were central to the work process of making glass panes by the hand-blown cylinder method. Comprising between 35 and 40 percent of the workers in window-glass plants, these craftsmen codified their control of production in the rules of LA 300. Membership rules limited entry to the crafts by requiring that new apprentices have a father, an uncle, or a brother already in the trade. Once admitted to an apprenticeship, a young man then had to spend four or five years learning the craft, the expected code of behavior, and the expectations of the union. LA 300 also established "Rules for Working" which governed virtually every aspect of production, including crew size, work pace, when certain tasks could be performed, and when the plants shut down for the summer. Through such rules and bylaws, the window-glass workers became one of the elite trades of the labor movement—highly paid, organizationally solid, and capable of passing their status and privileges to their sons, brothers, or nephews.[5]

Conditions had not been so kind to Belgian window-glass workers who were concentrated in the towns in the Charleroi basin—Jumet, Lodelinsart, Gilly, Dampremy and Charleroi. There, the industry began melting the raw materials in tanks heated by natural gas rather than in clay pots. This new technology encouraged continuous production on a much larger scale. First introduced in Belgium in 1874, industrialists rapidly adopted tank technology and concentrated the industry in larger corporations. In 1880, the Charleroi area had forty glass plants employing 4,447 workers; by 1896 it had only twenty plants but employed 9,763 workers.[6] Belgian employers used this to solidify their control over labor markets in the industry. They forced skilled workers to sign long-term labor contracts and they increased the number of apprentices and the length of their apprenticeship, giving companies an ample supply of cheap labor. The physical environment of the factories aided employer control; high brick walls surrounded their factories, allowing entrance only through a small gate or through a saloon owned by the firm. The heat and unhealthy atmosphere invited drinking, and drinks for thirsty glassworkers were recorded in a huge ledger and deducted from the workers' earnings.[7]

Efforts to organize workers in the Belgian plants met harsh treatment by the companies and by the government, as well as infiltration by agents of the state. Belgium limited suffrage to wealthy property owners who made up less than 10 percent of the male population, denying glassworkers a political voice. In southern Belgium, industrialists dominated the region at election time and forged connections with government officials to minimize state regulation of labor issues. Courts complemented this power; legal proceedings arising from labor conflict typically ended in favor of employers.[8]

Controlling conditions at home did not eliminate problems for Belgian glass corporations. These companies faced stiff challenges in both European and American markets. Protective tariffs in Germany, France, and other countries limited Belgian exports, creating problems for glassworkers and their employers.

Companies in the Charleroi area reduced wages to between one-fourth and one-half of American wages in order to stay competitive, but still produced more glass than they could sell. As a result, they also curtailed production, leaving some twelve hundred glassworkers without employment. LA 300, learning of the plight of the glassworkers, started a subscription drive to "relieve the distress of the Belgians" in 1880.[9]

The Knights of Labor reacted less favorably when low-paid Belgian craftsmen began immigrating to the United States in the early 1880s. In the early 1880s, American manufacturers hoped to expand production to capture the huge domestic market for window glass. As late as 1886, they accounted for only 42 percent of sales in the United States. Taking advantage of the poor wages and working conditions in Belgium, American employers recruited Belgian craftsmen to factories in Baltimore, Zanesville, Ohio, and Meadville, Pennsylvania.[10] LA 300 raised initiation fees for immigrants and threatened to strike if union members lost jobs. More promising for the Knights of Labor, however, in 1884 LA 300 sent emissaries Isaac Cline and Andrew Burtt to Europe to investigate conditions of glassworkers. Witnessing the poorly organized efforts of glassworkers in the Charleroi area to gain union recognition, Cline and Burtt recommended that the Knights send an organizer to Belgium to establish assemblies of glassworkers and to create a Universal Federation of Window Glass Workers.[11]

Belgian glassworkers flocked to the Eureka Assembly of the *Chevaliers du Travail* (Knights of Labor) in 1884 and 1885 in an effort to gain the type of wages and working conditions won by their counterparts in the United States. Unfortunately for them, they confronted a highly disciplined and powerful group of employers who exerted considerable influence over government authorities in the region. Insisting upon wage reductions and layoffs to deal with unstable markets, the employers' actions precipitated a disastrous strike. Despite the moderate counsel of the *Chevaliers du Travail*, workers rioted, sacking and burning several glass factories. Courts blamed the Eureka Assembly for the destruction and sentenced several of its leaders to twenty years in prison.[12] Nevertheless, the *Chevaliers du Travail* survived the debacle and became an alternative organization for labor activity in Belgium for the next generation, an organization that focused on militant, but politically unaffiliated trade-union activity. In a country where the labor movement had close ties to the Belgian Workers' party, the Knights of Labor remained outside those circles. Instead, the *Chevaliers du Travail* became a defensive, craft-oriented labor union that kept a safe distance from the more centralized and reformist socialism of the mainstream of the Belgian labor movement.[13]

The unique character of the Charleroi labor movement came in part from the strong regional identity of the glassworkers and miners in the area. Workers there defined themselves first as "Carolingians," which set them apart from others in a variety of ways, from their Walloon dialect to their general acceptance of a mixed-sex workplace. Even the Socialists from the province who had some national stature, Jules Destree and Alfred Defuisseaux, were seen as dissidents by the party leadership. Separation from the mainstream of the Belgian Workers' party, however, did not signify a complete rejection of socialist ideas or politics at the local level. Indeed, Defuisseaux drew upon the events of 1886 when writing his enormously popular socialist tract, *"Le Catechisme du Peuple."* While the *Chevaliers du Travail* avoided submission to either the Catholic or the Socialist labor federations, Charleroi glassworkers supported working-class mobilization. They championed direct economic action and the general strike, exemplified by the massive walkout of male and female glassworkers in 1895. Likewise, local workers participated in Socialist-led demonstrations that succeeded in obtaining universal male suffrage in 1894, and the city elected Socialist councilmen into the twentieth century. Finally, Charleroi workers developed a strong cooperative society, *La Concorde*, which had over fifteen thousand members and helped control prices for groceries and other commodities.[14]

This revitalized labor movement did not solve the glassworkers' problems. Through the 1890s, the *Chevaliers du Travail* won improvements in wages and working conditions in the Charleroi area, but the glass factories chronically operated at less than full capacity. At a time when the American industry was constantly expanding, Belgian glassworkers typically split shifts and worked only half of the week. Although wage rates were high, total earnings were not.[15] Moreover, Belgian corporations sought to implement any new technological improvements, particularly those that threatened the status of skilled workers. In contrast, window-glass factories in the United States remained far less concentrated and centralized, enabling smaller and less technologically advanced companies to find a market niche. Thus, Belgian emigrants flocked to America seeking new opportunities.

This was the environment that Edgar Quinaut sought to escape after 1900. Edgar was born into a glassworking family in Jumet in 1878, the son of Melchior and Josephine. He witnessed the emergence of the *Chevaliers du Travail* and the strikes of 1886 and 1895, and he may have participated in the Socialist demonstrations for universal male suffrage in the 1890s. The Quinauts were prosperous enough that in 1898 Edgar could purchase a substitute for his obligatory service in the Belgian army. In 1903, he married Clara Lambiotte, a twenty-three-year-old daughter of a glassworker, and the couple gave birth to two children in Jumet. Like many Belgian glassworkers, Quinaut, a cutter, considered moving. Probably he made several trips, perhaps to France or Germany, although some of his fellow craftsmen considered opportunities in Russia. In 1907, he followed many Belgians to America where he may have worked for a time in plants in Indiana, Ohio, or southwestern Pennsylvania, places with strong Belgian enclaves. In 1912 he arrived in Salem, West Virginia, a community that had several Lambiotte families (his wife's surname) and would come to the aid of his family two years later.[16] To understand why northcentral West Virginia would become home to so many Belgian glassworkers we must return to the transnational nature of markets, technologies, corporate initiatives, and labor strategies.

Belgians and the Transformation of American Window-Glass Manufacture

Local Assembly 300 had approached its European mission in the 1880s with conservative objectives. Organizer A. G. Denny reported that his goal was "restraining contract labor from coming to this country." Much of the work of the Universal Federation of Window Glass Workers attempted to regulate a transnational labor market by establishing rules limiting admission to union jobs in other countries, especially during strikes. In October 1886, a Berkshire County, Massachusetts, firm wrote to Belgium for blowers to replace the company's union men, but the *Chevaliers du Travail* refused to allow their members to take their union cards so that they could move to those jobs. In those cases when Belgian immigrants managed to obtain work at non-union American factories, LA 300 could mete out harsh discipline; the union pulled the cards of Frank Wery Sr. and Jr. for working as "black sheep."[17]

For a time, this attempt at international labor market regulation seemed to work. At the request of Belgian leader Albert Delwarte, LA 300 prevented the recruitment of American strikebreakers by Charleroi factories during the strike of 1886; meanwhile complaints in the United States against foreign labor declined noticeably. In fact, in the wake of the disastrous Belgian strikes, LA 300 offered transportation and jobs to some six hundred to seven hundred skilled glassworkers. American manufacturers were in the process of expanding production to capture the huge domestic market, actually doubling their pot capacity between 1882 and 1888. This created a temporary shortage of skilled labor, which the defeated Belgian *Chevaliers du Travail* supplied.[18] Of course, once Americans opened the floodgates for glassworkers victimized in their homelands, it became difficult to close them. In 1889, LA 300 raised the initiation fee for immigrants from one hundred to four hundred dollars, which represented several months' earnings, and limited new apprenticeships to United States citizens. In this more competitive transnational environment, the experiment in international labor market regulation collapsed.[19]

Adding to LA 300's growing fears of overproduction was the recomposition of the industry. The discovery of natural gas in Pennsylvania, Ohio, and Indiana spurred local boosters in those areas to make generous offers of land and low fuel rates to attract manufacturing industries. This occurred simultaneously with the adoption of the continuous tank by American employers, borrowing from their Belgian counterparts. The tank, which used natural gas as the fuel of choice, encouraged a larger scale of production because the steady heat enabled factories to melt much greater quantities of the batch. Although a decade behind his Belgian counterparts, Pittsburgh glass manufacturer James Chambers decided to build a new factory utilizing the tank in the late 1880s. First, he took a trip to Belgium to study the technology. Chambers's new plant in Jeannette, Pennsylvania, opened in 1889 with a complement of seventy-two blowers, seventy-two gatherers, twenty-eight cutters and sixteen flatteners. The actual capacity of 108 blowers was more than three times the average size of American factories. Over the next decade, tank factories would garner the lion's share of the industry, increasing from just 8% of the total capacity in 1889 to 68% in 1898.[20]

The reorganization of the industry had serious repercussions for LA 300. Immigrants and their children flocked to the new opportunities in the gas belt while older members remained concentrated near the Pittsburgh headquarters. This created tensions within LA 300, as workers in the gas-belt areas charged that Pittsburgh-based union leaders set policies that worked to the detriment of newer factories. Regional factionalism thus took on an ethnic character as immigrant union members struggled for jobs and control of LA 300. Compounding these tensions were important changes in the industry structure. First, the economic depression of the 1890s and the resulting stagnation of new construction meant that the window-glass industry was vastly overextended. Output had been at 66% of the existing capacity in 1890, but was only 36% of capacity in 1900. As a result, many glassworkers were periodically out of work. Second, the appearance of the industry's first marketing trust, the American Window Glass Company, triggered a period of intense competition and the demise of numerous small companies that had recognized and bargained with LA 300.[21]

By the end of the century, skilled Belgian glassworkers were exploring new strategies to deal with the problems facing them in a competitive industry. During the turmoil of the 1890s, Belgians had captured a leading role in LA 300. Because they had gravitated to the new gas-fueled plants, they were situated in factories that had the greatest staying power during the depression. The large Belgian faction helped elect a new president, Simon Burns, and he rewarded them with three of the five spots on the executive board in 1899.[22] To improve their working conditions and to recapture the control they had formerly wielded over the production process, Belgians used their influence in LA 300 to encourage cooperative production. The ongoing immigration of glassworkers from the Charleroi region infused the growing cooperative sentiment of Belgian socialism into developing union strategies in America. Thus, as a way to keep alive their craft traditions, Belgians turned to producer cooperatives, particularly in remote areas where small factories might carve out a market niche. This had the added benefit of enabling Belgians to escape the ethnic tensions that plagued LA 300.[23]

Opportunities for cooperative production were plentiful in the United States. Local boosters in small, gas-belt towns competed to recruit potential users of natural gas. Favorable fuel and land costs meant that starting a factory was within the reach of a group of skilled workers who had commanded fairly high industrial wages. Moreover, LA 300 commanded resources that could facilitate cooperative production. Glassworkers had experimented with cooperatives as early as the 1880s, and the transformation of the industry only added a new impetus, furthered by the presence of Belgians on the executive board. By September 1900, LA 300 had loaned $29,000 to seven separate cooperative plants. President Burns felt that the union's participation in the cooperatives would provide jobs for members and help the union regulate output for the benefit of the industry's workers.[24]

Although many of the cooperatives began in Pennsylvania, Ohio, and Indiana, the development of natural gas fields in West Virginia made it an ideal location for skilled workers hoping to start their own plants. Blessed with the natural resources necessary for glass production, many towns in the state developed a booster mentality that believed manufacturing industries would be an ideal complement to coal, oil and natural gas extraction. Northcentral West Virginia also benefited from its proximity to the large numbers of skilled craftsmen in southwestern Pennsylvania and eastern Ohio. For Belgians, the Mountain State reminded them of their homeland, a region of coal mining and glass production. Thus, one of the more enduring Belgian cooperatives, the Banner Window Glass Company, moved from Vincennes, Indiana, where it originated in the 1890s, to southern West Virginia after the turn of the century.[25] By that time, however, Belgians had already established a cooperative network in the northcentral part of the state.

Craft Communities in the Hills

Ironically, the first cooperative window-glass factory in West Virginia was not Belgian, but French. Drawing on the long history of producer associations in their homeland, a group of French glassworkers chartered the Lafayette Window Glass Company in the village of North View, just outside of Clarksburg, in 1898. Although not part of the original ownership team, Belgian workers hoping to escape the transformation of their industry made up nearly half of the francophone neighborhood surrounding the Lafayette factory. Soon after, groups of Belgians began their own plants; in 1904 they established the Clarksburg Cooperative Window Glass Company in the neighboring town of Adamston, and the Peerless Window Glass Company that located next to the Lafayette plant.[26] Over the decade, Belgians significantly expanded their cooperative activities, and West Virginia was the principal beneficiary. The Banner Glass Company moved from Indiana to South Charleston, while other groups of Belgians established two cooperatives in Salem (twelve miles west of Clarksburg), and one each in Sistersville and Weston. By 1910, West Virginia accounted for about one-third of the hand-blown window-glass producers in the country.[27]

The Belgian communities that took shape in northcentral West Virginia were the creation of a transnational network of craftsmen responding to technological changes, corporate initiatives, and labor strategies in the window-glass industry. Belgian glassworkers, virtually all of whom were from the Charleroi area, had been arriving in a steady stream beginning in the 1880s. By the time Edgar Quinaut's family arrived in the United States, they could move within an ethnic, craft community with a well-developed institutional framework. Edgar was already a member of the National Window Glass Workers (NWGW), the successor to LA 300, but French and Belgian craftsmen still referred to the union as Local Assembly 300. He also joined a West Virginia branch of *La Prevoyance*, a Belgian mutual benevolent association and insurance society founded in Hartford, Indiana, in 1895 by Belgians. Within two years Quinaut had become a shareholder in the Modern Window Glass Company, purchasing twenty shares for $1,000.[28] Edgar Quinaut certainly qualifies as an unusually fortunate working-class immigrant in the early twentieth century, but he was hardly atypical among the Belgian glassworkers in West Virginia.

These craftsmen were still a mobile group, trying to maintain their traditional work culture. Membership ledgers of the NWGW trace the movement of skilled craftsmen around the country in search of a place to ply their trade. Despite their high pay, the instability of the hand-blown portion of the industry meant that few could permanently settle; indeed, home ownership rates for these immigrant craftsmen were lower than for the unskilled workers in the industry.[29] Some of the craftsmen who purchased shares in the cooperatives also bought small lots to build homes close to the factories, but many were "tramping artisans" who moved from one factory to another when the plants shut down for the summer. These more mobile workers tended to be younger, and they frequently boarded with established Belgian families. But glassworker neighborhoods in northcentral West Virginia also accommodated the craftsmen with the trappings of a more transient culture—hotels and boardinghouses, saloons, and pool halls.[30]

Transiency was not a barrier to the establishment of vibrant craft communities among the Belgians. In North View, Adamston, and Salem, it was common to hear French spoken as a principal language. Moreover, these ethnic enclaves reproduced cultural practices reminiscent of their communities in the Charleroi area. Of particular importance was the celebration of the New Year's holiday, during which the youngest couple in the area would visit the next youngest and receive special drinks and toasts. Then the older couple would repeat the process with the next oldest, and so on until a complete circle of the community had been completed. For more routine entertainment, the Belgians built social clubs that hosted parties and dances every Saturday night. Belgian youths loved to dance, but "the mothers of young Belgian girls chaperoned the dances" to maintain the proper decorum. Clubs also provided opportunities for playing cards or drinking beer and wine among their fellow immigrants.[31]

Belgians also contributed to a vital cultural life in their new homes. In Clarksburg and Salem they established dramatic clubs that produced plays in French for the local community, occasionally attracting others to their performances. Another activity that did not face language barriers involved music. Glassworkers provided the director and comprised the bulk of the musicians in community bands in Clarksburg and Salem. Smaller ensembles provided music for the weekly community dances while the entire band was required for local parades and events. One Clarksburg glassworker, Adrian DeMeester, recalled that between 1906 and 1953, "I did more god darn parading around this town than you can shake a stick at."[32] Successive waves of Belgian immigrants maintained other cultural traditions. Of note were the highly artistic glassworkers who, in spare moments in the plant, made a variety of special items ranging from glass canes to dippers. Omar Lambiotte recalled that his father saved pieces of colored glass to make trinkets. Others remember cooking clubs to maintain particular Belgian treats. Aside from New Year's celebrations, Belgians also looked forward to summer when the various ethnic social clubs would hold a festival that included prizes for the best preserves and pastries. Finally, there were the sporting events which included bowling and bicycle racing, and the ever present cardplaying and pigeon races for which the Belgian community was noted.[33]

The location of the plants at the distant edges of small towns and villages limited Belgian interaction with the dominant society while sustaining local craft communities. Few French-speaking workers contributed to the growing animosity toward immigrants in northcentral West Virginia. Instead, local animosity focused on the blacks, Italians, and Poles who worked in the nearby mines. Before 1910, Salem and Clarksburg newspapers praised Belgians as "the most skillful" and respectable of workers, and the towns were delighted to have attracted the glass industry. Even when members of the group stepped out of line, the Belgian community took responsibility for handling the problems. For example, Belgians in North View turned over one of their glassworkers to authorities when they discovered that he had deserted his wife and refused to pay support. Likewise, when five Lafayette Company workers were arrested in a house of prostitution, the cooperative assumed responsibility for monitoring their conduct during the busy glassmaking season.[34]

These communities were in many respects conservative and self-reliant defenders of the craftsmen's empire. Belgians made little effort to build alliances with other workers. They were hostile to other wage earners who intruded into their neighborhoods. Indeed, North View was in turmoil in 1904 over an interracial romance, and a near riot occurred when an African American man yelled at a young French-speaking girl.[35] Belgians worked hard to distance themselves from the hostility directed toward other immigrants. Mindful of the growing unrest about which local newspapers complained, North View glassworkers tried to prevent a zinc works from being built in their village asserting that it would bring Italians and Poles into their peaceful neighborhood.[36]

Despite being so attentive to defending their communities, Belgians had a limited presence in local politics. High rates of transiency and citizenship requirements hindered participation, but even established glassworkers demonstrated little evidence of interest in local elections. Despite comprising a significant portion of the population in the independent villages of Adamston and North View, no Belgians appeared on political slates before 1910. In part, this apparent indifference reflected the strong craft and community-oriented identities that these immigrants had developed in Belgium. In the Charleroi area, glassworkers mobilized in a militant fashion around issues of particular concern, but preserved their independence and distance from larger political movements. In their neighborhoods and cooperative factories in northcentral West Virginia, Belgians had substantial control. Their benevolent association, *La Prevoyance*, insured them against disasters, the NWGW protected their wages and working conditions, and their clubs skirted local ordinances against enjoying a "continental Sunday."[37]

Technology, War, and the Transformation of Belgian Identity

The transnational nature of the window-glass industry, however, intruded into these craftsmen's paradises. Even as skilled glassworkers took refuge in remote locations with abundant natural resources and used decentralized markets to establish their cooperatives, new technologies and corporate strategies threatened their existence. In 1903, the American Window Glass Company

(AWGC) began using the Lubbers cylinder glass-blowing machine that created glass cylinders mechanically and eliminated blowers and gatherers from the process. Production flaws limited the use of the Lubbers machine, but it further fragmented the craft-union solidarity in the industry; blowers and gatherers had been the two largest crafts. By 1905 LA 300 ceased to exist, a victim of market pressures, technological innovations, and ethnic hostilities. Increasingly, workers clinging to traditional hand-blown methods worked at the margins of the industry in widely dispersed and remote locations.[38]

Although skilled craftsmen replaced LA 300 with the National Window Glass Workers in 1908, the AWGC's use of the Lubbers machine posed a grow-ing challenge by the time Edgar Quinaut's family arrived in Salem in 1912. The Lubbers machine substituted lower paid machine operators for high-paid crafts-men but also enabled manufacturers to greatly increase output because the machine-made cylinders dwarfed any that could be made by hand. Thus, AWGC plants cut labor costs by anywhere from 25 to 50 percent, enabling the com-pany to lower prices and capture a larger share of the domestic market. The competition faced by the cooperatives steadily undermined the craft elitism of glassworkers; wages tumbled and plants closed for longer periods each sum-mer, until the annual earnings of craftsmen approached those of semi-skilled workers in the mechanized plants. Moreover, the prospect for job security seemed no brighter than it had a decade earlier.[39]

Shrinking opportunities changed the glassworker communities of northcentral West Virginia. No longer were craftsmen able to move at will for better opportunities. In the decade after 1910 many glassworkers stayed in Salem or Clarksburg because they had nowhere else to go. By 1920, the home ownership rates of craftsmen outstripped all others in the industry, even though few had been born in West Virginia. Edgar Quinaut again provides an example; shortly after his wife, mother, and children escaped Belgium during the First World War, he put down more permanent roots in Salem by purchas-ing a house for $2,650, half of which he paid in cash at the time of purchase. Increasingly, those clinging to these craft communities were immigrants. In Clarksburg in 1920, immigrants made up a higher percentage of window-glass craftsmen than they had in 1910; with their children they comprised over 55% of the skilled workers.[40]

Under these circumstances, the identity of the Belgian craftsmen took a radical turn. They redoubled their efforts to build new cooperative plants for their fellow craftsmen despite the long-term prognosis, adding a cooperative plant in Clarksburg, another in Salem, and one more a bit further west in Pennsboro. Equally important, they borrowed from their past cultural experiences in Belgium, as well as from ongoing transnational networks, and developed a vibrant socialist culture. The Belgian community opened cooperative stores for consumers in North View and Salem, and these stores worked closely with local branches of the Socialist party. Belgians in both Salem and Clarksburg also began to issue Socialist newspapers and host Socialist speakers.[41] Because these plants were located in small, incorporated towns, the Belgians could also exert a disproportionate influence in electoral politics once they chose to get involved. In Adamston, Belgians contributed to the election of a Socialist mayor and city council in 1912 and 1915, victories that included three glassworkers. North View chose a Progressive ticket in 1913 that included two Lafayette Company glassworkers. Between 1913 and 1916, the Socialist party in Salem was the only serious rival of the Industrial party. Glassworker neighborhoods gave between 24% and 38% of their votes to Socialist candidates in the 1912 and 1914 national elections.[42]

The onset of World War I, however, interrupted the drift of these Belgian craft communities toward Socialism. In one sense, transnational concerns reoriented the focus of the glassworkers. The war drew Belgians more into the mainstream of the towns in which they lived as the support of the people of Salem for the predicaments of Belgians trapped in the war zone demonstrated. Previously, the local newspapers rarely contained any news about the sizeable Belgian enclaves. During the war, as the Belgians interacted more with others in Salem, their attachment to an alternative political party and political opposition waned, eventually experiencing an even larger rift when party leaders opposed intervention on the side of the allies. With family members in Belgium suffering under German assault, many young glassworkers in northcentral West Virginia enlisted in the United States army, hoping to see action in their homelands.[43]

In addition, market conditions temporarily improved for Belgian glassworkers. Wartime demand for glass and the regulation of fuel actually halted the decline of the hand-blown portions of the industry. Belgian glassworkers thrived through 1918. The hand plants benefited from the proportional allotment of fuel, which helped offset the production advantages of the more technologically advanced plants by limiting their ability to operate.[44] In the postwar years, this market regulation, which involved cooperation between the union and the companies, collapsed. The removal of government regulation of fuel restored the production advantage to the more advanced mechanized plants. But by then the Belgian union members had lost clout. Workers and management at the Buckeye Window Glass Company, looking to take advantage of a strong market, sued both the National Window Glass Workers and the Manufacturers' Association for violating antitrust laws. This suit lasted four years and helped destroy the hand-blown segment of the industry.[45]

A third factor undermining the Socialist inclinations of Belgians in northcentral West Virginia involved changes associated with the consolidation of Clarksburg, which diminished the influence that Belgians in North View and Adamston could exert during elections. Clarksburg absorbed the formerly independent townships, limiting the ability of Belgians and other skilled glassworkers to elect candidates of their choosing in a city-wide election. Meanwhile, the consolidated local government cracked down on labor and Socialist activities during the patriotic upsurge generated by the war. This, in turn, led to increased police surveillance of immigrant groups, another factor that narrowed the opportunities for glassworker politics. Finally, with the end of the war, Clarksburg shifted to a city manager form of government, a structural change that further removed political power from particular neighborhoods.[46]

None of these factors, however, matched the significance for the Belgians of further technological changes in the industry. During World War I the two companies that would come to dominate the industry—Libbey-Owens-Ford and Pittsburgh Plate Glass—began using new machines that allowed flat glass to be drawn in continuous sheets, thereby eliminating not only blowers and gatherers but also flatteners from the process. Although introduced in 1916, the war postponed widespread usage. By 1919, this new technology had intruded into the very heart of the hand-process industry; the two giants operated plants in Clarksburg and South Charleston, West Virginia. This last step on the path toward making window glass a mass-production industry destroyed the remaining vestiges of the hand-blown process by 1927. With the demise of the majority of the craft positions, the cutters formed their own small craft union, the Window Glass Cutters League of America in 1923. This would remain a small union of about one thousand members into the 1920s and 1930s.[47]

Belgian Glassworkers in a Mass Production Industry

By the mid-1920s, mechanized, mass-production factories had replaced the hand-blown window glass plants of the craftsman's era. However, the industry did not disappear from north-central West Virginia. Pittsburgh Plate Glass Company opened a large plant in Clarksburg that made windshields for the automobile industry, and several of the smaller plants converted to the new technologies. The four Rolland brothers, French immigrants and former craftsmen, founded the Fourco Glass Company, purchasing the factory in Adamston and the old Lafayette and Peerless plants in Northview among several other plants. They produced window glass in the area for another forty years.[48] Although employment in the region dropped precipitously in the late 1920s, by the late 1930s the number of jobs in the window-glass industry had rebounded, and West Virginia continued to play an important role in glass manufacturing.[49]

What did the transformation of the industry mean to the vast majority of the proud Belgian craftsmen who had settled in northcentral West Virginia?

For the cutters, the opportunity to continue their craft remained. Indeed, Belgian and French immigrants, with such names as Joris, Mayeur, Jacquet, Wery, Lefevre, Bastin, and Zabeau, dominated the cutter positions in the Clarksburg and Salem areas. Others were not so fortunate. A study conducted by the U.S. Department of Labor in 1929 suggested that only about 11% of the former craftsmen found a home in the mechanized plants. Oral history interviews with Belgian ex-craftsmen in the 1970s drew similar bleak conclusions. Many remembered that skilled glassworkers resisted taking jobs in the new factories, rejecting the faster pace, more intense supervision, and authoritarian styles of the mass-production corporations. They recalled the hard times facing the Belgian craftsmen, and claimed that some even committed suicide.[50]

This portrait of decline and principled resistance did not accurately capture the fate of the Belgians in northcentral West Virginia, however. Of the 60 percent of skilled glassworkers who remained in Clarksburg, for example, most had returned to the glass industry by 1935. Despite initial bouts of unemployment, almost three of every five glassworkers managed to obtain jobs in the mechanized plants. Particularly in the Fourco plants in the old French and Belgian neighborhoods, ex-craftsmen continued to work in the industry. Some few became supervisors, but most filled regular production jobs.[51] Ironically, as craftsmen became mass-production workers, they experienced little decline in their earning power. Because the hand plants had shortened the work year to avoid overproduction and had reduced wages to remain competitive with the mechanized plants, overall earnings for production workers in the mechanized plants compared favorably with the wages of now obsolete craftsmen.[52]

While working in the machine plants made sense for Belgian craftsmen whatever indignities their craft identities suffered, it also made sense for employers in the industry to hire former union members. Indeed, the Pittsburgh Plate Glass Company was more likely to hire ex-craftsmen than any other group of workers with experience in the industry, and the ownership of the Fourco plants obviously exhibited some ethnic loyalty to French and Belgian workers. In part, mechanized plants rehired former skilled workers because the company still valued their knowledge of the production process. Many former flatteners, blowers, and gatherers had superior insights for monitoring conditions at the tank, the drawing chamber, or the annealing lehr, even though the process was mechanized. The skills in handling glass acquired by these workers helped prevent breakage and damage. Finally, the huge window-glass companies probably felt they had little to fear from ex-union members. Pittsburgh Plate Glass and Libbey-Owens-Ford had handily defeated the last desperate attempts of the NWGW to exert some influence on the industry.[53]

Unions returned to the industry in the 1930s, however, and the remnants of the once powerful craft unions contributed to a new style of mass-production unionism. The passage of the National Industrial Recovery Act in June 1933 provided workers with an opportunity to build a new window-glass union. The Window Glass Cutters League (WGCL) took advantage of the resurgence of unionism in West Virginia associated with the United Mine Workers to expand its organizing beyond its craft. Many of the cutters in the Clarksburg and Salem areas were Belgians, and they helped organize production workers into "miscellaneous locals." By 1934, the WGCL had organized about twelve thousand miscellaneous workers, vastly outnumbering the craftsmen in the union.[54] Such organizing successes brought problems, however. Sensing that they might quickly lose control of their union, tensions arose over union policies. With no easy way to settle disputes, in July, the miscellaneous workers formed their own organization, the Federation of Flat Glass Workers (FFGW) with the blessing of the WGCL.[55]

Although begun with the support of the WGCL, relations between the two unions rapidly deteriorated. Production workers in the FFGW had to strike frequently in its early years to establish their bargaining power, strikes that inevitably threw the cutters out of work. Belgian cutters, such as Jules Michaux, Joseph Mayeur, and F. M. Lefevre resented the loss of work that they thought resulted from the more confrontational policies of the FFGW. When the FFGW bolted from the American Federation of Labor to join with the Congress of Industrial Organizations, the cutters felt betrayed.[56] Charges and countercharges flew back and forth, claiming that each organization was promising to recruit scabs to destroy the other. By 1937, there was little trust on either side.

Although there were Belgians were in both organizations, they played a more prominent role in the WGCL. In keeping with their craft traditions, the Belgian cutters were prepared to defend their apprenticeship system and their control over the trade. Cutters were willing to assist other workers in their efforts to build a union, but the WGCL expected that the FFGW would accept a more subordinate position in the relations between the two unions, and that it would negotiate with the companies in a fashion consistent with the style and goals of the WGCL. Several Cutters League officials even referred to the FFGW as the "Junior League."[57] In contrast, Belgians in less skilled production jobs bristled at the elitism of their more favored countrymen. Especially at the Fourco plants, the large numbers of formerly skilled Belgian workers contested the leadership of the Cutters League, and earned the grudging admiration of the cutters for the solidarity and discipline they demonstrated during the tumultuous years of 1936 and 1937.[58]

Not surprisingly, there was a distinct ethnic community flavor to the revival of unionism in North View and Adamston. The local leader of the cutters, Jules Michaux, noted that local French and Belgian merchants distributed groceries to striking glassworkers, and even donated "a keg of beer" to those on picket duty. During more routine times, Belgians played an important role in attaching their traditional community activities to the new union; they sponsored trips and picnics, and helped create baseball and basketball teams for members of the Rolland and Adamston local unions. Especially noteworthy among the new union's recreational accomplishments was the presence of many of its members in the local VFW band, an obvious link to the Belgian craftsmen of the past.[59] Clearly, there continued to be a lingering transnational flavor to labor organization in the window-glass industry.

Edgar Quinaut and his family were part of the ongoing transnational nature of the window-glass communities in northcentral West Virginia. He was still paying dues to *La Prevoyance* in 1951, a testament to the lingering importance of the Belgian mutual benevolent association in Clarksburg, where he had moved sometime in the 1930s. Meanwhile, he maintained a bank account in Belgium that also lasted well into the 1950s, a half-century after his move to the United States. Quinaut's sense of himself owed a good deal to both his ethnic background and to the transformation of his craft. Both characteristics had enabled him to move between continents with ease, but developments on both sides of the Atlantic Ocean continued to impact his life. For many Belgian-Americans like Quinaut, technological changes, corporate initiatives, labor strategies, politics, culture, and even wars in Belgium might intrude into their new homes in the hills of West Virginia.

The story of Edgar Quinaut and his countrymen should add several insights to our thinking about immigration and ethnic history in the early twentieth century. First, it suggests that we should acknowledge that the era of the "new immigration" and mass production continued to include highly skilled immigrants who were still central to craft production processes. The impact that these immigrants had on communities was quite different. Belgian glassworkers, for example, entered communities in northcentral West Virginia near the top of the occupational ladder. They developed flourishing, if insular, ethnic enclaves determined to protect privileges, not build broad alliances within the working class. Even the turn to Socialism masked conservative ends. Second, the story of Belgian glassworkers illustrates just how complex and contingent were the forces that shaped the social, cultural, and political outlook of immigrant workers, both in their homeland and in their adopted land. In an era of constant trans-Atlantic movement, we need many more particular stories of groups of workers to complete that historical picture.

NOTES

1. *Salem (W.Va.) Express*, 21 Aug., 23 Oct., 27 Nov., 11 Dec., 25 Dec. 1914; 15 Jan., 12 Feb., 17 Dec. 1915.

2. This is described in Ken Fones-Wolf, "From Craft to Industrial Unionism in the Window-Glass Industry: Clarksburg, West Virginia, 1900-1937," *Labor History* 37 (winter 1995-96): 28-49; Fred Barkey, *Cinderheads in the Hills: The Belgian Window-Glass Workers of West Virginia* (Charleston: West Virginia Humanities Council, 1988), 13-9.

3. Among the best examples are: Alan M. Kraut, *The Huddled Masses: The Immigrant in American Society, 1880-1921* (Arlington Heights, Ill.: Harlan Davidson, 1982); John Bodnar, *The Transplanted: A History of Immigrants in Urban America* (Bloomington: Indiana University Press, 1987); John J. Bukowczyk, *And My Children Did Not Know Me: A History of Polish-Americans* (Bloomington: Indiana University Press, 1987); Gwendolyn Mink, *Old Labor and New Immigrants in American Political Development, 1875-1920* (Ithaca: Cornell University Press, 1986); Donna Gabaccia, *From the Other Side: Women, Gender, & Immigrant Life in the U.S. 1880-1920* (Bloomington: Indiana University Press, 1994); and Matthew Frye Jacobson, *Whiteness of a Different Color: European Immigrants and the Alchemy of Race* (Cambridge: Harvard University Press, 1998).

4. Ken Fones-Wolf, "A Craftsman's Paradise in Appalachia: Glass Workers and the Transformation of Clarksburg, 1900-1933," *Journal of Appalachian Studies* 1 (fall 1995): 67-85; Steve Babson, *Building the Union: Skilled Workers and Anglo-Gaelic Immigrants in the Rise of the UAW* (New Brunswick: Rutgers University Press, 1991); and Peter Friedlander, *The Emergence of a UAW Local, 1936-1939: A Study in Class and Culture* (Pittsburgh: University of Pittsburgh Press, 1975).

5. Richard John O'Connor, "Cinderheads and Iron Lungs: Window-Glass Craftsmen and the Transformation of Workers' Control, 1880-1905," (Ph.D. diss., University of Pittsburgh, 1991), chaps. 1-2; David Montgomery, *Workers' Control in America: Studies in the History of Work, Technology, and Labor Struggles* (New York: Cambridge University Press, 1979),15-6; Ken Fones-Wolf, "From Craft to Industrial Unionism," 30-3.

6. Maurice Brigotte, *Histoire Industriel de Charleroi* (Mont-sur-Marchienne, n.p., 1984), 129-32.

7. Leon Watillon, *The Knights of Labor in Belgium* (Los Angeles: Institute of Industrial Relations, 1961), 7-8; "Report of James Campbell," 9 Sept. 1888, in LA 300, Minutes, Reel 7, Joseph Slight Papers, Microfilm edition (originals in the Ohio Historical Society, Columbus, Ohio).

8. Watillon, *Knights of Labor in Belgium*, 9-10; Carl Strikwerda, "Interest-Group Politics and the International Economy: Mass Politics and Big Business Corporations in the Liege Coal Basin, 1870-1914," *Journal of Social History* 25 (1991): 279.

9. LA 300, minutes, 16 July 1880, Reel 1, Slight Papers; Pierre-Jean Schaeffer, *Charleroi 1830-1994: Histoire d'une Metropole* (Ottignies: Editions Quorum, 1995), 113-4.

10. LA 300, minutes, 16 Dec. 1881, 7 July 1882, 30 July 1886, Reel 1, Slight Papers.

11. Watillon, *Knights of Labor in Belgium*, 8-13; LA 300, minutes, 18 July 1884, 3 Oct. 1884, Reel 1, Slight Papers; Schaeffer, *Charleroi*, 116-7.

12. Marcel Liebman, *Les Socialistes Belges, 1885-1914: Revolte et L'organisation* (Brussels: Vie Ouvriere, 1979), 54-5; Watillon, *Knights of Labor in Belgium*, 15-6.

13. Carl Strikwerda, *A House Divided: Catholics, Socialists, and Flemish Nationalists in Nineteenth-Century Belgium* (New York: Rowman and Littlefield, 1997), 162, 194; Patricia Penn Hilden, *Women, Work, and Politics: Belgium, 1830-1914* (New York: Oxford University Press, 1993), 256-61; Watillon, *Knights of Labor in Belgium*, 2-5, 17-8.

14. Strikwerda, *House Divided*, 147, 194-5; Hilden, *Women, Work, and Politics*, 253-61; Liebman, *Socialistes Belges*, 68; *Report of an Enquiry ... into Working Class Rents, Housing, and Retail Prices ... in the Principal Industrial Towns of Belgium* (London: HMSO, 1910), 47-56.

15. *Report of an Enquiry*, 50-1; *Histoire Industriel du Charleroi*, 135-6.

16. The information on Edgar Quinaut comes from documents in the possession of Clara McCann, a descendant of Edgar Quinaut. Included are the marriage certificate of Edgar and Clara Quinaut, 24 Feb. 1903, with notations of the subsequent birth of their children; a certificate from the Belgian army, 15 Sept. 1898; a bankbook for Clara Lambiotte for the years 1886 to 1905; and certificates of ownership of shares of the Modern Window Glass Company of Salem, 8 Jan. 1914, among other documents. The information about the mobility of the window-glass craftsmen of Jumet comes from the interviews in Barkey, *Cinderheads in the Hills*, 23-35. The existence of at least two other Lambiotte families in Salem comes from the manuscript census schedules, 1910 census, Harrison County, West Virginia. Oscar Lambiotte, a glassblower, was two years older than Clara, and he arrived in the United States in 1901.

17. LA 300, minutes, 4 Sept. 1885, Reel 1; 1 Oct. 1886, 16 Apr. 1887, Reel 7, Slight Papers; Report on the "Universal Federation of Window Glass Workers Held at Charleroi from August 1st to August 4th, 1888," in LA 300, minutes, 15 Sept. 1888, Reel 7, Slight Papers.

18. LA 300, minutes, 21 May 1886, Reel 1; 6 and 23 July 1886, 19 April 1889, Reel 7, Slight Papers; Norman Ware, *The Labor Movement in the United States: A Study in Democracy, 1860-1895* (New York: Vintage Books, 1964), 198-9; Richard O'Connor, "Cinderheads and Iron Lungs," chap. 3.

19. LA 300, Minutes, 29 Mar., 12 and 19 Apr. 1889, Reel 7, Slight Papers.

20. LA 300, Minutes, 19 Apr. 1889, Reel 7, Slight Papers; O'Connor, "Cinderheads and Iron Lungs," 175. The full implications of this change are explored in Richard O'Connor, "Technology and Union Fragmentation in American Window Glass, 1880-1900," (University of Pittsburgh, 1991, paper in the author's possession).

21. Much of this comes from the excellent work of Richard O'Connor. See his "Technology and Union Fragmentation," and his "Cinderheads and Iron Lungs." Also see *Report of the Sixth National Convention of the Window Glass Workers, LA*

300, July 12-22, 1892 (Pittsburgh, 1892), 16-7, 29-30; *Report of the Eighth National Convention ... 1896* (Pittsburgh, 1896), 26-9; E. H. Gillot, *A History of Trade Unions in the Window Glass Industry* (Columbus: Window Glass Cutters League of America, 1943).

22. LA 300, minutes, 11 Mar. 1899, Reel 7, Slight Papers; O'Connor, "Cinderheads and Iron Lungs," 184-94.

23. For the cooperative sentiment in the Belgian Workers party, see *Report of an Enquiry*, 55-6; Strikwerda, *House Divided*, 178-9; Hilden, *Women, Work and Politics*, 320-33.

24. LA 300, Minutes, 5 May 1899, 1 Sept. 1900; "President's Report" [1899], Reel 7, Slight Papers. For the early cooperative efforts of LA 300, see Norman Ware, *Labor Movement in the United States*, 320-33.

25. On the Banner Company, which moved to South Charleston in 1908, see Barkey, *Cinderheads in the Hills*, 29.

26. *Clarksburg (W.Va.) Telegram*, 30 Sept. 1898, 28 Oct. 1898; *Clarksburg (W.Va.) News*, 1 Sept. 1899, 14 Mar. 1904, 29 Aug. 1905. For the tradition of producer associations in France, see Bernard H. Moss, *The Origins of the French Labor Movement 1830-1914: The Socialism of Skilled Workers* (Berkeley: University of California Press, 1976), 3-6.

27. LA 300, Minutes, 7 Oct. 1911, Reel 8, Slight Papers; Barkey, *Cinderheads in the Hills*, 29; Robert Lookabill, "The Hand Window Glass Workers of West Virginia: A Study of His Skill, Union Organization, and Life Style," (master's thesis, Marshall University, 1971), 56.

28. Quinaut's dues book for *La Prevoyance* dates his membership from 18 Nov. 1912. Stock certificates show that he bought 20 shares of the Modern Window Glass Company on 8 Jan. 1914. The deed of sale for Quinaut's house, which he bought from Louis and Camille Mottet, was dated 1 September 1916. Copies of the originals, supplied by Clara McCann, are in possession of the author.

29. Membership ledgers of the National Window Glass Workers are contained in Series 7 of the Records of the Window Glass Cutters League of America, hereafter cited as WGCLA Records, in the West Virginia and Regional History Collection, West Virginia University, Morgantown, hereafter cited as WVRHC. Home ownership percentages were calculated for Clarksburg from the U.S. Census manuscript schedules, 1910, for Harrison County, West Virginia. The rates for skilled glassworkers were 13.6%, lower than the rate for laborers in the industry.

30. Manuscript Census schedules, *Thirteenth Census of the U.S. 1910*, for Harrison County, available on microfilm, WVRHC.

31. George Villain and George DelForge interviews, in Barkey, *Cinderheads in the Hills*, 23-4, 29; and Dave McKay, "Belgian Glass Workers in Mt. Vernon, Ohio," in *Glassworkers* 1, no. 3 (30 Oct. 2000): 1.

32. *Clarksburg News*, 22 Oct. 1906; *Clarksburg Telegram*, 3 Feb. 1905; *Salem Express*, 23 Oct. 1914; Adrian DeMeester interview in Barkey, *Cinderheads in the Hills*, 26.

33. Philemon D. Sabbe and Leon Buyse, *Belgians in America* (Tielt: Lannoo, 1960), 261-4, 275-82; interviews with George Villain, Adrian DeMeester, George DelForge, Artur LaChapelle, and Omar Lambiotte in Barkey, *Cinderheads in the Hills*, 23-35.

34. *Clarksburg News*, 17 July 1908, 9 Apr. 1906, 22 Nov. 1906.

35. *Clarksburg News*, 1 Sept. 1905; *Clarksburg Telegram*, 4 Oct. 1901.

36. *Clarksburg News*, 19 Feb. 1906, 21 Aug. 1908, 27 Aug. 1908.

37. Watillon, *Knights of Labor in Belgium*, 2-5, 17-8; Hilden, *Women, Work, and Politics*, 256-61; *Clarksburg Daily News*, 6 Apr. 1905, 5 Apr. 1909.

38. Gillot, *History of Trade Unions*; LA 300, Minutes, 10 Nov. 1900, 8 Mar. 1902, Reel 7, Slight Papers; O'Connor, "Cinderheads and Iron Lungs," chap. 5. Among the other locations where hand-blown factories located were Okmulgee, Oklahoma, Ft. Smith, Arkansas, and Shreveport, Louisiana. See "List of Factories Producing Window Glass by the Hand Method during the Blast of 1915-1916," *The National*, June 1916, 31-2.

39. LA 300, Minutes, 6 Aug. 1911, 6 Jan. 1912, Reel 8, Slight Papers. Also see Ken Fones-Wolf, "Craftsman's Paradise," 70.

40. These figures were derived from manuscript census schedules for Clarksburg and Adamston. For 1910, I compiled the nativity of glassworkers by occupation for 244 individuals; for 1920, my sample included 482 window-glass workers. Home ownership by the craftsmen, which had lagged behind less skilled workers in the industry in 1910, was 38% by 1920. I also checked these samples for persistence in the 1925 and 1935 Clarksburg city directories. Nearly 60% of the skilled workers were still in Clarksburg in 1935, a rate higher than any other group.

41. LA 300, Minutes, 6 Feb. 1912, Reel 8, Slight Papers; *Salem Express*, 13 Nov. and 4 Dec. 1914; 9 Apr., 2 July, and 16 July 1915. Also see M. S. Holt to *Appeal to Reason*, 2 Nov. 1911, in Rush Dew Holt Papers, Box 183, folder 4, WVRHC.

42. *Clarksburg Exponent*, 6 Jan. 1911, 2 Jan. 1912, 3 Jan. 1913, 2 Jan. 1914; *Salem Express*, 20 Mar. 1914, 19 Mar. 1915; Frederick Allen Barkey, "The Socialist Party in West Virginia from 1898 to 1920: A Study in Working Class Radicalism" (Ph.D. diss., Univ. of Pittsburgh, 1971), 248-53.

43. After running very close to the Industrial party in Salem elections in 1914 and 1915, the Socialist party nearly disappeared by 1916. *Salem Express*, 6 Nov. 1914, 9 Apr. 1915, 9 Nov. 1916. For Belgians enlisting in the U.S. Army, see The *National*, June 1918, 13-4.

44. The *National*, Aug. 1918, 19-21, Dec. 1918, 12-3.

45. The *National*, Dec. 1922, 2, Feb. 1923, 3-11. For more on this transition period, see Ken Fones-Wolf, "From Craft to Industrial Unionism."

46. Much of this is covered in Fones-Wolf, "Craftsman's Paradise," 76-8.

47. Gillot, *History of Trade Unions*; Fones-Wolf, "Craftsman's Paradise," 76-7.

48. See the correspondence of Harry Nixon, secretary of the Window Glass Cutters League of America to the locals in Salem and Clarksburg, in Series 3, Box 5, WGCLA Records, WVRHC.

49. West Virginia Bureau of Labor, *Annual Report for 1937* (Charleston, 1937).

50. *Monthly Labor Review*, Oct. 1929, 13-6; Barkey, *Cinderheads in the Hills*, 13-9.

51. Compiled from a sample of 170 NWGW members in the 1920 manuscript census schedules for Harrison County; 106 were still in Clarksburg in 1935. Occupations in 1935 were compiled from the Clarksburg city directory for that year.

52. The *National*, Oct. 1922, 28; West Virginia Bureau of Labor, *Biennial Report*, 1929-30, 19.

53. Barkey, *Cinderheads in the Hills*, 15-8; Trevor Bain, "The Impact of Technological Change on the Flat Glass Industry and the Unions' Reactions to Change: Colonial Period to the Present," (Ph.D. diss., Univ. of California, Berkeley, 1964), chap. 3.

54. *Flat Glass Worker*, Sept. 1934, 4; Barkey, *Cinderheads in the Hills*, 16-8.

55. Lowell E. Gallaway, "The Origin and Early Years of the Federation of Flat Glass Workers of America," *Labor History* 2 (1962): 96-9.

56. The correspondence in the records of the Window Glass Cutters League of America records is illuminating; see, for example, Joseph Mayeur to Harry Nixon, 21 Apr. 1936, Ser. 3, Box 3; Jules Michaux to Nixon, 1 Jan., 11 Jan., 23 Jan., and 7 Nov. 1936, Ser. 3, Box 5; F. M. Lefevre to Nixon, 27 Feb. 1936, Ser. 3, Box 6, all in WGCLA Records, WVRHC.

57. *Flat Glass Worker*, Oct. 1934, 16-7, June 1935, 12; Joseph Mayeur to L. J. Stenger, 22 July 1935, Stenger to Mayeur, 29 July 1935, in Ser. 3, Box 1, WGCLA Records, WVRHC.

58. Of the 25 names of Rolland FFGW members appearing in the *Flat Glass Worker*, twelve were either French or Belgian. For the conflict and the grudging admiration of the Cutters, see Jules Michaux to Harry Nixon, 11 Jan. 1936, Ser. 3, Box 5, and F. M. Lefevre to Nixon, 27 Feb. 1936, Ser. 3, Box 6, WGCLA Records, WVRHC.

59. Michaux to Nixon, 11 Jan. 1936, Ser. 3, Box 5, WGCLA Records, WVRHC; *Flat Glass Worker*, Nov. 1935, 9; Jan.-Feb. 1936, 7; Mar. 1936, 13, Apr. 1936, 15; July-Aug., 1936, 22.

Section III:
Immigrant Coal Miners

African American Miners of Lillybrook, West Virginia. Rufus "Red" Ribble Photograph, West Virginia and Regional History Collection,West Virginia University Libraries, Morgantown, W.Va.

Black Migration to Southern West Virginia

Joe William Trotter Jr.

The Great Migration of blacks to northern, southern, and western cities is receiving increasing scholarly attention, but large numbers of blacks moved to the southern Appalachian coalfields of Kentucky, Tennessee, Virginia, and especially West Virginia. The African American population in the Central Appalachian plateau increased by nearly 200 percent between 1900 and 1930, from less than forty thousand to over 108,000.[1] Black migration to Southern Appalachia, as elsewhere, was deeply rooted in the social imperatives of black life in the rural South, as well as the dynamics of industrial capitalism. This essay examines the origins, sources, and consequences of black migration to the Mountain State. It also suggests how southern blacks helped to organize their own movement and transformation into a new class of industrial workers.

Black migration to West Virginia accelerated as the Mountain State underwent a dramatic industrial transformation. The entire state produced only five million tons of coal in 1887, but coal production in southern West Virginia alone increased to nearly forty million tons in 1910, about 70 percent of the state's total output. As coal companies increased production, the state's black population increased from an estimated 25,800 in 1880 to over sixty-four thousand in 1910.[2] Like industrialization in other southern states, bituminous coal mining helped to transform the region's largely subsistence economy into a dependent industrial economy, with growing links to national and international markets .[3] Between the 1890s and early 1930s, blacks made up over 20 percent of the state's total coal mining labor force.

African American migration to the Mountain State built on antebellum and early postbellum roots. Booker T. Washington was among ex-slaves who migrated into the coalfields and worked in the mines. During the Civil War, Washington Furguson escaped from slavery and followed Union soldiers into the Kanawha Valley. After the Civil War, he sent for his wife, Jane, and her children, including the young Booker T., "who made the trip overland in a wagon, there being no railroad connection as yet with old Virginia." Booker T. Washington later described his tenure in the mines as an unpleasant experience. "Work in the coal mines I always dreaded. . . . There was always the danger of being blown to pieces by a premature explosion of powder, or of being crushed by falling slate. Accidents from one or the other of these causes were frequently occurring and this kept me in constant fear."[5]

Although blacks had entered the region in the antebellum and Reconstruction eras, it was not until the railroad expansion of the 1890s and early 1900s that their numbers dramatically increased, giving rise to a new industrial proletariat. Black workers helped to lay track for every major rail line in the region. In his assessment of black labor on the Chesapeake and Ohio (which produced the black folk hero John Henry), sociologist James T. Laing concluded that "this important road was largely built by Negro laborers from Virginia." Upon completion of the Chesapeake and Ohio in 1873, many blacks remained behind "to work in the newly opened coal mines of the New River district." The ex-slave James Henry Woodson from nearby Virginia eventually took a job on the labor crew of the Chesapeake and Ohio Railway shops, and thus paved the way for his young son Carter G. Woodson's brief stint in the mines of the Kanawha-New River field. The younger Woodson later moved out of coal mining, earned a Ph.D. degree from Harvard University, and founded the Association for the Study of Negro Life and History.[6]

In 1892, blacks played "fully as large a part" in the building of the Norfolk and Western Railroad as they did in constructing the Chesapeake and Ohio. As in the case of the Chesapeake and Ohio, following the completion of the Norfolk and Western, many black railroad men "remained to work in the coal fields" of the Pocahontas Division. Black labor on the Virginian Railroad and the subsequent opening of mines in the Winding Gulf field followed a similar pattern. "When the Winding Gulf Field ... opened up through the building of the Virginian Railroad in 1909 the Negro again played the part of pioneer."[7] While a few individuals like Carter G. Woodson and Booker T. Washington eventually moved out of coal mining, gained substantial education, and became part of the national black elite, most black migrants finished out their careers as part of the expanding black industrial proletariat. Under the impact of World War I, working-class black kin and friendship networks would intensify, bringing a new generation of southern black workers into the coal industry.[8]

Spurred by the labor demands of World War I, the black population in southern West Virginia increased by nearly 50 percent, from just over forty thousand in 1910 to nearly sixty thousand in 1920. The percentage of West Virginia blacks living in the southern counties increased from 63 to nearly 70 percent. At the same time, the black coal mining proletariat increased from eleven thousand in 1915 to over fifteen thousand during the war years, rising from 20 to nearly 25 percent of the labor force, as immigrants declined from 31 to 19 percent. Led by Virginia with over 34 percent in 1920, blacks from the Upper South states accounted for 56 percent of the state's black total.

Black migration to southern West Virginia during World War I was part of the first wave of the Great Migration of blacks northward out of the South. As elsewhere, the majority were young men between the primary working ages of twenty and forty-four, though the sex ratio evened out over time (as did the white ratio). Nonetheless, a substantial imbalance continued through the war years, at 125 males to every one hundred females in 1920. One contemporary observer argued that the Mountain State not only received the earliest, but also the "best" of the migrants. "We got the vanguard . . . those who came voluntarily and were not encouraged to leave on account of strained relations or the strain of living." In reality, however, the majority of blacks entered West Virginia precisely because of the "strain of living" and often "strained relations" in other parts of the South.[9]

In the Upper South and border states, black farmers abandoned the land in growing numbers. During World War I, John Hayes moved his family from rural North Carolina to McDowell County, his daughter tersely recalled, "because he got tired of farming." For similar reasons, in 1917, John Henry Phillips moved his family from a small farm in Floyd County, Virginia, to Pageton, McDowell County. During World War I, Salem Wooten's family owned a farm in Henry County, Virginia, near Martinsville. The family raised wheat, corn, some livestock, and especially tobacco for the market.[10]

Tobacco farming, Wooten recalled, was "back-breaking labor. Tobacco is a delicate crop and it's a lot of hard work. . . . If you did that all day, it was very tiresome." With thirteen boys and five girls in the family, the Wootens managed to make ends meet during the war and early postwar years. The young men, however, "wanted to get away from the farm." The elder Wooten fought in vain to keep his sons on the land. Shortly after his discharge from the army in 1918, the oldest son migrated to southern West Virginia, setting in motion a process that would eventually bring seven of his younger brothers into the coalfields.[11]

With the labor demands of the bituminous coal industry intersecting with the boll weevil and destructive storms on southern farms, hundreds of black sharecroppers and farm laborers from the Deep South also migrated to southern West Virginia. The Deep South states of Alabama, Georgia, South Carolina, and Mississippi sent increasing numbers of black migrants to southern West Virginia. Indeed, among contributing states, the Deep South state of Alabama was third, making up over 6 percent of West Virginia blacks in 1920.

Under the deteriorating agricultural conditions in the Deep South, some white landowners eased their tenacious grip on black farm laborers and helped to stimulate out-migration. In a revealing letter to the U.S. Department of

Justice, Alexander D. Pitts, U.S. Attorney for the Southern District of Alabama, explained: "There has been no corn (and little cotton) made and this country only raises cotton and corn, you can readily see that the negroes have nothing to eat. The planters are not able to feed them and they are emigrating."[12]

Black miners averaged $3.20 to $5.00, and even more, per eight-hour day, compared to a maximum of $2.50 per nine-hour day for southern industrial workers. Black southern farm laborers made even less, as little as $0.75 to $1.00 per day. It is no wonder, as one migrant recalled, some blacks moved to southern West Virginia, when "they heard that money was growing on trees."[13]

In 1916, Thornton Wright's family moved from a sharecropping experience in Montgomery, Alabama, to the coal mining community of Accoville, Logan County. At the same time, a Union Springs, Alabama, migrant wrote from Holden, Logan County, "I make $80 to $90 per mo. with ease and wish you all much success. Hello to all the people of my home town. I am saving my money and spending some of it." Writing in a detailed letter to his friend, another Alabama migrant wrote back from Omar, Logan County, "You can make I dollar heaire quicker than you can 20 ct theaire in Alla."[14]

Important social, cultural, and political factors reinforced the attractiveness of West Virginia as a target of black migrants. Racial lynchings were fewer, education opportunities were greater, and voting was not restricted by race as elsewhere in the South. In his letter back home, one migrant, W. L. McMillan, enclosed a flyer announcing a political rally, bearing the bold captions, "Republican Speaking Mr. Colored Man Come Out And Bring Your Friends to Hear." "Now listen," McMillan concluded, "I will vote for the president on the I I of this mont Collered man tick[e]t stands just as good as white man heare." Although it frequently overstated the case, during the 1920s, the Bureau of Negro Welfare and Statistics (BNWS), a state agency, repeatedly emphasized the political and social attractions of West Virginia.[15]

Though most blacks came to West Virginia from agricultural backgrounds, many had already made a substantial break with the land. As opportunities in southern agriculture steadily declined, rural blacks increasingly moved into southern nonfarm industries, especially lumber, coal, and railroad work, before coming to West Virginia. Before bringing his family to Pageton, McDowell County, John Henry Phillips had alternated between work in a local sawmill and farm labor. Salem Wooton recalled that one of his brothers worked in a furniture factory in Martinsville, Virginia, before migrating to southern West Virginia. Before migrating to Coalwood, McDowell County, Pink Henderson and his father were coal miners in the Birmingham district of Alabama. Alabama coal operators were infamous for the highly unjust contract labor and convict lease systems of employment. Taken together, these systems placed miners—mainly blacks—at a severe disadvantage, protected management, and helped to drive numerous Alabama miners to West Virginia. Commenting on the low wages in Alabama mines, Henderson stated: "That's why we came to West Virginia. They wasn't paying nothing [in Alabama]. They was paying more here in West Virginia mines than they was down there."[16] Since they entered the mines from industrial or semi-industrial backgrounds, black men like the Hendersons, Phillips, and Wooten experienced a less radical change than farm laborers did.

In addition to the economic conditions from which they came, the recruitment and advertising campaigns of coal companies provided important stimuli to the black migration. In the spring of 1916, the United States Coal and Coke Company, a subsidiary of the U.S. Steel Corporation, advertised for workers at Gary, McDowell County: "Wanted at once / 1000 Miners and Coke Drawers / I I mines and 2000 coke ovens working Six Days Per Week / Five Percent Increase in Wages / Effective May 8, 1916." At the height of World War I, such advertising intensified. In the summer of 1917, the King and Tidewater Coal and Coke Company at Vivian, McDowell County, frantically announced: "10 Automobiles Free / Men Wanted: miners and Day Men Money without limit to be made with Ten Automobiles given away free."[17]

Professional labor recruiters for the coal companies also encouraged southern blacks to move to the coalfields. During World War I, E. T. McCarty, located in the Jefferson County Bank Building, Birmingham, Alabama, recruited black coal miners for major southern West Virginia coal producers. His clients included the New River Coal Company and the New River and Pocahontas Coal Corporation. In Bessemer, Alabama, the renowned Jones and Maddox Employment Agency also served a variety of coal companies in the region. These agents carefully calculated their messages, skillfully aiming to uproot blacks from their tenuous foothold in the southern economy: "Do you want to go North where the laboring man shares the profits with the boss? Are you satisfied with your condition? Are you satisfied with your pay envelope? Are you making enough wages [to] take care of you in the times of distress? If you are not satisfied we want you to come to see us."[18]

Coal companies also enlisted the support of middle-class black leaders. Especially important was the local black weekly, the *McDowell Times*, which circulated in West Virginia and nearby Virginia. During World War I, the *McDowell Times* editorially proclaimed: "Let millions of Negroes leave the South, it will make conditions better for those who remain." In lengthy articles, the *Times* celebrated the movement of blacks into the various coal camps like those of Glen White, Raleigh County. "The old saying that 'All roads lead to Rome' surely has its modern analogy. . . . 'All railroads seem to lead to Glen White' for every train drops its quota of colored folks who are anxious to make their homes in the most beautiful spot in the mining district of West Virginia." The *Times* columnist, Ralph W. White, stated simply: "To one and all of them we say WELCOME."[19]

Despite the optimistic portrayals of the *McDowell Times*, a substantial degree of private and public coercion underlay the recruitment of black labor. Operators often advanced the migrants transportation fees, housing, and credit at the company store. Using privately employed Baldwin-Felts detectives, some coal operators were notorious for their violent control of black workers. One black miner recalled, "I can show you scars on my head which were put in there by the Baldwin-Felts men in 1917. There was four of them jumped me until they thought me dead, but I didn't die. They kicked two or three ribs loose—two or three of them—on Cabin Creek."[20]

The operators' autonomy over company-owned land was strengthened in 1917 when the West Virginia legislature enacted a law to "prevent idleness and vagrancy. . .during the war and for six months thereafter. All able bodied men between 18 and 60 years of age, regardless of color, class or income must toil thirty-five hours each week to support themselves and their dependents."[21] Failure to work as prescribed could result in arrests and sentences to work for the county or city for six months. Neutral in its class and racial provisions, however, the law received the enthusiastic endorsement of middle class black leaders, like T. Edward Hill who approvingly exclaimed: "So the boys who 'toil not' in McDowell County have 30 days to make up their minds [to work in the mines or on public road crews]. . . . Don't crowd boys."[22]

Moreover, West Virginia had passed a prohibition law in 1914, and some of the prohibition arrests, convictions, and sentences to hard labor on county road projects were scarcely veiled efforts to discipline and exploit the black labor force. Even the local black weekly soon decried the arrest of what it condescendingly called "a lot of ignorant men and depriving their families of support for months and in some cases years." According to the state commissioner of prohibition, southern West Virginia had the highest incidence of arrests, convictions, and sentences to hard labor on county road projects .[23]

Although some black miners felt the impact of public and private coercion, most migrants chose southern West Virginia voluntarily, using their network of kin and friends to get there. After arriving, they often urged their southern kin and friends to join them. Acute contemporary observers understood the process. In his investigation of the great migration, the U.S. attorney for the Southern District of Alabama reported that at least 10 percent of those who had left had returned, but half of the returnees had come back for relatives and friends. "It is the returned negroes who carry others off."[24]

Coal companies soon recognized the recruitment potential of black kin and friendship networks, and hired black miners to recruit among relatives and friends. During World War I, the Rum Creek Collieries Company hired Scotty Todd as a labor recruiter. On one trip back to Alabama, the company gave Todd enough money to bring fifty men to West Virginia. Several relatives and friends returned to the state with Scotty Todd, including his younger brother Roy. At Hollow Creek, McDowell County, the company added a second and then a third shift. When one newcomer asked why, the superintendent's reply, although highly paternalistic, revealed the familial pattern of black migration: "If you stop bringing all your uncles and . . . aunts and cousins up here we wouldn't have to do that. We got to make somewhere for them to work . . . They can't all work on day shift. They can't all work on evening shift."[25]

As suggested above, coal mining was an overwhelmingly male occupation, with few opportunities for black women outside the home. Yet, black women played a crucial role in the migration process. Before migrating to southern West Virginia during the war years, Catherine Phillips married John Henry who worked in a nearby sawmill in rural western Virginia. Catherine raised crops for home consumption, performed regular household chores, and gave birth to at least three of the couple's eight children. In 1917, she took care of the family by herself for several months, while John Henry traveled to southern West Virginia, worked in the coal mines, and finally returned for her and the children.[26]

Nannie Bolling, more than a decade before she moved with her family to southern West Virginia, married Sam Beasley in rural North Carolina. Sam eventually travelled to Gary, McDowell County, and worked in the mines for several pay periods, leaving Nannie to take care of the couple's four children until he returned for them. In a family group, including her husband, four children, and one grandparent, Vallier Henderson travelled from Jefferson County, Alabama, to McDowell County during World War I. The Hendersons traveled with a party of three other Alabama families, along with their household furnishings, and the trip took nearly seven days by rail. Upon reaching McDowell County, the families made a time-consuming and arduous horse and wagon trip into the mountains of Coalwood.[27] Black women—desiring to hold their families together, escape rural poverty, and gain greater control over their destinies—played a key role in the migration to southern West Virginia.[28]

Involving a web of legal entanglements and debts, some blacks found it more difficult than others to escape southern sharecropping arrangements. In such cases, their kin and friends served them well. Notwithstanding deteriorating conditions in the southern economy, southern landowners and businessmen often resisted the black migration. They feared a permanent loss of their low-wage labor pool. Thus, for many black migrants, white resistance necessitated a great deal of forethought, planning, and even secrecy. In his effort to ascertain the character and extent of black migration from Mississippi, Jasper

Boykins, a U.S. deputy marshall, reported: "It is very difficult to get the names and addresses of any of the negroes going away. It seems that this movement is being conducted very quietly."[29] Another investigator likewise observed: "I, myself, went to see the families of several negroes who have left and they are loath to tell where these people have gone. Of course, I did not tell them what I want to know. . . . they are secretive by nature."[30] Black migrants were by no means "secretive by nature," but many of them were secretive by design, and for solid reasons. The coercive elements of southern sharecropping would die hard.

Yet, not all black migrants to southern West Virginia received the blessings of their kin. In deciding to leave their southern homes, some young men moved despite the opposition of their fathers who sought to keep them on the land. Scotty Todd and his brother moved to West Virginia when their father rejected their effort to bargain: they had requested a car in exchange for staying on the farm.[31] Salem Wooten's father also fought a losing battle to keep his sons on the land. The oldest son "slipped away" and his brother later vividly recalled the occasion: "My father sent him over in the field to do some work. . . . And he packed his clothes, what few he had, and slipped them over there at the edge of the field and worked a little bit, well something like a half an hour in the field. Then he went to the cherry tree, ate all the cherries he could eat. Then he came down the tree and got his little suit case and he had to cross Smith River to get what we called the Norfolk and Western Railroad Train. . . into Roanoke [VA] from there into West Virginia . . . He had money enough . . . He came to McDowell County."[32] Such family tensions undoubtedly punctuated the lives of numerous blacks as they made their way into the coalfields during the war and early postwar years.

Whereas the vigorous recruitment of black workers characterized the war years, in the economic downturn of the early 1920s, black miners suffered rising unemployment. The Bureau of Negro Welfare and Statistics reported that the two years from July 1, 1921, to June 30, 1923, "were the most unsettled and dullest in the coal industry of this state for many years." Numerous black miners like John Henry Phillips moved to farms in Virginia and North Carolina, until work in West Virginia was "more plentiful and wages higher." At the same time, other black miners left the state for Pennsylvania and other northern industrial centers.[33]

More important, as the United Mine Workers of America accelerated its organizing activities in the aftermath of World War I, coal companies intensified their efforts to retain a solid cadre of black labor. As early as June 1920, the Williamson Coal Operators Association addressed a full page advertisement to black workers: the statement emphasized "the discrimination practiced against their race in the unionized fields," where the United Mine Workers held contracts

with the operators of the northern Appalachian mines. Logan County coal operators developed a pamphlet for black workers that exaggerated the virtues of
coal mining in the area. "You are now living in the best coal field in the country,
working six days a week in perfect harmony and on the seventh day resting,
where there are churches and schools furnished by the coal company, while in
the so-called Union fields, churches and schools are not furnished . . . You are
getting better pay than any other field and better coal."[34]

During the early postwar years, the Bureau of Negro Welfare and Statistics (BNWS) reinforced the operators' lively campaigns to keep black workers.
Under its black director, T. Edward Hill, an attorney and business manager of
the *McDowell Times*, the bureau often served the labor needs of the bituminous
coal industry. In 1921 for example, the bureau proudly proclaimed credit for
deterring over one hundred black men from joining the violent "Armed March"
of miners on Logan and Mingo Counties. Equally important, the bureau recognized the cyclical swings of the coal industry. When work was "irregular and
wages reached a certain minimum," the bureau observed that hundreds of black
miners moved to nearby southern farms until work resumed at higher wages. In
an effort to help stabilize the black labor force, the BNWS advocated the permanent resettlement of southern blacks on available West Virginia farm land.[35]

As the coal industry recovered between roughly 1923 and 1928, black
migration to the region also resumed. The black population in southern West
Virginia increased from close to sixty thousand in 1920 to nearly eighty thousand in 1930. By 1925, the black coal mining labor force had increased to an
estimated 20,300, about 27 percent of the labor force, as immigrants continued
to decline to less than 14 percent. When black workers left the area during the
economic downturn and coal strikes of the early postwar years, other blacks,
some serving as strike-breakers, had slowly filled their places. It was during this
period that the Deep South states of Alabama, Georgia, and South Carolina
dramatically increased their numbers. Alabama moved up from third to second
place in the number of West Virginia blacks born elsewhere. Blacks born in
Alabama now made up nearly 10 percent of the number born in other states.
Unlike the black migration to the industrial North, however, the Upper South
and border states of Virginia, North Carolina, Tennessee, and Kentucky continued to dominate the migration stream to West Virginia .[36]

Established black kin and friendship networks played a key role in stimu-
lating the new cycle of black migration into the coalfields. Born in Leesville,
Virginia, Sidney Lee visited relatives in the region for several months off and
on, before moving to Omar, Logan County, in 1926. Beginning at age fifteen,
Lee had alternated between work on the Virginian Railroad and farm labor,
before taking his first permanent job loading coal in southern West Virginia.

Lester Phillips (son of John Henry and Catherine Phillips) returned to southern West Virginia to work in the mines shortly after his sister married a Pageton, McDowell County, man during the late 1920s. Salem Wooten's oldest brother, after migrating to southern West Virginia from Virginia in the early postwar years, assisted seven of his younger brothers to enter the coalfields, most arriving during the mid-to-late 1920s. The youngest, Salem Wooten, was the last to arrive. He migrated during the early 1930s. According to Elizabeth Broadnax, she and her mother moved from North Carolina to Capels, McDowell County, during the 1920s because her brother lived and worked there.[37]

The growing importance of black kin and friendship networks was also reflected in the rising number of West Virginia-born black miners. In increasing numbers southern-born fathers taught their West Virginia-born sons how to mine coal. This process gained momentum during the 1920s. In 1923, Virginia-born miner James B. Harris took his fifteen-year-old son into the mines at Giatto, Mercer County. The young Charles T. Harris entered coal mining from a coal mining family, he later recalled, "as a career. I never even thought about it. Just coal mining was all I knew. My father was a coal miner." Three years later, with his father and cousin, Preston Turner loaded his first ton of coal at the Winding Gulf Colliery Company. Under the shadow of the impending Depression, Lawrence Boling entered the mines of Madison, Boone County, in 1930. While Gus Boling had hoped to educate his son, he now relented and carried the young man into the mines. Lawrence Boling later recalled: "My dad and I talked it over. . . . Things were tough in the mines . . . I seen I didn't have a chance to go to college even if I finished high school. So I decided at that point that I wanted to work in the mines and would be helping him too. I went in with him . . . He was responsible for me for a certain length of time."[38]

During the 1920s, like most of their white counterparts, Afro-Americans entered the mines primarily as unskilled coal loaders. They worked mainly in underground positions, called "inside labor," as opposed to outside or surface works. In 1922 and again in 1927, the BNWS reported that more than 90 percent of black miners worked as manual coal loaders or as common day laborers. The percentage of black laborers declined during the Great Depression. Yet, according to Laing's survey of twenty coal-mining operations, over 75 percent of black miners continued to work in such positions in 1932.[39]

Coal loading was the most common, difficult, and hazardous job in the mine. Yet, blacks often preferred it because it paid more than other manual labor jobs and "provided the least supervision with the greatest amount of personal freedom in work hours." As one black miner recalled, coal loaders could make more money because they were paid by the ton, and could increase their wages by increasing their output.[40] On the other hand, while the average wage-rates for coal loading were indeed higher than most outside jobs, inside work was subject to greater seasonal fluctuations and greater health hazards than outside positions.

Although coal loading was classified as unskilled work, it did require care and skill. For the novice especially, the apparently simple act of loading coal into a waiting train car could not be taken for granted. Watt Teal's father taught him techniques for preserving his health as well as his life. As an important component of his informal apprenticeship, Watt Teal learned how to carefully pace his work. Indeed, he concluded, "There is a little art to it . . . After all you could load it the wrong way and get broke down and you couldn't do business. . . . So [at first] you get so much on the shovel and start off and get used to it and then you can gradually pick up more on the shovel."[41]

Coal loading involved much more than merely pacing the work, though. It took over an hour of preparation before the miner could lift his first shovel of coal. The miner deployed an impressive repertoire of skills: the techniques of dynamiting coal, including knowledge of various gases and the principles of ventilation; the establishment of roof supports to prevent dangerous cave-ins; and the persistent canvassing of mines for potential hazards. Referring to the training he received from his brother, Salem Wooten recalled: "The first thing he taught me was . . . my safety, how to set props and posts. Wood posts were set up to keep the slate and rocks from caving in on you . . . safety first."[42]

Wooten's brother also taught him techniques for blasting coal: how to drill holes with an auger and place several sticks of dynamite in them properly, how to judge atmospheric conditions and be acutely sensitive, not only to his own safety, but to the safety of fellow workers as well. Salem Wooten also learned the miner's distinctive vocabulary of terms like "bug dust," particles of coal remaining after machines undercut the coal; "kettlebottom," a huge fossilized rock, responsible for numerous injuries and even deaths, when it dislodged from the roof of mines; and the frequently shouted "Fire! Fire in the Hole!" warning fellow workers of an impending dynamite blast.[43]

Coal loading was not the only job that blacks entered. In small numbers, they worked in skilled positions as machine operators, brakemen, and motormen. In its 1921-22 report, the Bureau of Negro Welfare and Statistics proudly announced its success, although modest, in placing "three machine men, two motormen . . . [as well as] 57 coal loaders and company men." Labor advertisements sometimes specified the broad range of jobs available to Afro-Americans: "Coal Miners, Coke Oven Men, Day Laborers, Contract Men and Helpers, Motormen, Track Layers, Machine Runners, Mule Drivers, Power Plant Men, and other good jobs to offer around the mines." According to state-wide data, the number of black motormen and machine men (or mechanics) increased nearly

150 percent, from 218 in 1921 to 536 in 1927. Although their numbers declined thereafter, some blacks retained their foothold in skilled positions through the 1920s. Among these, machine-running was the most lucrative. Between 1926 and 1929, for example, Roy Todd and his brothers worked as machine operators at the Island Creek Coal Company, at Holden, Logan County. On this job, Roy Todd recalled, he made enough money to buy a new car, bank one hundred dollars monthly, pay his regular expenses, and still have "money left over."[44]

However skillful black loaders may have become, coal loading took its toll on the health of black men. Some men literally broke themselves down loading coal. Pink Henderson painfully recalled: "My daddy got so he couldn't load coal. He tried to get company work [light labor, often on the outside] but the doctor turned him down, because he couldn't do nothing. He done broke his self down. . . . My brothers done the same thing. They used to be the heavy loaders." Moreover, all coal loaders, black and white, careful and careless, were subject to the inherent dangers of coal mining: black lung, then commonly called "miners' asthma," the slow killer of miners caused by the constant inhalation of coal dust; explosions, the most publicized and dramatic cause of miners' deaths; and slate falls, the largest and most consistent killer of miners. All miners and their families had to learn to live with the fear of death, although few fully succeeded. As one black miner and his wife recalled, reminiscent of Booker T. Washington's experience in the early prewar years: "That fear is always there. That fear was there all the time, because . . . you may see [each other] in the morning and never [see each other] any more in the flesh."[45]

As Afro-Americans abandoned southern life and labor for work in the coalfields, the foregoing evidence suggests that their rural and semirural work culture gradually gave way to the imperatives of industrial capitalism. New skills, work habits, and occupational hazards moved increasingly to the fore, gradually supplanting their older rural work patterns and rhythms of "alternating periods of light and intensive labor." Indeed, with the dramatic expansion of their numbers during World War I and the 1920s, black miners increasingly experienced southern West Virginia as a permanent place to live and labor.[46]

The working lives of black women also underwent change in southern West Virginia, but it was less dramatic for them than it was for black men. Along with their regular domestic tasks, working-class black women nearly universally tended gardens. Although the men and boys cleared and broke the ground, women and children planted, cultivated, harvested, and canned the produce: corn, beans, cabbage, collard and turnip greens, supplemented by a few hogs, chickens, and sometimes a cow.[47] Gardening not only nourished the bodies of black men, women, and children, it also symbolized links with their rural past. The pattern soon became deeply entrenched in the economic and cultural traditions of the region. Not yet eleven years old, while confined to a local hospital bed, a young black female penned her first verse, illuminating the role of black women in the life of the coal fields: "When I get [to be] an old lady, I tell you what I'll do, I'll patch my apron, make my dress And hoe the garden too."[48]

Although Afro-American coal mining families gained a significant foothold in the bituminous coal industry, not all blacks who entered the coal-fields were equally committed to coal mining life. Some of the men were indeed gamblers, pimps, and bootleggers. Middle-class black leaders attacked these men as "Jonahs" and "kid-glove dudes," who moved into the coalfields, exploited the miners, and, often, moved on.[49] Like European immigrants, other black men used coal mining as a means of making money to buy land and farms in other parts of the South. On the eve of World War I, for example, Ike Mitchell came to West Virginia from South Carolina. After two years, he had saved two thousand dollars in cash from his job in the Kanawha-New River coalfield. During the early war years, he took his money, returned his family to South Carolina, bought land, and began raising cotton for the market. In its 1921-22 report, the Bureau of Negro Welfare and Statistics noted that some black miners continued to work, sacrifice, and save in order "to buy a farm 'down home,' pay the indebtedness upon one already purchased, or, after getting a 'little money ahead,' return to the old home." Again in 1923-24, the bureau reported that several hundred blacks in the mines of McDowell, Mercer, and Mingo Counties either owned farms in Virginia and North Carolina themselves or had relatives who owned farms there. In order to curtail the temporary and often seasonal pattern of black migration and work in the mines, the BNWS accelerated its campaign for the permanent resettlement of blacks on available West Virginia farm land.[50]

If some black workers entered the region on a temporary and often seasonal basis, shifting back and forth between southern farms and mine labor, it was the up and down swings of the business cycle that kept most black miners on the move. Although there was an early postwar economic depression in the coal economy, as noted above, it was the onslaught of the Great Depression that revealed in sharp relief the precarious footing of the black coal mining proletariat. In December 1930, the black columnist S. R. Anderson of Bluefield reported that "more hunger and need" existed among Bluefield's black population "than is generally known. It is going to be intensified during the hard months of January and February."[51] In the economic downturn that followed, their numbers dropped from 19,600 in 1929 to 18,500 in 1931, though fluctuating only slightly between 26 and 27 percent of the labor force. Heretofore the BNWS had advocated black farm ownership as a mode of labor recruitment for the coal industry; it now advocated farming as a primary solution to permanent unemployment for a growing number of black miners. [52]

As unemployment increased during the late 1920s and early 1930s, the advice of the Bureau of Negro Welfare and Statistics notwithstanding, intra-regional movement accelerated. Unlike the earlier downturn, when many black miners moved to nearby southern farms and to northern industrial centers, most now struggled to maintain their foothold in the coal mining region. Their desperation is vividly recorded in the "Hawk's Nest Tragedy" of Fayette County. In 1930, the Union Carbide Corporation commissioned the construction firm of Rinehart and Dennis of Charlottesville, Virginia, to dig the Hawk's Nest Tunnel, in order to channel water from the New River to its hydroelectric plant near the Gauley Bridge. As local historian Mark Rowh has noted: "Construction of the tunnel would mean hundreds of jobs, and many saw it as a godsend." Unfortunately, it would prove the opposite. [53]

Requiring extensive drilling through nearly four miles of deadly silica rock, in some areas approaching 100 percent pure silica, the project had claimed the lives of an estimated five hundred men by its completion in 1935. Afro-Americans were disproportionately hired on the project and they were the chief victims. They made up 65 percent of the labor force and 75 percent of the inside tunnel crew. Official company reports invariably underestimated the number of casualties on the project. Even so, company reports highlight the disproportionate black deaths among the work crews. According to P. H. Faulconer, president of Rinehart and Dennis, for example, "In the 30 months from the start of driving to the end of 1932, a total of 65 deaths of all workmen, both outside and inside the tunnel occurred, six whites and fifty-nine colored." Although the firm was aware of a safer, wet-drilling method, it elected to use the more efficient, but lethal dry-drilling process, allowing workers to use water "only when state inspectors were expected at the scene."[54] The depression was not only a period of extensive unemployment, as the Hawk's Nest calamity demonstrates, it was also a time of excessive labor exploitation.

If unemployment pressed some men into the lethal Hawk's Nest Tunnel, it also required substantial contributions from black women. While he worked on a variety of temporary jobs during the early Depression years, Pink Henderson recalled that his wife "canned a lot of stuff," kept two or three hogs, raised chickens, and made clothing for the family. In 1930, the U.S. Census Bureau reported that 57.6 percent of black families in West Virginia were comprised of three persons or less, compared to 37.5 percent for immigrants and 40.8 percent for American-born whites; but the actual difference in household size was offset by the larger number of boarders in black families. During the late 1920s, and early 1930s, for example, Mary Davis not only enabled her own family to survive hard times, she also aided the families of unemployed coal miners at her boarding house restaurant. "We were pretty fortunate," her son later recalled, "and helped a lot of people."[55]

Under the impact of the Great Depression of the 1930s, blacks shouldered a disproportionate share of the unemployment and hard times. Their percentage in the state's coal mining labor force dropped from over 22 percent in 1930 to about 17 percent in 1940. The depression and World War II also unleashed new technological and social forces that transformed the coal industry, and stimulated massive out-migration in the postwar years. Although coal companies had installed undercutting machines in their mines during the 1890s, the handloading of coal remained intact until the advent of the mechanical loader during the late 1930s. Loading machines rapidly displaced miners during the 1940s and 1950s. As one black miner recalled, "The day they put the loading machine on our section, the coal leaders went in to work but the boss was already there and he said that the men not on his list could pick up their tools and leave." A black miner recalled that the mine management "always put them [loading machines] where blacks were working first." Black men, he said, could not "kick" against the machines.[56]

Mechanization decimated the black coal mining labor force. The percentage of black miners dropped steadily to about 12 percent in 1950, 6.6 percent in 1960, and to 5.2 percent in 1970. By 1980, African Americans made up less than 3 percent of the state's coal miners. To be sure, the white labor force had also declined, dropping by nearly 36 percent, but the black proportion had declined by over 90 percent. Under the leadership of John L. Lewis, the United Mine Workers of America adopted a policy on technological change that reinforced the unequal impact of mechanization on black workers. As Lewis put it, "Shut down 4,000 coal mines, force 200,000 miners into other industries, and the coal problem will settle itself."

As the state's black coal mining labor force declined, racial discrimination persisted in all facets of life in the Mountain State. In 1961, according to the West Virginia Human Rights Commission, most of the state's public accommodations—restaurants, motels, hotels, swimming pools, and medical facilities—discriminated against blacks. Moreover, applications for institutions of higher learning contained questions on race and religion, designed to exclude so-called undesirable groups. Finally, and most importantly, as blacks lost coal mining jobs, they found few alternative employment opportunities. The state's Human Rights Commission reported that, "Numerous factories, department stores, and smaller private firms had obvious, if unwritten, policies whereby blacks were not hired or promoted to jobs of importance or positions in which they would have day-to-day contact with white clientele."

Building upon the traditions bequeathed by preceding generations, many African Americans again responded to declining economic and social conditions by adapting migration strategies. Many moved to the large metropolitan areas of the Northeast and Midwest. Smaller networks of West Virginia blacks emerged in cities like Cleveland, Chicago, Detroit, and New York. Others moved to the nearby upper South and border cities of Washington, D.C., and Alexandria, Virginia. Still others moved as far west as California. Indicative of the rapid out-migration of West Virginia blacks, the state's total African American population dropped from a peak of 117,700 in 1940 to 65,000 in 1980, a decline from 6 to 3 percent of the total.

Still, other West Virginia blacks remained behind and struggled to make a living in the emerging new order. The dwindling number of African Americans did not sit quietly waiting for things to change under them. Charles Brooks, a black miner from Kanawha County, served as the first president of the Black Lung Association, which in 1969 marched on the state capital in Charleston to demand compensation for miners suffering from the disease. In 1972, the Black Lung Association also played a key role in the coalition of forces that made up Miners for Democracy, a rank-and-file movement that resisted the growing autarchy of the United Miner Workers of America's top leaders like Tony Boyle. As early as the mid-1930s, along with blacks elsewhere in America, West Virginia blacks had reevaluated their historic links to the Republican party and found it lacking. They joined the Democratic party and helped to buttress the volatile New Deal coalition of northern urban ethnic groups, organized labor, and devotees of the so-called "solid south." As suggested by their disproportionately declining numbers in the coal industry, however, the black alliance with the Democratic party produced few lasting benefits in the Mountain State.

Although characterized by enduring patterns of class and racial inequality, the history of African Americans in West Virginia is not one but many stories. The first generation faced the challenge of transforming themselves from slaves into citizens in the larger body politic. While this goal was only partially realized and would persist over the next century, the next generation confronted its own unique challenge. During the late nineteenth and early twentieth century, African Americans in the Mountain State faced the difficult transition from life in southern agriculture to life in coal mining towns. Despite important class and gender differences, between black men and women and between black workers and black elites, African Americans built upon the traditions of their predecessors, bridged social cleavages, and protected their collective interests. Like preceding generations, the current generation is reckoning with the impact of mechanization, the decline of the coal industry, and the massive out-migration of blacks to cities throughout the nation. How well they succeed in building upon the lessons of the past is yet to be seen.

Black migration to West Virginia was inextricably interwoven with the larger processes of industrialization and class formation in modern industrial

America. Their experiences were shaped by the dynamics of class, race, and region. Yet, until the decline of the coal industry, southern West Virginia between World War I and the Great Depression offered a unique setting for the development of black life. Blacks in the Mountain State faced fewer incidents of mob violence, less labor exploitation, and, since they retained the franchise, fewer constraints on their civil rights than their southernmost kinsmen. In 1918, for example, three black men, one a coal miner, served in the state legislature from southern West Virginia.[56] Nonetheless, their socioeconomic footing remained volatile, as reflected in the significant economic contributions of black women, work in the deadly Hawk's Nest Tunnel, and substantial geographic mobility throughout the period. Still, through their southern kin and friendship networks, black coal miners played a crucial role in organizing their own migration to the region. They facilitated their own entrance into the industrial labor force, and to a substantial degree shaped their own experience under the onset of industrial capitalism.

Notes

Portions of this article have appeared in Joe William Trotter Jr., *Coal, Class, and Color: Blacks in Southern West Virginia, 1915-32* (Urbana: University of Illinois Press, 1990). Reprinted by permission of University of Illinois Press.

1. Ronald L. Lewis, "Migration of Southern Blacks to the Central Appalachian Coalfields: The Transition from Peasant to Proletarian," *Journal of Southern History* 55, no. 1 (Feb. 1989): 77-102; Robert P. Stuckert, "Black Populations of the Southern Appalachian Mountains," *Phylon* 48, no. 2 (summer 1987): 141-51.

2. Ronald D Eller, *Miners, Millhands, and Mountaineers: Industrialization of the Appalachian South, 1880-1930* (Knoxville, Tenn.: University of Tennessee Press, 1982), 128-40; David A. Corbin, *Life, Work, and Rebellion in the Coal Fields: The Southern West Virginia Coal Miners, 1880-1922* (Urbana: University of Illinois Press, 1981), 1-7; Darold T. Barnum, *The Negro in the Bituminous Coal Industry* (Philadelphia: University of Pennsylvania Press, 1970), 1-24; Sterling D. Spero and Abram L. Harris, *The Black Worker: The Negro and the Labor Movement* (1931; reprint, New York: Atheneum, 1968), 206-45; Ronald L. Lewis, *Black Coal Miners in America: Race, Class, and Community Conflict, 1770-1980* (Lexington, Ky.: University Press of Kentucky, 1987), chap. 7; West Virginia Department of Mines, *Annual Reports* (Charleston, W.Va.: 1909, 1910).

3. John A. Williams, *West Virginia and the Captains of Industry* (Morgantown, W.Va.: West Virginia University, 1976), 109-29; Charles Kenneth Sullivan, "Coal Men and Coal Towns: Development of the Smokeless Coalfields of Southern West Virginia, 1873-1923" (Ph.D. diss., University of Pittsburgh, 1979); Otis K. Rice, *West Virginia: A History* (Lexington, Ky.: University Press of Kentucky, 1985), 184-204; Corbin, *Life, Work, and Rebellion*, 3-4; Eller, *Miners, Millhands, and Mountaineers*, 132-40, 165-68; Randall G. Lawrence, "Appalachian Metamorphosis: Industrializing Society on the Central Appalachian Plateau, 1860-1913" (Ph.D. diss., Duke University, 1983), 28-42, 64.

4. Corbin, *Life, Work, and Rebellion*, 8, 43-52; Eller, *Miners, Millhands, and Mountaineers*, 129, 165-75; Barnum, *The Negro in the Bituminous Coal Mining Industry*, 1-24; Lawrence, "Appalachian Metamorphosis," 224-8; Price V. Fishback, "Employment Conditions of Blacks in the Coal Industry, 1900-1930" (Ph.D. diss., University of Washington, 1983), 44-51; Lewis, *Black Coal Miners in America*, chap. 7; Kenneth R. Bailey, "A Judicious Mixture: Negroes and Immigrants in the West Virginia Mines, 1880-1917," *West Virginia History* 34 (1973): 141-61. On the exclusion of blacks from northern industries, see William H. Harris, *The Harder We Run: Black Workers since the Civil War* (New York: Oxford University Press, 1982), 29-50; Philip S. Foner, *Organized Labor and the Black Worker, 1619-1973* (New York: International Publishers, 1974), 64-135; Spero and Harris, *The Black Worker*, 53-115; U.S. Bureau of the Census, *The Negro Population in the United States, 1790-1915* (1918; reprint, New York: Arno Press 1968), 85; U.S. Bureau of the Census, *Negroes in the United States, 1920-1932* (1935; reprint,

New York: Arno Press 1966), 45; *Fourteenth Census of the U.S.* (1920), vol. 2, 636-40.

5. Booker T. Washington, *Up From Slavery* (1901; reprint, New York: Bantam Books, 1967), 26-8; R. G. Hubbard, et al. (Malden Homecoming Committee), to Booker T. Washington, 29 May 1913, in B. T. W. Tuskegee Records, Lecture File, Boxes 811 and 816, Booker T. Washington Papers (Library of Congress); Louis R. Harlan, *Booker T Washington: The Making of a Black Leader* (New York: Oxford University Press, 1972), 28

6. James T. Laing, "The Negro Miner in West Virginia" (Ph.D. diss., Ohio State University, 1933), 64-9; J. M. Callahan, *Semi-Centennial History of West Virginia* (Charleston, W.Va., 1913), also quoted in Laing, 64; A. A. Taylor, *The Negro in the Reconstruction of Virginia* (Washington, D.C.: Associated Publishers, 1926), also quoted in Laing, 64-5.

7. Laing, "Negro Miner," 64-9; Callahan, *Semi-Centennial History of West Virginia*, also quoted in Laing, 64; Taylor, *The Negro in the Reconstruction of Virginia*, also quoted in Laing, 64-5.

8. Corbin, *Life, Work, and Rebellion*, 64-5; Lewis, *Black Coal Miners in America*, chap. 7; and Trotter, *Coal, Class, and Color*, chap. 3.

9. Ralph W. White, "Another Lesson from the East St. Louis Lynching," *McDowell Times*, 20 July 1917; Carter G. Woodson, *A Century of Negro Migration* (1918; reprint New York: AMS Press, 1970), 147-66.

10. Lester Phillips and Ellen Phillips, interview by author, 20 July 1983; Salem Wooten, interview by author, 25 July 1983; see also Reginald Millner, "Conversations with the Ole Man: The Life and Times of a Black Appalachian Coal Miner," *Goldenseal* 5 (Jan.-Mar. 1979): 58-64; Tim R. Massey, "I Didn't Think I'd Live to See 1950: Looking Back with Columbus Avery," *Goldenseal* 8 (spring 1982): 32-40; Eller, *Miners, Millhands, and Mountaineers*, 165-75; Corbin, *Life, Work, and Rebellion*, chaps. 7, 8, and 9; Fishback, "Employment Conditions," 72-82, 116-20.

11. Wooten, interview.

12. Robert N. Bell, U.S. Attorney, Northern District of Alabama, to U.S. Attorney General, 25 Oct. 1916; and Alexander D. Pitts, U.S. Attorney, Southern District of Alabama, to Samuel J. Graham, U.S. Assistant Attorney General, 27 Oct. 1916, both in Department of Justice, Record Group No. 60, Straight Numerical File No. 182363 (Washington, D.C., National Archives). Thelma 0. Trotter, conversation with author, 1 Aug. 1983; Solomon Woodson, conversation with author, 9 Nov. 1985.

13. Florette Henri, *Black Migration: Movement North, 1900-1920* (Garden City: Anchor Press Doubleday, 1975), 132-73; Laing, "The Negro Miner," chap. 4; Eller, *Miners, Millhands, and Mountaineers*, 168-72; Corbin, *Life, Work, and Rebellion*, pp. 61-3; Roy Todd, interview by author, 18 July 1983.

14. Thornton Wright, interview by author, 27 July 1983; W. L. McMillan, Omar, W.Va., to R. L. Thornton, Three Notch, Ala., 2 Nov. 1916, Department of Justice, Record Group No. 60, Straight Numerical File no. 182363; "Migration Study,

Negro Migrants, Letters Fr. (Type script), 1916-18," in National Urban League Papers, Series 6, Box 86 (Washington, D.C., Library of Congress).

15. McMillan to Thornton, 2 Nov. 1916; West Virginia Bureau of Negro Welfare and Statistics (WVBNWS), *Biennial Reports* (Charleston, W.Va.), 1921-22, 5, and 1925-26, 8.

16. Phillips and Phillips, interview; Pink Henderson, interview by author, 15 July 1983; Wooten, author; Lewis, *Black Coal Miners in America*, chaps. 3 and 4; McMillan to Thornton, 2 Nov. 1916; "From Alabama: Colored Miners Anxious for Organization," *United Mine Workers Journal (UMWJ)*, 1 June 1916; Rev. T. H. Seals, "Life in Alabama," *UMWJ*, 15 Sept. 1924; and "The Horrors of Convict Mines of Alabama, " *UMWJ*, 19 Aug. 1915. Bell to U.S. Attorney, 25 Oct. 1916; Pitts to Graham, 27 Oct. 1916; "Memorandum: Willie Parker" (recorded by Edwin Ball, General Manager, Tennessee Coal, Iron, and Railroad Company) and "Statement of Tom Jones," all of the preceding in Department of Justice, Record Group No. 60, Straight Numerical File No. 182363.

17. "Wanted at Once . . . ," 12 May 1916 and "10 Automobiles Free," 25 May 1917, both in *McDowell Times*; "Safety First," "Go North," "Wanted," and "Employment Office," in U.S. Department of Labor, Box 2, folder 13/25, Record Group No. 174 (Washington, D.C., National Archives).

18. Bell to U.S. Attorney General, 25 Oct. 1916; Pitts to Graham, 27 Oct. 1916; "Labor Agents Succeed in Inducing Negroes to Leave Southern Farms," *Atlanta Constitution*; "Memorandum: Willie Parker"; "Statement of Tom Jones"; "Early Surveys ... Migration Study, Birmingham Summary," National Urban League Papers, Series 6, Box 89 (Washington, D.C., Library of Congress); "Safety First"; "Go North"; "Wanted"; and "Employment Office."

19. "The Exodus," 18 Aug. 1916; "Southern Exodus in Plain Figures," 1 Dec. 1916, both in *McDowell Times*; Ralph W. White, "Another Lesson . . . ," 20 July 1917; "Colored Folks Enjoying Universal Industrial and Social Advancement." 28 July 1917, in *McDowell Times*.

20. *Conditions in the Coal Fields of Pennsylvania, West Virginia, and Ohio* (Washington, D.C.: GPO, 1928); for excerpts of the committee hearings, see *UMWJ*, 1 Mar. 1928; "Testimony of J. H. Reed," in West Virginia Coal Fields (Washington, D.C.: GPO, 1921), 479-82.

21. "Idlers between Ages of Eighteen and Sixty Will Be Forced to Work," *McDowell Recorder*, 25 May 1917; T. Edward Hill, "Loafers and Jonahs," *McDowell Times*, 25 May 1917; "Dig Coal or Dig Trenches Is the Word to the Miner," *Raleigh Register*, 12 July 1917.

22. Hill, "Loafers and Jonahs."

23. "Educate All the People," 16 April 1915; "To Whom It May Concern," 29 Jan. 1915; "Good People of McDowell County Outraged," 17 May 1918, all in *McDowell Times*; State Commissioner of Prohibition, *Fourth Biennial Report* (Charleston, W.Va.), 1921-22.

24. Wooten, interview; Pitts to Graham, 27 Oct. 1916.

25. Todd, interview; Watt B. Teal, interview by author, 27 July 1983; Laing, "The Negro Miner," chap. 4.

26. Phillips and Phillips, interview; Campbell, interview by author, 19 July 1983; Bell to U.S. Attorney General, 25 Oct. 1916; Pitts to Graham, 27 Oct. 1916; WVBNWS, *Biennial Report*, 192324, 22-3; "Adams-Russel," 14 July 1916, and "Gannaway-Patterson," 22 Dec. 1916, both in *McDowell Times*; *The New River Company Employees Magazine* 2, no. 3 (9 Nov. 1924): 9-10.

27. William M. Beasley, interview by author, 26 July 1983; Henderson, interview; Thomas D. Samford, U.S. Attorney, Middle District of Alabama, to U.S. Attorney General, 2 Nov. 1916, and Samford to U.S. Attorney General, 21 Oct. 1916, in Department of Justice Record Group, No. 60, Straight Numerical File No. 182363.

28. Wright, interview.

29. Jasper Boykins to U.S. Attorney General, 16 Oct. 1916, Department of Justice, Record Group No. 60, Straight Numerical File No. 182363. For a discussion of coercive elements in southern agriculture, see Jay R. Mandle, *The Roots of Black Poverty: The Southern Plantation Economy after the Civil War* (Durham, N.C.: Duke University Press, 1978).

30. Pitts to Graham, 27 Oct. 1916.

31. Todd, interview.

32. Wooten, interview.

33. WVBNWS, *Biennial Reports*, 1921-22, 57-8, and 1927-28, 17-9; Phillips and Phillips, interview; Laing, "The Negro Miners in West Virginia," *Social Forces* 14 (1936): 416-22; Laing, "The Negro Miner," chap. 5.

34. "Discrimination gainst the Negro," *Bluefield Daily Telegraph*, 20 June 1920; "Negro Tricked into Logan County . . ." *UMWJ*, 15 June 1921, includes extensive excerpts of the operator's pamphlet to black workers.

35. WVBNWS, *Biennial Reports*, especially the reports for 1921-22, 38-41, and 1923-24, 29-35.

36. WVBNWS, *Biennial Reports*, 1923-24, 39-45; Children's Bureau, U.S. Department of Labor, *The Welfare of Children in Bituminous Coal Mining Communities in West Virginia* (Washington, DC: GPO, 1923), 5; U.S. Bureau of the Census, *The Negro Population in the United States, 1790-1915*, 85; *Negroes in the United States, 1920-32*, 45; *Fourteenth Census of the U.S.*, vol. 2, 636-40.

37. Sidney Lee, interview, 19 July 1983; Phillips and Phillips, interview; Wooten, interview; Eliza Broadnax, "'Make a Way out of Nothing': One Black Woman's Trip from North Carolina to the McDowell County Coalfields," interview by Randall G. Lawrence, *Goldenseal* 5, no. 4 (Oct.-Dec. 1979): 27-31.

38. North Dickerson, interview by author, 28 July 1983; Charles T. Harris, interview by author, 18 July 1983; Preston Turner, interview by author, 26 July 1983; Lawrence Boling, interview by author, 18 July 1983.

39. WVBNWS, *Biennial Report*, 1921-22, 57-8, and 1927-28, 17-9; Laing, "The Negro Miner," 195.

40. Laing, "The Negro Miners in West Virginia," 416-22; Laing, "The Negro Miner," chap. 5; Dickerson, interview.

41. Teal, interview; Laing, "The Negro Miner," chap. 5. For general insight into the miner's work, see Carter G. Goodrich, *The Miner's Freedom* (1925; reprint, New York: Arno Press, 1971), and Keith Dix, *Work Relations in the Coal Industry: The Handloading Era, 1880-1930* (Morgantown, W.Va.: West Virginia University, Institute for Labor Studies, 1977), chaps. 1 and 2.

42. Wooten, interview; Harris, interview; Leonard Davis, interview by author, 28 July 1983.

43. Wooten, interview. While some scholarly accounts refer to the particles left by the undercutting machine as "buck dust," black miners used the term "bug dust." Indeed, the nickname of one black miner was "Bug Dust." See Laing, "The Negro Miner," 171; Keith Dix, *What's a Coal Miner to Do?: The Mechanization of Coal Mining and Its Impact on Coal Miners* (Pittsburgh: University of Pittsburgh Press, 1988), chap. 1; and Goodrich, *The Miner's Freedom*, xx.

44. WVBNWS, *BiennialReport*, 1921-22, 58-9, and 1927-28, 17-9; "Safety First"; "Go North"; "Wanted"; "Employment Office"; "Wanted Sullivan Machine Men," *Logan Banner*, 8 June 1923; Todd, interview; Beasley, interview. See also Dix, *Work Relations,* chap. 1; Laing, "The Negro Miner," 264-65; Fishback, "Employment Conditions," chap. 6; and Dix, *Work Relations in the Coal Industry*, chap. 1.

45. Henderson, interview; Fishback, "Employment Conditions," 182-229; Eller, *Miners, Millhands, and Mountaineers*, 178-82; Walter Moorman and Margaret Moorman, interview by author, 14 July 1983. For recurring reports of black casualties, see "Six Miners Killed in Explosion at Carswell," *Bluefield Daily Telegraph*, 19 July 1919; "Gary (Among the Colored People)," 11 Dec. 1923, 2 Jan. 1924; "Compensation for Six Injured Miners," 10 Dec. 1923; "Russel Dodson Killed Monday by Slate Fall," 14 July 1925; "Walter McNeil Hurt in Mine," 22 July 1925, all in the *Welch Daily News*; "Negro Miner Is Killed at Thorpe," 12 June 1929; "Colored Miner Killed Friday in Slate Fall," 5 Mar. 1930; "McDowell County Continues Out in front in Mine Fatalities," 24 July 1929; "Negro Miner Electrocuted in Tidewater Mines," 9 Oct. 1929; "Hemphill Colored Miner Killed in Mining Accident," 8 Jan. 1930, all in *McDowell Recorder*.

46. For a discussion of these processes in the urban- industrial context, see Peter Gottlieb, *Making Their Own Way: Southern Blacks' Migration to Pittsburgh, 1916-30* (Urbana: University of Illinois Press, 1987); James R. Grossman, *The Land of Hope: Chicago, Black Southerners, and the Great Migration* (Chicago: University of Chicago Press, 1989); Earl Lewis, *In Their Own Interests: Race, Class, and Power in Twentieth-Century Norfolk* (Berkeley: University of California Press, 1991); and Joe William Trotter Jr., *Black Milwaukee: The Making of an Industrial Proletariat, 1915-45* (Urbana: University of Illinois Press, 1985).

47. Boling, interview; Campbell, interview; Beasley, interview; and Harris, interview; "Annual Garden Inspection at Gary Plants," 17 July 1925, and 23 July 1925; "Annual Inspection of Yards and Gardens: Consolidation Coal Company,"27 July 1925, all in *Welch Daily News*; Agricultural Extension Service, *Annual Reports* (Morgantown, W.Va.), 1921-32, especially "Negro Work" and "Extension Work

with Negroes"; "The Annual Garden and Yard Context Complete Success," *The New River Company Employees Magazine* 3, no. 1 (Sept. 1925): 3-4 and 2, no. 2 (Oct. 1924): 8-9; "55 Individual Awards Made Today in Yard and Garden Contests," *McDowell Recorder*, 31 July 1929.

48. The Peters Sisters, *War Poems* (Beckley, W.Va.: n.p., 1919), 7.

49. See note 21 above, especially Hill, "Loafers and Jonahs."

50. "How a Coal Miner Can Save Money," *McDowell Times*, 19 Feb. 1915; Laing, "The Negro Miner," chaps. 3 and 4. Also see "Local Items," *McDowell Times*, 26 Mar. 1915; WVBNWS, *Biennial Report*, 1921-22, 5-11, 38-41, and 1923-24, 8-10, 39-45; "Kimball (Colored News)," *Welch Daily News*, 28 Jan. 1924; "Among Our Colored," *The New River Company Employees Magazine*, various issues, 1924-30; "Agricultural Extension Work in Mining Towns," Agricultural Extension Service, *Annual Reports*, 1921-26.

51. S. R. Anderson, "News of the Colored People," *Bluefield Daily Telegraph*, 28 Dec. 1930; WVBNWS, *Biennial Reports*, 1929-32, 12-14.

52. WVBNWS, *Biennial Reports*, 1929-32, 4-7; Laing, "The Negro Miner," 254, 503-4.

53. Martin Cherniack, *The Hawk's Nest Incident: America's Worst Industrial Disaster* (New Haven: Yale University Press, 1986), 18-9, 89-91; Mark Rowh, "The Hawk's Nest Tragedy: Fifty Years Later," *Goldenseal* 7, no. 1 (1981): 31-2.

54. Cherniack, *Hawk's Nest Incident*, 18-9, 90-1; Rowh, "The Hawk's Nest Tragedy," 31-2.

55. Henderson, interview; Davis, interview; *Fifteenth Census of the United States* (1930), vol. 6, p. 1428.

56. This and the remaining portions of this essay are based on my essay in Jack Salzman, ed., *Encyclopedia of African American Culture and History* (New York: Macmillan Publishing Company, 1996).

"Native White, African American, and Italian Track Crew." West Virginia and Regional History Collection, West Virginia University Libraries, Morgantown, W.Va.

'Here Come The Boomer 'Talys':
Italian Immigrants And Industrial Conflict In
The Upper Kanawha Valley, 1903-1917

Frederick A. Barkey

In 1900, West Virginia was the most native-born state in the Union. However, over the next decade, this demographic phenomenon would change dramatically as the Mountain State's rapidly developing industrial sector created a need for labor that could not readily be supplied by the state's population base. In response to that need, employment agencies and representatives of railroads, factories, coal and lumber companies vigorously recruited immigrant workers both in Europe and at American ports of entry. These efforts attracted so much foreign labor that by 1910, only fourteen states in this country had added more European immigrants to their population than West Virginia.[1]

The rapid influx of immigrants into the Mountain State during the first decade or so of the twentieth century transformed the ethnicity of several segments of the state's industrial workforce. This was particularly true in the case of coal miners. In 1890, only 13.4 percent of West Virginia's coal miners were foreign-born (mostly northern European) as compared to 60 percent of the miners in Pennsylvania and Illinois, and over 30 percent in Ohio and Indiana.[2] However, by 1915, almost half of West Virginia's miners were recent immigrants, mainly form southern Europe. So extensive was this influx that by the time of America's entrance into World War I, West Virginia's mine workforce was the most foreign-born of any southern state.[3]

By far the most numerous of the immigrant groups to flood into the West Virginia coalfields at the turn of the last century were Italians. Phillip Conley first documented the extent of this ethnic group's participation in the state's mining industry. In his pioneering *History of the West Virginia Coal Industry*, Conley estimated that by 1915, there were over twice as many Italian miners as any of the twenty-seven or so nationality groups involved in the extraction of the Mountain State's coal.[4] In fact, there were so many Italians in West Virginia before World War I that for a number of years officials of the Italian government were stationed in both the northern and southern part of the state to look after them.[5]

Historians have been slow to explore the significance of the high concentration of Italians or any other immigrant group in the coal mine workforce of

West Virginia. What little we do know has reinforced the long-standing image of these and other southern and eastern European immigrants in America as anonymous, desperately poor individuals fleeing their old-world peasant communities for a chance at a better life in this country. Bewildered and unable to speak English, they were met at ports of entry by employment agents or representatives of private firms and whisked away to the mountains where they had little idea of where they were or what they were going to do. Parceled out to coal, lumber, railroad, and construction companies, they are seemingly powerless to resist exploitation. However, despite this background, they earn respect for their hard work and are assimilated rather easily, by the second generation, into the emerging industrial culture of the state.[6]

The purpose of this article is to broaden our understanding of the immigrant experience in the Mountain State. By focusing on the significant group of Italians who were drawn to the mines in the Fayette County towns of Boomer and its neighboring coal communities, this discussion attempts to move beyond chronicling the impact that the West Virginia industrial environment had on such immigrants. Rather than seeing them as essentially helpless victims of overpowering economic and social forces, this study views these Italian miners as the possessors of beliefs, skills, and traditions that enabled them not only to take important initiatives on their own behalf, but also to influence institutions and values that were emerging in the state's industrial working class.

The town of Boomer is located on the north side of the Kanawha River about thirty miles southeast of Charleston. The community was named for John Boomer Huddleston whose family had migrated into the area in the late 1700s.[7] Boomer is bordered on its east side by the metal producing town of Alloy (formerly Boncar) which lies a little over a mile away on Route 60 and less than a mile on its west by the coal camps of Harewood and Longacre. In a number of ways Boomer, Harewood, and Longacre, along with the nearby commercial center of Smithers, have constituted one interrelated area.[8]

An excellent seam of coal measuring between five and six feet in thickness ran through the hills above Boomer, Harewood, and Longacre. This coal was first mined commercially in 1894 at Harewood by W. R. Johnson who had been involved for a number of years in the operation of the Crescent mines at nearby Montgomery on the south side of the Kanawha River.[9] Johnson and his backers in Montgomery were attracted to Harewood when the Kanawha and Michigan Railroad was completed from the old salt town of Malden just east of Charleston to the headwaters of the Kanawha River at Gauley Bridge in 1893. This K & M extension held the promise of great profits due to the fact that it provided a dependable year-round link to the coal markets of the Midwest.[10]

The completion of the Kanawha and Michigan attracted other budding entrepreneurs. First of all, there was William Masters, a prominent Fayette County merchant turned coal operator. Masters was a long-term resident of the Fayette County town of Ansted where he owned land, operated a general merchandise store, and a gristmill from 1820 through 1895. In 1893, Masters decided to try his hand at the coal business and subsequently opened a mine at Winona on Keeney's Creek in the Nuttal Magisterial District of the county. Building upon the success he achieved at Winona, Masters decided to expand and determined that the Boomer area was a hot prospect for development. In 1895, he formed the Boomer Coal and Coke Company and opened the first of several mines that would dot the hills above the community.[11]

Also drawn to the profit potential of the greater Boomer area was Samuel Dixon, who, after consolidating his coal and rail holdings in 1906 into the New River Company, became one of the most influential figures in southern West Virginia mining. Dixon had come to Fayette County from England in 1877 and was employed for many years as a bookkeeper and mine foreman. By 1893, Dixon had worked his way up to the position of president and general manager of the coal operation he had bought into near Mount Hope, which bore the name of one of his partners, Symington Macdonald. Four years later, Dixon, Macdonald, and C.D. Blake began mining near Harewood at a place that Dixon named Longacre after a coal community in his native Yorkshire, England.[12]

By 1903, the rich coal deposits at Boomer, Harewood, and Longacre were acquired by Ohio capitalists. From the very beginning much of the coal that was produced in this section of the upper Kanawha River was shipped to the Buckeye State where it was sold to brokers in Columbus and Cincinnati. While some of this Kanawha coal was used to heat homes and businesses in the Midwest, a good deal of the product was shipped out in the form of an excellent grade of coke that helped fuel furnaces in Ohio metals industries.[13] In 1901, a southern Ohio syndicate doing business in the state as the Sunday Creek Coal Company decided to acquire their own sources for what was becoming a rising tide of quality West Virginia coal. Operating in the Mountain State as the Kanawha and Hocking Coal Company, the Sunday Creek interests opened nine mines around Cedar Grove in Kanawha County, eighteen miles southeast of Charleston, and five mines at Harewood and Longacre.[14] Two years later, a northern Ohio syndicate controlled by Cleveland steel millionaire and U.S. Senator Marcus A. Hanna purchased and began expanding the mining property at Boomer.[15]

Shortly after the Hanna interests took control of the Boomer Coal and Coke operations, they and the management of the nearby Kanawha and Hocking mines began to recruit Italian immigrants as a key component of their respective workforces. Although immigrants had been filtering into Fayette County for a decade or more before 1900, only a few were from Italy. However, by 1905, what had once been a trickle now became a veritable flood as Italians poured into the county.[16] The trigger for this influx and its heavy concentration in the Boomer area appears to have been the labor relations climate that developed in the area as a result of West Virginia's participation in the strike which erupted in the hard coal region of eastern Pennsylvania in May of 1902.

The coal strike of 1902 in West Virginia is sometimes pictured as sympathy action taken in solidarity with the miners in the Anthracite region.[17] However, in southern West Virginia, at least, the strike was basically over local issues including union recognition and the need to spread the reach of the United Mine Workers into the upper Kanawha and lower New River valleys.[18] During the strike, the Boomer Coal and Coke Company did everything it could to thwart union organizing while keeping its production going full tilt. Among other things, the company prohibited meetings on its property and obtained blanket court orders restraining any actions that allegedly interfered with the individual employment contract of its miners. Despite these strategies, Boomer's coal production was continually disrupted by demonstrations and work stoppages.[19] Moreover, by the end of the struggle, Boomer's essentially native-born workforce had been organized into a local union of the UMWA.[20]

Adding to the tensions engendered in the Boomer area by the coal strike was the fact that, although the conflict officially ended in the fall of 1902, clashes between labor and management continued in several nearby areas of Fayette and Raleigh Counties for a year or two. During that period, UMWA organizers periodically passed through the Boomer area seeking local allies and financial support for their efforts to bring union coverage to more of the miners in the region. Taking over the Boomer coal property in this kind of atmosphere, the Hanna interests apparently determined that greater reliance on immigrants would provide a more dependable, production-oriented workforce.[21]

Whatever the central reason for recruiting them may have been, a steady stream of Italian immigrants began to arrive in the Boomer, Smithers, Harewood, and Longacre area. These newcomers were drawn from many sections of Italy, but some communities in the Old Country contributed more emigrants than others. In the first place, the great majority of Italian immigrants in the upper Kanawha valley appear to have come from southern Italy.[22] This should not be surprising considering the fact that southern Italy supplied at least a million and a half emigrants to the United States between 1880 and 1920. Known collectively as the Messogiorno, these southern provinces had been marked for decades by difficulties for peasants and artisans. A rapidly increasing population combined with changing markets and land use patterns along with excessive taxation and a lack of educational opportunities made it difficult for the southern Italian working class to improve itself or even survive without supplemental employment. Increasingly, peasant-class males in many parts of the region engaged in ever wider searches for day or seasonal employment until it seemed logical to emigrate, at least temporarily, somewhere in the Atlantic world's Western Hemisphere.[23]

Although the Messogiorno consists of the three provinces of Campania, Calabria, and Sicily, it was the latter two regions that produced the most immigrants to the upper Kanawha valley. Most of these Sicilian emigrants appear to have made their way to the port of Palermo from communities in the very center of that island.[24] In contrast to many southern Italians who came to America, a significant number of these Sicilians began their long journey with vocational skills that made them prime candidates for recruitment to the Appalachian region. There was, for instance, Luigi Curatolo, who, along with his brothers Salvatore and Guiseppe, had entered the sulfur mines around Valguarnera at the tender age of eight or nine. These brothers expected to spend the rest of their lives like their families before them laboring in such mines.[25] However, by the first decade of the twentieth century, competition in international markets from America was reducing employment opportunities in Sicily's sulfur mines and propelling young men of the Curatolos' generation out of the country which in Luigi's case meant Longacre, West Virginia.[26]

Even more important in terms of the number of southern Italians who ended up in the Boomer area was the province of Calabria which occupies most of the foot of the Italian boot. Many sections of Calabria contributed native sons to the exodus of souls who passed through Naples on their way to the United States. However, the community of San Giovanni in Fiore and the nearby town of Cacurri produced a continuing chain of emigrants that together constituted a core of the Italian population in the greater Boomer area.[27]

Smaller but still significant clusters of immigrants who reached the upper Kanawha valley came from the northwestern sections of Italy. The three provinces of Piedmont, Lombardi, and Liguria which make up this region had a reputation for generating many fewer emigrants than the Messogiorno. In reality, however, the rate of exodus per thousand residents in northwestern Italy was close to that of the country's southern provinces. In part, this higher than expected emigration rate can be attributed to the fact that, although the northwest was the most industrialized and urbanized section of the country, there were still many agricultural communities where resources and production technique were inadequate for a population that, despite a considerable exodus during the first two decades of the twentieth century, continued to grow.[28]

For many of the peasant farmers from northwestern Italy, the struggle that led to the decision to migrate was similar to that of Dina Dalporto, a longtime resident of Longacre. Dina was a native of the small town of San Ginese, which is situated in the border area between Tuscany and Liguria. She recalls the difficulty her mother and father had raising a growing family there at the turn of the last century.

> After a few more years the family grew larger and father and mother were forced to work from daylight till dark. Mother's work was never done; we had a little farm and could not afford to hire anyone…so time passed on a little harder. Father was working for his children (but) could not get all what they needed and was forced to go and borrow money from his neighbors.

Dina's older brothers and sisters began to emigrate to America where Fresno, California, and Longacre, West Virginia, were the most common destinations.[29]

Once in America, Italians traveled to the Boomer area by a number of well-established routes. One of the most common of these appears to have been by rail from New York to Cincinnati, and from there by riverboat down the Ohio and up the Kanawha Rivers. Their arrival by this method always attracted a great deal of local attention. As Dave Tamplin, a life-long resident of Boomer recalled, "As a general rule, the steamboat would come in on Sunday. We kids used to come out here on the riverbank and watch them get off the boat and go up the hollow loaded down with everything they had in the world. It sure was a sight."[30] As more and more Italians made that trip up Boomer hollow, they soon filled up the clusters of houses which the company built at what became known as "Little Italy." In less than a decade, there were over a thousand Italians settled in Boomer and nearby coal camps making this area the largest concentration of such immigrants in contiguous communities in West Virginia.[31]

If the Boomer Coal and Coke Company and the Hocking Valley interests recruited the Italians in the hope, as tradition has it, that they would constitute a more docile, controllable workforce than their American-born counterparts, they would soon be disillusioned. They would learn what several employers in the upper Kanawha valley were already discovering—that Italians could respond aggressively and with remarkable solidarity to injustice. For example, in the first week of July 1905, the foreman of a crew grading a section on the construction of the Deepwater Railway near the town of Page in Fayette County reprimanded an Italian laborer by viciously knocking him down an embankment. The foreman's action incensed many of what the *Fayette Journal* described as "Dago friends" of the assaulted laborer. About half of these Italians threw down their tools, grabbed rocks, and proceeded to attack the foreman and his assistants. Additional Italians and several blacks from nearby railroad construction sites joined the fray. In the pitched battle that followed, the Italians and their allies were carrying the day until William Nelson Page, the Deepwater line's president, received word of the trouble and immediately summoned Fayette County law officers who put down the rebellion and arrested eleven of the instigators. Over the next week, Page expelled about five hundred Italians from his properties at Deepwater, Page, and Kincaid, and vowed that his operation would hire no more such immigrants.[32]

A little less than four years after the incident at Page, the Boomer Coal and Coke and the Kanawha and Hocking Companies discovered for themselves just how militant Italian workers could be. The trouble that would tear apart the communities in the area was precipitated by the effects of the depression that staggered the United States in 1907. In the Mountain State this so-called "Banker's Panic" was anything but the short-term economic setback that it is sometimes pictured.[33] The effects of the national crisis hit West Virginia hard by 1908 when unemployment rates rose and the working class began to suffer.[34]

The situation for West Virginia mine workers and their families became particularly serious. While many coal operators tried to keep their mines going through the economic crisis, few could run at more than 10 or 20 percent of their normal capacity. Throughout the Kanawha and New River regions, miners complained about having very little work through much of 1908. As Cleveland Toney of the Fayette County community of Dothan recalled:

> I'd get up every morning at five o'clock to see if the whistle would blow, but that would happen only once or twice a month. At that rate a man might make five or six dollars a month; and, out of that, they'd take fifty cents for the doctor and fifteen cents for hospital insurance.[35]

Even in those places where work was steadier, the miners could afford only the barest necessities and the ingenuity of their wives was taxed to provide an even halfway decent table for their families. The United Mine Workers of America recognized the miners' plight and temporarily reduced their union fees in order to retain as many members as possible.[36]

In December of 1908, the Coal Operators on Paint Creek in Kanawha County demanded a modification of the labor agreement they had negotiated the previous spring. These operators claimed that it was impossible for them to compete in the depressed coal market, especially when the UMWA had lost the nearby Cabin Creek mines in 1906 and had not yet organized the competition in the New River coalfields. The Paint Creek operators followed up their announcement with an immediate wage reduction. This action provoked a strike by two thousand miners who were determined to protect their contract.[37] A week later, the strike was settled through a compromise worked out by Governor William O. Dawson in which the union was granted payroll deduction of union dues (checkoff) in exchange for the miners being paid on the basis of the long ton rather than the standard two thousand pounds. This settlement was implemented shortly after it was approved by a referendum of the affected miners.[38]

The peace brokered by Governor Dawson was very short-lived. Many of the other mine operators in the upper Kanawha valley resented the so-called Paint Creek Modification which they claimed put them at a distinct disadvantage in the continuing depressed coal market. Therefore, in April of 1909, a number of these companies posted notices at their mines that they would begin on May 25 to calculate their workers' wages based upon the long ton.[39]

The actions of the coal operators in the Upper Kanawha valley forced the hand of President Ben Davis and the executive board of UMWA District 17. A special convention was called for April 20 in Charleston. After a lively debate and some very strong opposition, the delegates agreed to offer the Paint Creek Modification to any unionized operator in the district. Over the next several weeks only the operators of two small mines took the union up on its offer. It was abundantly clear that at this point most coal operators wanted nothing to do with granting the union the security of a checkoff system for dues, claiming it would be too expensive to implement. The union argued that such a position was ludicrous in light of the fact that the coal operators routinely docked the miners' pay for all sorts of things.[40]

The refusal of the Kanawha valley coal operators to accept the Paint Creek formula left District 17 officials with what they believed was no alternative but to go on strike. President Ben Davis launched a series of rallies to drum up support and scheduled a meeting for late May in Boomer. More than two thousand miners attended the rally where Davis explained the union's position and how important the miners in that area would be to the success of any work stoppage in the district. The meeting was followed by a circular letter to all UMWA locals in the district designating May 25 as the beginning of the strike.[41]

The Long Ton Strike, as it came to be called, idled between five and six thousand miners but lasted only about a week. President Davis quickly came to the conclusion that he had gotten himself into a bad spot. For one thing, Tom Lewis, the president of the UMWA, believed that allowing the Paint Creek operators to deviate from their 1908 labor agreement was a bad idea and informed Ben Davis that the national union would not support the strike.[42] Second, Davis began to suspect that operators might not be too anxious to settle the strike if they came to the conclusion that it would serve to whittle down what was an obvious surplus of coal.[43] And finally, Davis began to worry that the events of the conflict might fragment the operators' organization and consequently imperil the viability of the yearly negotiating conventions that had established all of the district's labor agreements since 1902. Therefore, President Davis struck a deal by which the miners would return to work on the long-ton pay basis while the other issues in dispute could be settled by a jointly agreed upon arbitration panel.[44]

The overwhelming majority of District 17 miners obeyed the return to work order of President Ben Davis. The Italians in the Boomer area, however, refused. As far as they were concerned, the strike was still on and, as if by magic, they produced an amazing supply of rifles that they had apparently been accumulating for some time. The immigrant strikers quickly mobilized themselves and, when approximately four hundred native white and black miners attempted to return to their work places, the Italians prevented them by an intimidating show of force.[45]

The aggressive blocking of the mine sites, as well as other immediate actions by the Italian strikers in the Boomer area were labeled riots by Fayette County newspapers. In some ways these events do seem similar to spontaneous peasant revolts that were common in Italy and other parts of Europe. On the other hand, one perceptive witness had a different take on things. "Everyone called it a riot; and even though it looked like all hell had broken lose, I think there was more to it," mused life-long Boomer resident Dave Tamplin.[46] In fact, there did appear to have been some well-thought out strategies involved. For example, a contingent of Italians proceeded to gain control of the vital rail line in the community and, in the process, drove off a crew of workers who were doing minor repairs on some rolling stock. In addition, a group of Boomer Italians marched to Harewood in order to close down the Kanawha and Hocking central blacksmith shop that was vital to the ongoing operation of all the mine properties in the Boomer area.[47]

The next day, the Italians decided to demonstrate their strength to management; in so doing, they tapped tactics they had doubtlessly used in the Old Country. The strikers proceeded to the mine offices at Boomer parading behind a large red and black flag upon which was emblazoned in gold lettering the words, "Victory or Death." Along the line of march the Italians sang songs interspersed with whoops, shouts, and rifle fire. After marching for some time in front of the management building, the Italian entourage proceeded to a level bottomland along Bowman Creek that flowed through the community and began to conduct a meeting. Thinking he might seize this moment to reason with his Italian workers, Boomer coal's superintendent, A.J. Gillie, rushed to the meeting spot and began to address the crowd. Gillie discovered immediately that he could not have picked a worse moment. The Italians were in no mood to listen to any company representative and Gillie was forced to retreat with rifle shots whizzing over his head.[48]

Back in the safety of his office, the badly shaken mine superintendent swore out arrest warrants for those Italians he believed to be leaders of the aggression and telephoned Sheriff Dickinson of Fayette County for immediate assistance in restoring order. The sheriff and two deputies arrived that evening. One of the latter, a Mr. Perry, was dispatched to size up the situation and was immediately taken hostage by the strikers, and held for several hours before being released.[49] At ten o'clock that night, when the Italians began firing shots toward the Boomer coal offices, Sheriff Dickinson declared that the situation was completely out of control and called to Montgomery for immediate assistance. Fifty armed deputies were rushed to Boomer aboard the packet boat Cuba. The sheriff also sent word of the trouble to Guiseppe Carldari, the Italian government's consular agent in Fairmont.[50]

Even with reinforcements, Sheriff Dickinson hesitated to move against the strikers. He discovered that they were well entrenched in rock forts which they had thrown up above their homes near the Number Three mine tipple. By the next morning, another fifty deputies arrived along with the peacemaker of that era, a Gatling gun, which had been loaned to the county by Baldwin Felts agents working for the Norfolk and Western Railroad. Now assured of superior firepower, the sheriff launched a successful assault against the strikers. Thirteen ringleaders, including a recent arrival, eleven-year-old Sam Yockaway (Yaquinta) were arrested and sent to Montgomery for safekeeping.[51]

The day after Sheriff Dickinson's victory, Guido Vincenzo arrived from the Italian consulate office in Fairmont. He met with his fellow countrymen and heard their version of what had transpired. Later that day, Vincenzo and most of the strikers proceeded to the Boomer Coal Company office where he conveyed the Italians' offer to return to work immediately upon the sheriff's release of their countrymen who had been arrested. Superintendent Gillie, apparently still seething over his previous encounter with the strikers, would have none of it and plunged into the crowd of Italians, identifying nine more individuals he dubbed troublemakers and insisted that the sheriff place them under arrest. At this juncture, a lively and protracted discussion between Vincenzo and the authorities ensued, the gist of which was the consul's argument that the Italians had been misinformed and mislead by UMWA representatives. The two sides were finally able to work out an arrangement whereby the arrested strikers would be released on bail of one hundred dollars per individual. In return, the Italians would return to work as soon as practical. Before he left, Vincenzo retained the well-known Fayette County law firm of Osenten McPeak, and Horan to represent the arrested strikers at their subsequent trials.[52]

A few days after the Italian Long Ton Strike was settled, Ben Davis secured from the coal operators throughout the district a pledge to return to the terms and conditions of the 1908 labor agreement, including the use of the two-thousand-pound ton as the basis for the miners' pay.[53] In light of this development, it could be argued that had the Boomer area Italians shown a little patience and gone back to work with the rest of the district, they would have gotten what they wanted without creating so much trouble. In fact, Adam Littlepage, Kanawha County's pro-labor state senator, apparently acting on behalf of Ben Davis, had told them that when he addressed a public meeting in Smithers just after the Italians initiated their strike.[54]

Setting aside the fact that few, if any, of the Boomer Italians were UMWA members and, therefore, under no compunction to obey President Davis's return to work order, the problem with the above argument is that the stakes in the Long Ton dispute were higher for these immigrants than they were for native-born miners. It was one thing for American miners to be willing to accept the long ton pay basis in exchange for future benefits that might be achieved from a union strengthened by the security of a contractual dues checkoff system; it was quite another thing for the Italians. The typical Italian miner needed to earn as much money as possible as quickly as possible. Back in Italy there were almost always parents, siblings, wives, children, or sweethearts to be brought to America or assisted in the Old Country until the immigrant could return and build with them a better life.[55]

While coal mining was unquestionably one of this country's most dangerous occupations, it was on the other hand theoretically a great opportunity for Italian immigrants. On a good day in a West Virginia coal mine, an Italian could earn more than he could in a week in the Old Country. Moreover, because he was paid by the ton, the harder the immigrant was willing to work, the more he could make. On the other hand, it was almost always a challenge for Italian miners to earn what they needed. In the first place, southern European immigrants usually had far fewer resources than American-born miners when their employment began. This was especially true of immigrants from the Messogiorno who brought 40 percent less money with them to America than their fellow countrymen from other parts of Italy.[56] As a result, Italians more often than not began their jobs in debt. In addition, Italians and other foreign miners were often assigned the worst places in the mine and were exploited by their fellow coal diggers. Angelo Ulissi of Longacre explained to researcher John Cavalier how the latter could occur:

> One way in which I was rooked was by others stealing my cars. As you know, each miner was issued those checks with his number on them. After I had loaded a car, I hung one of my checks on it. In the course of the long journey to the tipple, someone would remove my check and put his in its place, so I would lose that car.[57]

Adding to the Italian immigrant's problems was the fact that it was difficult for miners, generally in southern West Virginia, to get more than 180 or 200 days of work per year.[58]

Despite these challenges, Italian coal miners' hard work and frugality allowed them to save at a rate that astonished the U. S. Department of Labor. This agency estimated that Italian immigrants saved more money at the same wage than any other foreign national group.[59] It is little wonder that the Italians in the upper Kanawha valley were upset with the use of the long ton as the basis for pay since it would have in effect meant an 11 percent reduction in wages.[60] The only thing that could upset the Italians more was the possibility that there might be no jobs at all, as an incident that occurred at Rush Run on the New River illustrates.

A month after the Boomer area Long Ton Strike ended, a group of Italian coke- oven tenders at Rush Run became very upset when the coal company began to move an automatic coke drawing and loading machine onto their property. During the first week of July in 1909, the Rush Run Italians armed with beer bottles, home-made knives, and a few pistols, proceeded to the home of their foreman, John Elliott, to express their anger at what they were sure would be the loss of their jobs once the coke drawing machine was set up. With Elliott agreeing to act as spokesman, the Italians proceeded to the residence of William Burns, the company superintendent. When Burns was called out to face the angry Italians and refused, a number of shots were fired at the house. The protestors also tore down the fence around Burns' house and set it on fire. The terrified superintendent reportedly raced out of his back door and sprinted to nearby Thurmond where he sought the assistance of Fayette County deputy sheriffs who were stationed there. The deputies gathered up a posse and sped to Rush Run where they disarmed the Italians and arrested Elliott and seven of the protest ringleaders. Despite Elliot's later claim in court that he and the Italians were merely following an Old World tradition of a bonfire and community celebration, those arrested were sentenced to six months in jail.[61]

As the events surrounding the Long Ton Strike demonstrate, the activism of Italian miners in the Boomer area was peripheral or even detrimental to spreading the influence of the United Mine Workers in southern West Virginia. However, by the end of the great Paint Creek and Cabin Creek Strike of 1912 through 1914, that situation would change and the Italians would become an integral part of the union's struggle. This transformation apparently began in April of 1912 when a strike broke out over the operators' refusal to grant either a wage increase or the checkoff of union dues.[62] To encourage the miners to support the strike, District 17 officials scheduled several mass meetings, one of which was to be held at Smithers. At least two thousand miners from Boomer,

Harewood, Longacre, Cannelton, and Carbondale attended this meeting and heard two of the national union's Italian organizers and several local Italian union members make a special appeal to their fellow countrymen to stand firm in the strike and work more closely with the UMWA.[63]

The presence of Italian speakers at the Smithers strike-support meeting greatly upset the mine operators in the Boomer area for it added substance to their growing belief that the Italian workers were increasingly susceptible to "outside forces" which were the source of much of the current trouble at the mines. The operators maintained that most of their American-born miners understood the economics of the district's competitive situation and would have returned to work except for the fact that the Italians were demonstrating, making threats, and sending nasty notes to anyone who reportedly was even thinking of working. Furthermore, the operators warned that the Italians were ready to invade nearby Paint, Cabin, and Kelly's Creeks and, if this happened, it would likely upset the fragile peace the parties had been enjoying for the past several years.[64]

As it would turn out, the Boomer area coal operator's warnings would be more prophetic than they knew. Although at first it would not be generally realized, as the whole strike potential appeared to diffuse when a new contract with a two and a half cents per ton wage increase was worked out at a joint conference in Charleston. However, as in the case of the Long Ton Strike, the agreement quickly fell apart when the Paint Creek operators announced that there was no way that they could possibly afford a wage increase. Anticipating a long and bitter struggle, the district's coal operators began to import more Baldwin Felts mine guards and saw to it that they were equipped with high-powered rifles and machine guns. As miners rushed to collect their own firearms, confrontations were inevitable.[65]

As the level of conflict began to rise in the late spring and early summer of 1912, the Italians from Boomer and elsewhere in the Cabin Creek District became increasingly critical of the UMWA's ability to match the combativeness of the coal operators. In the first place, the Italians were some of the most fearless and enthusiastic frontline soldiers in the struggle, as attested by the fact that they were among the first killed and arrested. Less than a month after the first pitched battle of the strike which took place on May 17 in Mucklow on Paint Creek, a Boomer Italian was killed and his black comrade was wounded by Baldwin Felts guards who were patrolling along the creek near Wacomah. Moreover, when the Baldwin guards and local law enforcement officials followed the strikers' tracks back to a house in Wacomah, everyone they picked up there was Italian.[66] Not long after this incident, two Italian miners were killed and five others were beaten by a contingent of Baldwin guards, prompting an inquiry of Governor Glasscock requested by the Italian consul in Fairmont.[67]

Italians were also involved in spreading the strike. An example of this kind of initiative occurred in late July of 1912 when Governor William Glasscock stationed National Guard troops along Paint Creek in response to a plan from the sheriff of Kanawha County for assistance in keeping order. Shortly after the troops were deployed, the governor was forced to dispatch part of them to nearby Boone County where strike trouble had escalated into violence, including the wounding of Sheriff A. H. Sutphin. No sooner had the troopers arrived in Boone County than they were attacked at the community of Sterling by contingents of Italians from Boomer and some Greeks from the Clear Creek area of neighboring Raleigh County.[68] Moreover, by the second week of September, the Italians had walked off their jobs raising the fear that an additional 1,400 armed strikers would now have to be dealt with.[69]

In addition to being among the shock troops of the Paint Creek-Cabin Creek struggle, the Italians were vital to the logistics of keeping munitions and other vital supplies flowing into the strike zone. The Boomer area Italians and their native-born comrades developed a number of routes for moving such items. One of the most common supply trails was to cross the Kanawha River to Morris Creek which is located a little southeast of Montgomery. From there, supplies were carried over the mountains into the scenes of the fighting on Paint Creek.[70] Smaller loads of supplies were frequently ferried across the river directly into the strike zone. This was a much riskier enterprise as Wyatt Thompson, the editor of the Socialist Party newspaper in Huntington, found out when he volunteered to smuggle arms to the strikers.

> My humble duty was the delivery of high powered rifle ammunition secured for the miners by their good friend, O.J. Morrison…I had just delivered a couple of suitcases full to the south side of the river…and was stepping into the john boat to be rowed back to the north bank when the soldier turned a spotlight on us from the high river bank…I had my back to them and I also had on a belt with holster and revolver. I eased the gun from the holster and flipped it into the river. And, I don't think they ever did believe the story I told them of wearing the holster to carry tools in.[71]

Meanwhile, the effectiveness of the arms-smuggling network was becoming clear to state authorities. In late August, Governor William Glasscock had rushed five companies of the West Virginia National Guard to stop the shootings and destruction of property on Cabin Creek where the strike had spread earlier that month. When the violence continued to escalate, the governor declared martial law and dispatched one thousand guardsmen under the command of Adjutant General Elliott to both creeks. Four days later, at six o'clock in the morning, nine companies of troops swept through the strike zone and collected fifteen hundred rifles, numerous bushel baskets of pistols, six or seven machine guns and two hundred thousand rounds of ammunition. The military authority apparently realized that many of these supplies had come from Boomer and sent Colonel Ford and several aides to talk to Mr. Huddie, the mine superintendent, about the key leaders among the miners. Colonel Ford was informed that the core of the union members in the community were Italians and that their leader was an "effective fellow" by the name of Giacomo.[72]

Not long after Colonel Ford's scouting trip to Boomer, a contingent of Baldwin Felts guards and the Fayette County sheriff arrived in Boomer with the objective of gaining control of the community. When the intentions of the Baldwin Felts guards became clear, an Italian sharpshooter stationed on the first mine tipple began firing at them. The guards and deputies took shelter at the weigh house and signaled their tormentors that they wished to parley. The Italians who came down to talk were told that the guards had been summoned to Boomer because management had been informed that there would be attempts to burn the company tipples. The Italian spokesman advised the sheriff that the property would be well looked after by those who worked there and that no other help was necessary. That evening, the Baldwin Felts detectives decided to return to Huntington.[73]

On September 17, Governor Glasscock extended the martial law zone to include parts of Boone, Fayette, and Raleigh Counties. It was rumored by good authority that this extension was designed in large part to stop the flow of arms and supplies that were entering the strike zone from the Italian communities on the north side of the Kanawha River. It was further rumored that the governor was contemplating extending the military jurisdiction to Montgomery and some surrounding areas where supplies and arms were often hidden until they could be moved to the strike front.[74]

The rumored extension of martial law to Montgomery greatly distressed the leadership of that community. The city fathers feared that military rule would be a disaster for business. Therefore, a delegation was sent to Charleston to plead with the governor to postpone any action on an extension until the community could try to correct the problems that were causing him concern. Moved by the entreaties of the Montgomery delegation, Glasscock allegedly agreed that he would withhold any action until a town meeting could be held to address the issues involved.[75]

The meeting in Montgomery to discuss the threat of martial law drew a large crowd of citizens topped off by such luminaries as Mayor T. J. Davis; Judge M. L. Simms; Bert Hastings, a former district UMWA officer; prominent businessmen, including K. E. Smart; and Dr. Luther and Samuel Montgomery, the brothers for whose family the town was named. Since stopping the flow of arms was presumed to be the main objective of the governor's extension of military rule, the citizens decided that the best strategy was to get the residents of the area, including the Italians, to turn in all their weapons. The guns would then be registered and stored until the trouble was over. A citizens' committee was appointed to supervise the process and a deadline of one week established to complete the task. A cautionary note of advice was given to the committee by a perceptive citizen who pointed out that the governor was no fool and doubtless understood that, since there was probably two or three guns for every man, woman, and child in the Montgomery area, a comparable number of weapons would have to be turned in if the collection effort was to be taken seriously.[76]

Fortunately, the efforts of the Montgomery citizens' committee did produce a large quantity of arms, including weapons allegedly procured from a majority of the Italian miners in the Boomer area. Word went back to the governor detailing the scale of this wonderful response and assuring him that the armaments were in safe and, one can presume, cold storage at the Montgomery Bottling and Ice Company. The governor was satisfied enough by these developments that, not only did he not impose martial law on Montgomery, but even removed it from the Italian communities on the north side of the river.[77]

As the Paint Creek-Cabin Creek strike wore on, the Italians also played a significant role in the conflict between coal operators and the union over the importations of replacement workers. From the very beginning, most operators were determined to keep their mines open. A number of mine owners sought to replace strikers by claiming that the men they began hiring were obtained only to make needed repairs on tipples and other above-ground facilities. When this and other ploys failed to obtain enough local labor, the operators increasingly turned to recruiting workers from out of state. This "importation of transportation," as the replacement workers came to be called, picked up significantly after mid-October of 1912 when Governor Glasscock believed conditions in the district had settled down sufficiently to justify the removal of the National Guard.[78]

Due perhaps to the fact that the election campaign of 1912 was in full swing, and the strike leaders, most of whom were Socialists, did not want to give state authorities an excuse for interfering with what looked like a victory for their party in the strike district, little was done about the increasing flow of replacement workers.[79] However, within a few days of the election, there were demonstrations against replacements at locations on both creeks. Some of these demonstrations were carried out by strikers' wives who persistently harassed replacements until they left the district. The strikers quickly became more aggressive in their tactics and began to attack the trains that were transporting the scabs. Thus, on November 13, 1912, although a trainload of replacements was able to slip up Cabin Creek, it faced a hail of bullets on its return trip. On the fourteenth, the strikers mobilized their forces and placed them in strategically significant numbers to stop the next trainload. The strikers then detached the cars loaded with scabs and sent them back to Charleston pulled by an auxiliary engine commandeered from a nearby siding.[80]

Although there are no reliable statistics on the matter, many of the replacement workers were themselves Italian immigrants. As was the case with most of their traveling companions, these Italians knew little or nothing of what they were getting into in West Virginia. However, once enlightened by the strikers and their supporters about the nature of the conflict and provided with a reasonable alternative, these immigrant replacement workers were often willing and anxious to leave the district. Especially effective in achieving this result with fellow countrymen were several Italian activists, the most notable of whom was Rocco "Rock" Spinelli.[81]

Twenty-year-old Rocco Spinelli arrived in Longacre sometime in 1908. Three years later he moved to Eskdale on Cabin Creek where he meet Nellie Elizabeth Bowles. The couple was married in late May of 1912 and became increasingly involved in strike support activities. In a remarkable show of bravery and daring, the Spinellis went from camp to camp talking to Italian replacements, beseeching them to come out of the creek.[82]

The Spinellis were ultimately able to convince fifty-four Italians to follow them down to the Kanawha River. There the husband and wife team booked passage for the replacements on a packet boat to Charleston.[83]

Care of the replacement workers "liberated" by the Spinellis was taken over by UMWA representatives who housed them in a tent community on Charleston's Capital Street until the union could make arrangements to send them out of state. While they were in Charleston, the replacement workers attracted a great deal of attention from curious citizens of the city. A few of the Italians could speak a little English and the stories which they told had a familiar ring to those who understood the techniques of the labor recruiters of the era. Rather typical was the case of a young man from Chicago who said that he had been informed that, if he would go to West Virginia, he would have a nice house, free fuel to heat it, and a good job as a timekeeper. However, after three days of back-breaking pick and shovel mining, he was more than ready to follow the Spinellis out of Cabin Creek.[84]

By the middle of November, Governor Glasscock had once again dispatched units of the state's militia into the strike zone. These troops immediately began arresting strikers they claimed had been involved in blocking the importation of replacement workers. The great majority of those so charged were Italians, including Angelo Belloti, Antonio "Tony" Stafford, Rock Oliver, Larry Cepriant

(Cepriani), and, of course, Rocco and Nellie Spinelli.[85] To legalize these arrests (the civil courts are opened, but staffed by Socialists), a subsequent declaration of martial law was made retroactive by stating that "offenses against the civil law prior to the proclamation of November 15, 1912, shall be regarded as offenses under military law." Furthermore, the military court that would try those arrested was given broad authority to impose sentences "as in their judgment the offenses may merit." Apparently, the offenses of the Italians all merited five to seven years in the state penitentiary.[86]

Resolution of the Paint Creek-Cabin Creek strike would fall to the newly-elected Republican governor, Henry D. Hatfield, who took office in 1913. Hatfield was a physician from McDowell County and part of the feuding family, two of whom, by the way, had been killed in 1911 by an Italian in a shoot-out at Boomer over beer distribution. The new governor was without question popular with rank-and-file coal miners. He had been instrumental in establishing three hospitals in the coalfields and frequently used his own funds to help equip them. Moreover, as a state legislator, he had fought for bills to improve safety and sanitary conditions for miners. The new governor had also worked to abolish mine guards and to forbid deputy sheriffs from serving in that capacity.[87]

Many Italians shared the initial enthusiasm for Doctor Hatfield and joined their fellow coal diggers in flocking to his inauguration. Italians in the Boomer area chartered the last two cars of a special Kanawha and Michigan train, attached Italian and American flags to them, and proceeded to the ceremony in Charleston accompanied by H. D. Periullo, the Italian consulate in Fairmont.[88] The new governor only enhanced his status with the Italians when early in his administration, he toured the strike zone by himself, treating the sick and pardoning dozens of prisoners, a number of whom were their fellow countrymen.[89]

By mid-April of 1913, Governor Hatfield had developed the terms by which he was determined to settle the strike. He proposed that the operators establish a nine-hour workday, pay on a semi-monthly basis, allow miners to elect checkweighmen, maintain the prevailing wage rates of the central competitive fields, and end discrimination in rehiring. Further negotiations were required to assure the union that it had the right to pursue its organizational efforts and that "no discrimination" applied to union membership and not just to miners who refused to shop at the company store.[90] Under pressure from the governor and an ongoing investigation into the strike by the U. S. Senate, the Paint Creek operators accepted the settlement and agreed to check off for union dues. However, on Cabin Creek, the operators held out till August, and when they did sign off on the agreement, it was without a checkoff system. In the meantime, the leaders of recently-created District 29 in Beckley and the coal operators along the New River achieved essentially the same agreement.[91]

Although the upper Kanawha valley appeared relatively calm in the wake of the Hatfield settlement, a high level of dissatisfaction persisted. Many miners felt that their district and national officials had steamrolled the ratification convention even to the point of having some delegates who were opposed to the settlement arrested when they attempted to attend the meeting.[92] There was additionally the widespread belief that miners should have voted for themselves on the settlement and that many only went back to work because Governor Hatfield threatened to use his martial law power to deport them. Miners were also complaining that a number of coal operators were not hiring strike activists back, were not paying correctly, were still using the widely condemned mine guards, and had not recognized the union. In addition, miners from District 29 added their voices to the rising chorus of discontent and threatened to strike.[93]

The post-Hatfield Settlement turbulence increased in intensity over the next three years. This growing unrest owed as much to an internal conflict over the proper direction which the union should take as it did to relations between labor and management. The origin of this union schism can be found in the increasingly militant industrial union perspective of such rank-and-file strike leaders as Frank Keeney, Fred Mooney, Lawrence Dwyer, Charles and Will Lusk, and John Workman. This transformation in the UMWA was noted by George Williams, a major recruiter of replacement workers for the coal operators. He testified before the U. S. Senate committee investigating the strike in 1913: "I went up the creek and investigated myself before we brought in transportation. And, I saw it was not a question of fighting, as I knew of fighting unionism in the past, it was merely the Industrial Workers of the World introduced under the name of the United Mine Workers."[94] In a similar vein, a commission of distinguished citizens designated by Governor Glasscock to look into the causes of the strike noted in their report, "The wildest theories concerning the rights of property were propounded and admitted by the strike organizers. Doctrines ranging upon anarchy were upheld with such effect that men who before were living peacefully and in comparative prosperity, purchased Winchesters, revolvers, blackjacks, and other murderous weapons to shoot down coal barons."[95]

The more militant strike leaders denied that they were members of the Industrial Workers of the World. However, most of them were left-wing Socialists who believed that many of the IWW's ideas were right on the mark. For instance, the IWW's emphasis upon direct action at the workplace, including the use of the general strike, which they believed to be a wholly appropriate strategy to combat this country's increasingly powerful and diverse industrial complex. In addition, the IWW's commitment to direct action would strengthen the workers sense of sacrifice and solidarity. As Wyatt Thompson saw it, "The general strike is simply putting into effect the old labor motto, 'an injury to one is an injury to all'."[96] Equally important was the IWW's leadership in criticizing the craft form of labor organization and the call to workers to create industrial unions that would be the building blocks of a new society by providing a training ground "in which rank and file decide all questions for themselves."[97]

The philosophy and tactics of the militant Socialists had a familiar ring to many Italians in the upper Kanawha valley. The very years which marked the surge of immigration into southern West Virginia were also a time when a movement of revolutionary syndicalism was growing in Italy. In many places in the Old Country, this syndicalist movement built upon anarchist roots and other forms of rebel protests which won a majority of the delegates to the Congress of the Italian Socialist Party at the time of the General Strike of 1904 and had gained control of several labor chambers by 1906. Even more than their counterparts in the American Socialist movement, these Italian syndicalists maintained that participation in electoral and parliamentary activity should be replaced by direct action through unions with a truly revolutionary orientation.[98] And, while it is difficult at this point to make links between specific Italian syndicalists and the left-wing West Virginia Socialists opposing the Hatfield settlement, the connection appears considerable.

Infused with the anarcho-syndicalism of their homeland, the Italians of the upper Kanawha valley joined the militant Socialists in accusing the regular District 17 officers of demonstrating their conservative, bourgeois mentality by being party to the Hatfield settlement and "selling out" the rank and file. Beginning in the spring of 1914, each convention of District 17 was marked by increasing turmoil as activists like Frank Keeney, Fred Mooney, and the Lusk brothers worked to oust the administration of Thomas Cairns and to refashion the union body into an organization controlled by the rank and file.[99] At the same time, local unions sympathetic to the rebels' objectives began petitioning UMWA President John P. White to seek the recall from West Virginia of national representatives Thomas Haggerty and Joe Vasey, and the removal of Thomas Cairns as district president.[100]

The officials of District 17 realized that the challenge of the militant Socialists was growing so serious that counter measures were necessary. As one of the district officials put it, "It is time to take the bull by the horn and give these disorganizers and disrupters the same dose (of medicine) that they have gotten in Illinois, Iowa, and Kansas, namely expulsion."[101] The special targets of such expulsion were Frank Keeney, Fred Mooney, William Ray, and Walter Deal, all of whom were to be brought up on charges of violating their union oaths. Fred Mooney claimed that he and the other rebels were "shadowed" wherever they went and were hounded to death through the pages of the *Miner's Herald*, a newspaper the district leaders had established to counter the *Labor Argus* of Charleston and the *Labor Star* of Huntington, both of which championed the militant socialist position. The district also fired Harold Houston as the union's legal counsel because of his sympathy with the rebels.[102]

Undaunted, the rebels in District 17 were able to force a special convention in the summer of 1915 to consider charges that District President Tom Cairns, aided by Thomas Haggerty, had used fraudulent means to win office in December of 1914. When the rebels' charges were finally brought to a vote on July 14, they failed to be sustained by four votes. Irate, the rebels bolted their convention and headed for Charleston's Grant Hotel where they established a new UMWA district to which they gave the number 30 and claimed as the only legitimate representative of the miners in West Virginia.[103] Within days, the new district's ranks were swollen by miners who had left District 29 in disgust over the exoneration of their organization's president on similar charges. Miners from the Coal River section of nearby Boone County also joined District 30 and by the end of the month, representatives of seventy-six local unions had gathered in Eskdale to support the new organization.[104]

One of the first actions of District 30 was to attempt to secure recognition from the national union. Frank Keeney, Lawrence Dwyer, and John Workman laid the new district's case before the UMWA's National Executive Board in Indianapolis during the second week of September 1915. The heart of the rebels' claim as the only legitimate representative of West Virginia coal miners was that the existing districts increasingly viewed themselves as junior partners in the American capitalist system and existed only to collect dues and keep the mining corporations happy.[105] Unimpressed, the national executive board turned the rebels down, stating that District 30 had no standing as a legitimate suborganization of the union. Furthermore, the board warned that any local unions that continued to recognize District 30 would lose their charters. In addition, the national office of the UMWA sent a special commission to Charleston with the authority to expel and seek the arrest of any officer of District 30 who continued to use the union's name. Disappointed but undaunted, Keeney and his colleagues decided to take their claim to the general convention of the UMWA which was scheduled for January of 1916.[106]

When UMWA President White learned that delegates from District 30 would present their case to the national union, he devised a plan to head off what was sure to be a significant floor fight at the convention. White persuaded Mother Jones to arrange a pre-convention meeting for him with the delegation from District 30.[107] At the subsequent meeting the District 30 committee included an influential Italian activist, John Bruttinate. White told the delegation that it was of utmost importance to the prospects for a wage increase that the

coal operators not see the union divided. The District 30 delegates agreed provided that the officers of all districts in southern West Virginia resigned until a
supervised election could be held. Allegedly, Lawrence Rogers of 29, Tom Cairns
of 17, and Keeney of 30, all signed the peace proposal on January 21, 1916, and
a committee was appointed to set up the election process. However, when the
convention ended with no word from the committee on the election, Keeney
and his comrades returned to West Virginia believing that they had been set
up.[108] Keeney maintained that John White could still have rectified the situation
by wiring District 30 no later than February 2 of the national office's intention to
keep its agreement. When no word came, one hundred delegates met at Eskdale
on February 3 to establish a new organization, the West Virginia Mine Workers.[109]

The new union delegation lost no time in institutionalizing the principles
for which they had been fighting. The rebels elected officers who, they boasted,
represented the ethnic and racial elements characteristic of the mine workforce
in the region. Rock Oliver and Tony Stafford, for example, were chosen to serve
on the West Virginia Mine Workers executive board. The Eskdale Convention
also selected a committee to draft a constitution for the new union which would
then be submitted to the rank and file for final approval. In this and other actions the rebels declared that their union "shall be a movement of the men who
dig the coal. The miners themselves shall govern the new organization. In every
matter vital to their interests, they alone shall have a voice. Officials shall be the
servants and not the masters of the union."[110]

For the West Virginia Mine Workers, nothing better symbolized the contrast between their philosophy and that of the regular UMWA district leaders
more than the democratic manner by which the secessionists pledged all future
contracts would be obtained. First, the secessionists produced signed petitions
to convince the operators that the WVMW had the largest following among the
miners in the Cabin Creek and Coal River areas. Next, the new organization
elected their scale committee which was charged to solicit input from local
unions and negotiate a tentative agreement. The agreement was then referred
back to local unions for any recommended changes. This latter process took
more than four weeks during which there was allegedly none of the "ramming
down the throat processes" which the secessionists claimed was characteristic
of the Haggerty- Cairns style of leadership. Finally, the agreement was to be
amended as necessary in a joint convention of operators and miners and then
resubmitted to the local unions for final approval. Although slower and more
cumbersome, it was claimed that this process would produce not just a contract, but democratic compact.[111]

Despite the optimism of its founders, the West Virginia Mine Workers
lasted barely two months. Erosion of support was evident from the beginning.

The new organization's leadership blamed this falling away on misrepresentations and strong-arm tactics used by the UMWA. While there is some evidence to support this claim, the larger problem appears to have been that many of the miners in the West Virginia Mine Workers became increasingly uneasy about the idea of a dual mine workers' union.[112] This sentiment mushroomed when word got around that Districts 17 and 29 of the UMWA had been placed in the hands of appointed trustees after all. Discontent reached a critical point in early April 1916 when the UMWA called a strike on Cabin Creek and Coal River to demonstrate that the West Virginia Mine Workers could claim only one-third of the miners in those places. The UMWA appeared to be correct as the strike was reasonably successful in spite of some strenuous efforts by the WVMW to get the miners back to work. Seeing the handwriting on the wall, the West Virginia Mine Workers, in a plan brokered by Mother Jones, agreed that they would abide by the results of a referendum conducted on Cabin Creek and Coal River to determine whom the miners wanted to represent them.[113]

The miners of Cabin Creek and Coal River mine regions voted overwhelmingly in favor of returning to the ranks of the United Mine Workers of America. While this referendum represented a rejection of a separate or independent mine workers' union, it did not necessarily symbolize a rejection of the revolutionary Socialist leaders and the principles which had inspired their secessionist movement. In fact, by the end of 1916 the miners of District 17 had turned to that leadership for direction. Under the supervision of tellers from the national union, Frank Keeney, William Petry, and Fred Mooney were elected into the top positions of the district. Moreover, even though these leaders and their allies had to make a tactical retreat, they had apparently lost little of their enthusiasm for the efficacy of militant industrial unionism as the proper vehicle for a reshaping of the American social order. As they took office they relished the news that a recent general strike in Belgium had been so successful and even helped to expand the franchise to workers in that country.[114]

As a result of the Paint Creek-Cabin Creek Strike and its turbulent aftermath, the Italians had increasingly become an integral part of coal mine union movement in the upper Kanawha valley. By 1913, Italians were regularly elected into top local union positions at Boomer and, within a year or so, they were represented on the executive board of District 17.[115] Furthermore, under the Keeney administration, Italians would be appointed as district organizers. The most notable of the latter was Tony Stafford who became a major force in extending the UMWA into Raleigh County.

The integration of Boomer Italians into leadership positions in a left-wing socialist-dominated administration in District 17 is a reflection of the major theme which undergirds this essay. These immigrants were not individuals so hindered by conservative Old World social psychologies that they were unable to improve their social and economic conditions through cooperative and collective behavior. Perhaps their situation will prove to be exceptional. Only continued and, hopefully, comparative research on other Italian groups in West Virginia will finally decide the issue. However, some things we do know about them provide hints as to why they seem to deal so effectively as a group with challenges in their new world environment.

In a number of ways the Boomer Italians defy conventional wisdom about such immigrants. To use one important example, these immigrants are supposed to be mainly young, single males who will return to the home country as soon as possible. However, in 1910 a little over 45 percent of the Italian male immigrants in Boomer were thirty or older which would suggest a certain degree of maturity. In addition, well over half of the Italian males in the Boomer area were married and over half of all the households in the communities consisted of a married couple, their children and one or two close relatives from which it might be fair to infer that these immigrants may have been more commited to a permanent future in America.[116] This older, more settled population may also have come to this country with considerable experience in associational activities since Calabria, the province of origin for so many of them, possessed one of the highest concentrations of rural voluntary organizations in Italy.[117]

If these social characteristics have produced a proclivity towards a class-consciousness already developed in Italy, then the experience of Boomer Italians in the coalfields of southern West Virginia would surely have intensified it. In fact, their recognition in the Kanawha coalfields of a familiar form of class-consciousness seems to have helped them transcend ethnic normal boundaries and become a force that shaped events as much as it was shaped by them. This tendency was recognized by a number of their American counterparts. For example, Duff Scott, whose brother Brandt was the Socialist justice of the peace in Cabin Creek, captured something of this impact when he claimed:

> They (the Italians) played a big part in these things (strike). I recall one time we got whipped bad in the early days of the Cabin Creek-Paint Creek strike and we was down at Cabin Creek Junction and we seen a gang comin' from the river. My brother said, "Oh, boy, we got 'em now. Here comes the Boomer Talys and things are gonna get hot."[118]

NOTES

1. *Parkersburg Sentinel,* 2 Sept. 1910; Bureau of the Census, *Thirteenth Census of the United States Taken in the Year 1910, Population* (Washington, D.C.: GPO, 1916). For the most thorough discussion to date of the recruitment, deployment, and exploitation of immigrant miners in West Virginia, see Kenneth Bailey, "A Judicious Mixture: Negroes and Immigrants in the West Virginia Mines, 1890-1917;" *West Virginia History,* 34 (Jan. 1973): 141-61.

2. Evelyn L. K. Harris and F. J. Krobs, *From Humble Beginnings: West Virginia State Federation of Labor,* 1903-1957 (Charleston: West Virginia Labor History Publication Fund, 1960), 16-20.

3. Elizabeth Cometti, "Trends in Italian Emigration," *Western Political Quarterly* 1 (1958): 4.

4. Phillip Conley, *History of the Coal Industry of West Virginia,* (Charleston: West Virginia Education Association Foundation, 1960), 81-4.

5. *Fayette Journal,* 17 June 1909.

6. W. P. Tams, *The Smokeless Coal Fields of West Virginia* (Morgantown, W. Va.: West Virginia Univ. Press, 2001), 61-3; Walter Thurmond, *The Logan Coal Fields of West Virginia* (Morgantown: West Virginia Univ. Library, 1964); Harry M. Caudill, *Night Comes to the Cumberlands: A Biography of a Depressed Area* (Boston: Little, Brown and Co., 1963), 103-4. For a discussion of the similarities between pre-industrial folk cultures of Southern Italy and Southern Appalachia, see Margaret R. Wolfe, "Aliens in Southern Appalachia, 1900-1920: The Italian Experience," *Virginia Magazine of History and Biography* 87 (Jan. 1974), 141-61.

7. Fayette County Chamber of Commerce, *History of Fayette County West Virginia* (Oak Hill, W. Va.: Fayette County Chamber of Commerce, 1993), 86-8.

8. Carl Chafins, "The Italians of Boomer" (seminar paper, Marshall University Graduate College, May 1993); David Tamplin, interview by Fred Barkey, 18 July 1969, Boomer, W. Va.; Shirley Donnally, interview by Fred Barkey, 20 July 1969, Oak Hill, W. Va. (Tamplin was a life-long resident of Boomer. Donnally was a well-known local historian of Fayette County; interviews in author's collection).

9. John Cavalier, *Smithers, W.Va.,: A History* (n.p.).

10. J. T. Peters and H. B. Garden, *History of Fayette County* (Charleston, 1926), 272-4.

11. Peters and Carden, *History of Fayette County,* 448-98.

12. John Cavalier, *Panorama of Fayette County* (Parsons, W. Va., 1985), 261.

13. Peters and Carden, *History of Fayette County,* 273-5.

14. *Annual Report of the Commission of Mines* (1903).

15. *Fayette Journal,* March 5, 1903. Both a written document and tradition date the Hanna acquisition of the Boomer property in 1902. However, the date appears to be 1903. *Fayette Journal,* May 1903.

16. The scale of the late-nineteenth-century influx of Italians into Fayette County can be seen in data from the Twelfth and Thirteenth U.S. Censuses.

17. Maier B. Fox, *United We Stand: The United Mine Workers of America: 1890-1990* (Washington, D.C.: United Mine Workers of America, 1990), 64-5.

18. *The Charleston Gazette,* 20 June 1902.

19. *The Fayette Journal,* 26 June, 21 Aug., 28 Aug., and 25 Sept. 1902.

20. The miners from Boomer and Longacre belonged to UMWA Local Union 1831. Harewood's local was 2018. *Minutes of the Joint Convention of Operators and Miners of the Kanawha District* (Huntington, April 14-15, 1903), Kanawha Coal Operators Papers, West Virginia Department of Archives and History, The Cultural Center, Charleston, W. Va.

21. *The Charleston Gazette,* 3 March, 14 March 1903; *Fayette Journal,* 26 February 1903.

22. The Italian immigration from southern Italy to the Boomer area for the period 1903 to 1915 appears to be at approximately a four-to-one ratio with those from northern Italy. Declaration of Intention Records, Department of Archives and History, Cultural Center, Charleston, W. Va. Originals available at the Fayette County Courthouse.

23. Dino Cinel, "The Seasonal Emigration of Italians in the Nineteenth Century from Internal to International Destinations," *Journal of External Studies* 10 (1982): 43-68.

24. See Declaration of Intention Records, Archives and History, Charleston, W. Va.

25. Chafins, "Italians of Boomer."

26. Jurg K. Siegenthaler, "Sicilian Economic Change since 1860," *The Journal of European Economic History* 2 (1973): 363-415.

27. The San Giovanni-Cacurri nexus apparently provided native sons to northcentral West Virginia. Some of the immigrants to the Boomer area had first come to Fairmont or Clarksburg. Sam LeRose, interview by Fred Barkey, 18 September 2001, Saint Albans, W. Va.; Zot DelRio, interview by Fred Barkey, 15 June 1985, Clarksburg, W. Va. (author's collection); Charles H. McCormick, "The Death of Constable Riggs: Ethnic Conflict in Marion County in the World War I Era," *West Virginia History* 52 (1993): 33-9.

28. Franco Ramella, "Emigration from an Area of Intense Industrial Development: The Case of Northwestern Italy," in *A Century of European Migrations, 1830-1930,* ed. Rudolph J. Vecoli (Urbana: Univ. of Illinois Press, 1991), 261-74.

29. Dina Dalporto, "True Life of a Mother," unpub. memoir of Dina Dalporto, 20 April 1926, Longacre, W. Va. (author's collection).

30. Dave Tamplin, interview.

31. Otis Rice, *Charleston and the Kanawha Valley* (Woodland Heights, Pa.: Windsor Publications, 1981), 76-7. There were more Italians employed by the Fairmont Coal Company of Marion County. However, they were not as concentrated as those in the Boomer area. See *Annual Report of the West Virginia Department of Mines, 1908* (Charleston: Tribune Printing Co., 1909), 93, 117.

32. *The Fayette Journal,* 16 March, 6 July 1905.

33. Oscar T. Barck and Nelson M. Blake, *Since 1900: A History of the United States in Our Times* (New York: Macmillan Co., 1952), 56-60.

34. *Charleston Gazette,* 19 and 25 Jan. 1908; Wheeling *Intelligencer,* 3 February 1908; *Huntington Dispatch,* 6 Oct. 1908.

35. Cleveland Toney, interview by Fred Barkey, 19 July 1968, Dothan, W. Va.

36. Thomas Felts to Justus Collins, 22 March 1908, Bluefield, W. Va., Justus Collins Papers, West Virginia and Regional History Collection, West Virginia Univ., Morgantown, W. Va.
37. *Labor Argus,* 24 July 1908.
38. *Fayette Journal,* 26 April 1909.
39. *Charleston Gazette,* 12 April 1909; *Montgomery News,* 28 May 28 1909.
40. *Fayette Journal,* 4 June 1909.
41. *Bluefield Evening Leader,* 28 May 1909; *Fayette Journal,* 28 May 1909.
42. *Huntington Advertiser,* 26 May 1909.
43. *Fayette Journal,* 28 May 1909.
44. *Fayette Journal,* 3 and 4 June 1909.
45. *Charleston Daily Mail,* 6 June 1909.
46. Dave Tamplin, interview.
47. *Charleston Daily Mail,* 7 and 8 June 1909.
48. *Fayette Journal,* 8 June 1909.
49. *Fayette Journal,* 10 June 1909.
50. *Charleston Gazette,* 9 June 1909.
51. *Fayette Journal,* 10 and 17 June 1909; Guy Yockaway, interview by Fred Barkey, 15 June 2001, St. Albans, W. Va. (author's collection).
52. *Fayette Tribune and Free Press,* 17 June 1909; *Fayette Journal,* 17 June 1909.
53. *Charleston Gazette,* 10 June 1909.
54. *Fayette Tribune and Free Press,* 17 June 1909.
55. Ibid.
56. Chafins, "Italians of Boomer," 11-13.
57. Cavalier, *History of Smithers.*
58. Chafins, "Italians of Boomer," 15.
59. Ibid.
60. *Fayette Tribune,* 27 May 1909.
61. *Fayette Journal,* 8 July 1909.
62. Fox, *United We Stand,* 148-9.
63. *Charleston Daily Mail,* 24 April 1912.
64. *Charleston Daily Mail,* 26 April 1912.
65. Charles B. Crawford, "The Mine War on Cabin Creek and Paint Creek, West Virginia, 1912-1913." (master's thesis, University of Kentucky, 1939), 22-3; John R. Commons et al., *History of Labour in the United States*, Vol. 2 (New York: Macmillan Co., 1935), 330; *Huntington Socialist and Labor Star,* 4 Aug. 1912.
66. *Fayette Sun,* 30 July 1912.
67. Fox, *United We Stand,* 148.
68. *Charleston Daily Mail,* 30 July 1912.
69. The Italians remained on strike despite strenuous efforts by District President Tom Cairns and William Craigo. *Fayette Sun,* 13 Sept. 1912.
70. For a good description of this conduit, see Adjutant General Elliott to William E. Glasscock, 17 February 1913, National Guard Papers, West Virginia Department of Archives and History, Cultural Center, Charleston, W. Va.

71. Wyatt Thompson to Price Williams, West Virginia Labor History Association Collection, West Virginia Department of Archives and History, Cultural Center, Charleston, W.Va. Though sparse, this correspondence is an invaluable source on Thompson's life and attitude on a variety of subjects.

72. David Tamplin, interview by Alicia Tyler, time and place unknown (author's collection).

73. Ibid.

74. *Fayette Sun*, 17 Sept. 1912.

75. *Fayette Sun, 8* Oct. 1912.

76. *Montgomery News,* 1 Oct. 1912.

77. *Fayette Sun,* 8 Oct. 1912.

78. *Kanawha Citizen,* 5 Oct. 1912; Crawford, "The Mine War," 41.

79. The Socialists carried the Cabin Creek Magisterial District in Kanawha County and the adjoining Fells Magisterial District in Fayette County which includes the Italian communities. This meant that all local officials including law enforcement were party members. Frederick Allan Barkey, "The Socialist Party in West Virginia from 1898-1920: A Study in Working Class Radicalism" (Ph.D. diss., University of Pittsburgh, 1971), chap. 4.

80. Crawford, "The Mine War," 22-3; *Huntington Herald Dispatch,* 17 Sept. 1912.

81. Joe Mino, interview by Fred Barkey, 28 May 1968, Eskdale, W.Va. (author's collection).

82. U.S. Bureau of the Census, *Thirteenth Census of the United States taken in the Year 1910, Population* (Washington, D.C.: GPO, 1916); Fells Magisterial District; Kanawha County Marriage Records, Book 5, 112; Nellie's birth is found in Birth Records, Kanawha County, 14 Feb. 1890.

83. *Kanawha Citizen,* 22 November 1912.

84. Ibid.

85. *Kanawha Citizen,* 27 and 30 Nov. 1912.

86. John Brown, *Constitutional Government Overthrown in West Virginia* (Charleston: privately printed, 1913), 14; Broce Reed, Testimony before Senate Committee on Education and Labor, in *Conditions in the Paint Creek District, W.Va.,* 63rd Cong., 1st sess., vol. 1 (Washington, D.C.: GPO, 1913), 25.

87. Shirley Donnally, *Historical Notes on Fayette County, W. Va.* (Oak Hill, W.Va., n.d.), 77; *Parsons Advocate*, 14 March 1968; *National Cyclopedia of Biography*, Vol. 53 (1971): 36.

88. *Fayette Sun*, 25 March 1913.

89. Edward M. Steel, *The Court Martial of Mother Jones* (Lexington, Ky.: University Press of Kentucky, 1995), ix, 25.

90. *Appeal to Reason*, 21 June 1913.

91. *Raleigh Register,* 5 May 1913.

92. *Fayette Sun*, June 5, 1913.

93. *Appeal To Reason*, 21 June 1913.

94. Testimony, George Williams, U.S. Senate, Committee on Education and Labor, *Conditions in the Paint Creek District, West Virginia*, Vol. 2 (Washington, D.C.: GPO, 1913), 185.

95. West Virginia, Mine Investigation Commission, *Report of the West Virginia Mine Investigation Commission* (Charleston: Tribune Printing Co., 1912), 10.

96. *Huntington Socialist and Labor Star*, Aug., July, and Nov. 1913.

97. Wyatt Thompson, "How Victory Was Turned into Settlement," *International Socialist Review* 14 (July 1913): 17.

98. Thomas R. Sykes, "The Practice of Revolutionary Syndicalism in Italy: 1905-1910" (Ph.D. diss., Columbia Univ., 1974), i-x.

99. *The Argus-Star*, 10 Feb. 1916.

100. Ibid.

101. Wheeling *Intelligencer*, 23 Jan., and 30 March 1914.

102. *Miner's Herald*, 19 and 26 Sept. 1912.

103. *Charleston Gazette*, 18 July 1915.

104. *Argus-Star*, 6 May 1915, 13 April 1916.

105. *Argus-Star*, 6 May 1915, 13 April 1916.

106. *Fayette Journal*, 1 July 1915. John White also claimed that any unwarranted interference on his part would threaten the long-standing principle of local autonomy that was so important to the UMWA.

107. *Fayette Tribune*, 8 Feb. 1916.

108. *Argus-Star*, 10 Feb. 1916.

109. *Argus-Star*, 30 March 1916.

110. *Argus-Star*, 13 April 1916.

111. Wyatt Thompson, interview by Fred Barkey, Oct. 13, 1968, Columbus, Ohio.

112. *Argus-Star*, 30 March 1916. For example, miners at Kayford Number Nine on Cabin Creek complained that they could not live up to their contract for fear of being shot.

113. *Montgomery News*, 10 June 1916.

114. *Charleston Daily Mail*, 28 Dec. 1916.

115. James Dean was president of the local union at Boomer in 1913 and he and his brothers were members of the District 17 executive board. *Montgomery News*, 17 Jan. 1913.

116. James Owsten, "The Boomer Italians and the Socialist Vote in the Election of 1912," (humanities paper, Marshall University Graduate College, 1985).

117. The power of the mine community to create class consciousness is dealt with in detail in David Alan Corbin, *Life, Work, and Rebellion in the Coal Fields: The Southern West Virginia Miners, 1880-1922* (Urbana: Univ. of Illinois Press, 1981).

118. Duff Scott, interview by Fred Barkey, 23 Feb. 1968 (author's collection).

"Cemetery for the Polish and Italian Victims of the Monongah Explosion, 1907."
West Virginia and Regional History Collection, West Virginia University Libraries,
Morgantown, W.Va.

Uneven Americanization: Italian Immigration to Marion County 1900-1925

William B. Klaus

Citizens of Fairmont, West Virginia, observed Columbus Day in 1912 by granting the "compatriots of Christopher Columbus," as the *Fairmont Times* dubbed Italian immigrants, the "freedom of the city." The day showcased Americanized Italian solidarity. The "sturdy" and "intelligent" natives of the "Sunny Land" staged a parade that was headed by both Italian and American flags. Five hundred members of Italian civic societies reportedly marched along the city streets in an orderly procession. A reporter for the *Fairmont Times* conspicuously noted the sobriety and orderliness of the Italians who participated in the event's festival, speeches, and other performances. The celebration's message was clear: the city's Italians themselves had taken up the task of Americanization and were worthy of joining the city's sober, law-abiding middle class.[1]

The celebration did not resonate with all Italian immigrants in Marion County, home of Fairmont and several other smaller independent cities and coal company towns. Three years after the first gala Columbus Day in Fairmont, and just eight miles to the west, between three hundred and six hundred Poles, Russians, "Croatians" (used then as a catch-all for Serbs, Hungarians, and Slovenes), and Italians started a wildcat strike to retaliate against the coal operators' new practice of deducting the cost of dynamite primer shots, which were purportedly being wasted through carelessness, from the miners' wages. On February 15, 1915, the strikers congregated between coal camps in the county's Lincoln District and marched along dirt roads behind both an American flag and a red flag. They armed themselves with makeshift weapons and admonished more to join. The message of this particular "parade" was more explicit than the one that marked Columbus Day. The miners carried a banner that read, according to one account, "United We Stand; Divided We Fall. Give Us Justice; Or Nothing At All."[2]

The U.S. census, naturalization records, and extant records of the Italian Catholic parishes in Marion County confirm the underlying meaning of the starkly contrasting parades: Two versions of ethnic solidarity had coalesced from the multifaceted experience of Italian immigrants in Marion county. One group was

Chart 8.1
Italian Immigrants and their Children, Marion County, 1900 – 1920

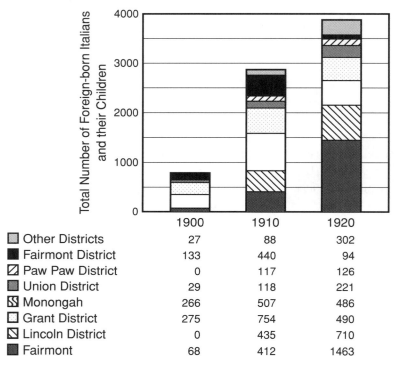

	1900	1910	1920
☐ Other Districts	27	88	302
■ Fairmont District	133	440	94
▨ Paw Paw District	0	117	126
☐ Union District	29	118	221
▨ Monongah	266	507	486
☐ Grant District	275	754	490
▨ Lincoln District	0	435	710
■ Fairmont	68	412	1463

Source: U.S. Manuscript Census schedules, 1900, 1910 and 1920, for Marion County, W. Va.

made up of the Italian merchants, miners, glassworkers, and women who lived in Fairmont and, to a lesser degree, Monongah and the county's other independent towns (see chart 8.1). Many of them migrated to Marion County around the turn of the century, just as the county was undergoing an industrial expansion, and some of them formed the social infrastructure that underlies the enduring Italian-American presence in northern West Virginia. The Italians who lived in the scattered coal company towns that made up Fairmont's hinterland took a different route to Marion County. A large number of them arrived later than their urban counterparts, and the enormous power of the coal industry limited their public acts of self-determination to working-class conflicts. The main difference between the two groups was not necessarily a matter of working-class consciousness alone. Coal miners lived in both the city and in the countryside in Marion county, and many coal miners pledged allegiance to the American flag just as fervently as Italian merchants. The generational lore of Italian immigrants who were experienced in American ways, the channels of immigration from Italy to Marion County, and attitudes toward Catholicism divided the city-dwelling Italians from their country-dwelling counterparts.

Italians in both groups had been an integral part of the industrial expansion that took place in Marion County in the 1910s. The county's coal industry recovered from the Panic of 1893 and underwent a process of expansion and consolidation. The number of operations in the Fairmont coalfield peaked in the 1920s, but overdevelopment, the concentration of investment in the coal industry alone, mine mechanization, and the resulting pervasive labor discord started the coalfield into a drawn-out tailspin starting just after World War I. Ignoring signs of overdevelopment, the county's industrial elite continued to push for further expansion of the coal industry, and Fairmont, which reached a population of 17,851 in 1920 and was the state's sixth largest city, remained a booming commercial and financial hub for decades. The city also grew into a manufacturing, retail, and service center that included a variety of glass manufacturers, a box factory, and an assortment of retail services. Surrounding Fairmont was, by 1910, a patchwork of satellite independent cities and towns, coal company towns, and farms, all of which were interconnected by a network of trolley car lines (funded by the county's coal barons and built, in part, by Italian laborers in the 1910s).[3]

Though the Italians held a variety of occupations and lived in diverse settings, the coal industry was the dominant force that pulled Italians into the county. It employed about 70 percent (1,023) of the Italian-born males of working age in 1910 and 72 percent (852) in 1920. By 1923, the county contained one of the largest populations of Italian coal miners in West Virginia: 1,153.[4] Yet the coal industry's long domination of Marion County did not necessarily limit Italian identity to a working-class consciousness alone. The experience of Italians was more multifaceted than the disproportionate number of Italian coal miners would suggest.

The details of the 1915 wildcat strike and the 1912 Columbus Day parade underscore just how uneven Americanization was among Italian immigrants in Marion county. The exact number of Italians involved in the 1915 wildcat strike remains uncertain, but it is known that their numbers were fewer than the other ethnicities that took part in the episode. Thirty of the 134 individuals indicted for participating in the strike's violence were Italian. Some contemporaries suspected that the smaller number of Italians had masterminded the strike. This is not surprising, considering that the "black hand" had already gained notoriety in the region, and the *Fairmont Times* had given dogged coverage to the group's murderous plots. One historian suggests that the theory of Italian leadership might have some merit, but one ethnic group working alone could not have marshaled the wills of so many other ethnic groups for several days.[5]

The strike was bound to fail because the miners were ignorant of organized work stoppages, and they lacked the backing of the United Mine Workers of America or any other labor group. Moreover, the county's powerful elite could not tolerate such rebellion for long. Judging from the tone of the *Fairmont Times*, the particular display of red flags, which was perceived as a symbol of anarchy, alarmed and vexed the law abiding citizens more so than the work stoppage and various acts of vandalism. Only scant evidence suggests that the strikers had tangible connections to such national anarcho-syndicalist organizations as the Industrial Workers of the World or "Wobblies." Individual Italian radicals who organized small groups were not uncommon in coal mining regions. Perhaps such an individual was responsible for sparking the strike, but the strike's lack of organization suggests an unfolding of events more similar to a peasant revolt than an ideological battle.[6] Irregardless of the strike's impetus, the county's leaders could not let such a display of rebellion stand. The coal operators called in mine guards, and a posse of thirteen, led by Constable William Ross Riggs and accompanied by only one Slavic interpreter, set out from the county seat of Fairmont on February 20, with arrest warrants in hand, to pacify what some perceived as a mob threatening the county's fundamental stability.[7]

The trip that Constable Riggs's posse took to meet up with the strikers reveals something of the nature of Marion County's industrial landscape. The posse started out from its urban base in Fairmont and took a trolley eight miles west to the town of Farmington in the county's Lincoln District. The original plan involved making arrests in coal camps that were several miles from Farmington, marching the prisoners back to the town, then returning to Fairmont on a regularly scheduled trolley. The county constable at Farmington, knowing the attitude of the strikers and fearing a violent confrontation, warned off the posse, but they proceeded undaunted. The plan fell apart when the posse met and clashed with the strikers while on the way to arrest individual miners accused of vandalism.[8]

In other words, thirteen armed white lawmen rushed into an area controlled by hundreds of foreign-born strikers, many of whom did not speak English. Their route by trolley and dirt road led them from their base in Fairmont, to a smaller, but still "safe" independent town, then finally, on foot, into a hinterland controlled by coal companies and, for the time being, foreign-born miners brandishing red flags and makeshift clubs. Though the physical distance that they traveled was relatively short and interconnected by established transportation routes, the posse crossed a distinct social border between the urban landscape of Fairmont and the city's rural-industrial hinterland.

The ill-conceived plan emboldened the strikers and cost Constable Riggs his life. The posse's arrest of a fellow miner provoked the strikers, who grew into a mob. The strikers liberated the prisoner who had already been taken, trapped the posse, and proceeded to assault them. Riggs, who had gained fame for enforcing prohibition, barely escaped, but was mortally wounded and died days later on February 24. The miners' "victory" was bound to be temporary. The strikers now faced a local government that resolved to avenge the death of a local hero, and an estimated five hundred armed volunteers scoured the countryside, confiscating numerous pistols, knives, clubs, and one red flag. The strikers inevitably exhausted their resources, and all of them disbanded by March.[9]

The strike is a remarkable contrast to the Columbus Day festivities, held annually from 1912-1915, when county and city officials willingly turned over control to Italians. The exact origins and planning of the day's celebration are unclear, but a few details can be gleaned from newspapers. The *Fairmont Times* cites the "Christopher Columbus Society" for planning the event, and describes five hundred members of other Italian civic organizations marching in the parade, which was probably an exaggeration, considering that Fairmont's population of foreign-born Italians and their offspring was 412. City officials even swore in Tom (also known as "Tony") Deligatti, described as "one of the best known Italians of the city," as an honorary sheriff for the day. A few details about Deligatti himself can be pieced together from the manuscript census and from city directories. The 1900 census lists Deligatti as a coal miner who lived in Fairmont. Sometime between 1900 and 1910, he took ownership of a fruit stand. In 1920, the Deligattis' household included a twenty-four-year-old son, Frank, who was the owner of a tailor shop.[10] The parade showed that the city embraced Italians who, like Deligatti, had become fixtures in the city's day-to-day marketplace by 1910. The sentiments and the patriotism showcased on Columbus Day were not imposed; rather, Italians had achieved a sufficient number and status to take figurative control of the city.

Two different social processes shaped the standpoints of Italians who brandished red flags and marched along dirt roads and Italians who pledged allegiance to both the American and the Italian flags and marched along city streets. Italians were certainly split by stark divisions of class and gender. Italian merchants, coal miners, skilled craftsmen, mothers, boarding- house proprietresses, and the native-born children of Italians, all experienced immigration to Marion County in particular ways. The diversity of the social and economic conditions included within the county added to the social stratification of Italians. The social landscape of northcentral West Virginia was not a common denominator.

What knowledge and experiences the Italians did share stemmed from their common origins in Italy. It is generally accepted that a disproportionate number of Italian immigrants came from southern Italy, and northcentral West Virginia is not an exception. Studies of Italian immigration have also shown that immigrants from particular Italian regions often had common destinations in the United States, but most studies of Italian immigrants have focused on large urban areas. Extant naturalization records for largely rural Marion County show a remarkably consistent pattern. During the period of 1908-1935, 1,251 Italians declared their intention to become citizens of the United States. Of those declarations, 1,008 list identifiable towns in Italy (the remaining entries are either omitted, illegible, or ambiguous). The bulk of immigrants were *contadini* from Calabria. Four hundred twenty-nine or 43 percent of Italians applying for citizenship hailed from the southern region. The next three largest regions represented in the naturalization records span the area south of Rome and north of Naples: Molise (196), Campania (132), and Abruzzo (79).[11]

That most of the Italians in Marion County originated from southern Italy is unsurprising. More compelling is the pattern of emigration from particular towns and provinces to such a relatively small, perhaps even unobvious, destination as Marion County. Of those Italians from Calabria, 236 originated from the province of Cosenza, and 172 of them came from one village, San Giovanni in Fiore. Likewise, 118 of 142 Italians from the province of Reggio Calabria hailed from the coastal city of Caulonia. Together, immigrants from just the two towns of San Giovanni in Fiore and Caulonia made up a full one-third of the Italians who petitioned for naturalization in Marion County during the years 1908-1935.[12] Several factors could have caused such a pattern. The Italians could have been recruited to Marion County by padrones, Italians working as domestic and international labor agents. It is well known that immigrants also formed chains of emigration in which kinship and local identity were links. It is likely that padrones, chain emigration, and the coal industry's powerful draw, together formed a nexus between Italy and Marion County.

With one notable exception, most of the regions represented in the naturalization records show a disproportionate number of petitioners working in coal. Sixty-four percent of immigrants from the province of Cosenza listed their occupation on the petition for naturalization as coal miners. Just over half of immigrants from the region of Molise identified themselves as coal miners as well. Thirty-eight of the sixty-four immigrants from the village of Bagnoli del Trigno (in the present-day province of Isernia) worked in the county's glass industry. One particular glass manufacturer, Owens Bottle Factory, which started

Chart 8.2
Regional Origins of Marion County Italians, 1908–1935

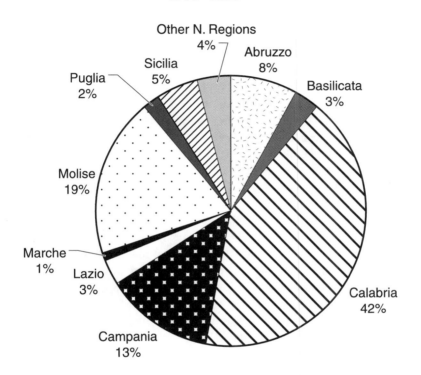

production in Fairmont sometime after 1910, employed at least eighty Italian immigrants in 1920, causing the number of Italians employed in glass to rise above the number employed in coal.[13] A number of immigrants from Bagnoli del Trigno probably worked in the coal industry, but did not apply for naturalization. Still, the trend of immigrants from a particular town working in the glass industry underscores the diversity of Fairmont's economy.

The concentration of Italians from one region also suggests that the Italian identity of Marion County is better understood as a *Calabrian* or southern Italian identity rather than simply "Italian." This does not imply that the Italians were a homogenous group of peasants. The historian Rudolph Vecoli succinctly describes the Italian countryside as "rural cities," complete with social stratification. Still, some generalizations and comparisons are useful in understanding

how the southern Italians perceived Marion County. They were, Vecoli continues, clannish and disinclined toward factory labor, and a vast majority of
Calabrians worked in agriculture. One study of the province of Cosenza showed
that only 1 percent of the population worked in industries.[14] One can imagine
that Marion County was remotely familiar to Calabrians. Most Italians were engaged in a single occupation: coal. In Marion County, most Italians experienced
a set class system of coal operators and other land owners, which was analo-
gous to the vestiges of southern Italy's feudal system. Moreover, a large number of them lived in what was, more or less, a rural setting. The city of Fairmont
was, perhaps, a new social setting for both the immigrants who arrived there
directly and the smaller number of immigrants who remained in the county's
countryside and later moved to the city.

When, where, and through what channels an Italian immigrant arrived in
Marion County determined, more than their common origins, whether they
marched behind the American flag or a red flag in 1915. As a whole, the population of Italians consistently kept pace with the expansion of the county's coal
industry. Starting in 1900, the Fairmont coalfield entered into a period of expansion of coal production and consolidation of coal interests. By 1910, new mines
had opened in the county's Lincoln District, site of the 1915 wildcat strike, and
the mines operating in the Grant District had increased production. During the
period of 1900-1910, the production of coal doubled from just over five million
tons to twelve million. Consequently, the number of Italians living in the Grant
and Lincoln Districts rose considerably in the years 1906, 1907, and 1909.[15]

Italians who had immigrated early in the century and lived in the county
or elsewhere in the United States for ten or more years gravitated toward
Fairmont and the county's other independent towns. In 1920, 579 of the 1,062
foreign-born Italians who had immigrated before 1910 lived in Fairmont or
Monongah. About 40 percent of the foreign-born Italians living in Fairmont had
immigrated to the United States before 1905. The city's diverse economy explains why the Italian population accumulated and grew independently of the
coal industry's changing demands for labor.

By comparison, any measurement of the number of Italians living in
the county's unincorporated places must take into account the population's
dramatic turnovers. The 1910 census lists 475 Italian coal miners who immigrated to Lincoln and Grant Districts between the years 1905-1910, five
years of unparalleled growth in the county's Italian population. By 1920,
the number of Italians who immigrated in that same period had dropped
to 131, but they were soon replaced with yet another wave of immigration
during the period of 1910-15, when the 1920 census records an influx of
188 foreign-born Italians.[16]

Such rapid turnovers are not surprising, considering that most of the Italians who migrated to the Lincoln District in the peak year of 1909 were either single men or married men whose wives remained in Italy. The 1910 census lists seventy-six foreign-born Italians who reported immigrating in the year 1909. Only two of them were women: one of them a wife and the other a seventeen-year-old woman who worked as a clerk in a company store. Forty-one of the remaining seventy-four men were married and listed as boarders, with their wives presumably remaining in Italy. Compared to the Italians who lived in Fairmont, the population that migrated to Marion County's industrial countryside were more transient and more closely tied to the coal industry.[17]

Evidence in the manuscript census also suggests that the Italians who immigrated to the Lincoln and Grant Districts had been either outright recruited by coal officials or had found their way to Marion County through a padrone. The 1900 census records no Italians living in the Lincoln District. The seventy- four Italian miners listed in the 1910 census lived in contiguous dwellings that did not exist in 1900. A somewhat larger enclave of 337 Italians (98 female and 239 male) existed in the Grant District in 1920, though the years of immigration reported by the census are not as uniform as the Lincoln District. The enclaves in both Lincoln and Grant Districts lived in coal company housing.[18] The exact mechanism or individuals behind this pattern remain unclear, but it is apparent that some particular agent had sought out the Italians and had been brought into the area to serve the purposes of the coal industry.

The 1907 Monongah mine disaster temporarily slowed Italian immigration to the region and gives further evidence that coal operators actively sought out a transient supply of Italian labor. On December 6, 1907, the worst coal mine disaster in American history killed a reported total of 361 miners. One hundred seventy-one of them were foreign-born Italians. Subsequently, the 1910 census records a sharp decline in the number of Italians who reported 1908 as their year of immigration. The report made by the Monongah Mines Relief Committee, which oversaw the distribution of relief payments to widows and survivors, shows close ties between Italian miners and kin remaining in Italy. The disaster widowed a total of 112 foreign-born Italian women and left a total of 207 fatherless children. The relief committee located seventy-four of the Italian widows and 122 of the fatherless children living in Italy. The Italian regions of miners killed at Monongah generally coincide with the naturalization records, with one slight variation. The relief committee identified 119 Italian miners whose closest living relatives lived in Italy. The three regions most represented among the dead were Molise (68), Calabria (28), and Campania (10). Twenty-eight miners were from the town of Duronia del Sannio in the region of Molise.[19] In short, a large majority of the

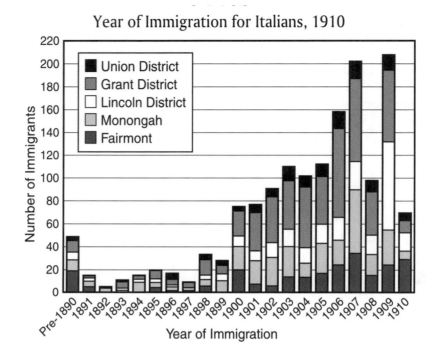

Year of Immigration for Italians, 1910

Italian miners killed in the Monongah disaster were transient laborers from the region of Molise.

Italians who immigrated early in the century and lived in the cities of Fairmont or Monongah had greater opportunities for social mobility and for achieving a higher social status. Scouring newspapers, city directories, and the manuscript census yields numerous Horatio Alger-like stories. Tom Deligatti, Fairmont's "Honorary Sheriff" for Columbus Day, 1912, is one notable example. Like Deligatti, Camillo Salvati immigrated to West Virginia in 1882 and worked constructing railroads. He migrated north to Monongah, worked in the mines, and bought a home in Monongah. The 1910 census lists Salvati as the owner of a general store, and a story in the *Fairmont Times* cites Salvati as a pioneering entrepreneur who rebuilt Monongah after the 1907 disaster and had revived the town's Italian heritage.[20]

For some Italian immigrants, coal mining was neither transient nor necessarily oppressive. Some of them who started in the coal industry before 1900, when mining was still a job that required a miner's skill and knowledge, led relatively stable lives. Angelo Sazrie, for example, immigrated to the United States in 1892 and worked alternately in Marion County as a stone mason and

Chart 8.4
Year of Immigration for Italians, by Residence in Marion County, 1920

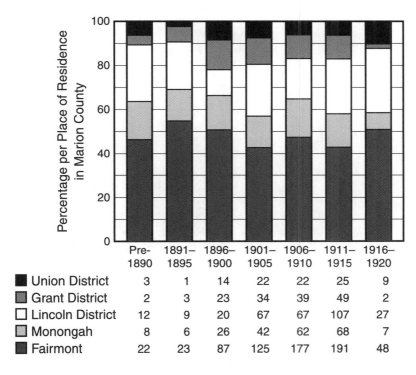

	Pre-1890	1891–1895	1896–1900	1901–1905	1906–1910	1911–1915	1916–1920
■ Union District	3	1	14	22	22	25	9
▨ Grant District	2	3	23	34	39	49	2
☐ Lincoln District	12	9	20	67	67	107	27
▦ Monongah	8	6	26	42	62	68	7
■ Fairmont	22	23	87	125	177	191	48

as a coal miner. He, his wife, who had followed Sazrie to America in 1895, and his six children lived on the outskirts of Fairmont and were homeowners for more than twenty years. In 1920, Sazrie had reached the age of sixty-three and lived with his wife, his nineteen-year-old son, who worked as both a coal miner and a student, and four other children, all of them attending school. Sazrie's neighbor in 1920 was Dominick Stingo, who had immigrated to West Virginia sometime in the 1880s. At the age of seventy-one, Stingo had retired from the coal industry after working in the Fairmont coalfield for at least twenty years. The Stingos' expansive household included ten grandchildren, two daughters-in-law, and their husbands, both of whom were also coal miners, all living under one roof.[21] Whether or not Sazrie and Stingo immigrated to Fairmont with the intention of permanently settling there is uncertain. Irregardless of their intention, their long careers and tenure show that some Italian miners, like Italian

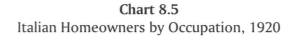

Chart 8.5
Italian Homeowners by Occupation, 1920

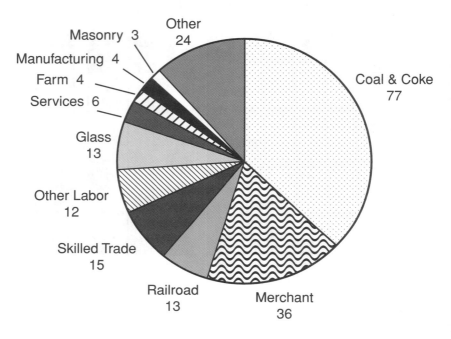

Other 24

Masonry 3

Manufacturing 4

Farm 4

Services 6

Glass 13

Other Labor 12

Skilled Trade 15

Railroad 13

Merchant 36

Coal & Coke 77

Total = 207

Source: U.S. Manuscript Census schedules, 1920, for Marion County, W. Va.

merchants, had become stable members of the larger community of Fairmont. The main difference between them and the more numerous miners in the county's hinterland was that the former arrived earlier and, apparently, of their own accord.

Acknowledging that only a small fraction achieved such success or apparent stability, the aggregate of Italians in the county shows that those who lived in Fairmont had immigrated earlier and had the ability to establish roots in the community. The pattern of homeownership among Italians supports the observation. One-third or 207 of the 663 Italian households owned (free or mortgaged) homes in Marion County in 1920. (see chart 8.5) One hundred seventeen of the Italian households were in Fairmont, and nineteen were in Monongah. About 40 percent of the Italian heads of households who owned

Chart 8.6
Year of Immigration for Italians, 1920

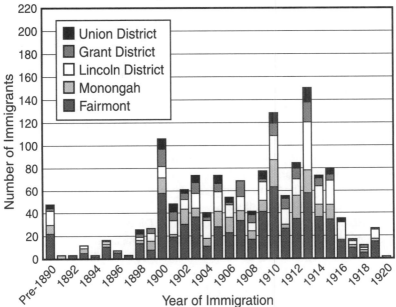

Source: U.S. Manuscript Census schedules, 1920, for Marion County, W. Va.

homes (80) had immigrated to Marion County before 1900, and two-thirds of them (136) had immigrated by 1905. Moreover, homeownership was not strictly limited to Italian merchants. Seventy-seven Italian coal miners owned their homes in 1920—the largest single group of the total population of Italian homeowners.[22] (see chart 8.6)

The number of Italian homeowners suggests that some of the immigrants perceived Marion County to be their permanent home. Accordingly, they set about creating institutions that cultivated their community and identity. National parishes, for example, were both wanted by Catholics and not unusual in West Virginia, despite the relatively sparse and transient nature of the state's Catholic population in the 1920s. The official Catholic Directory lists only three Italian parishes in West Virginia during the 1920s: Wheeling, Fairmont, and Clarksburg. Several other smaller parishes included a predominance of Italians, were known as Italian Parishes, but were not listed as such.[23] The church of Our Lady of Pompeii in Monongah, for example, was known as a predominantly Italian parish, and the Diocese of Wheeling-Charleston occasionally classed it as such. The small number of Italian Catholic parishes did not unite Italians with other European Catholics, nor did they unite all Italians themselves. Rather, attitutdes towards Catholicism were a touchstone for Americanized Italian ethnic identiy in Marion County.

Clashes between various ethnic groups belonging to the same parish, and a longing for priests of a particular ethnicity, were more common than a desire for national parishes. In 1923, a Catholic from Williamson, in southwestern West Virginia, asked the diocese for a priest who would "fit in with the surroundings." He meant that the mostly Irish and German Catholics in Williamson no longer tolerated their Polish and Hungarian priests.[24] In Clarksburg, Czechs refused to merge with a Polish parish and petitioned the diocese for a Slovak priest. They were confident that their proposed parish was sound and that their particular request was judicious, even though they numbered only a few dozen.[25] The bishop received these requests even as he continuously recruited badly-needed clergy to the diocese. Ethnicity was a divisive issue, regardless of the small size.

Father John J. Swint, the bishop of the Diocese of Wheeling-Charleston, which encompasses the entire state of West Virginia, thought that it was particularly important to minister to Italians. In May 1924, Father S. Forestier, M. S., provincial of the La Salette Fathers, a community of missionaries, offered to form an Italian parish somewhere in the diocese. With the state's highest concentration of Italians in 1924, Fairmont was the logical place. Swint accepted, writing:

> [The Fairmont Italians] are like the ordinary run of Italians. Most of them are not practical. However, I find that with non-Italian priests, fairly good results can be obtained among them. I believe they have never had a fair chance. They are not antagonistic, but rather ignorant. I have by no means lost faith in them, and have a strong conviction that, if we only save the children of the present generation, the next generation will be good Catholics.[26]

By July, the La Salette Fathers were laying plans to take over the city's Italian parish, St. Joseph's, that had already been formed in Fairmont in 1909. The parish had floundered into the 1920s, even as the population of Italians had increased. The La Salette Fathers sent two priests with instructions to take a census of Fairmont's Italians and begin the process of ministering to the next generation of Italians and building up the parish.[27]

Forestier's initial enthusiasm for Fairmont waned after one year. In one long letter to the bishop, he cataloged numerous reasons why. Foremost, the number of Italians were roughly half of the expected population. The priests had reported to Forestier that no more than seventy-five Italian families lived in the city together with single, male miners. The parish had conducted 102 baptisms, thirty-three marriages, and ten funerals. These figures suggested an estimate of 1,700-1,900 Italians, not "a population of 3000 or more [Italians] that I had been told was at Fairmont," Forestier wrote. The Italians were scattered, too. Families on the city's east side refused to travel to the west side. Twenty-five families lived along the Monongahela River, which runs through the city, and they refused to walk the distance, too. The problem, Forestier concluded, was that Fairmont needed three churches, rather than one, to serve far fewer Italian Catholics than indicated by initial estimates of the Italian population. He was justifiably discouraged.[28]

Where did the Italians go? The predecessors of the two La Salette priests had taken haphazard censuses of their parish. In the years 1920-1922, St. Joseph's reported to the diocese that an even three thousand Italians and their native-born children lived in Fairmont. The number is dubious. The 1920 Federal Census records 1,463 foreign-born Italians and their native-born children living in Fairmont. Later, the La Salette priests recorded a more conservative population of between thirteen to fourteen hundred.[29] The La Salette Fathers' 1925 estimate of between seventeen hundred and nineteen hundred foreign-born Italian Catholics and their families was sound.

The formation of the Italian parish also coincided with a series of coal strikes that followed after the coal operators resolved to rid the area of the United Mine Workers of America. The La Salette Fathers were tolerant of the Italian miners in their parish, but Father Forestier and the La Salettes stopped short of supporting the miners as a class. "The labor conditions render the work of the Fathers...difficult," Forestier wrote to Bishop Swint. In sum, the growing group of unemployed or striking Italian miners could support neither a priest nor a church building, and the church could not depend upon their future employment. In particular, the parish had started a mission in a coal town known as Watson, located just south of Fairmont. "Unless the labor situation is settled, that mission [in Watson] may just as well be abandoned," Forestier concluded.[30]

Despite Forestier's dour assessment and the pervasive labor discord, some Italians in Fairmont rallied behind their parish. After yet another year lapsed, Forestier redoubled the La Salettes' commitment to Fairmont, selected two multilingual Swiss priests, and sent them to bolster the Italian parish. The impetus came from the Italians themselves. After receiving Forestier's glum report in 1925, Bishop Swint traveled to Fairmont and investigated the matter on his own. He concluded that the Italian parish's base of financial support was uncertain. Hearing word of the bishop's plan to abandon their national parish, some Italians appealed to the Bishop and sent a copy of their parish's donated income, most of which came directly from Italians. The amounts, sources, and distribution of St. Joseph's income are telling of the parish's function in the Italian community (see table 8.1). The amount of income generated by dances amounted to about one-third of the total income. Holidays and saints' days, too,

Table 8.1
1924 Income Collected by St. Joseph's Parish,
Fairmont, West Virginia

Source	Amount	Percentage of Total
Estimated 7 Dances	$1,078	34%
Individually-named Donors	$862	27%
Sunday Collections	$815	25%
Holiday Collections: Christmas Easter St. Joseph Day St. Anthony Day	$166	5%
St. Joseph Society, Monthly Donations	$140	4.5%
Unspecified	$121	3%
Total Income	**$3,182**	

Source: Fairmont, W.Va., to Rt. Rev. John J. Swint, D.D., Wheeling, W.Va., [no month or day] 1925, DWC.

can be counted as festive events. Italian Catholicism in Fairmont facilitated leisure and, at the same time, Italian ethnicity.[31] The appeal changed the bishop's attitude. "I am willing to let your Fathers make another trial of the Italian Parish in Fairmont," the bishop wrote to Forestier.

> I believe the people have been somewhat stirred up and will be more generous in supporting the church. In fact, they pledged themselves to the full salary of a priest if I would consent to give them a priest again who can speak Italian.[32]

The Italians had convinced the Bishop that Catholicism was an integral part of their lives and their community.

The list of donors, and the apparent health of the Italian parish beyond 1926, was due to the diverse social makeup of its parishioners. None of the named individual donors included in St. Joseph's 1924 income were miners (see table 8.2). The list did include a real estate broker and a landlord, a proprietor of a men's furnishings store, a carpenter, and a banker.[33] Parish records also confirm that a diversely-employed Italian community was at the core of

Table 8.2
Occupations in Fairmont, 1910 and 1920

Occupation Type	1910	1920
Coal and Coke	155	111
Common Labor	95	41
Glass	45	141
Masonry	43	12
Construction	34	17
Railroad	27	34
Merchant	14	33
Skilled Trade	12	26
Services	6	37
Municipal Labor	5	9
Domestic	3	3
Machinist	2	6
Manufacturing	—	25
Professional	—	6
Musician	—	5
Farm	1	5

Source: Author's Census Database.

St. Joseph's in the mid-1920s. One way to gauge the parish's social makeup is to couple prolonged church activity with the occupations of one generation. The La Salettes began keeping accurate parish records in 1924, the same year in which the population of Italian coal miners in the county peaked. One hundred five households baptized a child at St. Joseph's during that year. A sample of those children who were later confirmed or married in the same or neighboring parish includes forty-seven individuals. The households in which they grew up included a variety of occupations: thirteen miners, a mold maker and three laborers at Owens Bottle Company, a glass blower, a teamster, a chauffeur, a confectioner, a shoemaker, two barbers, four grocers, a mechanic, a carpenter, and a box maker. Ten of the households identified in the sample do not show up in the city directory or the 1920 census. Judging by the city-wide employment of Italians, they were likely employed in coal. Parish records alone do not gauge the religious attitudes and participation of either miners or otherwise occupied Italians. It does suggest, however, that the viability and longevity of Fairmont's Italian parish stemmed more from ethnic identity than any one particular class. The La Salette Fathers' indifference toward miners and their issues as a class may have been, in the long run, a winning strategy to build up a viable parish. After all, Italian Catholicism in Fairmont was not a homogeneous religion of miners.[34]

By contrast, the relationship between priests and Italian Catholics in the hinterland bordered on mutual and outright hostility. More often than not, the diocese simply did not invest its stretched resources in outreaches to the coal miners who lived in the hinterland. In February 1923, Father Thomas H. Collins, an Irish priest, wrote to Bishop Swint and requested the annexation of Downs, a small coal-mining town three miles near Collin's parish in Farmington, a part of the infamous Lincoln District. Upon inspection of the place, Collins found one-hundred foreign Catholic families and four English-speaking families.[35] Collins' request was no simple matter. Downs lay at the outskirts of another parish, St. Patrick's, in Mannington. Father Kluser, Mannington's German priest, viewed Downs as a volatile place populated by infidels and radicals. "I always kept an eye on the people at the Rachel mine in Downs," he wrote to the bishop. His concern was not necessarily for the people's spiritual well being.

> I found that nearly all of these people are foreigners who care nothing for religion and many of whom are absolutely antagonistic to all religion. Many of those to whom I happened to speak, and who call themselves Catholics, belong, according to their statement, to the "Russian Orthodox Church." They are genuine Boshiviki [sic].

Kluser asserted that his neglect of Downs merely reciprocated the people's disdain for the church and their inclination toward radicalism. "Several of them told me right in my face: 'We don't care for any Church, for the Church is doing nothing for our economic relief; it always stands by the capitalists.' I considered myself lucky that I got out [of Downs] without being whipped."[36]

Father Collins's view on the church's proper role among the ill-tempered miners was more compassionate, but not necessarily aligned with the class. "It does no good to tell the coal miners who are on strike that they are in the wrong," Collins asserted. "It [is] best to let the operators and men discuss the question and settle among themselves and take no part on either side."[37] His stance was not so simple and passive, for he had aligned his ministry with the charitable graces of coal operators, not Downs's miners. A coal operator persuaded Collins that the "foreigners" at Downs neither wanted nor needed a church, and the "English-speaking" Catholics—in other words, the Irish Catholics—attended church at Farmington. Besides, the company owned an unused schoolhouse. The coal operator promised his own and his company's money toward its purchase—only if Collins waited until the next spring. Collins acquiesced, deferring to the supposed wisdom and power of a coal company.[38]

Such financial relationships between coal companies and churches were not uncommon. New England Fuel and Transportation Company offered the bishop of Wheeling land and a loan to build St. Anthony's Church in Grant Town, in Marion County's Grant District. The agreement stipulated that the loan would be paid off through payroll deductions. The coal company promised to sway its workers to attend mass, so long as the diocese manned the parish with a suitable, complacent priest.[39] In such direct and indirect ways, the coal industry exerted an enormous power over Catholic churches in Marion County.

What, then, underlies the difference between the Italians who used Columbus Day to showcase their involvement in Fairmont's marketplace and the Italians who brandished red flags? In one important way, both groups had a common impetus: they had adapted their ethnicity to match their particular living conditions in Marion County.

The Italians who lived in Fairmont either had more knowledge of American society or had access to individuals who possessed such knowledge. The Italian parish formed in Fairmont was one of several means to impart that knowledge to recent immigrants and to future generations. Some historians have argued that Italian Catholicism was a poor agent of Americanization. Strains of anti-clericalism, cult rituals, and the irreligious nature of Italian religion, they suggest, produced the opposite effect of Americanization.[40] The Italian parish in Fairmont does not fit this mold. The Italians of Fairmont were quite willing to work with the church hierarbhy, so long as it provided an Italian-speaking priest. The Bishop, too, met the Italians' demands, so long as they demonstrated their fiscal ability to support their church. Judging by the Italian's dogged pursuit of a national parish, they willingly took up the task of tailoring an Americanized version of their ethnic solidarity. The social space taken up by the Columbus Day parade, and later by the Italian parish, gave them the status of being a fixture in the larger social fabric of northcentral West Virginia.

Coal company housing, irreligion, the narrow avenues of immigration through padrone and labor recruiters, all limited the knowledge and experience of Italians living in the hinterland. Compared to Fairmont, the countryside lacked a generation of Italians who established deep roots in the marketplace and the community. Miners who had immigrated before 1900 certainly lived among the miners who were recruited into the region in mass numbers, but the countryside also lacked the institutions and community leaders that would have formed a nexus between those more experienced immigrants and new immigrants. The one social interaction that they shared, directly or indirectly, was work. It is not surprising, then, that the only collective action available to the Italians living in Marion County's hinterland was based upon class interests.

In this light, marching behind a red flag was a sensible way in which Italians adapted their preindustrial culture to their surroundings. The 1915 wildcat strike is similar to the common, unplanned, and fervent peasant uprisings that swept across parts of Europe, including southern Italy. Italian socialists were also common members of immigrant groups, though no one Italian radical can be identified in Marion County. Yet focusing too closely on the strike's radical overtones, and the possible involvement of perhaps even a handful of radicals, blurs the broader social context of the channels of immigration to Marion County. Given the high concentration of Italian immigrants from one region and, in some cases, one town, it is conceivable that many of the Italians who took part in the strike knew one another on a face-to-face basis before they immigrated. The relatively small size of the Italian population in Marion County, as compared to major urban places, probably enhanced the chances of immigrants having an intimate knowledge of their peers. One can infer that a padrone or a labor agent of the coal industry had promised the Italians decent work and housing. The Italians had immigrated to their destination and discovered disparities between what had been promised and the social reality that they encountered. Their actions stemmed from their common experience of immigrating to America through channels laid out by the coal industry.

The historical problem of "Americanization" underscores the solidarity and the fragmentation among Italians in northcentral West Virginia. The word is packed with meanings. Some historians construe the word as, more or less, a nativist attack upon the culture of immigrants. In West Virginia in the 1920s, politicians, religious leaders, educators, and the coal industry colluded to form a bulwark against unions and to create a more compliant working class.[41] Other historians of West Virginia have focused on the connection between ethnicity and class conflicts, though few would go so far as David Corbin's assertion that, during the coal wars of the 1920s, working-class consciousness among coal miners outweighed any divisions of ethnicity.[42] Historians of the state have just begun to understand how immigrants took the matter of Americanization into their own hands and, through civic groups, religion, subtle acts of rebellion, and various other informal channels, applied their preindustrial experiences to life in West Virginia. The best understanding of "Americanization" encompasses both the intervention of nativists and the grassroots resources that inclined immigrants toward altering their customs to match their surroundings. In this sense, Italian immigrants living in Marion County's city and country were themselves agents of Americanization, even though some of them refused assimilation into the coal-based society and demanded "justice" or "nothing at all."[43]

It is also clear that Americanization was more a local than a national process. Most studies of immigrant history are either implicitly or explicitly framed within a local context. Studies of Italian immigrants have typically focused on major urban places, though there has been some effort to study the many Italians who settled in rural regions.44 Even at the local level of a largely rural, but still industrial, state, the forces acting upon immigrants, and the ways in which they responded, were multifaceted. The bustle of American metropolises fostered a particular construction of Italian ethnicity in the early twentieth century. The scattered coal towns and middling-to-small cities of Marion County in West Virginia's Fairmont coal-field fostered several versions of Americanized Italian ethnicity.

NOTES

1. *Fairmont(W.Va.)Times*, 14 October 1912.
2. For a discussion of the strike and how it related to the prohibition movement in West Virginia, see Charles H. McCormick, "The Death of Constable Riggs: Ethnic Conflict in Marion County in the World War I Era," *West Virginia History* 52 (1993), 33-58; Fairmont *West Virginian*, 27 February 1915.
3. For an overview of the development of the Fairmont coal- field, see Michael E. Workman, Paul Salstrom, and Philip W. Ross, *Northern West Virginia Coal Fields: Historical Context*, Technical Report Number 10 (Morgantown, W.Va.: Institute for the History of Technology and Industrial Archeology, West Virginia University, 1994) 14-6, 36-7.
4. Population numbers are derived from a database, compiled by the author, of all Italians and their progeny who lived in Marion County and are listed in the 1900, 1910, and 1920 U.S. Manuscript Census schedules for Marion County, available on microfilm in the West Virginia and Regional History Collection, West Virginia University, Morgantown, West Virginia. When possible, the names and residences of Italians were cross-referenced with extant city directories. Levi B. Harr and C. L. Michael, *The Fairmont City Directory, 1901* (Fairmont, W.Va.: Index Printing Co., 1901); *R. L.Polk & Co.'s Fairmont Directory, 1913-1914* (Pittsburgh, Pa.: R.L. Polk & Co., Publishers, 1914); *Polk's Fairmont City Directory (West Virginia), 1925-1926* (Pittsburgh, Pa.: R.L. Polk & Co., Publishers, 1926); Database compilation hereafter cited as Author's Census Database; West Virginia Department of Mines, *Annual Report* (Charleston: Tribune Printing Company), 1924.
5. McCormick, "Death of Constable Riggs," 5. *Fairmont Times*, 15 February-31 March 1915.
6. John Bodnar, *The Transplanted: A History of Immigrants in Urban America* (Bloomington: Indiana University Press, 1985), 107; for a sample of the anti-radical sentiment, see *Fairmont Times*, 15 February 1915, and *West Virginian*, 22 February 1915.
7. *Fairmont Times*, 22 February-31 March 1915; *West Virginian*, 22 February-31 March 1915.
8. Ibid.
9. Ibid.
10. *Fairmont Times*, 14 October 1912; Author's Census Database.
11. The place of origin was arrived at through a database of Italian immigrants listed in the Marion County, West Virginia, *Naturalization Records* (1908-1935), West Virginia and Regional History Collection, West Virginia University, Morgantown, West Virginia (hereafter cited as WVRHC).
12. Ibid.
13. Ibid; Author's Census Database.
14. Rudolph J. Vecoli, "Contadini in Chicago: A Critique of the Uprooted," *The Journal of American History* 51 (Dec. 1964), 404. See also an explanation of the social stratification of one Calabrian town in Joseph Lopreato, "Social Stratification and

Mobility in a South Italian Town," *American Sociological Review* 26 (Aug. 1961), 585-96; John Bodnar, *The Transplanted*, 32-3, 45; Dino Cincel, *From Italy to San Francisco: The Immigrant Experience* (Stanford: Stanford University Press, 1982), 22-3; 26-8; William A. Douglas, *Emigration in a South Italian Town: An Anthropological History* (New Brunswick, N.J.: Rutgers University Press, 1984), 12-21.

15. Workman, Salstrom, and Ross, *Northern West Virginia Coal Fields*, 8-13; Author's Census Database.

16. Author's Census Database.

17. Ibid.

18. Ibid.

19. Monongah Mines Relief Committee, *History of the Monongah Mines Relief Fund: In Aid of Sufferers from the Monongah Mine Explosion, Monongah, West Virginia, December 6, 1907* (Fairmont: Monongah Relief Committee, 1910), 179.

20. *Fairmont Times*, 1 February 1915; Author's Census Database.

21. Author's Census Database.

22. Ibid.

23. *The Official Catholic Directory* (New York: P.J. Kendy and Sons, Publishers, 1920-1929); *Annual Reports*, 1920-1929, Diocese of Wheeling-Charleston Archive, Wheeling, W.Va., hereafter cited as DWC.

24. W. B. Blottman, Williamson, W.Va., [to Rt. Rev. John J. Swint, Wheeling, W.Va.], 1923, Bishops' Correspondence, DWC.

25. Rudolf Kacinec, Clarksburg, W.Va., to Rt. Rev. John J. Swint, D. D., Wheeling, W.Va., 7 May 1924, Bishops' Correspondence, DWC.

26. John J. Swint, Bishop of Wheeling, Wheeling, W.Va., to Rev. S. Forestier, 7 May 1924, Bishops' Correspondence, DWC.

27. S. Forestier, M. S., Altamont, N.J., to Right Reverend John J. Swint, D. D., 5 May 1924, 7 July 1924, Bishops' Correspondence, DWC.

28. S. Forestier, Nashua, N.H., to Rt. Rev. John J. Swint, D. D., Wheeling, W.Va., 6 October 1925, Bishops' Correspondence, DWC.

29. *Annual Reports*, 1920-1929, DWC; Bureau of the Census, *Fourteenth Census of the United States. State Compendium, West Virginia: Statistics of Population, Occupations, Agriculture, Manufactures, and Mines and Quarries for the State, Counties, and Cities* (Washington, D.C.: GPO, 1925), 27, 30-1.

30. S. Forestier, Nashua, N.H., to Rt. Rev. John J. Swint, D. D., Wheeling, W.Va., 6 October 1925, DWC.

31. S. Forestier, Nashua, N.H., to Rt. Rev. John J. Swint, D. D., Wheeling, W.Va., 12 December 1925; [St. Joseph's Parishioners], Fairmont, W.Va., to Rt. Rev. John J. Swint, D. D., Wheeling, W.Va., [no month or day] 1925, DWC.

32. John J. Swint, Bishop of Wheeling, Wheeling, W.Va., to Rev. S. Forestier, 12 Dec. 1925, Bishops' Correspondence, DWC.

33. Author's Census Database; [St. Joseph's Parishioners] Fairmont, W.Va., to Rt. Rev. John J. Swint, D. D., Wheeling, W.Va., [no month or day] 1925, DWC.

34. St. Joseph's Parish Baptismal, Confirmation, Marriage, and Death Records, St. Peter the Fisherman, Fairmont, West Virginia; Author's Census Database. After

St. Joseph's closed in 1998, its records were transferred to St. Peter's in nearby Fairmont.

35. Thomas H. Collins, Farmington, W.Va., to Rt. Rev. J. J. Swint, Wheeling, W.Va., 2 and 8 February 1923, Bishops' Correspondence, DWC.

36. C. J. Kluser, Mannington, WV, to Rt. Reverend Bishop John J. Swint, D. D., Wheeling, WV, 5 February, 1923, Bishops' Correspondence, DWC.

37. Thomas H. Collins, Farmington, W.Va., to Rt. Rev. J. J. Swint, Wheeling, W.Va., 8 February 1923, Bishops' Correspondence, DWC.

38. Thomas H. Collins, Farmington, W.Va., to Rt. Rev. J. J. Swint, Wheeling, W.Va., 3 April 1923, Bishops' Correspondence, DWC; Idem, 5 September 1923.

39. St. Anthony's, Grant Town, DWC.

40. Bodner, *The Transplanted*, 154; Vecoli, "Prelates and Peasants: Italian Immigrants and the Catholic Church," *Journal of Social History* 2 (spring 1969), 268.

41. John Hennen, *The Americanization of West Virginia: Creating a Modern Industrial State, 1916-1925* (Lexington: The University Press of Kentucky, 1996), 1; 74-6.

42. David Alan Corbin, *Life, Work, and Rebellion in the Coal Fields: The Southern West Virginia Mine Wars, 1880-1922* (Chicago: University of Illinois Press, 1981), 77.

43. James R. Barrett, "Americanization from the Bottom Up: Immigration and the Remaking of the Working Class in the United States, 1880-1930," *Journal of American History* 79 (December 1992): 997.

44. Rudolph J. Vecoli, ed., Italian *Immigrants in Rural and Small Town America* (New York: American Italian Historical Association, 1987).

Section IV:
Representations of
Ethnic Work Communities

The "Top Mill" (Wheeling Iron and Nail Company), circa 1877. Notice the open sides of the mill near the cluster of puddling furnace chimneys, left of center in the image. Detail, "Wheeling Iron Works – Top Mill," plate in Eli L. Hayes, ed., Illustrated Atlas of the Upper Ohio River and Valley from Pittsburgh, Pa. to Cincinnati, Ohio (Philadelphia, 1877). Image reprinted, with permission, from the David Rumsey Map Collection, www.davidrumsey.com.

Wheeling Iron and the Welsh:
A Geographical Reading of *Life in the Iron Mills*

Anne Kelly Knowles

In April 1861, the *Atlantic Monthly* published a remarkable novella titled *Life in the Iron Mills,* by Rebecca Blaine Harding (1831 – 1910), a writer known today by her married name, Rebecca Harding Davis.[1] Set in fictionalized antebellum Wheeling, it is the tale of a Welsh iron puddler named Hugh Wolfe and Deborah, a fellow immigrant who loves him. Unlike the other mill workers, Hugh is an artist whose talent finds expression in carving wild female figures from korl, a waste material at the mill. The dramatic turning point in the story comes when the works manager brings several visitors to observe Hugh and the other work-men during their night shift. The visitors talk in a desultory way about the hard life of labor. Then Mitchell, a man of superior intellect and appreciation, stumbles on one of Hugh's sculptures. While the middle-class characters debate the mean-ing of "the korl woman" and heartlessly encourage Hugh to pursue his dreams, Deborah steals Mitchell's wallet, thinking that the money will enable Hugh to buy wood and sculptor's tools so that he can become a real artist. Instead, Hugh is accused of the crime and put in jail. He commits suicide while awaiting transport to prison.

In Davis's telling of this melodramatic story, Hugh the iron puddler is imprisoned by industry long before he lands in the Wheeling jail. The greater crime is society's bland acceptance of Hugh's miserable poverty and the way work at the rolling mill brutalizes his finer sensibilities as it sickens his body with consumption. The environment in which he works is a literal hell. Davis describes it through the eyes of Deborah as she walks along the cinder path to the mill in the dead of night to deliver Hugh's meal of bread, salt pork, and ale:

> The mills for rolling iron are simply immense tent-like roofs, covering acres of ground, open on every side. Beneath these roofs, Deborah looked in on a city of fires, that burned hot and fiercely in the night. Fire in every horrible form: pits of flame waving in the wind; liquid metal-flames writhing in tortuous streams through the sand; wide caldrons filled with boiling fire, over which bent ghastly wretches stirring the strange brewing; and through all, crowds of half-clad men, looking like revengeful ghosts in the red light, hurried, throwing

masses of glittering fire. It was like a street in Hell. Even Deborah muttered, as she crept through, "'T looks like t' Devil's place!"[2]

Davis's harsh depiction of workers' lives shocked *Atlantic Monthly* readers. It gained her a certain notoriety that launched her career as a writer for popular magazines. Over one hundred years later, Davis gained new fame when feminist writer Tillie Olsen republished *Life in the Iron Mills* with a long biographical introduction.[3] Olsen hailed Davis as one of the first American realists and as an important, too-long neglected female American writer. Since then, many other feminist scholars and literary critics have examined Davis's life and her fiction. They have praised her as a pioneer literary figure, reinforcing Olsen's appraisal of the quality of her work and her importance as perhaps the first American author to write in what became known as the realist style.

Literary scholars have not plumbed all the depths of Davis's tale of industry, however, for they have not asked whether her realism penetrates beyond the level of style. How accurately does the novella portray the author's thinly disguised hometown? As a historical geographer of immigration and industrialization, I find *Life in the Iron Mills* to be an astonishing piece of place history. Where the portrait of Wheeling and its people bends away from the truth suggested by other historical evidence, the very distortion reveals important aspects of the author's life and the structure of social relations in her time.

Wheeling in Rebecca Harding's Youth

Rebecca Harding lived in Wheeling, Virginia (later, West Virginia), from age five through most of her adolescent and early adult years, until her marriage to L. Clark Davis in 1863. During her youth, Wheeling was transformed from a quiet market town, which saw occasional visitors along the National Road and light traffic along the Ohio River, into an industrial boom town of over thirteen thousand people. While Wheeling had a number of glassworks (see chapter 5 in this volume) and other industries by 1850, it became dominated by ironworks, most notably large rolling mills that refined pig iron and produced finished iron products. The first rolling mill was built by Pittsburgh ironmaster Peter Schoenberger between 1832 and 1834 in the north end of town. It set the stamp for Wheeling iron by specializing in cut nails.[4] By the late 1840s, demand for relatively cheap manufactured nails was growing rapidly, thanks to accelerating westward expansion and the popularity of wooden "balloon-frame" houses. The rising market for nails, combined with expectations for the completion of the Baltimore & Ohio Railroad through Wheeling, inspired a burst of new rolling mill construction between approximately 1849 and 1853 (see figure 9.1). Three of the six mills built during this period made nails exclusively.[5] By 1860,

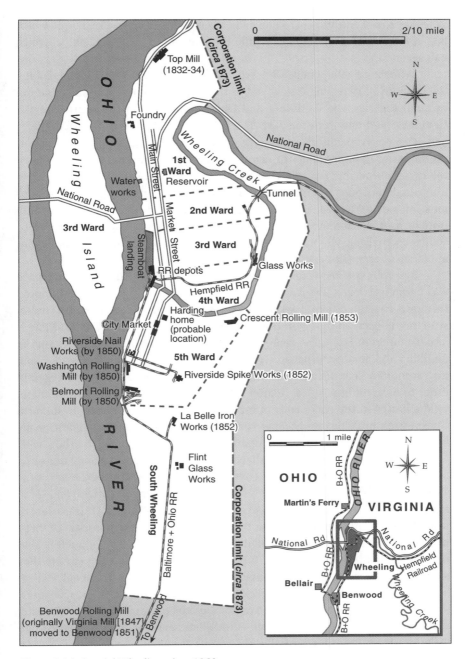

Figure 9.1 Industrial Wheeling, circa 1860.

Wheeling's concentration of rolling mills was exceeded only by Pittsburgh, which had at least fifteen rolling mills within the city limits, and Philadelphia, which had seven.[6]

Wheeling's rolling mills were typical of their day. They were located along the Ohio River, Wheeling Creek, and/or the route of the two railroads that ran through the city, the Baltimore and Ohio Railroad from the south and the Hempfield Railroad from the east. The key locational concern for rolling mills and other heavy manufacturing plants in this period was proximity to transportation rather than proximity to raw materials. Blast furnaces, which produced the raw pig iron that fed Wheeling's mills, had to be located near deposits of iron ore, limestone, and either coal or forests to be turned into charcoal. For most of the 1850s, Wheeling's rolling mills and foundries shipped in pig iron from furnaces located up and down the Ohio River, in northwestern Virginia, or southwestern Pennsylvania. Not until 1859 was the first blast furnace built nearby, at Martin's Ferry, Ohio.[7]

The rolling mills were also typical in their design.[8] The main workspace was a long rectangle about one hundred feet wide and two to three hundred feet long, covered by a roof, with open sides, just as Davis describes. This drafty structure housed all the operations involved in refining pig iron and turning it into useful products. At the center, or off to one end, of the structure stood the puddling and heating furnaces, where skilled men called puddlers worked pig iron at molten heat in small furnaces, stirring it to expose the mass oxygen in order to burn off impurities. Nearby were the roll trains, whose massive metal rollers flattened the pasty balls of red-hot refined iron into sheets of uniform thickness or into elongated shapes such as railroad rails. Nailworks additionally had rows of nail machines, where operatives stood or sat, punching thousands of nails a day from small strips of sheet iron. Judging from the occupations and numbers of workers listed in the population and manufacturing censuses for 1850 and 1860,[9] each of Wheeling's mills employed between fifteen and three hundred men, depending on the year and economic conditions. (This is a far cry from the thousand men Davis puts at the rolling mill where Hugh works.) Of these men, roughly 30 percent were skilled puddlers, heaters, rollers, moulders, and their assistants. Perhaps another 20 percent were nailers and the cutters they supervised. The remaining 50 percent were unskilled laborers who hauled, loaded, and did myriad other tasks at the beck and call of skilled workers and managers.

The proportion of skilled men in all industrial trades is higher in Wheeling than in other iron towns of the late antebellum period, particularly when one includes the scores of men listed in the census as engineers and machinists. Although the latter skills were employed at keeping the steam engines that ran Wheeling's mills in good working order, their numbers were probably swollen in

1860, as that was the year when the Baltimore and Ohio Railroad was building its bridge across the Ohio River at Wheeling.[10]

Ironworkers lived in all parts of the city, though the sequence of households in the 1860 population census indicates that workers tended to cluster along particular streets in each ward, just as wealthier professional and shopkeeping families tended to be neighbors.[11] Rebecca Harding Davis's family belonged to the middle class. In 1860 her father, Richard W. Harding, was city treasurer. His family lived in the Fifth Ward, the heart of the iron district, in a house valued at one thousand dollars – not the grandest in Wheeling by any means, but commodious and probably nicely appointed. Nearby lived a German machinist and an engineer from Pennsylvania, while in a boardinghouse a few doors down lived three rollers from Ireland. A large proportion of male industrial workers in 1860 Wheeling had been born in Germany, England, Ireland, Scotland, Wales, or France.[12] Davis would have heard many foreign languages on the streets of her neighborhood.

She also would have seen workers in a wide range of economic circumstances. According to the 1860 census, Wheeling's industrial labor included many propertyless ironworkers, cotton mill girls (like her character Deborah), and glassworkers, as well as skilled workers worth three thousand dollars or more. About one-third of men and boys in skilled iron occupations are listed as having no personal or real property. These included teenagers and young single men living with their parents and siblings. Their wages probably contributed to the family's wealth. In many such households, the parents have at least one hundred dollars in personal property, some more. Sons' income may help explain why most of those families lived in single-family dwellings. The truly poor tended to live in boardinghouses or to share one dwelling between several families, though the census shows no house crowded with six families as Davis says the Wolfes' house was.[13] A few score of elite industrial workers – rollers, heaters, puddlers, nailers, engineers, and machinists – ranked as members of the middle class. Some of them were wealthier than Rebecca's father.

Comparing occupational data from the 1860 census to information about the productive capacity of Wheeling's rolling mills suggests that the mills may have been operating well below capacity in 1860 (see table 9.1). J. P. Lesley's figures for Wheeling, based on his survey of ironworks managers in 1855-1857, show that at full production, the city's rolling mills could have employed at least 600 puddlers, heaters, and their helpers, between 80 and 120 men at the roll trains, and up to 350 men at nail machines. The census figures are not quite one-third of those numbers. While both sources are flawed,[14] they give credence to Davis's depiction of industrial poverty. It may be that Wheeling's ironworkers suffered significant periods of unemployment in the wake of the 1857

Table 9.1
Employment at Wheeling's Rolling Mills, circa 1860
Employment capacity of rolling mills[1]

Rolling Mill	Puddling Furnaces	Heating Furnaces	Total	Roll Trains	Nail & Spike Machines
Top Mill	NA	NA	14	2	15
Crescent	NA	NA	27	5	
Benwood	15	3	18	2	43
La Belle	15	3	18	2	41
Washington	14	4	18	2	
Riverside	NA	NA	10	3	
Belmont	NA	NA	21	2	40
TOTALS	44	10	126	18	139

Estimated labor at full capacity, two shifts daily, versus census occupations

	Lesley	1860 population census[2]
Puddling and heating furnaces	252 men, 252 helpers	135
Roll trains	36 rollers, 36 catchers, 36 helpers	51
Nail machines	278 feeders, 70 nailers	123
		(one nailer per four machines)

1. Figures from J. P. Lesley, *The Iron Manufacturer's Guide to the Furnaces, Forges, and Rolling Mills of the United States.* New York: John Wiley, 1859. Pp. 254-55.
2. 1860 U.S. manuscript census for Virginia, Ohio County, Wheeling. National Archives and Research Administration (hereafter NARA) M653 (Eighth Census of the United States), roll no. 1368; Marshall County, Benwood district, roll no. 1360. Labor for puddling and heating furnaces includes puddlers, boilers, heaters, and helpers listed in household of man with one of those occupations; roll train labor includes rollers and one hooker; nail machine labor, nailers and feeders.

depression, which hit many iron producers hard. How much a skilled puddler such as Hugh would have suffered is a point to which I will return.

Literary Realism in *Life in the Iron Mills*

Literary critics from Henry James to Sharon M. Harris, Davis's most recent biographer, have emphasized the gritty realism of her fiction. James disliked her style intensely. In his 1867 review of one of her novels, he accused Davis of "injudicious straining after realistic effects which leave nature and reality at an infinite distance behind and beside them."[15] Scholars' subsequent understanding of realist fiction has become much more nuanced and theoretical. Studies of *Life in the Iron Mills* examine the novella's narrative structure; its literary devices and metaphoric richness; the gender identities of Hugh, Deborah, and the androgynous narrator; the story's religious and moral messages, and more.[16] The crux of the story's significance for literary scholars, however, rests on its being regarded as "a precocious text in the movement known as literary realism."[17] Realism, according to Alan Trachtenberg, was "not so much a single consistent movement as a tendency among some painters and writers to depict contemporary life without moralistic condescension."[18] Laborers, mill girls, prostitutes, slums, poverty, disease – all of which became targets of moral and sanitary reform in the late nineteenth century – were common figures and environments in realist fiction. Davis, scholars claim, was one of the first American writers to tackle these unsavory subjects. Some also claim that her depictions of industrial life in *Life in the Iron Mills* are the equal of many later works by much more famous male authors.

Establishing Davis's place in the realist canon has led scholars to give considerable attention to distinguishing her realist observations from the romantic and sentimental elements in her writing and determining why realism was important to Davis herself. Sharon Harris believes that the accurate depiction of brutal industrial conditions and of working-class characters was central to Davis's literary theory of the "commonplace," a theory that Davis articulated in her fiction decades before William Dean Howells and Hamlin Garland formally expressed the same ideas in their theoretical writings on realism and naturalism.[19] According to Jean Pfaelzer, the main force behind *Life in the Iron Mills* is the author's "struggle to find an aesthetic language to express the ineffable nature of industrial reality."[20] Kirk Curnutt praises "the power of Davis's expose of working conditions in Wheeling, Virginia . . . . Welding documentary details into long, iron-hard descriptive passages, she forges a startling style: conjunctive images like 'the pig-pens, the ash-heaps covered with potato skins, the bloated and pimpled women at the doors' . . . prefigure the clarity and focus of labor-class photographers like Alfred Stieglitz and Walker Evans."[21]

Tillie Olsen considered *Life in the Iron Mills* not only Davis's best work, but a rare source of information about early industrial workers. "To those of us, descendants of their class, hungry for any rendering of what they were like, of how they lived, Rebecca Harding Davis's *Life in the Iron Mills* is immeasurably precious. Details, questions, Vision, found nowhere else – dignified into living art. . . . Without intention, she was a social historian invaluable for an understanding access to her time."[22] Olsen was astonished at the reach of Davis's imagination, given the constraints upon women in antebellum America.

> It is almost impossible for us at a later, freer time, to conceive of the difficulties of accumulating the dense accretion of significant details out of which *Life in the Iron Mills* springs so terribly to life (details that could come no more out of books than does Wolfe, or for that matter, Clarke, Kirby, May, Mitchell [middle-class characters in the story]).

> Perhaps only once was Rebecca able to take Deborah's night walk to the "city of fires"; she would not have been permitted to go unescorted, or to linger, or to initiate or participate too actively in any conversation. . . . How did she come then by the observation, the knowledge of the incomparable rainy night mill scene with its seizing descriptions and its unequaled encompassing of various class attitudes? How, too, did she come to know the fetid, kennel-like room where the Wolfes lived, with its slimy moss-covered earthen floor; and the dress, the differing talk and beings of the potato eaters?
>
> She must have had to use "trespass vision," eavesdrop, ponder everything, dwell within it with all the resources of intellect and imagination; literally make of herself (in Henry James' famous phrase) "one on whom nothing is lost."[23]

Olsen confessed that her appraisal of the novella and Davis's life was based more on her impressions and emotional response than on scholarly research. She is Davis's most breathless admirer, but most of those championing Davis in recent years have implicitly accepted the notion that she did not have extensive personal experience with industrial workers or workplaces, that she led the kind of sheltered life one would expect of the eldest daughter of a middle-class businessman and civic leader. All but one of the literary scholars, whose work I read, interpret the narrator of *Life in the Iron Mills* as Davis herself. They see the narrator's pose at the opening and closing of the story – seated at a desk, looking out the window onto the busy streets below – as an autobiographical snapshot as well as a symbol of Davis's domestic isolation. How did she know, in Olsen's phrase, "what is happening here," what life in an iron town, iron-making, and the lives of mill workers were really like?

The Place Rebecca Harding Knew

Sharon Harris gives a partial answer to that question. Harris argues that other scholars have been too surprised by the quality of "Life in the Iron-Mills." It was not a sudden, unprepared-for achievement, because Davis served a literary apprenticeship as a writer for the town's newspaper, the Wheeling *Intelligencer*. Sometime in the late 1850s, several years before Davis wrote the novella, the newspaper's editor, Archibald Campbell, engaged her to write reviews, poems, and editorials. Harris notes that Davis published one intriguing editorial on women's rights, titled "Women and Politics," on February 2, 1859.[24] She says nothing more about the newspaper or how Davis's years writing as a journalist may have affected her fiction.

Davis belittled her journalistic writing when her publisher, James Fields, pressed her to explain how she came to write so well. "'Whatever I wrote before the Iron Mill story I would not care to see again,'" she replied, "'—chiefly verses and reviews written under circumstances that made them unhealthful.

I would rather they were forgotten.'"[25] An apprenticeship, however, teaches skills and gives the receptive trainee a certain kind of eye. To get some idea of how working for the *Intelligencer* might have influenced Davis, I read several months of the paper's editorials and local news items from early 1860. I found striking similarities between their content and style and *Life in the Iron Mills*, which Davis was writing or planning to write at that time (she submitted the manuscript in December 1860). One commentary that appeared in the local news section on January 7, 1860, comes remarkably close to the argument and diction of *Life in the Iron Mills*:

> THE POOR. — The chill winds of winter are bearing the old burden of sighs and beseechings to the ears of the merciful, who have to spare from their abundance. . . . We all know that, when at night we lie down to dreams in warmth, many beings, created for divine purposes, and in the same image as ourselves, will shiver until dawn lights them to new struggles and miseries. We know, every day, that hunger and cold are gnawing at the vitals of persons from whose touch we may shrink, passing us in the streets, and that within a stone's throw of our comfortable places of resort, there are cold hearths and aching hearts. We are not certain ever that the thin, imploring hands which stretch out towards us from the wayside, deserve not to be held up, or that the tear that glistens in the sunken eye is pumped up for the occasion . . . .
>
> Let those who doubt go in person where actual cold and hunger are. Seeing for themselves the insufficient rags, the sucked bones, and the hoarded crusts, and hearing the low complaints against fate, and inhaling the noxious atmosphere which gathers down upon misery everywhere, they may settle the account of nature with their conscience and with God.[26]

"Let those who doubt go in person where actual cold and hunger are." It is a short step from this indirect command to the forceful opening incantation of Davis's story, where the narrator pulls the reader close, saying, "Stop a moment. I am going to be honest. This is what I want you to do. I want you to hide your disgust, take no heed to your clean clothes, and come right down with me, — here, into the thickest of the fog and mud and foul effluvia. I want you to hear this story. There is a secret down here, in this nightmare fog, that has lain dumb for centuries: I want to make it a real thing to you."[27]

Did the woman who wrote, "Stop a moment. I am going to be honest," also write the following *Intelligencer* notice calling for labor at one of the city's rolling mills?

> MEN WANTED. — Norton, Acheson & Co. advertise for a number of workmen at their mill, for the "drag down." We hope those for whom the advertisement is intended will know what "drag down" means. We don't.[28]

The blunt style typical of the 1860 *Intelligencer's* local news may have been Davis's emerging voice or the established style of her editor. Reports on the weather, life along the Ohio River, and incidents in town also have much the same tone as Davis's prose. Even if she did not contribute to the local news column, it is possible that Campbell influenced her style. The many echoes of *Life in the Iron Mills* that I found in the paper suggest that Davis scholars could learn a good deal by attending more closely to her apprenticeship in journalism. Her involvement with the *Intelligencer* could help fill the gap in knowledge left by the frustratingly few extant letters and autobiographical writings from the years leading up to the publication of her most famous work.

The newspaper also contains much grim news reflecting the stagnant economy in late antebellum Wheeling in the aftermath of the 1857 depression. Only when the Civil War drove up demand for ordnance, rails, and other iron wares did the iron economy spring back to life.[29] In January 1860, the Wheeling city council met to consider a proposal for publicly funding a House of Refuge and Reform for the Poor.[30] Nearly every issue of the thrice-weekly paper mentions poor people jailed or fined for petty theft of clothes, food, or money. One story tells of a town drunk who pounded on someone's door, hollering for food, until someone finally gave him a loaf of bread. The Harding family lived one block from the city market. Within a few doors of their home was a boardinghouse that domiciled single young laborers, most of them listed in the census without a penny to their name.[31] If Davis was sealed up in a protective bubble of middle-class propriety within her home, she at least would have read about the city's unfortunates in the newspaper. I suspect she wrote about them for the paper as well.

Even with the windows shut, Davis, like all residents of Wheeling, would have smelled the sulphurous emissions given off by the coal-burning glass and ironworks and heard the constant patter of coal soot softly striking the windowpanes. Perhaps, like other ladies in the town, she carried a handkerchief on social calls "for the express purpose of preventing [her] gloves from becoming soiled in opening gates and pulling at the door-bells." This detail of daily life comes from James E. Reeves's *Physical and Medical Topography . . . of the City of Wheeling*, published in 1870. It was Reeves's official report as city health officer to the mayor and city council. Reeves confirms Davis's physical descriptions of the urban environment. The "mephitic odors" given off by crumbling vaults in the impoverished Catholic cemetery were only the beginning of the city's environmental problems. One and a half miles upstream from Wheeling, along Wheeling Creek, was the village of Fulton, a place "remarkable for its slaughter-houses, tanneries, etc." All the "foul drainings" from this "village of concentrated odors" were poured into the creek, as were the effluvia from the Third and Fourth

Wards' "soap and tallow chandler establishments, the gas works, oil refineries, private and public sewers. . . ." Although heavy rains flushed out the "accumulations of filth . . . from its banks and eddies," most of the time Wheeling Creek stank.[32] It ran a few blocks from Davis's family home.

Heavy rain was a mixed blessing, particularly in the low-lying wards of Centre Wheeling and South Wheeling, parts of which were below the level of the Ohio River bank. In these lowlands, impervious clay soils prevented water from percolating down. Standing water was common, mud "abundant" and well worked by hogs that were allowed to roam the streets and back alleys. In these poorer districts, where mill workers were concentrated, few streets were paved. None of the city's miles of alleys were. Along those alleys, the domain of servants and the poor in so many North American cities in this period, Reeves found "wretched hovels," some "partly underground." Without drainage, they became soaked with surface water and sewage. Such conditions would certainly promote the growth of mildew and perhaps even the "green, slimy moss" Davis ascribes to the Wolfes' cellar habitation.[33]

The most stunning images in Reeves's report come in his description of the effects of coal soot. Although many streets were shaded by trees, including the poplars Davis mentions at the opening of her story, the trees were scarcely able to breathe because of the greasy soot and poisonous fog that hung over the city. They would have been "faded" indeed.

> Grass grows with difficulty in Wheeling, and many of the green yards in front of the houses are the result of much care. Neither do tender plants live in summer without constant washing; the leaves become coated with soot, the stomata choked, and respiration ceases. Indeed, Wheeling has acquired almost as much fame for its coal smoke and soot as for its mud, fogs, and manufactures. With every breath, the sooty particles enter the lungs and discolor the bronchial secretions; and housekeepers in the vicinity of the foundries, mills, and similar establishments are compelled to keep their windows continuously closed to keep out the soot. Some of the furnaces are positive nuisances from the quantities of carbon they emit as smoke.[34]

Judging by topographical maps, the steep hills immediately to the east and north of Wheeling probably trapped the smoke and held it over the town except on days of exceptional wind.[35]

Reeves goes on to assure his patrons that, "notwithstanding the obstruction of light caused by the smoky, sulphurous atmosphere in which the city is almost constantly enveloped, and the clouds of sooty particles from hundreds of furnace stacks, there does not . . . seem to be any unusual tendency to pulmonary phthisis or other respiratory trouble among the masses. . . ." His many years of medical practice in rural West Virginia convinced him that nowhere in the countryside were there "so few deaths from 'consumption' as in Wheeling."[36] Elsewhere in his report, however, Reeves provides evidence that undermines this assertion. His statistical summary of the causes of death in Wheeling from 1854 to 1868 shows that, aside from outbreaks of cholera, typhoid fever, scarlet fever, and puerperal fever, and disturbingly numerous deaths from eclampsia (a deadly syndrome affecting pregnant women), the majority of deaths were credited to respiratory diseases, including pneumonia, pulmonary phthisis, and the "indefinite" killers called "'Consumption,' 'Inflammation of the Lungs,' 'Lung Disease,' etc. . . . ."[37] Perhaps Reeves was trying to assuage the hurt done to Wheeling's reputation by Rebecca Harding Davis in her depiction of a doomed, consumptive ironworker. The city was undeniably blackened by industry, Reeves confesses, but he insists that it was not full of the likes of Hugh Wolfe.

Davis begins *Life in the Iron Mills* with the line, "A cloudy day: do you know what that is in a town of iron-works?" She certainly did. Her description of Wheeling's foul atmosphere is even more evocative than Reeves's:

> The idiocyncracy of this town is smoke. It rolls sullenly in folds from the great chimneys of the iron-foundries, and settles down in black, slimey pools on the muddy streets. Smoke on the wharves, smoke on the dingy boats, on the yellow river, — clinging in a coating of greasy soot to the house-front, the two faded poplars, the faces of the passers-by. The long train of mules, dragging masses of pig-iron through the narrow street, have a foul vapor hanging to their reeking sides. Here, inside, is a little broken figure of an angel pointing upward from the mantel-shelf; but even its wings are covered with smoke, clotted and black.[38]

Davis records the environmental degradation caused by heavy industry with the same eye for telling detail, and the same moral outrage, that informed Friedrich Engels's descriptions of the physical deformities typical of those in certain industrial occupations in Manchester and Birmingham, England, fifteen years before.[39] What Davis knew of Wheeling as a place came from years of living there, native knowledge that may have been augmented and sharpened by her work for the *Intelligencer*. She wrote best about what she knew firsthand, from the smell of the mule teams hauling pig iron down Market Street to the soot that blackened figurines on the mantel.

What She Knew Less Well: Iron-Making Technology and the Welsh

Davis is less sure about industrial processes and the lives and thoughts of laboring people. Her lack of personal knowledge is reflected to some extent in her prose. Literary scholars have been fascinated by the two distinctive narrative styles employed in *Life in the Iron Mills*. While they differ in their interpretation

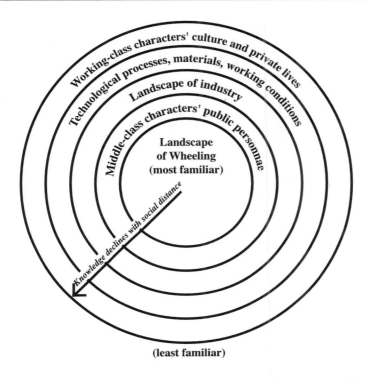

Figure 9.2 The scope of Rebecca Harding Davis's knowledge in "Life in the Iron-Mills."

of just what the styles mean and why Davis used them, there is general agreement that one style is masculine, direct, and aggressive, while the other is feminine, emotional, and persuasive. Scholars of literature see these alternating styles as Davis's challenging exploration of the conventional dichotomy between the public and private spheres and the gender roles they embodied.[40] I see in her two styles also the difference between writing based on direct, personal knowledge and writing based on imagination and invention. In her aggressive, direct addresses to the reader, Davis thrusts the realities of Wheeling before our eyes. The intense descriptive passages burn with her intent to force the comfortable bourgeoisie to see what she sees and condemn the injustice that vision reveals. Where the writing becomes more impressionistic, sentimental, or fantastic, Davis is entering less familiar territory; namely, the interior of the rolling mill or the culture and private lives of her working-class characters (see figure 9.2).[41]

Davis tells us in her brief autobiography and in a few letters that she loved to walk.[42] Olsen and others have assumed that she could not have walked often within view of Wheeling's rolling mills because such industrial, masculine places would have been off-limits to a respectable woman. I would assume the opposite; that, as a nearly middle-aged woman of independent mind, Davis would have included the ironworks frequently in her rambles around town. If she needed an excuse or a male companion, she could have accompanied Archibald Campbell when he went to report on a mill accident or her father when he went to call on one of the works managers. Seeing did not necessarily mean understanding, however. Someone (whether Davis or Campbell) who did not know the meaning of industrial terms such as "drag down"[43] could not be expected to understand industrial crafts such as puddling, whose details workers held close as trade secrets. Davis's brief description of puddling – "ghastly wretches stirring the strange brewing" in "wide caldrons filled with boiling fire" – evokes Shakespeare more than puddling itself.[44] It would have been difficult for a woman to gain entry to the clannish world of male ironworkers. Walt Whitman, who also worked as a journalist, shows a much better understanding of iron-making technology in several poems written in the 1850s. In "A Song of Occupations," for example, he precisely catalogs

> Iron-works, forge fires in the mountains or by river-banks, men around feeling the melt with huge crow-bars, lumps of ore, the due combining of ore, limestone, coal,
>
> The blast-furnace and the puddling furnace, the loup-lump at the bottom of the melt at last, the rolling-mill, the stumpy bars of pig-iron, the strong, clean-shaped T-rail for the railroads. . . .[45]

Puddling was a kind of stirring and boiling, though it was done in upright, boxy furnaces rather than open cauldrons. As Davis adds a little later, a puddler "dug into the furnace of melting iron with his pole,"[46] pushing and then stirring up to three hundred pounds of pig iron for half an hour or more as it softened and eventually boiled in blazing heat. Puddling was the most physically demanding of all occupations in the iron industry. It took a terrible toll on men's bodies. Puddlers were prone to heat stroke, cataract, and retinal and choroidal lesions due to exposure to extreme, dry heat, as the puddler stood just a body's length from the furnace. One puddler wrote, "My palms and fingers, scorched by the heat, became hardened like goat hoofs, while my skin took on a coat of tan that it will wear forever." Puddlers' intense labor caused chronic muscle strain and exhaustion. A British metallurgist estimated in the early nineteenth century that in Wales, the birthplace of puddling, "The majority [of puddlers] die between the ages of forty-five and fifty years."[47]

While puddlers may have contracted consumption (now called tuberculosis), its weakening effect would have made it impossible for a workman to continue puddling once he was truly ill. Nor would an experienced puddler like Hugh Wolfe have had thin muscles and weak nerves. Men in his occupation required exceptional physical strength and endurance. They often built up massive muscles in the upper body. Davis took poetic license in giving Hugh the classic disease of artists in the nineteenth century. It is interesting, however, that the medical report of James E. Reeves notes that "nailers consumption" was fairly common in Wheeling. He describes it as a form of chronic pneumonia that nailers developed after even just a few years of "shaping and sharpening the bits that cut the nails. These men spend much of their time at the *grind stones*, which revolve with great speed, and breathe an atmosphere loaded with mineral particles."[48]

Davis's central metaphor and most striking image is the korl woman. She is a crouching, life-size figure that Hugh carved from korl, a waste material that Davis describes as "a light, porous substance, of a delicate, waxen, flesh-colored tinge." "In the neighboring furnace buildings," she writes, blocks of korl lay in "great heaps." Korl is an imaginary amalgam of furnace slag, a glassy by-product of the smelting process that was sometimes beige; and the light, porous, dark-gray cinders that were scraped out of puddling and heating furnaces at rolling mills after each "turn." Neither material would have existed in large blocks, nor would either be amenable to carving, except perhaps by blow-torch.[49] By inventing korl, Davis satisfied the need for emotional accuracy in her story. The korl woman symbolizes the desperate hunger Davis perceived in the faces of mill workers, a hunger for something more than toil and poverty. Asked to explain the statue, Hugh can only stammer, "She be hungry. . . . Not hungry for meat. . . . Summat to make her live, I think, – like you."[50] The statue also has strong metaphorical resonance with the story's two main characters. It is made from waste material, as Hugh is a cast-off from American society. The statue's bold, wild face and groping hand mirror the desperate, sacrificial love that Deborah feels for Hugh.

While sorting invented technical details from historical fact is fairly straightforward, Davis's depictions of the Welsh and the ranks of skilled ironworkers are more difficult to assess. She does strike the right note in casting her puddler as a Welshman. The Welsh were a dominant minority in skilled iron-making occupations throughout the antebellum period and were a particular presence among puddlers at rolling mills in Pittsburgh and other iron towns.[51] Although the 1860 census of Wheeling and Benwood lists only twenty-five Welshmen with occupations, they are all iron- workers, twenty-three of them puddlers, boilers (a synonym for puddler), or their helpers.[52]

Davis may also have chosen a Welsh identity for Hugh and Deborah for the sake of novelty, for outside of the iron and coal industries, the Welsh were a very small, highly localized minority within the stream of British immigration in the early nineteenth century.[53] What she says about the Welsh, however,

suggests that she either shared or wanted to challenge the kinds of racial stereotypes that were typically ascribed to the Irish. For example, when she intro-
duces the Wolfes as Welsh immigrants, she writes,

> You may pick the Welsh emigrants . . . out of the throng passing the windows,
> any day. They are a trifle more filthy; their muscles are not so brawny; they
> stoop more. When they are drunk, they neither yell, nor shout, nor stagger,
> but skulk along like beaten hounds. A pure, unmixed blood, I fancy: shows
> itself in the slight angular bodies and sharply-cut facial lines. . . . [The Wolfes']
> lives were like those of their class: incessant labor, sleeping in kennel-like
> rooms, eating rank pork and molasses, drinking – God and the distillers only
> know what; with an occasional night in jail, to atone for some drunken excess.
> Is that all of their lives? – of the portion given to them and these their dupli-
> cates swarming the streets to-day? – nothing beneath? – all?[54]

Although Hugh and his family are clearly meant to be representatives of their
class first and their nationality second, Davis continually reminds the reader of
their ethnicity through her use of dialect. I must confess that, as a Welsh speaker,
I find some of her dialect painful, though it is no less accurate, no more demean-
ing than the dialect her Irish characters speak. Deborah's speech is farthest from
educated English, as she has had not even Hugh's few months of schooling: "'Hur
can eat the potatoes, if hur's hungry,'" is typical of her language. And yet the one line
spoken by a Welsh ironworker other than Hugh – "'Hyur comes t' hunchback, Wolfe'"
– comes close to the sound of a typical accent in industrial South Wales today.[55]

What matters most in literature, of course, is character. Hugh's character
is singled out as exceptional among millworkers. He avoids masculine entertainment and craves a finer way of life. The other men enjoy cockfights, drink
heavily, fight often, and scorn education. While at work the men shout, "as they
had to do, to be heard over the deep clamor of the mills." They trade boisterous
"jeers and drunken choruses."[56] This is more stereotyping. But in characterizing ironworkers as aggressively masculine, Davis echoes the view of articulate
workers and antebellum ironworks managers.

Thomas Wright, a journeyman engineer in England, wrote two volumes
about "the inner life of workshops" in heavy industry, "a life behind the scenes
– that is known only to the initiated." He describes pranks of initiation and a
culture of drink in the machine shops and rolling mills of England in the 1860s.
The men and boys in his stories inhabit industrial spaces that they possess in
every way except as owners of capital.[57] James J. Davis, a Welsh-born puddler
who went on to serve as secretary of labor from 1921-1930, claimed to love his
demanding work at the mill. Puddling "is not a job for weaklings," he writes
with typical bravado in his autobiography. It takes "mental knowledge" to judge

when the iron has "come to nature" in the furnace, as well as "great muscular skill like that of the heavyweight wrestler, besides great physical endurance to withstand the terrific heat."[58] He expresses what Welsh labor historian Gwyn Alf Williams called "the sheer **pride** of ironworkers, the overweening pride of skilled men, the secretive pride of those . . . who nursed their craft lore in an industry which counted about forty separate 'trades'" in the mid-nineteenth century.[59] Experienced puddlers, rollers, and heaters earned some of the highest wages in nineteenth-century industry.[60] While Rebecca Harding Davis was writing *Life in the Iron Mills*, Pittsburgh puddlers and boilers were organizing the country's first ironworkers union. By 1867, the boilers of Wheeling were well represented by two "sub-forges" of the union. It was called the Sons of Vulcan.[61]

The same pride that gave a powerful sense of identity to skilled ironworkers made them difficult to control. Ironworks managers in the North and South complained about workers' drinking, their clannishness, and their unreliability. Shenandoah Valley ironmaster William Weaver summarized the problem posed by the industry's relatively scarce skilled labor in 1825 when he wrote that "no reliance could be placed in the free White laborers who are employed about Ironworks in this country," for in "moments of the greatest pressure and necessity, the proprietor must either make them advances which they will never repay, or they leave his service to the ruin of his business."[62] Skilled workers were more plentiful by 1860 and some suffered spells of unemployment in the depths of depression before the Civil War. But I doubt whether even at that time an experienced Welsh puddler would have been quite as wretchedly poor and alienated as Hugh Wolfe. His character does remind me, however, of a real Welshman I happened to encounter while researching the strict, conservative Welsh settlement in rural Jackson and Gallia Counties in Ohio, downriver from Wheeling. Nathaniel Edwards emigrated to Jackson County with his parents and siblings in 1865. He soon fled to Cincinnati, where he hoped to pursue his artistic ambitions as a sculptor. He died of consumption in 1871.[63]

Middle-Class Perceptions of Ironworks

Davis's indictment of industrial capitalism was unusual coming from an American woman, but her perception of rolling mills as dark, satanic places was quite conventional for a member of the middle class. When the Scottish poet Robert Burns visited the huge Carron Foundry on the River Clyde around the turn of the nineteenth century, he responded as most visitors did. He was stunned – though he wrote with typical wit and understatement,

We cam' na here to view your warks,
In hope to be mair wise,
But only, lest we gang to hell,
It may be nae surprise. . . .[64]

Throughout the nineteenth century, educated people wrote of large iron works as hellish places. One could see the lurid glow of blast furnaces from miles away. Blasts of pressurized air, forced into the crucible to feed the fire with oxygen, made furnaces roar like "volcanos breathing out their undulating pillars of flame and smoke." Iron towns like Merthyr Tydfil, in South Wales, were likened to Pompeii: "smoking ruins . . . prey to the devouring element" of fire. Two-ton forge hammers crashed, strikers' hammers banged, and men yelled themselves hoarse to be heard above the clamor on the shop floor.[65] In open-sided rolling mills, depicted almost as industrial cathedrals in contemporary paintings and lithographs, men strained like Hercules to manipulate hundredweights of molten iron. No wonder American ironworkers named their first union the Sons of Vulcan.

Centers of large-scale iron manufacturing were extreme environments. The largest ironworks, such as Dowlais and Cyfarthfa in South Wales, employed five thousand men or more. Such places were unprecedented in human experience. They were thrilling to many workers but repellent, or almost lasciviously fascinating, to at least some middle-class observers. Historical geographer John Stilgoe summarized the latter view when he wrote that, while the farmer "caresses the soil, urging it to bear fruit in its own time," the artifice of iron-making

> embodies rape, and abortion and transmutation too. Artifice thrusts into the very womb of mother earth, into infernal dark, and wrenches living rock from living rock. Smelting, forging, and casting torment the aborted fetuses with fire. Earth, air, fire, and water combine in an unholy alchemical alliance from which husbandmen stand away, shielding their eyes. . . . All the mystery of making obscures the places of artifice. Only the artificers understand. Onlookers stand back and hope for success, and are afraid.[66]

Stilgoe, writing in 1982, used language not unlike the terms Welsh preachers used to attach sin and immorality to their country's burgeoning iron district in the nineteenth century. The Welsh iron district, its religious critics claimed, harbored all the sins associated with the big city as well as the vices peculiar to intensely industrial and masculine places, namely overweening pride, alcohol, and ungodliness.[67]

Davis's "city of fires," where "crowds of half-clad men, looking like revengeful ghosts in the red light, hurried, throwing masses of glittering fire," fits the image of almost erotic danger that recurs in observations of ironworks. Such depictions suggest that heavy industry inspired particular kinds of anxiety in middle-class men and women. Davis's iron town is different from the industrial Sodom and Gomorrah feared by Calvinistic Welsh preachers, for she ultimately condemns capital rather than labor. Hers is a moral landscape in which benighted workers struggle against desperation without hope of improving themselves. They are criminal because they belong to the uneducated working class; they are filthy in body and spirit; they are minions of darkness inhabiting "t' Devil's place" who can never lift themselves from the grinding labor that leaves them utterly spent at the end of each twelve-hour shift. And yet Davis's observations are concrete as well as moral. The devil's place is carefully observed. I imagine Davis standing with a small group of privileged observers, like the reporter, doctor, mill owner, and wealthy visitor in her story, raptly watching puddlers at work. Artist John Ferguson Weir captured just such a scene when he painted the owner of the West Point Foundry entertaining visitors at his mighty cannon works during the Civil War. Among the visitors are two women. Gloved and hatted, they gaze at a team of brawny men struggling to hold still a huge bucket of molten iron as they tip its contents into the mouth of a cannon mold.[68]

Historical Geography as a Context for Literature

I came to *Life in the Iron Mills* hoping to find evidence of the social history of antebellum ironworkers and their families. At first I was put off by Davis's over-wrought style, her moralizing, the errors in her depictions of iron-making technology, and her apparent unawareness of the economic and social status of skilled ironworkers. But as I spent more time with the text and compared it to other historical sources, I felt a growing respect for Rebecca Harding Davis. Like her literary admirers, I think Davis strove for accuracy and that she achieved it in many parts of her novella. She paints the most detailed portrait of a late antebellum iron town that I have come across in many years of researching the industry. Her depictions of the rolling mill where Hugh works and the hovel where he sleeps are glimpses of rarely described environments. Where narrative elements diverge from historical conditions, they reveal the social distance between a middle-class woman and the working people she meant to portray sympathetically.

Literary scholars typically contextualize their subjects by considering when they wrote, whom they knew, what they read, and how their work was received by contemporary readers and critics. Rarely do scholars of literature as carefully consider where writers lived and worked or the places they depict in their prose and poetry. I believe that geographical contextualization can enrich one's understanding of any writer. It is essential to grasping the full meaning, inspiration, and achievement of literature by writers whose work is embedded in place, as Rebecca Harding Davis's *Life in the Iron Mills* certainly is. The novella was her best work in part because she poured into it her years as a child and young woman witnessing the industrial transformation of her intimately familiar hometown. Sharon Harris notes that much of women's literature in the mid-nineteenth century was a literature of place based on realistic observation, the one platform of superior knowledge women could claim with confidence.[69] I have no doubt that a historical-geographical reading of other realist authors, whether women or men, would reward the effort.

Learning about the geographical context of an author's life and work also deepens one's pleasure when one returns to the literary text. Having seen Wheeling, walked its streets and mapped them, I can more vividly visualize the town Davis wants me to see. I walk closer behind Deborah as she trods the cinder path toward the mill, and can imagine more of the noisy, smelly, bumptious, heartbreaking life along Market Street outside Rebecca's window.

Acknowledgements

I would like to thank Lee Maddex for reading the draft manuscript and providing very helpful information about industrial Wheeling; Edward K. Muller and Trevor Harris for their critical suggestions; and those in attendance during presentations of an earlier version of this paper at a joint Regional Research Institute/Department of History colloquium, West Virginia University, and the Department of Geography, Ohio University.

Map Sources

Main map in Figure 1: *White's New County and District Atlas of the State of West Virginia* (Philadelphia, 1873): 39-40; J. P. Lesley, *The Iron Manufacturer's Guide* (Philadelphia, 1859): 254-5; "Bird's-Eye View of the City of Wheeling" (1870); Oliver I. Taylor, *Directory of the City of Wheeling & Ohio County* (Wheeling, 1851); 1850 U.S. Census, Manufacturing Schedules, National Archives and Research Administration, T1132, roll #4 (Virginia 1850); location of wards, courtesy Ken Fones-Wolf. Inset: *Mitchell's County and District Map of the State of West Virginia* (Philadelphia 1873); Joseph S. Wood, "The Idea of a National Road," in Karl Raitz, ed., *The National Road* (Baltimore 1996): 95; "Martins Ferry," U.S. Geological Survey Topographical Quadrangle (July 1981).

NOTES

1. Rebecca Harding Davis, *Life in the Iron Mills*, ed. Cecelia Tichi (Boston: Bedford/St. Martin's, 1998). In this essay I follow the convention adopted by literary scholars of referring to the author by her married name, even though *Life in the Iron Mills* was published two years before she married L. Clarke Davis. Rebecca Blaine Harding published the story anonymously.
2. Davis, *Life in the Iron Mills*, 45.
3. Tillie Olsen, ed., *Life in the Iron Mills or The Korl Woman*, by Rebecca Harding Davis (New York: The Feminist Press, 1972).
4. Lee Maddex, "La Belle Iron Works," Historic American Engineering Record No. WV-47, typescript dated August 1990, 8; J. P. Lesley, *The Iron Manufacturer's Guide to the Furnaces, Forges, and Rolling Mills of the United States* (New York: John Wiley, 1859), 254-5.
5. Earl Chapin May, *Principio to Wheeling, 1715-1945: A Pageant of Iron and Steel* (New York: Harper & Brothers, 1945), 106-9; Lesley, *Iron Manufacturer's Guide*, 254-5.
6. Lesley, *Iron Manufacturer's Guide*. Although Lesley is the most reliable and comprehensive source for the number, size, and ownership of ironworks in the antebellum period, other sources give different tallies. The 1860 Census Manufacturing Schedules, for example, exclude some rolling mills that appear in Lesley and include others that do not, but that were probably built before his compendium was published. Company records can give more certain answers; however, for the antebellum period, they are scarce and rarely complete.
7. Lee Maddex, typescript list of blast furnaces in West Virginia, provided via email, 29 November 2000, and further email correspondence from Lee Maddex dated 1 May 2002. Wheeling mills were undoubtedly served by the many charcoal iron furnaces in the Ohio and upper Kentucky Hanging Rock Iron District. See Eugene B. Willard, ed., *A Standard History of the Hanging Rock Iron Region of Ohio,* 2 vols. (n.p.: Lewis Publishing Company, 1916); Vernon D. Keeler, "An Economic History of the Jackson County Iron Industry," *Ohio Archaeological and Historical Quarterly* 42 (1933): 132-244; Wilbur Stout, "The Charcoal Iron Industry of the Hanging Rock Iron District: Its Influence on the Early Development of the Ohio Valley," *Ohio Archaeological and Historical Quarterly* 42 (1933): 72-104.
8. The following description is based on Lesley, *Iron Manufacturer's Guide*, 254-5; Davis, *Life in the Iron Mills*, 45; and antebellum maps from various U.S. iron towns that show the footprint of furnaces within large rolling mills. Paintings of the interiors of rollings mills in early nineteenth-century Wales provide rare evidence of the interior architecture of mills.
9. U.S. Manuscript Census schedules, 1850 and 1860, for Ohio and Marshall Counties, Virginia, National Archives and Research Administration (hereafter NARA): Manufacturing schedules on microfilm T1132, roll no. 4 (1850) and roll no. 8 (1860); Population schedules on M653, roll no. 1368 (Ohio County, wares of Wheeling) and roll no. 1360 (Marshall County, Benwood district).
10. I am grateful to Lee Maddex for this insight.

11. For a discussion of how one can approximate the geography of census-takers' routes, see Michael P. Conzen, "Spatial Data from Nineteenth-Century Manuscript Censuses: A Technique for Rural Settlement and Land-Use Analysis," *Professional Geographer* 25 (1969): 337-43.

12. 1860 U.S. manuscript census, Ohio County, Wheeling, 5th Ward, M653, roll no. 1368. Richard and Rachel Harding and four of their five children are listed in household no. 2831. Rebecca is not listed. She may have been away from town that day, or even visiting a friend. Sometimes census takers scrupulously recorded only those who were physically present at the time of their visit. Thanks to local historian Margaret Brennan for directing me to the former site of the Harding home. Margaret Brennan, telephone conversation with author, Wheeling, W.Va., 9 March 2002.

13. Davis, *Life in the Iron Mills*, 42.

14. Where Lesley and his scouts did not confirm reports with personal inspection – which appears to have been the case for Wheeling – the figures in *The Iron Manufacturer's Guide* tend to be less reliable than for sites they did visit. J. Peter Lesley Papers, J. Peter and Joseph Lesley correspondence, 1856 – 1858, American Philosophical Society, Philadelphia; Benjamin Smith Lyman Collection, Series 1: Correspondence 1856-1892 (Lesleys), Box 14, W. E. B. DuBois Library, Special Collections and Archives, University of Massachusetts at Amherst .
    Census figures can never be counted on as 100 percent reliable. In the case of iron-making occupations, the Wheeling census takers identified far fewer helpers and apprentices than I would expect in a workforce of the city's size. Those workers may be among the many laborers of unspecified occupation in the census. Some occupations, such as catcher, are not listed at all. There is also no way of telling whether the census takers tallied occupants of dwellings during the day and night. If they missed night-shift workers, the count of ironworkers may be short by half.

15. Kirk Curnutt, "Direct Addresses, Narrative Authority, and Gender in Rebecca Harding Davis's *Life in the Iron Mills*." *Style* 28, no. 2 (summer 1994): 163, quoting Henry James, review of *Waiting for the Verdict*, by Rebecca Harding Davis, *The Nation,* 21 Nov. 1867, 183.

16. In addition to the literary studies cited below, see J. F. Buckley, "Living in the Iron Mills: A Tempering of Nineteenth-Century America's Orphic Poet," *Journal of American Culture* 16, no. 1 (1993): 67-72; William H. Shurr, "*Life in the Iron Mills*: A Nineteenth-Century Conversion Narrative," *American Transcendental Quarterly* 5, no. 4 (1991): 245-57; Jean Pfaelzer, ed., *A Rebecca Harding Davis Reader* (Pittsburgh: University of Pittsburgh Press, 1995).

17. Cecelia Tichi, "Introduction: Cultural and Historical Background," in Rebecca Harding Davis, *Life in the Iron Mills*, ed. Cecelia Tichi (Boston: Bedford/St. Martin's, 1998), 14.

18. Trachtenberg cited in Sharon M. Harris, *Rebecca Harding Davis and American Realism* (Philadelphia: University of Philadelphia Press, 1991), 6.

19. Harris, *Rebecca Harding Davis*, 3, 11-6.

20. Jean Pfaelzer, *Parlor Radical: Rebecca Harding Davis and the Origins of American Social Realism* (Pittsburgh: University of Pittsburgh Press, 1996), 24.

21. Curnutt, "Direct Addresses," 146.

22. Olsen, *Life in the Iron Mills*, 154, 156.

23. Ibid., 83-4.

24. Ibid.

25. Harris, *Rebecca Harding Davis*, 26.

26. Wheeling *Intelligencer*, 7 January 1860, 3.

27. Tichi, *Life in the Iron Mills*, 41.

28. Wheeling *Intelligencer*, 9 January 1860, 3.

29. On the impact of the 1857-1860 depression on the neighboring Hanging Rock Iron District in southern Ohio, see Anne Kelly Knowles, *Calvinists Incorporated: Welsh Immigrants on Ohio's Industrial Frontier* (Chicago: University of Chicago Press, 1997), 176-7.

30. Wheeling *Intelligencer*, 18 January 1860, 3. It is not clear whether this would have been in addition to "the poor house" to which other local news and commentaries refer around this time.

31. See note 12.

32. James E. Reeves, *The Physical and Medical Topography . . . of the City of Wheeling* (Wheeling, W.Va.: Daily Register, 1870), 18, 13.

33. Ibid., 17-9; James Borchert, *Alley Life in Washington: Family, Community, Religion, and Folklife in the City, 1850-1970* (Urbana: University of Illinois Press, 1980).

34. Reeves, *Physical and Medical Topography*, 18. His descriptions of the atmosphere in a coal-burning iron town are very similar to those in Anna Egan Smucker's autobiographical story, *No Star Nights* (New York: Knopf, 1989), about growing up in the steel town of Weirton, West Virginia.

35. Chicago Lithographing Company, "Bird's Eye View of the City of Wheeling, West Virginia, 1870," (Madison, Wis.: Ruger & Stoner, 1870), no scale, Ruger Collection, Library of Congress; U.S. Geological Survey, "Martins Ferry, Ohio," USGS Topographic Quadrant, 1: 24 000, 1 July 1981.

36. Reeves, *Physical and Medical Topography*, 49-50. Emphasis in the original.

37. Ibid., 38.

38. Davis, *Life in the Iron Mills*, 39-40.

39. Friedrich Engels's *The Condition of the Working Class in England* was first published in Germany in 1845. I used the London: Penguin Books, 1987 edition.

40. See, for example, Curnutt, "Direct Addresses."

41. I am obliged to National Public Radio for prompting this insight. In an interview excerpt included in a retrospective report on her play *A Raisin in the Sun*, playwright Lorraine Hansberry said that there was a permanent imbalance between white and black people's knowledge of each other. While blacks often witnessed the private lives and conversations of white people, whites never heard the personal conversations and concerns of blacks. Report on *All Things Considered*, broadcast 11 March 2002, WAMU FM, Washington, D.C.

42. Olsen, *Life in the Iron Mills*, 81, 118.
43. "Drag down" refers to the catcher's job in the rolling mill, which is catching hot lengths of iron as they emerge from the mill rollers and flipping them around for a reverse pass through the mill and back to the roller.
44. Davis, *Life in the Iron Mills*, 45. She alludes to the famous witches' scene in Shakespeare's *Macbeth*, Act 4, scene 1, where the three witches chant, "Double, double toil and trouble; / Fire burn, and caldron bubble."
45. Walt Whitman, "A Song of Occupations," stanza 5, in *Leaves of Grass* (New York: Signet Classic, 1958), 188. Whitman also describes ironworks and labor in "A Song of Joys": "O to work in mines, or forging iron, / Foundry casting, the foundry itself, the rude high roof, the ample and shadow'd space, / The furnace, the hot liquid pour'd out and running"; and in "Crossing Brooklyn Ferry": "Burn high you fires, foundry chimneys! cast black shadows at nightfall! cast red and yellow light over the tops of the houses!" (both in *Leaves of Grass*, 160,149). Olsen notes the difference between Whitman's descriptions and Davis's but does not explore them (*Life in the Iron Mills*, 164, n. 11).
46. Davis, *Life in the Iron Mills*, 49.
47. Chris Evans, "Work and Workloads during Industrialization: The Experience of Forgemen in the British Iron Industry, 1750-1850," *International Review of Social History* 44 (1999): 210-1, brackets in original; George M. Kober and Emery R. Hayhurst, eds., *Industrial Health* (Philadelphia: Blakiston's Son & Co., 1924), 178, 181, 621; James J. Davis, *The Iron Puddler* (Indianapolis: Bobbs-Merrill, 1922), 98-9. Davis gives by far the best account of the puddling process and its physical effects. His account is also unique as a puddler's autobiography.
48. Reeves, *Physical and Medical Topography*, 23.
49. This analysis is based on field trips to the sites of abandoned blast furnaces in Jackson and Gallia Counties, Ohio, in 1990-1992, and conversations with Robert B. Gordon, an expert in the metallurgy and industrial archaeology of nineteenth-century American iron. He knows of no term of art at all similar to "korl." See the technical discussions of iron-making, including a glossary of technical terms, in Gordon, *American Iron, 1607-1900* (Baltimore: Johns Hopkins University Press, 1996); and Gordon and Patrick M. Malone, *The Texture of Industry: An Archaeological View of the Industrialization of North America* (Oxford: Oxford University Press, 1994). Slag ran off in much more copious quantities at blast furnaces than at rolling mills, where smaller amounts of slag were pressed out of hot puddled iron by rotary squeezers. Wheeling had no blast furnaces. Lesley, *Iron Manufacturer's Guide*, 254-5; Maddex, "La Belle Iron Works"; May, *Principio to Wheeling,*106-9.
50. Davis, *Life in the Iron Mills*, 53-4.
51. Anne Kelly Knowles, "Labor, Race, and Technology in the Confederate Iron Industry," *Technology and Culture* 42, no. 1 (2001): 8-9.
52. 1860 U.S. manuscript census, Ohio and Marshall Counties, Virginia, M653, roll. no. 1368 and 1360.
53. Rowland Berthoff, *British Immigrants in Industrial America, 1790-1950* (Cambridge: Harvard University Press, 1953), 4-6. On the gross underestimation of Welsh

immigrants in official sources like those Berthoff used, see Knowles, *Calvinists Incorporated*, 1-41. Even by my higher estimates, the Welsh were a very small minority within British and total European immigration throughout the nineteenth century. On the Welsh in coal mining, see William D. Jones, *Wales in America: The Welsh in Scranton, 1860-1920* (Cardiff: University of Wales Press, 1993).

54. Davis, *Life in the Iron Mills*, 42.

55. Ibid., 44, 45. Evidence from early nineteenth-century Welsh immigrant obituaries suggests that the majority of Welsh ironworkers and coal miners emigrated from South Wales, where the country's iron and coal districts were concentrated; Knowles, *Calvinists Incorporated*, 17-29.

56. Davis, *Life in the Iron Mills*, 47-9.

57. A Journeyman Engineer [Thomas Wright], *Some Habits and Customs of the Working Classes* (London: Tinsley Brothers, 1867), 83 and passim. See also A Journeyman Engineer, *The Great Unwashed* (1868; reprint, London: Frank Cass & Co., 1970).

58. Davis, *The Iron Puddler*, 87, 92.

59. Knowles, *Calvinists Incorporated*, 59-60, quoting Gwyn A. Williams, *Merthyr Rising* (London: Croom Helm, 1978), 28.

60. Berthoff, *British Immigrants*, 28.

61. John William Bennett, "Iron Workers in Woods Run and Johnstown: The Union Era, 1865-1895" (Ph.D. diss., University of Pittsburgh, 1977), 42 ff.; *The Vulcan Record* 1, no. 1 (January 1868), Minutes from meeting of the Grand Forge, Iron City, 7 August 1867; *The Vulcan Record* 1, no. 2 (September 1868), Minutes from meeting of the Grand Forge, Buffalo, 5-7 August 1868.

62. Charles B. Dew, *Bond of Iron: Master and Slave at Buffalo Forge* (New York: Norton, 1994), 22.

63. Obituary of Nathaniel Edwards, *Y Cyfaill* (*The Friend*), September 1871, 291. On the Welsh in Jackson and Gallia Counties, see Knowles, *Calvinists Incorporated*.

64. Robert Burns, quoted in H. J. Fyrth and H. Collins, *The Foundry Workers: A Trade Union History* (Manchester: Amalgamated Union of Foundry Workers, 1959), 13.

65. Chris Evans, *The Labyrinth of Flames: Work and Social Conflict in Early Industrial Merthyr Tydfil* (Cardiff: University of Wales Press, 1993), 31-3; George Borrow, *Wild Wales: The People, Language, and Scenery* (London: J. M. Dent & Sons, 1906), 588; *Leigh's Guide to Wales and Monmouthshire* (London: M. A. Leigh, 1833), 299.

66. John R. Stilgoe, *Common Landscape of America, 1580-1845* (New Haven: Yale University Press, 1982), 267.

67. Knowles, *Calvinists Incorporated*, 87-90.

68. John Ferguson Weir, *The Gun Foundry*, Putnam County Historical Society, Cold Spring, New York. Weir's painting is reproduced in *Historical Atlas of the United States* (Washington, D.C.: National Geographic Society, 1988), 124-5.

69. Harris, *Rebecca Harding Davis*, 18.

"A Wide Variety of Cultures Converged in the West Virginia Coalfields." West Virginia and Regional History Collection, West Virginia University Libraries, Morgantown, W.Va.

Strange Tongues: West Virginia and Immigrant Labor to 1920

Kenneth R. Bailey

From the creation of the state, West Virginia's relatively small population was considered to be a detriment to developing the state's farmlands and natural resources. Hoping to rectify the problem, the West Virginia Legislature authorized the appointment of an immigration commissioner in 1864. The first immigration commissioner was Joseph H. Diss Debar who encouraged farmers to immigrate to West Virginia from his native Switzerland and other northern European countries. In addition, West Virginia state officials received numerous solicitations from labor agents in port cities such as Baltimore, Philadelphia and New York who sought a fee for directing immigrants to West Virginia.

Early efforts to stimulate immigration met only minor success due to a lack of adequate roads and rail transportation. West Virginia's abundant resources of timber and coal could not be exploited until transportation improved. The Baltimore and Ohio, completed through the state to Wheeling by 1852, had stimulated growth along its route, but the Civil War delayed efforts to develop railroads through central and southern West Virginia. Soon after the war the Chesapeake and Ohio opened up the coalfields and forests along the New and Kanawha Rivers. Later, the Norfolk and Western Railroad did the same for the Tug Fork and Guyandotte Rivers along the West Virginia-Kentucky border.

Coal and lumber companies quickly used up the available local, native labor. To expand, they turned to recruiting black workers from the South and immigrants from Europe (see table 10.1). Recruiting efforts took several forms. In order to attract black workers from the South, labor agents, some of whom were Baldwin-Felts detectives, would travel in company with black recruiters. The Baldwin-Felts Detective Agency, headquartered in Bluefield, West Virginia, supplied coal, railroad, and lumber companies with "guards" for their various properties. The guards were used to protect company properties, evict strikers, maintain order in the remote coal camps and, in this case, to help recruit new workers from the South. The Baldwin-Felts men did their work after the black recruiters had done theirs. The recruiters would speak at church gatherings and encourage men to come to West Virginia with glowing reports of high wages and the opportunity to escape Jim Crow conditions. Once convinced to board trains for West Virginia, the recruits would be locked in by the Baldwin-Felts operatives until they arrived in West Virginia.

Immigrants were attracted to the state in a number of ways. Some companies stationed independent labor agents in port cities such as New York, Philadelphia, and Baltimore, and paid the agents a fee for each worker that arrived in West Virginia. Other techniques included sending recruitment brochures to European countries describing the advantages of working in West Virginia and promising free transportation to the New World. Sometimes, an advance on wages was offered as an added inducement. Finally, family members of recent immigrants were encouraged to emigrate when they heard of the high wages being paid. Recruiters in both the American South and in Europe found a fertile field among those who sought to improve themselves economically and socially and saw work in the mines or timber operations as the way to accomplish their goals.[1]

Attracting and using immigrant labor created a conflict between the great need for workmen and existing prejudicial attitudes toward immigrants and blacks. West Virginia's population at the end of the Civil War, with the exception of a small number of blacks, was almost exclusively white, Anglo-Saxon, and Protestant. The power structure, public and private, reflected general negative attitudes toward immigrants, especially those from southern and eastern Europe. Newspaper articles, official documents, and actions by state officials and private companies reflected a dichotomy of need for, and disdain toward, the immigrant. Complaints about ill treatment of immigrants surfaced as early as 1891 when the Austro-Hungarian consul at Richmond, Virginia, complained to West Virginia Governor A. B. Fleming that his countrymen were being held against their will at a railroad construction camp in Mercer County, West Virginia. Again in 1894, Governor William A. MacCorkle received a complaint that 350 Italian laborers were being mistreated at a labor camp in Randolph County. While both instances were investigated, no charges were leveled at the alleged perpetrators and no details of the mistreatment were revealed.[2]

Charges that companies were holding workers and forcing them to work against their will persisted and were so numerous that in 1903 the Society for the Protection of Italian Immigrants sent Gino C. Speranza to West Virginia to investigate.[3] Speranza's visit stimulated the investigation of charges of peonage against several West Virginia companies. Peonage is a legal term meaning that a person is being held against his or her will in order to work off a debt. Unlike slavery, which is a permanent condition, the peon would, hopefully, be freed once the debt was paid. Immigrants fell prey to the practice of peonage when they accepted free transportation to West Virginia and food and lodging from companies for whom they worked. Bringing workers to West Virginia in this manner was called bringing them "on transportation" and each was expected to reimburse the company which footed the bill. Since many immigrants spoke no English, had no idea of the type of work they would be doing in the Mountain State, and had no training in mining or timbering, many desired to leave shortly after arriving and without paying their debts. West Virginia authorities used the boardinghouse law to hold them at work. An 1899 law passed by the West Virginia legislature allowed owners of boardinghouses to obtain warrants for the arrest of anyone defrauding them for food and lodging. Coal and timber operators used this statute before local justices of the peace to charge immigrants for transportation, lodging, and food. The justices of the peace would charge the immigrants and turn them over to the operators to work off their debts, thus leading to the charges heard by Speranza and others who sought to improve the lot of immigrants.[4]

In 1907, reports of peonage caused United States Secretary of State Elihu Root to complain to Governor William M. O. Dawson about the practice and to ask for an investigation. Dawson later sent a special message to the 1907 session of the legislature detailing the results of the investigation. Dan Cunningham, a federal marshal who looked into the allegations, found that a number of men had been brought to West Virginia by the William Ritter Lumber Company to build an extensive lumberyard in Wyoming County. The men had been secured from Bureau Number 7 of the Southern Immigration Labor Company of New York City. There were a number of nationalities and races included in the group, and on the job the men were known only by numbers, rather than by names. Cunningham's investigation revealed that peonage had, indeed, occurred in Wyoming County.[5]

Governor Dawson denounced the conditions of lawlessness in the coalfields, and lack of law enforcement which allowed peonage and other acts of cruelty to occur, but he offered little in the way of a solution to the problem. Rather, his remarks blamed the immigrants themselves for their problems:

> These laborers are of different nationalities; unable to speak our language and unable to protect themselves; many are brutal and vicious; and, their manhood and spirit crushed by centuries of oppression in the foreign lands, they confuse liberty with license. But they are human beings. Our duty, the instincts of humanity, justice, our own safety as a people, and our good name, all demand they be treated justly, and that if the law has been violated that the offenders be adequately punished, and if there be need of further legislation it be promptly furnished.

Dawson emphasized that the state had a huge need for labor, but the system of using labor contractors produced an undesirable class of labor. He noted that he had received a letter from a coal operator that suggested the state offer

Table 10.1

Comparison of Total West Virginians by Nationality and Number of Each Who Worked in the Mines 1910, 1920, and 1930

Nationality	1910 Total	1910 Miners	1920 Total	1920 Miners	1930 Total	1930 Miners
Albania			2			
American (White)	1,099,745	28,301	1,319,218	56,913	1,461,544	66,022
Armenia			41			
Asia (Other)			76			
Australia			33			
Austria	8,360	1,210	5,115	2,095	5,969	843
Belgium	800	10	938	67	1,480	40
Bohemia		26		31		48
Bulgaria	61	19	98	117	199	109
Canada	854		54		2,658	
Central Am & Islands			160			
China	90		98		86	
Croatia		55		165		190
Czechoslovakia			1,549		7,381	
Denmark	67	1	121	7	270	2
England	3,505	391	3,435	343	11,910	490
Finland	127		289		271	
France	535	28	633	53	1,979	46
Galatia				15		3
Germany	6,327	312	3,798	268	19,804	296
Granish				81		36
Greece	787	340	3,186	731	4,197	532
Guinea Negro		4				
Hebrews				3		
Holland	60					
Horwat		12		387		194
Hungary	5,939	4,016	6,260	4,128	8,275	3,503
India	36		7		18	
Ireland	2,290	146	1,459	154	9,113	225
Italy	17,286	7,599	14,147	6,412	32,190	4,225
Japan	3	2	10		9	
Jugoslavia			2,802		5,225	
Lithuania		428	717	417	2,023	641
Litvitch		140		126		50
Luxembourg			6			
Magyar		5				
Mexico			80		191	233
Montenegro				133		74
Negroes	64,173	12,087	86,345	18,391	114,893	23,523
Netherlands			66		249	
Newfoundalnd			6			
Norway			51		194	
Palestine			20		3,384	
Poland		1,895	5,799	2,568	14,857	2,474
Portugal			17			17
Roumania	259	296	625	314	1,311	269
Russia	5,143	1,077	3,911	1,528	5,388	1,137
Scotland	1,088	179	998	99	4,316	171
Servia		16		135		170
Slavish		1,899		795		1,284
Spain	464	5	1,543	440	2,397	836
Syria		60	1,235	63		27
Sweden	278	22	326	44	924	21
Switzerland	600		545		1,819	
Turkey	1,146		180	37	671	16
Unknown	216	7,545		331	1,433	52
Wales	880	9	704	35	2,312	33
Total	1,221,119	68,135	1,466,701	97426	1,728,940	107,832

Sources: General statistics taken from *United States Census for 1910, Vol. III (Population); 1920, Vol. II (Population);* and *1930, Vol. III, Part 2 (Population).* Miners figures from *West Virginia Department of Mines Annual Reports.*

inducements to suitable immigrants from the British Isles, Sweden, Norway, and Poland to offset the huge number of Italian immigrants to the state.[6]

The United Mine Workers Journal added its voice to the debate on the quality of the immigrants being brought to the United States. An April 1907 article described the early wave of northern Europeans as being those who helped settle the country. The paper lamented a new group of immigrants:

> The classes of people which today arrive on our shores from the European South and West, viz., the Italian, the Slavish races, the Russian and Polish Jews, and even the Greeks, Armenians and Bulgarians, who are crowding in upon our territories in the East, are by far not the class of people that would join us or participate in our struggle for the maintenance of our standard of living.[7]

Most of the union's concerns were directed at the impact that unorganized immigrant labor would have on its efforts to raise the standard of living in the United States for all workers rather than on ethnic prejudice. The union wanted to see the government direct immigrants to the large, unsettled areas of the West where they could make use of their skills in agricultural endeavors and where they could become productive members of society.[8] However, when it came to Oriental immigrants, the union publication expressed ideas that clearly demonstrated a racial and cultural bias. A January 1907 editorial in the UMWJ illustrates these feelings:

> The United States is cursed or blessed, just as you look at it, by several race problems that are worrying the intellects of the nation in an effort to arrive at a solution. In the southern as well as in several northern states the negro question is a burning issue. In the Rocky Mountain states, Utah, Idaho and Arizona are struggling with the Mormon question, while the Pacific coast states, California, Oregon and Washington are passing sleepless nights over the Chinese question, to which it seems will be added the Japanese question. And along these lines it is very amusing to read that the Japs are insulted because they are classed with the native American negro. The negro may be alien in race but he is civilized and is a believer in Christian civilization and has in times innumerable from Crispus Attucks to Mingo Sanders, fought and bled for the United States and is to all intents and purposes part and parcel of this nation. The Jap is on level and allied with all that is antagonistic to Christian morals, ideas and teachings. He is first, last and always a Jap, and in the event of his being given citizenship he will receive his political instructions from Tokio instead of Washington and will vote for the glory of the Mikado instead of voting for the good of his adopted country.[9]

An unsigned letter to the editor in the Charleston Gazette in November 1908 also reveals the general attitude toward immigrants. The writer complained that recent articles in the paper were supportive of protecting labor "but of the imported kind. The kind we hear jabbering in unknown tongues on Capital Street of a Saturday night." The writer then gave a brief history of immigration:

> Look at the evolution of labor in the past few years: first we had the Swedes, Germans and other **desirable** classes imported to act as a lever to cut down the wages of the native born laborer; then as they got wise in their generation and demanded more pay, a **cheaper** class was looked up, and when they also got wise, a dragnet was hauled among the lowest elements of Hungarians and Italians, and when they wear out as to rates, I suppose we have the little brown brother.[10]

Other complaints about eastern Europeans lamented the large sums of money that after each payday they allegedly mailed back to their relatives in Europe.[11] The amount of money sent from the United States annually to relatives in the country of origin was, in fact, staggering. In 1906, the U.S. Post Office reported that 2,757,409 money orders were sold. Over $62,400,000 was sent to twenty-nine countries with Italy, Great Britain, Hungary, Austria, Russia, and Germany being the largest recipients in descending order.[12] The *United Mine Workers Journal* interpreted sending money abroad as positive in that it allowed workers in the United States to raise the standard of living in, and to influence the cultures of, the foreign countries. However, in West Virginia many expressed outrage at the loss of capital to the foreign countries, particularly Italy and other countries of southeastern Europe. It is interesting that the amount sent to Great Britain, $10,497,744 was second only to the $16,239,134 sent to Italy, but was apparently more acceptable.

Another complaint against miners from southern Europe was that they were detrimental to safety in the mines. The chief of the West Virginia State Department of Mines, John W. Paul, joined in the criticism expressed in the media, when he suggested that substituting Welsh, German, or Scottish miners for Italians in the mines of West Virginia would solve many problems. The large number of accidents in West Virginia mines were blamed on the eastern and southern European immigrants. The 1907 *Annual Report of the Department Of Mines* claimed that men speaking languages other than English caused mining accidents because they were unable to understand verbal commands and because they were inexperienced.[13]

If the statistics are examined, however, it appears that immigrants were no more likely to be involved in accidents than native white or black miners (see table 10.2). In 1907, the year in which Paul made his comment, immigrants accounted for 39 percent of the total mine work-force, but only accounted for 40 percent of the accidents. American White miners had 44 percent of the accidents reported to the Department of Mines but made up only 36 percent of the total workforce. Black miners were 17 percent of the total mine force and had 17 percent of the accidents.[14] Even in 1908, a year which included figures on

Table 10.2
Total Mine Accidents
and Percentage of Accidents by Nationality

YEAR	White Am Employees	Percent of Total Accidents	Negro Employees	Percent of Total Accidents	Foreign Born Employees	Percent of Total Accidents	Total Number of Employees	Total Number of Accidents
1907	36%	44%	17%	17%	39%	40%	56,209	804
1908	39%	36%	18%	14%	43%	50%	60,484	1,467
1909	40%	40%	17%	25%	43%	35%	62,189	1,396
1910	42%	37%	18%	16%	41%	47%	68,135	1,297
1920	58%	57%	19%	19%	23%	24%	97,426	1,168
1930	61%	66%	22%	20%	17%	13%	107,832	3,372

*Figures for employment by nationality were not available for 1906.
**All figures from West Virginia Department of Mines Annual Reports.

West Virginia's worst mine disaster in December 1907, immigrants compared favorably with native whites in terms of safety. The explosion at Monongah killed more than three hundred men and boys in a mine complex where there was a heavy concentration of southeastern European immigrants. In 1908, white American miners made up 39 percent of the workforce and had 36 percent of the accidents, while immigrants made up 43 percent of the workforce and accounted for 50 percent of the accidents. Black miners had only 14 percent of the accidents and made up 18 percent of the total workforce.[15] It would appear that James Paul's comments may have been based on his prejudices rather than on the facts. In 1909, the West Virginia Department of Mines report contained statistics which demonstrate that the number of years of experience was a major factor in mine accidents. From 1901 to 1909, miners with fewer than two years of experience had 38 percent of all accidents and those with fewer than five years had 49 percent of the accidents.[16]

Statistics and facts notwithstanding, by 1907 coal operators and their friends in state government decided that West Virginia had to seek more "desirable" miners. Their approach to attracting more western European miners was to employ an immigration commissioner for the state of West Virginia. Attracting immigrants to the state, however, was not easy. They found that their efforts were resisted by organized labor, by problems with national immigration officials who claimed that West Virginia mines were unsafe, and by conflicts with national immigration laws.

As noted earlier, the West Virginia legislature had created the position of immigration commissioner to attract farmers to West Virginia, but after the term of the first commissioner, Joseph H. Diss Debar, the position had been largely ignored. In 1907, the legislature authorized the board of public works to appoint another commissioner, but failed to fund the position. Instead, the salary and office expenses were borne by coal companies. John Nugent, president of both the United Mine Workers District 17 and the West Virginia State Federation of Labor, was chosen as the immigration commissioner. Nugent resigned as president of District 17 shortly after his appointment and was forced from the presidency of the state labor federation within six months.[17]

John Nugent had high hopes of attracting what he called "practical" miners from the British Isles to work in West Virginia. Nugent, himself a Welsh immigrant, proposed to visit "England, Scotland, Wales and Ireland where the best class of laborers come from." He accepted the position of immigration commissioner, he told a reporter, because he believed that the introduction of English-speaking and British-trained miners into West Virginia would improve the coal industry's workforce[18]

One of Nugent's first acts as the immigration commissioner was to propose a trip to England to advertise opportunities for miners in West Virginia's coalfields.[19] Nugent's plans raised a storm of protest from labor groups and probably violated the most recent version of the Alien Contract Labor Law, enacted by the United States Congress in February 1907 to become effective on July 1 of that year.

Since the 1880s, various versions of the Alien Contract Labor Law had been passed to limit immigration by skilled workers who had been contracted for specific employment. The early statutes, enacted by concerted efforts of labor organizations, were aimed at corporations and businesses. The laws addressed the use of agents in foreign lands, advertisements, and contracts for labor. The 1903 statute made it illegal, for example, for any person to prepay transportation or assist or encourage the importation of an alien." The law did, however, allow states or territories to advertise their inducements for immigration.[20]

By the time that the West Virginia Legislature authorized appointment of an immigration commissioner, even the use of state agencies for the encouragement of immigration had come under attack. An opinion by the U.S. attorney general had been requested to determine the effect of the new law on state-induced immigration. West Virginia Governor Dawson, Nugent, and others were aware that their efforts might be thwarted by the change in the Alien Contract Labor Law effective in July 1907. In fact, in late May 1907 Governor Dawson tried to avoid potential criticism by sending Nugent to get the blessing of the federal commissioner of immigration for the West Virginia immigration effort.[21]

The governor had good reason to be concerned. The United Mine Workers of were struggling to organize West Virginia. The union officials claimed that imported labor was unneeded in West Virginia and elsewhere in the United States if coal operators would cooperate with unions who could provide the "practical" workers they needed.[22] Adding weight to the mine workers' protests, American Federation of Labor President Samuel Gompers wrote federal immigration officials protesting the importation of contract laborers into West Virginia and other states.[23]

In addition to the turmoil surrounding proposals to seek out more acceptable workers from abroad, West Virginia was dealing with the federal prosecution of alleged peonage against the William Ritter Lumber Company and the Raleigh Lumber Company. Because local federal officials were reluctant to prosecute powerful West Virginia interests for violating the peonage statutes, Deputy U. S. Attorney General Charles Russell was assigned the task. Securing a conviction was not easy, even with a plea of guilty from officials of both companies since the presiding judge, Alston G. Dayton of the northern district of West Virginia, never a labor supporter, made it clear that he found the whole proceeding distasteful. Actually Dayton was assigned the duty of hearing the case because the southern district judge, B. F. Keller, owned stock in the Ritter company and had to recuse himself. The Ritter company's plea agreement provided that Ritter would plead guilty in return for all charges against his employees being dropped, and that he would have a hearing before Judge Dayton to determine the amount of his fine. During the hearing, Dayton's actions handicapped the government's presentation. He limited the number of witnesses, reduced the number of charges to which Ritter had pled guilty from twenty to ten, and made his prejudices known. Dayton found excuses for the fact that Ritter had held men in peonage. One of his excuses was that few people even knew of the peonage statute; therefore, how was Ritter to know he violated the law? He also found it "inconceivable...to believe that [Ritter], for the paltry sums of money involved, went to New York and got these men, paid their transportation and got them into debt for the purpose of violating the law." Like Governor Dawson before him, Dayton blamed the victims for their plight. "I take into consideration the further fact that these people, the prosecuting witnesses, do not stand, from a moral standpoint, in the strongest light. [I do] not have sympathy with these fellows who did not go down there and keep their contracts and live up to their honest debts; but at the same time, this law, tender of the liberty of the people, makes this company technically a violator of the law. . . ."[24]

Whether or not Ritter knew in advance how friendly Judge Dayton would be is unknown. West Virginia's power structure was made up of businessmen, state government leaders, and federal officials, all of whom had close political, economic, and social ties. As noted earlier, Judge Keller had business dealings with Ritter's company and was replaced by Judge Dayton. The assistant district attorney on the case, H. D. Rummell, continued to represent coal interests while holding his federal post. It is not clear if the federal district attorney, Elliott Northcott, actually represented coal interests, but he, Judge Keller, Judge Dayton, and Rummell, all Republicans, owed their federal appointments to Senators Stephen B. Elkins and Nathan B. Scott. Northcott was closely aligned politically with Ritter's defense counsel C. W. Dillon. Dillon had served as the tax commissioner under Governor Dawson at the same time that Northcott was state chairman of the Republican party, and both men had been considered as possible successors to Governor Dawson.[25]

All things considered, U.S. Assistant Attorney General Charles Russell was lucky to get an indictment, let alone a verdict for the government. However, while he gained a successful guilty plea, Russell actually lost the case when Dayton reduced the number of charges and gave both the Ritter and Raleigh lumber companies minimal fines as punishment.[26]

Instances such as the trial for peonage and continued problems with immigrant labor, reaffirmed a general desire to bring more favorable immigrants to the state. West Virginia was not the only state hoping to stimulate immigration through official, state-sponsored programs, nor were such efforts exclusive to coal and timber operations. South Carolina, North Carolina, and Georgia sought workers for textile plants, and union workers feared that similar efforts would be made on behalf of Indiana glass manufacturers.[27]

In spite of ongoing peonage trials and virulent criticism from the United Mine Workers, John Nugent continued planning for a trip to England and Wales to recruit miners. Nugent met with U.S. labor officials such as Terence V. Powderly about his plans. Nugent was evidently successful in, if not receiving approval of his trip to Europe, at least avoiding active federal disapproval. On June 7, Nugent left for the British Isles.

Nugent spent three months in England and Wales, talking to coal miners and coal mine groups about the advantages of working in West Virginia. On his return, Nugent discovered that the United Mine Workers organization had flooded England with flyers warning miners about his trip and purporting to tell the truth about the mine situation in West Virginia.[28] Nugent was reportedly greatly saddened that his former coworkers would not support the recruitment of immigrant miners who could help organize West Virginia.[29]

He disclaimed personal knowledge of any miners who had heeded his call to immigrate. He had reports, according to an interview in a Charleston newspaper, that some English miners had come to the state as a result of his efforts and he knew of "thousands of others" who were saving their money to come to West Virginia.[30] He undoubtedly did not wish to admit aiding foreign miners to come to the state since the opinion of U.S. Attorney General Charles J. Bonaparte forbade state officials to have direct influence in encouraging immigration and assisting laborers to enter the United States.[31]

National labor officials continued their attack on Nugent and accused him of actively aiding English miners to immigrate. UMWA President John Mitchell and AFL President Samuel Gompers wrote the Bureau of Immigration and Naturalization demanding an investigation. In November, George E. Baldwin, an "immigrant inspector" for the United States Immigration Service, was assigned to the case. Baldwin was given letters reportedly written by English miners alleging that they had come to the United States aboard the SS *Baltic* under assumed names. When they got to their destination in West Virginia, they were held in peonage and could not leave until debts for travel, food, and lodging were paid.[32]

Baldwin first examined the manifest for the SS *Baltic*. He found the aliases of four of the English miners named in Mitchell and Gomper's complaint. He also found that John Nugent was a passenger on the same ship. According to Baldwin, "subsequent events have proven beyond the shadow of doubt that he was aware of this movement if not directly responsible for its promulgation."[33] Baldwin's next step was to visit West Virginia to talk to people on the scene.

In West Virginia, Baldwin learned that miners, state mine inspectors, and coal company officials were well aware that Nugent had been actively involved in bringing miners to the state in violation of the Alien Contract Labor Law. Nugent's activities were largely on behalf of the New River Coal Company which had provided most of the money for his salary. New River Coal Company President and General Manager Samuel Dixon was noted to be the force behind Nugent, and Dixon's mines had benefitted the most from Nugent's efforts. In fact, Baldwin found that Sam Dixon had himself traveled to England and brought back English miners for his coal operations.[34]

Baldwin requested and secured a meeting with Governor Dawson. On arriving in Charleston for the meeting, he found that John Nugent had accompanied the governor. In a lengthy interview, Baldwin was told that the governor had sent Nugent abroad to "seek nothing but that class of aliens of the English-speaking race who would amalgamate and become permanent residents and citizens." The governor admitted that he knew the orders might conflict with the Alien Contract Labor Law and noted that he sent Nugent to talk with U.S. Secretary of Commerce and Labor Oscar Straus to discuss the trip. He also admitted that he was aware that a decision on the use of state agencies to encourage immigration had been made, but the attorney general's opinion had not been made public at that time. Nugent's comments largely echoed those of the governor, and both of them refused to give details on how Nugent's trip was financed or the source of his salary.[35]

Oscar Straus sent copies of Baldwin's reports to U.S. Attorney General Bonaparte with the recommendation that they be turned over to the U.S. attorney for the district in which the mines were located to determine if the law had been violated.[36] While asking the U.S. attorney to look into the matter was undoubtedly the proper step, it meant that the matter would go no further. The close relationship between federal officials and local coal operators has been mentioned earlier and has been examined more fully in other research.[37] That relationship became evident, however, in conversations between George Baldwin and H. D. Rummell. Baldwin noted that Rummell provided him with a historical background on the development of the West Virginia immigration commissioner's position. Rummell was aware that the coal operators had talked of providing money for the office, but he was not sure if that had been done; "he would positively state, however, that no one of the mine operators **for** whom he was Counsel had contributed a dollar to the enterprise."[38] Baldwin then asked Rummell if he did not believe that Nugent's operations were in opposition to the U.S. attorney general's opinion on "assisted emigration." Rummell replied in the affirmative, but said he believed Nugent had violated neither the letter nor the spirit of the law.[39]

Neither Nugent nor Samuel Dixon were charged with having violated the Alien Contract Labor Law, not because they were not guilty, but because of the attitudes expressed by Rummell, coupled with the fact that the attorney general chose to prosecute Samuel Dixon for peonage instead. Charles Russell had some success in prosecuting West Virginia lumber baron William Ritter for peonage in 1907 and apparently chose to concentrate on similar charges against Dixon. Peonage was probably a better choice for an indictment since Russell had already had success in prosecuting those cases in other southern states and limited success with the Ritter Lumber Company case. Proving criminal intent to violate the Alien Contract Labor Law might have been difficult. Consequently, Dixon, a very powerful coal operator in the New River coalfield, was accused of holding some of the English miners who came to West Virginia on the SS *Baltic* until they paid for their transportation.[40] Dixon was tried in 1908 and, largely because of his influence and power, was found not guilty of the peonage charges.[41]

There is no evidence to show why Nugent was never indicted for his part in illegally assisting immigration. It is very likely that once Dixon had been indicted for peonage, it was considered less important to show that Nugent had violated the law, particularly in light of his quasi-state employment status. From 1907 to 1913 Nugent continued to work to encourage immigration from

England, Wales, and Scotland. He met with a singular lack of success. During testimony before the senate committee investigating the Paint Creek Strike in 1912-13, Nugent claimed that federal officials rebuffed his efforts to recruit miners for West Virginia. According to Nugent, the commissioner-general of immigration had ordered that West Virginia be denied assistance in acquiring immigrant workers until the mines met the (safety) requirements of the United Mine Workers of America. Not only would West Virginia be denied assistance in getting miners, but Terence Powderly, who was the federal official in charge of information distribution, told Nugent that the federal government would do all in its power to prevent immigrant miners from going to West Virginia.[42] The boycott worked. Mine employment in West Virginia grew from 60,484 in 1908 to 70,321 in 1913, but the number of English, Scottish, and Welsh miners dropped from 721 in 1908 to 590 in 1913. The increase between 1908 and 1913 was in the number of native white and Black miners.[43]

Official state involvement in immigration efforts ended when John Nugent left his position and accepted a job with the Consolidation Coal Company. The issue became moot when the outbreak of war in Europe in 1914 practically ended immigration to the United States until war's end. The Russian Revolution and the rise of socialism led Congress to take a much more restrictive attitude toward immigration, resulting in a national quota system in 1921. Figures for West Virginia's foreign-born population between 1900 and 1930 are illustrative of the impact that World War I, and then restrictive immigration laws had on the numbers of immigrants to the state. In 1900 there were 22,379 foreign-born whites and that had more than doubled to 57,072 in 1910. By 1920 there was modest growth to 61,906, while the figure actually declined to 51,520 in 1930.[44]

Negative attitudes toward southeastern European immigrants surfaced in West Virginia again during the "Red Scare." Newspaper articles frequently credited lawless activities to "Bolsheviks" and labor activities were scrutinized to determine if socialists were involved. Those with foreign-sounding names were suspect. In one instance, the *Charleston Daily Mail* noted that "Names of Foreign Origin" were signed to a protest of the 1919 state police bill from United Mine Workers Local 2901.[45] Obviously, names such as Smith and Jones were not considered "foreign-sounding."

An evaluation of West Virginia's response to immigration must recognize that there was a legitimate need to attract workers to develop the state. However, the early effort to attract small numbers of "yeoman" farmers quickly changed when huge numbers of workers were needed for the lumber and coal industries. The source of the largest number of immigrants, at the same time that the West Virginia coal industry was booming, was Italy, Hungary, and other southeastern European countries. White, Anglo-Saxon business operators and government officials allowed their religious and ethnic prejudices to color their attitudes toward these immigrants and, consequently, to affect how they treated them on and off the job. With few exceptions, those who were subjected to peonage were either of southeastern European origin, or black. Finally, the state of West Virginia failed in its attempt to use its official status to recruit workers because its collective bargaining stance made it a pariah with the federal officials in a position to control immigration, and also because its actions were in violation of the Alien Contract Labor Law.

Fortunately, in spite of their treatment and to the benefit of the state, thousands of southeastern Europeans opted to remain in West Virginia and raise their families. Over the years, children from these families have been influential in the development of the state and have become business and political leaders.

NOTES

1. For a discussion of recruitment techniques, see Kenneth R. Bailey, "A Judicious Mixture, Negroes and Immigrants in the West Virginia Mines, 1880-1917," *West Virginia History* 34 (January 1973).

2. J. W. Ewing to Louis Bourchers, 21 March 1891, A. B. Fleming Papers, Department of Archives and History, Cultural Center, Charleston, W.Va.; A. Raoogila to Governor William A. MacCorkle, 11 Dec. (no year), MacCorkle Papers, Department of Archives and History, Cutlural Center,Charleston, W.Va.

3. "Getting Evidence in the Labor Camps of West Virginia," n. d., Gino Speranza Papers (microfilm), Department of Archives and History, Cultural Center, Charleston, W.Va.

4. For a discussion of peonage in West Virginia, see Kenneth R. Bailey, "A Temptation to Lawlessness: Peonage in West Virginia, 1903-1908, *West Virginia History* 50 (1991), 25-45. The most complete study of peonage in the United States is Pete Daniels's *The Shadow of Slavery: Peonage in the South, 1901-1969* (Urbana: University of Illinois Press, 1972).

5. West Virginia, *Special Message of Governor Dawson Concerning Cases of Peonage and Labor Conditions to the Legislature of 1907* (Charleston: Tribune Printing Co., 1907).

6. *Special Message*, 32-5.

7. "Immigration Ideas," *United Mine Workers Journal*, 25 April 1907.

8. Ibid.

9. "Another Race Problem," *United Mine Workers Journal*, 5 Jan. 1907.

10 "Kelley and Luke Interested in Protecting Laborers—But of the Imported Kind," *Charleston Gazette*, 3 Nov. 1908.

11. "20,000 Miners Needed," *Raleigh Herald*, 1 Aug. 1907.

12. "Money Sent Away," *United Mine Workers Jounral*, 25 April 1907.

13. "20,000 Miners Needed," West Virginia, *Annual Report, Department of Mines* (Charleston: Tribune Printing Company, 1908), ix.

14. West Virginia, *Annual Report, 1907*.

15. West Virginia, *Annual Report, 1908*.

16. West Virginia, *Annual Report,1909*.

17. "Cabin Creek Is Falling in Line," *Labor Argus*, 2 May 1907; Evelyn Harris and Frank Krebs, *From Humble Beginnings: West Virginia State Federation of Labor 1903-1957* (Charleston: West Virginia Labor History Publishing Fund, 1960), 18-20.

18. *Labor Argus*, 7 May 1907; Harris and Krebs, *From Humble Beginnings*, 17 To qualify as "practical," a miner needed to satisfy the officers of the union that he possessed the requisite skills for coal mining. U.S. Immigration Commission, *Reports of the Industrial Commission on Immigration*, Vol. 15 (Washington, D.C.: GPO, 1901), 410.

19. U.S. Senate, Committee on Education and Labor, 63rd Cong., 1st sess., *Conditions in the Paint Creek District, West Virginia*, Vol. 2 (Washington, D.C.: GPO, 1913), 2078.

20. U.S. Department of Justice, *Official Opinions of the Attorneys-General of the United States*, 26 (Washington, GPO, 1908), 184.

21. George F. Baldwin to Immigration Commissioner, 7 Nov. 1907, RG 60, Department of Justice, National Archives, Washington, D.C., Box 379, Folder 97058-97257.

22. "The Immigration Conference Farce," *Labor Argus*, 26 Sept. 1907.

23. Samuel Gompers to Executive Council, AFL, 24 Sept 1907, John Mitchell Papers, Reel 12, Vining Library, WVU Tech, Montgomery, W.Va.

24. Bailey, "Temptation to Lawlessness," 39.

25. John Alexander Williams, *West Virginia and the Captains of Industry* (Morgantown: West Virginia University Press, 1976), 144-7, 235-6.

26. Bailey, "Temptation to Lawlessness," 25-45.

27. "Industrial Items," *United Mine Workers Journal*, 21 Feb. 1907.

28. "Unwarranted and Vicious Attack," *Labor Argus*, 10 Oct. 1907.

29. Ben F. Morris to Samuel Gompers, 11 Oct. 1907, Mitchell Papers, Reel 12, WVU Tech.

30. Ibid.

31. *Official Opinions of the Attorneys-General*, Vol. 26, 180-94.

32. George F. Baldwin to Immigration Commissioner, 7 Nov. 1907.

33. Ibid.

34. Ibid.

35. Ibid.

36. Oscar Straus to Charles J. Bonaparte, 14 Dec. 1907, RG60, Department of Justice, National Archives, Washington, D.C., Box 379, Folder 97058-97257.

37. Bailey, "A Temptation to Lawlessness," 36-7.

38. George F. Baldwin to Immigration Commissioner, 7 Nov. 1907.

39. Ibid.

40. George F. Baldwin to Immigration Commissioner, 6 Dec. 1907.

41. Bailey, "A Temptation to Lawlessness," 42.

42. *Conditions in the Paint Creek District*, Vol. 2, 2077-8.

43. West Virginia, *Annual Report of the Department of Mines 1908*, 92; *Annual Report 1909* (Charleston: News Mail Company, 1910), 93; *Annual Report 1910*, 104; *Annual Report 1911*, 120; *Annual Report 1912*, 116; *Annual Report 1913*, 127.1212

44. U.S. Bureau of the Census, *Thirteenth Census of the United States Taken in the Year 1910*, Vol 3, 1032; *Fifteenth Census of the United States: 1930*, Vol. 3, Part 2, 1266.

45. "Miners Union Threatens Strike and Bloodshed If Flag Law Is Upheld," *Charleston Daily Mail*, 12 March 1919.

"Striking Miners on Scotts Run Picket Line, 1931." West Virginia and Regional History Collection, West Virginia University Libraries, Morgantown, W.Va.

Americanizing Immigrant Coal Miners In Northern West Virginia: Monongalia County between the World Wars

Ronald L. Lewis

The twenty million mostly southern and eastern European immigrants who entered the United States between 1880 and 1920 nativist response deeply ingrained in American nationalism and ethnic prejudice. These "New" immigrants, as opposed to the "Old" immigrants from the British Isles and northwestern Europe, spoke foreign languages, were Roman Catholic, Orthodox, and Jewish, and often came from pre-industrial cultures. While they were welcomed by industrialists hungry for cheap, unskilled labor, the "New" immigrants stirred in Americans the sense that something must be done because they were so "un-American."

That something was "Americanization," a movement which took two general forms. One was a malevolent version which sprang from a convergence of ethnocentrism and a nationalistic desire for a more cohesive nation. Americanizers ranged across the conservative ideological spectrum from the Daughters of the American Revolution to the Ku Klux Klan, and they designed programs either to inculcate foreign immigrants with loyalty to America or reject them entirely. A second brand took shape among those who responded primarily to the desperate needs of newly arrived immigrants. Theirs was a humanitarian, reformist perspective on immigration, and they sought to narrow the gulf dividing poor immigrants from the rest of American society. "They concentrated less on changing the newcomers than on offering them a home," writes immigration historian John Higham; they offered assistance to help ease the transition, and organized educational programs and settlement houses to accomplish this end. Hence, "the impulse of fear and the impulse of love," Higham observes, were the polarities of the Americanization movement. "One current tended to soften the movement, orienting it toward the welfare of the immigrant, the other steeled it to an imperious demand for conformity."[1]

The polarity of malevolent to benevolent Americanization impulses were mirrored in industrializing West Virginia during the first decades of the twentieth century. In 1920, at the end of this immigration era, approximately 10 percent of the population of West Virginia were foreign-born. Although this is a modest figure, the vast majority of the new immigrants were concentrated in the state's three major coal subregions: the Pocahontas and Flat Top coalfield; the Kanawha and New River coalfield; and the Fairmont District of northern West Virginia (see table 11.1). The core of the Fairmont District was in Harrison, Marion, and Monongalia Counties along the Monongahela River. In Monongalia County, the focus of this essay, the entire range of Americanization impulses were evident. Morgantown was not only the county's civic and commercial center, and home to the state's university, it was also a service center for the coalfields on the west side of the river. Monongalia County was a hub of malevolent, pragmatic, and benevolent Americanization impulses which were not present elsewhere in the state.

The Monongalia coalfields were part of the greater Fairmont District, which is composed of six West Virginia counties in the Upper Monongahela River watershed: Barbour, Harrison, Marion, Monongalia, Preston, and Taylor. The Monongahela River itself is an extension of the Ohio River industrial and transportation nexus. Industrialization produced a population explosion in the district, particularly in the three largest counties of Harrison, Marion, and Monongalia. Their dramatic growth is reflected by the population expansion of the county seats, which were also the commercial centers: Clarksburg, Harrison County, from 6,742 in 1890 to 27,869 in 1920; Fairmont, Marion County, from 1,023 in 1890 to 17,851 in 1920; and Morgantown, Monongalia County, from 1,011 to 12,127 during the same period.[2] Solidifying their commercial power, each of these small cities built trolley lines during the first decade of the twentieth century which linked many nearby mining towns into the region's transportation network. This local network itself was tied into the national transportation system by the Baltimore and Ohio Railroad, whose tracks were on the east side of the Monongahela River, and the Monongahela Railroad whose tracks ran along the west side of the river. The railroads and the barges which plied the Monongahela River stimulated the development of local industries, especially coal which became the leading industry by 1900. Production increased from 1.13 million tons in 1890 to 21.5 million tons in 1920— about one-quarter of the state's total production. As the industry expanded during the first decade of the twentieth century, many small independent mines were consolidated into fewer, larger companies. By 1920 more than 20 percent of the entire workforce in the six county region was employed in the coal industry.[3]

On the eve of the industrial transition, in 1890, the population in the Fairmont District counties was overwhelmingly (over 95%) composed of white, Anglo-Saxon Protestants. The previous wave of immigrants to enter the region were the Irish who came as railroad workers in the 1850s, and they had long since been assimilated. Industrialization would change this homogeneity as foreign immigrants, and to a lesser extent African Americans, poured into the

Table 11.1

Distribution of West Virginia Coal Miners by Nationality

	1923		1925		1926	
	Number	%	Number	%	Number	%
Southern Territory						
Pocahontas District						
American White	21,101	54.9	22,230	55.1	23,680	55.7
Other Nationalities	8,123	21.2	6,832	16.9	6,885	16.2
African American	9,162	23.9	11,273	28.0	11,982	28.1
Total Miners	38,386	100.0	40,335	100.0	42,547	100.0
New River - Kanawha District						
American White	21,527	64.9	19,243	63.7	21,319	66.0
Other Nationalities	3,813	11.5	3,113	10.3	3,332	10.3
African American	7,835	23.6	7,844	26.0	7,648	23.7
Total Miners	33,175	100.0	30,200	100.0	32,299	100.0
Northern Territory						
Fairmont District						
American White	16,702	55.1	14,829	61.9	17,148	60.9
Other Nationalities	11,425	37.7	6,536	27.3	7,637	27.2
African American	2,192	7.2	2,590	10.8	3,356	11.9
Total Miners	30,319	100.0	23,955	100.0	28,141	100.0

Source: Compiled from the *West Virginia Department of Mines Annual Reports.*
Patterned after Sterling D. Spero and Abram L Harris, *The Black Worker: The Negro
and the Labor Movement* (New York: Columbia University Press, 1931), Table 23, 218.

area workforce, primarily becoming coal miners. The mining workforce in the
Fairmont Field grew from 12,681 to 26, 275 between 1910 and 1920. The 9,762
immigrants in the field represented 37.2 percent of the mine force in 1920.
Eastern Europeans represented 54.4 percent of the foreign-born coal miners,
and Italians accounted for the second largest at 35.2 percent. A significant increase in the number of African American miners also occurred by 1920, growing from a minuscule number to 8.4 percent of all miners in the Fairmont District.[4] Most came during World War I when there were severe labor shortages,
and their numbers would increase during the mid-twenties.

Monongalia County closely followed the same path of development as the Fairmont District generally, although somewhat later. Small "coal banks" dug at the outcrops supplied local demand for coal in Monongalia County prior to 1886 when the first commercial mine began operation. Real expansion did not occur until decades later during World War II when the unprecedented demand for coal prompted large-scale development of the coal industry. In 1900 just two coal mines employing 107 miners produced 82,148 tons of coal in Monongalia County. By 1919, however, 2,521 miners at sixty-one mines produced 2.15 tons of coal, and by 1921 tonnage soared to nearly 4.4 million tons.[5]

Most of this growth was attributable to the development of Scotts Run where, during the twenties, coal companies owned 75 percent of the taxable acres and thirty-six mines were in operation. In fact, this narrow, five-mile-long hollow was one of the most intensively developed coal districts in the United States, hosting at least seventy-three different coal companies between its inauguration in 1917 and its consolidation by one company in 1942.[6] The development of Scotts Run was a project of I. C. White, the state geologist and a Morgantown businessman, who lent his considerable talents to promoting the county's coal industry. In 1923, White published a promotional piece in *Black Diamond*, a leading coal trade publication, informing readers that the four commercial coal seams of Scotts Run located on the west side of the Monongahela River across from Morgantown contained twenty-five feet of coal. This commercially minable coal, he wrote, gave "this favored region the unique distinction of having more coal in its immediate vicinity than any other city of the world." This was more than mere hyperbole, however, for *Black Diamond* subsequently informed its readers that "in no section of West Virginia's many mining districts has the development of a coal field been more phenomenal" than Scotts Run.[7]

Scotts Run provided ready access into the Pittsburgh seam, considered by many experts to be the most valuable mineral deposit in the world. Just above the Pittsburgh, the Sewickley seam was considered the best quality locomotive coal in the nation. With the onset of World War I, the price of coal escalated rapidly in the national markets, and it is significant that the first commercial mine on The Run dates from 1917. Transportation was another key factor. Scotts Run flows into the Monongahela River, one of the most important interior waterways in the nation.[8] Between 1915 and 1925, after a complicated financial history, several small railroads which had laid tracks the length of Scotts Run were purchased by the Monongahela Railway. In 1921, 175 coal cars per day originated from Scotts Run mines and were transported over two sets of double tracks; by 1924 that number had reached an average of two hundred cars a day when the coal markets were slow.[9] Finally, Morgantown was a full-fledged service center for industrial development located on an emerging transportation nexus, and home to six banks willing to finance the development of Scotts Run. Together, these assets would assist Morgantown's growth "as the greatest coal center in northern West Virginia," White proclaimed.[10]

Rapid industrial development on Scotts Run brought an equally profound social transformation to this rural hollow as mining replaced farming as the chief means of earning a livelihood. Farmers and farm laborers comprised 66 percent of the heads of household in Cass District in 1880 and miners only 2 percent; by 1920 coal mining accounted for 63 percent and farming had declined to 21 percent. What this meant to people who had lived there for generations is suggested by an item published in a 1923 issue of *Black Diamond*, which described Cassville as "a sleepy little village that has been there for years. Its residents do not yet comprehend what has taken place in their little community to transform it into a great hive of industry, with rows of dwellings, stores, schools, churches, power houses, generating stations, and tipples that lie in an almost unbroken line for five miles."[11]

In 1890 only seventy-four out of the 15,705 people in Monongalia County were foreign-born; most of them were from the British Isles or northwestern Europe. That profile had changed dramatically by 1920, however, when 3,279 immigrants resided in the county; two-thirds of them lived outside of the city near industrial plants, and in the mining district west of the Monongahela River. Immigrants comprised approximately one-half of the 3,236 miners who worked in the county's seventy-three mines in 1920.[12] The number of foreign-born miners peaked at 3,147 in 1923 (see charts 11.1 and 11.2). Unlike many native whites, immigrants and African Americans did not have farms to return to when the mines were slow or shut down. Instead, they were totally dependent on the coal companies for the necessities of life.

Every aspect of life for the newly arrived immigrants was a challenge. Even getting here was an arduous process. The view of European immigration that American school children were traditionally taught, is of poor, oppressed Europeans leaning forward to catch their first glimpse of the Statue of Liberty in New York harbor. Once ashore their worries were behind them, because now they had officially joined in the pursuit of the American Dream. If they worked hard, prosperity would follow. For first generation immigrants from the British Isles or northern Europe, this may have been the case; for those many more millions from southern and eastern Europe, the story was infinitely more complicated. For the vast majority of them the American Dream was three generations away.

The story of Monongalia County immigrants Charles Luchok (Vassily Luczak) and Anna Manyak Luchok suggests the complexity of the experience. They were born in Mukachevo, Hungary, which was annexed by the Ukraine after World War II. Charles was a farmer, and Anna worked as a domestic for a family in Budapest. They were married, but with little opportunity available to them in their homeland, he left his wife and a young son behind with her parents and emigrated in 1903. Upon arrival in New York, he landed a job at a sugar refinery in Brooklyn, New York, then moved to the anthracite coalfields in northeastern Pennsylvania where he found work in the mines. Before long, he moved on to Lilly, a coal camp near Brownsville, Pennsylvania. In 1913, after ten years of labor, Charles had saved enough money to buy passage for Anna and their son to join him in America. In Lilly, two daughters and another son were born. In 1922 Charles Luchok and his family moved to the Monongalia County, West Virginia, coal camp of Jere on Scotts Run. Charles's only sister and her husband, George Lucaviski, also a Hungarian, lived there, and the family decided to join them. Charles's brother-in-law was a man of many trades: a miner, a butcher, and an expert carpenter who built houses to rent. Charles worked at Jere until the mine closed in 1933. Fortunately, Anna and he had purchased one of George's houses which provided a roof over their heads while Charles worked on WPA projects during the depression. Because they had been farmers in Europe, the Luchoks also managed to have enough to eat. Anna kept a cow for milk, and chickens for eggs. The men butchered hogs a few times a year, and the women made up sausages, hams, shoulders, and smoked meat. Farm culture from the old country, therefore, was not lost in the transition to industrial work; for those trapped by the Great Depression, agricultural skills were often a lifesaver. The Luchoks were among the more fortunate.[13]

Immigrants in Monongalia County not only drew on previous knowledge to survive, but actively attempted to reproduce their Old World lifeways in the new communities as best they could. Immediately, their preferred churches appeared wherever there were sufficient numbers to support them. These churches must have been noticeable structures sprouting up in that established Protestant landscape dominated by Methodist, Presbyterian, and Baptist spires since the late eighteenth and early nineteenth centuries. Roman Catholics began holding services as early as 1901 and built St. Francis Catholic Church in 1914. St. Mary's Greek Orthodox Church was constructed in 1915 to serve the growing Slavic community, but Russian immigrants split away during World War I to found the Greek Catholic Church in Westover, near Scotts Run. In 1918 Rev. Andrew Harsanyi came from Uniontown, Pennsylvania, to preach to Hungarian miners at the newly established Hungarian Evangelical and Reformed Church just across the Monongahela River from Scotts Run. A Hungarian Baptist church was established nearby in 1935. The Greek Catholic church was organized to serve the growing Greek community in 1928. The Tree of Life Congregation synagogue was erected in 1920 to serve Morgantown's Jews. These ethnic religious institutions marked major changes on the cultural landscape of Morgantown during the first decades of the twentieth century. All but the synagogue emerged at the periphery of the growing city to serve the new emergent immigrant work communities.[14]

Religion is, of course, one of the key ingredients of culture, and immigrant churches served as transitional institutions which helped retain the continuity of cultural tradition in the face of rapid change and forced adaptation. Religion was the source of many of the customs which were distinctive to the cultures of the newly arrived immigrants as well. Louis Birurakis, whose parents were from Greece, was born in Liberty on Scotts Run in 1926. He remembered that there were many customs among the immigrant Greek community which were carried over from the old country and persisted during his youth in the 1930s. Greeks celebrated holidays together. The Eastern Orthodox churches celebrated Christmas on January 6, and Easter also generally fell on a different day than the western churches. On New Year's Eve, Mr. Birurakis recalled, he and his young friends would visit the homes of other Greek families to sing. . . . We'd get together and go to each house and sing. And, of course, after singing, we'd go in and they'd . . . give us pastries and sometimes money. And after we were done, we'd divide it up." Baptisms were an important event in the community too. "When there was a baptism," Mr. Birurakis remembered, "that was a big thing with the Greeks. It was a big celebration, sometimes lasting a day or two. Weddings the same way. And they'd sing folk songs in Greek and have a big dinner, and drink a lot."[15]

Common among most immigrant groups, Greek parents expected their children to mate within their own ethnic group. "The parents that came from overseas," Mr. Birurakis said, "preferred that their children dated and married within the same nationality. And that's where I ran into trouble because I married an Italian girl. And it kind of hurt the family a little bit."[16] A social worker at Crown in 1932 remembered that children of immigrants married within their own nationality, "Hungarians to Hungarians and Russians to Russians."[17] Also, following the broader patterns of the immigrant experience in America, the children were far less conscious of ethnic solidarity. According to Mr. Birurakis, even though each group celebrated their own holidays together, and often helped each other, immigrant housing was mixed rather than segregated on Scotts Run. Through play and school the children lost their parents' ability and need to determine subtle nationality differences. The children played together, he related, and were not aware of what nationality the others were. Mr. Birurakis thought he could tell by the names who was Italian, but he was unable to determine the difference between many of the eastern European nationalities. Important as their identity was to the first generation, the cultural nuances generally were lost on their children.[18] John Luchok, who was born in 1921 to Hungarian parents, remembered that Jere coal camp was not segregated either. He remembered "a lot of different people" living there side by side. Across the street and a few doors away lived black families; on one side lived Hungarians, on the other Slovakians; and behind lived an Italian family. Luchok was unaware of any discrimination practiced within the camp toward anybody. He remembered some native-born whites "yelled about the blacks," and sometimes "they called us Hunkies." Nevertheless, racist or nativist behavior was not part of his daily world on Scotts Run.[19] This is a common refrain in numerous interviews with people of The Run.

Native whites viewed the first generation of immigrants with mixed emotions ranging from empathy to hostility. Isolated by their inability to communicate, and low educational and economic status, the immigrants became socially isolated, and isolation accentuated their emotional attachment to their native cultures. This intensification of feeling for the homeland and preserving the old ways became a problem for immigrants during World War I and its aftermath when nativism reached a fever pitch in "100 percent Americanism." This slogan was a compost of many nativist notions, but above all, John Higham writes, 100 percenters "belligerently demanded universal conformity organized through total national loyalty." It was not sufficient to passively assent; loyalty must be "carried forward with evangelical fervor."[20]

The Great War turned Americanization into a "great popular crusade," to use Higham's phrase.[21] "With startling suddenness," a prominent authority wrote in 1916, the war focused in the nation's consciousness the possibility that "the immigrants whom we have welcomed into our society . . . should be an integral part of that society and not foreign to it." Moreover, Americans came to sense that "assimilating this foreign element" had not proceeded as it ought to have, and might prove dangerous to national security.[22] One hundred percent Americanizers "opened a frontal assault on foreign influence in American life," according to Higham, in an attempt to "stampede immigrants into citizenship, into adoption of the English language, and into an unquestioning reverence for existing American institutions."[23] A widely adopted construction of Americanization was offered in 1920 by an authority at Columbia University who insisted that "all newcomers from foreign lands must as quickly as possible divest themselves of their old characteristics," and they must "utterly forget the land of their birth and completely lose from their memory all recollection of its traditions in a single-minded adherence to American life in all its aspects. *They must do the changing; the situation is not to be changed by them*."[24]

Taken up by the more reactionary segments of society, the crusade quickly slid into a general suppression of all unrest, "the dissolution of minority cultures," and finally culminated in immigration restriction legislation passed by Congress in 1921 and 1924. The crusade for Americanization reached a peak in the 1919 and 1920 Red Scare, a campaign led by U. S. Attorney General A. Mitchell Palmer to root out suspected Bolsheviks, particularly in the labor movement, and to deport alien radicals who challenged the status quo.[25]

The tides of national hysteria found expression in West Virginia and the northern coalfields. John Hennen, the authority on Americanization in West Virginia, found that the anti-radical crusade was taken up by business, government, education, and private organizations. At the 1919 meeting of the West Virginia Education Association, teachers were told that they should "teach that law and order must be supreme and inculcate in their students 'a loathing for that thing which is the antithesis of law and order—Bolshevism.'" Another educator declared that America had been admitting an "undigested mass" of foreign immigrants who had retained their old language and culture, and represented "'a dangerous element in our midst who had no sympathy with our Government, our institutions, and our ideals.'"[26] Industrial leaders welcomed immigrant labor, but they joined in the campaign to suppress radicalism. The president of the West Virginia Coal Mining Institute declared that it was not enough to simply Americanize foreigners. "Trouble in the coal industry," he said, "was largely the result of foreigners following a very few un-American Americans." These were the people who presented the biggest concern. Another coal operator declared that "we need to give the foreigner an American outlook, to let him gradually absorb Americanism without knowing it," in other words to be "inoculated" with Americanization in order to develop an immunity to the virus of radicalism.[27]

Hennen concluded that "radicalism" was broadened from Bolshevism to include all social criticism, and dissent in all forms especially from the working class. Cooperation based on class interests exhibited by labor unions in particular were tarred with the brush of foreign radicalism and crushed with the support of the government and public opinion. Like other states, West Virginia attempted to criminalize dissent. Sponsored by a delegate from Monongalia County, the most striking attempt was the 1919 flag bill which sought to ban the teaching of doctrines or displaying flags that were antagonistic to American democracy, or speaking, printing, or otherwise communicating ideas antithetical to American institutions or ideals.[28] No other group of West Virginia workers presented more concern to the Americanizers than the Fairmont District coal miners who had a higher percentage of eastern and southern European immigrants than any other mine force in the state. Moreover, unlike in the southern West Virginia coalfields where labor radicals were derived from the natives, immigrants were the labor radicals in the northern coalfields. Consequently, labor-capital conflict throughout the Fairmont District between 1900 and the 1930s was a social, political, and economic struggle fought on the battlefield of ethnicity.

As in most industries, immigrants were given little opportunity to advance themselves in the coal industry. The best jobs in the mines, such as machine runner, fire boss, or foreman, were generally beyond the reach of even those immigrants who were Americanized. It was the American-born children of immigrants who found personal advancement in coal mining.[29] Immigrants born in Great Britain or Germany were the exception to this rule, but this source of immigration had diminished to a trickle by the twentieth century. Most of the British and German miners came to America between 1850 and 1900 when the industry was expanding and their mining experience was at a premium; culturally they were easily assimilated into Anglo-America. Southern and eastern Europeans were very different culture bearers who spoke little or no English, and often had no coal mining experience. They were hired to be laborers rather than skilled workers. The coal industry was going through a transition from the hand-loading to the machine-mining system. Machine mines required a larger percentage of laborers and, as coal mining experience became less crucial and traditional, craftsmen lost control over production. As a result, craft miners were increasingly "deskilled," and the British and Germans found other employment or remained in their native countries. Their places were taken by southern and eastern Europeans, and to a lesser extent blacks from the Deep South.[30]

The immigrants were desperate for work, but they were not as docile as the operators had expected. The 1920s was a period of intense labor-capital conflict in the coalfields because of the collapse of postwar demand. The "war to make the world safe for democracy" ended in 1919, and with it government regulation of the industry. In order to maintain war production, a government brokered agreement between industry and labor recognized the United Mine Workers of America as the miners' agent, but that grudging compromise was retracted by industry after the war.[31] In northern West Virginia coal operators adhered to a nonunion policy prior to the war, and, after the armistice was signed, they awaited their opportunity to return to the antebellum status quo. One obstacle blocking their immediate return to prewar conditions in the Fairmont Field was the fact that C. W. Watson of Consolidation Coal Company, the dominant producer in the region, had recognized the union in 1918 in hopes of carrying the miners' votes during his campaign for the U.S. Senate. Watson failed in that quest, but he was forced to accept the union until there was an appropriate pretext for rejoining the nonunion operators. That pretext came in 1922. By then the war-heated demand for coal had cooled significantly, and President Warren G. Harding lifted federal regulation of the industry, thus opening the way for an "open shop" drive by the coal producers. In 1923 officers of the UMWA and the Central Competitive Field fashioned, and then early in 1924 signed, the Jacksonville Agreement which maintained the 1922 wage scale. Shortly thereafter, the Northern West Virginia Coal Operators' Association met with UMWA representatives in Baltimore and ratified the national accord. Both contracts were to last until 1927.[32]

In West Virginia, the Fairmont District operators were alone among the state's coal operators in signing the agreement, convinced that their companies could compete with nonunion labor in the southern West Virginia fields. They were wrong and, as coal prices plummeted to their lowest level in the market, the northern operators abrogated the national agreement, thereby precipitating a seven-year mine war in northern West Virginia. This disastrous series of strikes and lockouts lasted from 1924 to 1931. The northern West Virginia mine war was the longest strike in the state's colorful industrial history, and it cast the miners and their families into destitution, and many of the operators into bankruptcy.[33]

In 1928, with the UMWA in ruin, President John L. Lewis granted the districts the power to negotiate their own separate contracts. This left the door open for the National Miners Union, a stalking horse for the Communist Party, to organize the miners. Under the NMU banner, Scotts Run miners went out on strike in 1931 against further cuts in wages which already sagged below subsistence levels. An American Red Cross report called this strike "the most peculiar strike in history" because it was directed against consumers who paid too little to sustain a living wage, rather than against the operators.[34] After a month's stoppage, the Scotts Run operators recognized the UMWA, presumably rather than risk legitimizing the NMU. Operators in the adjacent southwestern Pennsylvania coalfields followed this strategy,[35] and the long, bitter, and frequently violent strike came to an end. The strike settlement proved to be the beginning of the UMWA's resurgence. The end of the seven-year mine war did not bring a return to prosperity, however, for by 1931 the Great Depression also had tightened its hold on the miners, many of whom had been without real work for years. Thus weakened, the nation's economic collapse fell on the miners with a merciless fury that drove most of them into abject poverty.

The mine war and the hard times which followed also fragmented the mining communities into hostile camps. Howard B. Lee, who served as West Virginia attorney general from 1926 to 1933, wrote that "a large number of strikers were of foreign birth and varying nationalities. They had come to this 'land of promise' to escape the earthbound drudgery" of their European homelands "only to find themselves hopelessly buried in America's black pits and embroiled in her endless labor wars." The attorney general indicated that this was particularly worrisome because many of them could "neither speak nor understand the English language, and were highly susceptible to radical influences." In fact, the immigrant strikers "regarded the scab workers as public enemies, and believed that the strike should be conducted in the same manner as their Balkan wars."[36] Lee witnessed just how much they hated strikebreakers when the governor sent him to Everettsville, Monongalia County, after the mine there was demolished by an explosion on April 30, 1927, which took 97 lives. There he saw "that snarling animal hatred felt by members of the miners' union for nonunion miners." The miners regarded the explosion as a "form of divine punishment" meted out to the scabs who had taken their jobs. As bodies were brought from the mine, Lee reported, they would utter: "There's another goddamned strikebreakin' scab son-of-a-bitch gone straight to hell."[37]

According to Michael Workman, an authority on the Fairmont District, confrontations during the twenties followed the same basic pattern: a coal company would declare its intention to operate nonunion; miners who refused to work nonunion were evicted from company houses; the companies would then hire mine guards and start production with replacement workers, "scabs" to the displaced union men; strikers set up temporary tent camps or barracks; picket lines and "marching the mines" followed as miners challenged the non-union policy; and violent outbreaks often resulted from confrontations between the strikers, scabs, and mine guards. During the twenties, local newspapers were full of reports of dynamiting, riots, and shoot-outs between union and nonunion miners. Often, newspaper descriptions of African American and immigrant strikers were less than flattering.[38]

Conservative newspaper editors like C. E. Smith of the *Fairmont Times*, who also was fully invested in the coal industry, blamed the strike violence on the foreigners. In fact, he claimed that the nonunion miners were predominantly natives, and "a typical strikers' picket line would show not more than 10 percent native born whites, 10 percent Negroes and the rest foreign born with the Italian type predominating."[39] Like the Ku Klux Klan, which he supported, Smith reserved his greatest hostility for foreigners and they responded in like manner; a businessman informed Smith that "he was a special object of attack in assemblies of the furriners." The editor also ran a network of company undercover agents who informed him that he was "marked man" by the "foreign element."[40]

The racialist tone of the Americanization rhetoric was hardly subtle even among those motivated by humanitarian impulses. Mrs. L. H. Cammack, chair of the West Virginia Federation of Women's Clubs, declared that West Virginia was "peculiarly fortunate" in having so few immigrants. Only 10 percent of the state's population were foreign born in 1920, she observed, and many had already become citizens.[41] Phil Conley was managing director of the American Constitutional Association, founded as a public relations project by the West Virginia Coal Operators, but he also edited the *West Virginia Review*, which boosted the state's business opportunities and other attractions, and emphasized the Anglo-Saxon purity of West Virginia natives. In the journal's very first issue he boasted that West Virginia's population was 89.9 percent white, "the highest percentage of native born white citizens to be found in any state in the Union." They represented "the best Anglo-Saxon blood to be found in America today." In a subsequent issue, another contributor touted West Virginia's "Pure-Blooded Americans," and claimed that "there is scarcely a trace of foreign blood to be found," in the state. With the exception of the coal districts, there were few foreigners or Negroes in these mountains, he pointed out.[42]

Following World War I, there was a prevailing sense among 100 percenters that they had failed in their efforts to assimilate foreigners. Instead of vainly struggling to make Americans of them, some nativists reasoned, perhaps it was best to avoid the problem and keep them out. The nativism of the postwar twenties thus turned toward hatred of Catholics, Jews, and other non-Anglo groups. Anglo-Saxonists associated crime, labor radicalism, and excessive alcohol consumption with foreign immigrants.[43] Anti-Catholicism surpassed every other hatred in the twenties, and nobody hated better or more than the Ku Klux Klan. The Klan of the twenties accepted the notion that America had fought the war to save the world for democracy, and all America got in return was "crime, moral chaos, and organized selfishness on a grander scale than before," all of which suffocated the moral purity of an earlier, purer Anglo-Saxon America. Influenced by the rise of Protestant fundamentalism, the Klan insisted on a Biblical Christianity which emphasized the differences between Protestants and Catholics.[44]

Michael Workman claims that many native coal miners in the Fairmont District who had gone back to work during the mine war of the twenties belonged to the Klan even though it was a clear violation of the UMWA's constitution for members to belong to the Klan. After trying to soft-pedal the issue early in the strike to avoid antagonizing native members, the UMWA "finally recognized the Klan as an adversary," and by August 1925 speakers were attacking the Klan at union rallies. C. E. Smith "claimed that the working miners were mostly natives and those who were striking, 'in overwhelming majority,' were aliens."[45] Presumably the West Virginia State Federation of Labor supported the UMWA's belated stand against the Klan, for it invited Edward T. Hill, director of the state's Bureau of Negro Welfare and Statistics, to address the state convention in 1924. Hill's speech is interesting because he points out that blacks joined with organized labor in support of restricting immigration.

"On the question of restricted immigration, the Negroes of the country are united with the American Federation of Labor and on that question we are also with the Ku Klux Klan," Hill told the delegates. "You support restricted immigration because most foreigners who come here are not accustomed to the American standard of living. . . . and they can work cheaper than you." Similarly, immigrants took the jobs available to blacks in the northern industrial centers so restricting immigration would free up "many thousands in the South from economic slavery and a social order only a little above physical slavery." But the Klan, Hill continued, "is for restricted immigration because of their theories that a branch of the white race which they call 'Nordics' is superior to all other races and their desire to keep Catholics and Jews out of this country." Hill said African American workers joined the UMWA in support of restricted immigration as a job protection measure, but condemned the Klan's "efforts to supplant organized government, to promote religious intolerance, racial antagonisms and bigotry. . . . We call upon them to preserve religious freedom and the rights of all men of all races under the law."[46]

Hill's position demonstrates why hostility often pervaded relations between native blacks and foreign-born whites. John Atkinson, the general superintendent of the Berry Mine on Scotts Run, informed the economist Abram L. Harris in 1925 that "the foreign Poles and Slavs have always opposed the hiring of Negroes as miners." When he tried to hire several black miners at the Berry mine, the foreigners threatened to strike. "He further said that the foreign element would drive the Negro out of his own country" and that "the Negro is a fool to turn 'red' with huskies and Russians whose first words in English are usually 'I won't work with a ——black——of a ——.'" Harris reported parenthetically that Mr. Atkinson was an Englishman who worked as a miner in Britain, but had been in American mines for twenty years.[47]

The number of Klan members in Monongalia County is unclear, but on May 31, 1926, Morgantown experienced its first (and only known) "Klavakade." The city's newspapers, the *Post* and the *New Dominion*, reported that "two to three thousand robed and hooded men and women marched in a huge parade down High Street through the center of downtown," and that "great crowds" had assembled along the streets to watch the parade. Spectators, who "appeared to take the spectacle good-naturedly," periodically applauded the marchers, and no incidents were reported. Klan men and women came from all over West Virginia, and from surrounding states, to participate in the Klavacade. The *New Dominion* reporter estimated that there were "some 400 to 500 men in the unit designated as Monongalia Klan No. 59." The line of march took the paraders to the West Virginia University football stadium where an estimated fourteen to fifteen thousand people gathered to watch the fireworks display, and to hear

Imperial Wizard Hiram Wesley Evans attack the Catholic Church for attempting "to secure control over the body politic in America," and asserted that "American labor owes to the Klan the present immigration law that practically prohibits the entry of the undesirable European labor to the shores of America."[48] The *Post* also carried the story on the front page, but in the adjoining column printed an article on the May 30 sermon by the Reverend W. E. Brooks, pastor of the First Presbyterian Church, denouncing Klan demagogy, and chastising those who accepted the lure of racial and religious superiority as unworthy of the gifts of religious freedom and equal rights bequeathed by the Founding Fathers.[49]

Generally, the racialism and anti-religious prejudice encountered by immigrants was more subtle than Klan diatribes. Local newspapers, particularly the *Fairmont Times*, often used derisively colorful language when reporting crimes committed within the ethnic communities. As might be expected, the greatest venom was reserved for crimes committed by immigrants against natives. When an Italian immigrant stabbed a mine foreman at Monongah in 1911, the local paper editorialized that foreigners were "being allowed too much latitude, and that trouble would result unless they were checked." Many of these foreigners, the editor continued, "believe they can do as they please in this country" and must be "taught their place in no uncertain manner by the authorities." Although conditions were worse in the mine towns, he continued, "it often occurs" that foreigners "become unruly, and rude upon the streets, much to the discomfort and disgust of the pedestrians."[50] The editors of the Morgantown papers were noticeably less nativistic than C. E. Smith of Fairmont, but they did speak out when local economic progress seemed threatened. Gilbert B. Miller, the editor of the *Post*, was a self-conscious booster of local business and political reform. A survey of Miller's columns shows an anxiety common among civic leaders that his hometown and county were falling behind in the national pursuit of progress. Throughout the twenties, the paper reported an ever growing number of violent episodes as evidence of the need for order. Foreigners were giving the county a bad image which would dissuade external investment in the local economy. Therefore, he applauded the creation of the state constabulary by Governor John J. Cornwell in 1919 as a necessary antidote to the increased radicalism among the miners, and he supported their use throughout Monongalia County during the strike of 1919.[51]

Ethnic relations plummeted to a new low with passage of prohibition legislation in 1912 closing the saloons, and the Yost Law in 1914, which provided for the law's enforcement. Few immigrants supported prohibition, and continued to secure their liquor from moonshiners and bootleggers; some became suppliers themselves. When mixed into the barrel of other grievances fermenting among immigrants, prohibition became a volatile cultural brew.

This became apparent in 1915 when coal miners at three operations near Farmington, Marion County, threw down their tools and went on strike. Between three and six hundred "Italians, Poles, Russians and a large contingent of Croatians or Serbo-Croatians," marching behind an American flag and a banner that read "Give Us Justice or Nothing at All" demonstrated at area mines in an attempt to stop work in the field. A posse led by Constable William Riggs dispatched to subdue the strikers instead found themselves surrounded by an angry mob of immigrant miners. According to one historian who has analyzed this episode, the miners attacked the posse and beat them with fists and clubs. The mob singled out Constable Riggs because he enforced the Yost Law, and he subsequently died from the brutal treatment he received. Close to fifty immigrants were sentenced to the state penitentiary for the attack.[52] The attack was not premeditated, but it confirmed the nativists' low opinions of the new arrivals.

Monongalia County did not have its equivalent of the Constable Riggs episode, but prohibition was an important source of friction between law enforcement and immigrants. One researcher has suggested that, like elsewhere in industrializing America, Morgantown's political and business elites were proponents of prohibition. West Virginia went dry in 1912, and prohibition advocates took particular aim at immigrant workers in their efforts to establish a reliable (pliable) workforce through Americanization. Prohibition played a major role in that campaign. Monongalia County industrialists and political leaders, particularly in the Republican Party, were leaders in the drive to close the saloons; they not only fashioned the law but also enforced it.[53]

There is little doubt that interest in prohibition among native Protestants accompanied the growth in the number of immigrants entering the workforce during the early twentieth century. Most of these immigrants were not eligible to vote in 1912 and, therefore, had no voice in the decision. For many conservative Protestant natives, immigrants, radical anti-American ideologies, and booze were inextricably intertwined. The state commissioner of prohibition, Frederick O. Blue, left little doubt of his position. In his 1916 book, *When a State Goes Dry*, he declared that "the great present-day problem of immigration to this country is that of assimilating these outlanders, ignorant of our tongue as of our institutions and ideals, into the fabric of the American nation." The fear of labor radicalism also was clearly in evidence: "From this mass of ignorance and prejudice comes a large, perhaps the largest part of the recruits who swell the ranks of the Industrial Workers of the World and kindred organizations." He laid the blame on the large number of foreign industrial workers for the labor problems, and "in the case of serious riots and disorders, the rioters are usually, if not always, intoxicated." Alcohol was dangerous for foreigners because they had come from nations where they had been oppressed, and in America these restraints were lifted. Inexperienced with freedom, foreigners "perverted ideas of liberty" and misinterpreted "license for liberty," the commissioner wrote.[54] By closing the saloons, prohibition would seriously diminish the flow of alcohol that drove immigrant workers wild, and pauperized their families.

Blue argued that foreigners had to be educated to American ideals and laws, and to that end the state of West Virginia printed pamphlets which explained the prohibition laws in several languages, and distributed them at work sites with the eager assistance of employers. Blue made it clear, however, that if education failed, foreigners would not be welcome: "It is necessary that the foreigner should understand when he comes to this land that he will be gladly received, provided he comes with the purpose of being a loyal citizen with respect for law and a desire to conform to American ideals and American institutions." He emphasized that American ideals would not be "surrendered to suit the personal habits or notions of the foreigner," and if the immigrant did not respect and conform to American ideals and institutions, "then there is no place for him in America."[55]

Here was progressive West Virginia's attitude toward immigrants in a nutshell: become like us, that is, socially respectable and economically reliable, or leave. These values were not only espoused by the business and civic leaders, but enforced by them as well. Many of the prohibitionists were either coal mine investors or owners. An examination of prohibition records in the Monongalia County courthouse led one scholar to conclude that prohibition was definitely intended to control foreign workers. Of the 622 indictments issued between January 1923 and January 1927, 348 were arrested for the possession of alcohol, and most of the defendants were immigrants who lived in mine camps. The manufacture or sale of alcohol accounted for 164 of the indictments, and again most of the arrests occurred in the mining communities, or in Jerome Park and Star City which were two other industrial neighborhoods with significant immigrant populations. Some ethnic establishments on Scotts Run distilled and sold their own liquor, such as the Liberty Coffee House, the Kismet Restaurant, and Kopen's restaurant in Osage.[56]

The story of assimilation for the first generation of immigrant miners in Monongalia County is not a happy one. It is common to think of assimilation in stages of three generations: the first generation arrives from the old country and struggles to survive on the "wrong side of the tracks"; the American-born second generation sheds its ethnic identity, acquires the skills and education to get ahead, and moves to the "right side of the tracks"; the third generation achieves in higher education, gets the best jobs, moves to the best part of town, and becomes ethnically invisible. But the long perspective foreshortens the degree and duration of anxieties, hardships, and hostility experienced by the first generation.

At Crown Mine, on the west side of the Monongahela River near Everettsville, the depression of the thirties found immigrant miners stranded in desperate conditions with no hope on the horizon. They had participated in the recent strikes, and bitterness between union and nonunion families formed a deep chasm among Crown's residents. Only one miner in five was native-born white, approximately one-third of the camp's population was African American, and the remainder were Russian, Austrian, German, Hungarian, or Italian immigrants "who spoke little or no English." William E. Simkin and his wife Ruth, recent graduates of Earlham College, a Quaker school in Indiana, worked with the American Friends Service Committee's child feeding and retraining program and moved to Crown Mine in 1932.[57] According to William Simkin, who ran a rehabilitation project at Crown in 1932, there were approximately 250 miners excluding the African Americans, nearly all of them foreign immigrants. Most had emigrated to America earlier when the mines were prosperous, but now found themselves trapped by the depression. Few had more than a smattering of English.[58]

Years later, Ruth Simkin remembered that blacks were segregated on "Colored Hill," but the rest of Crown residents, Russians, Latvians, Poles, Austrians, Hungarians, Italians, one Irish, and several Americans, occupied the remainder of the coal camp. While racism explains the segregation of blacks, it is also likely that the immigrants ostracized them because they had entered the camp as strikebreakers. Some of the immigrant families were fragmented within households as well. Ruth Simkin recalled that in some families "the children couldn't talk to their parents. They talked through the oldest children in the family. The oldest children in the family would get the parents' language and they would translate for the little ones."[59] As Ruth recalled, the farmers resented the miners because the mine changed the agricultural community by bringing in "all these foreigners and Blacks," and showed an "unacceptance of the foreigners." On one occasion, an immigrant died from drinking moonshine and "it was quite a problem finding a place to bury him." The sexton for a nearby church cemetery "absolutely refused" to permit his burial there observing that "his parents were buried there and he wasn't going to have one of them miners buried right next to them, or anyplace else." Finally, she found a small family cemetery where the man was permitted to be buried outside of the fence.[60]

The following night Ruth Simkin was up all night with an Italian woman having difficulty delivering her seventh child. The Simkins had the only phone in the camp, and she called for the doctor in Morgantown, eleven miles away over rough road. But he was on a call seventeen miles east of Morgantown, and as the only doctor who took relief calls in the county, they would simply have to wait for him to get there. He showed up at dawn to deliver the baby just when all seemed lost. According to Ruth, that was life in Crown, with "humanity facing their problems."[61]

Certainly there were plenty of problems for humanity to confront in the coalfields during this period, and the lack of, and even systematic denial of, proper health care was one of the most critical. The public health service, an agency predicated on not-for-profit preventative medicine, was totally inadequate relative to the public need. The county medical society represented the most formidable resistance to an expansion of the public health service and preventative medicine into the coalfields. Sandra Barney, an expert on the historical development of the medical profession in Appalachia, studied health services on Scotts Run during the 1920s and 1930s. She concluded that resistance from the Monongalia County Medical Society to the extension of public health to rural areas outside of Morgantown explains a great deal about the "inequitable distribution of medical resources within the county," and accounts for the deplorable health conditions to which many contemporary reformers alluded. Although the victims often were blamed for these deplorable conditions, the position of the county medical society demonstrates how the system itself discriminated against poor immigrants to ensure such an outcome.[62]

Handicapped by poverty, racism, and nativism, while living in crowded unsanitary company shack communities, all conspired to isolate coalfield residents from the opportunity to escape, and then justified discrimination against them as undesirables who should be isolated. The need to improve public health in the coal camps was thoroughly documented by progressive reformers of the 1920s and 1930s who pointed out the dangers from drinking water contaminated by raw sewage, refuse piles which became breeding grounds for vermin, the lack of running water, and housing unfit for human habitation.[63]

Coalfield residents also demanded improved health care for the coalfield; nearly one thousand rural residents petitioned the county court to establish a public health office in 1927, and the following year more than 1,200 sent another petition when the first was ignored.[64] But institutional resistance was strong. Although West Virginia created its first board of health in 1881, only one public health nurse had been hired to visit Monongalia County's schools by the early 1920s. By 1929, at the onset of the Great Depression, a grassroots movement for improved public health service arose throughout the county that was supported by one of Morgantown's newspapers, the *New Dominion*. There were few doctors in the county outside Morgantown, the paper editorialized, and those in "the thickly populated mining sections" should not "be sacrificed because public immunizations against contagions and infections can be given free." The medical community's primary concern was maintaining their traditional principle of "fee for service," and deflecting even the slightest government intrusion.[65] Barney found ample evidence of conscious discrimination among Morgantown physicians against the rural poor. For example, when the county nurse requested permission to run a birth control clinic on Scotts Run in 1933, the medical society proclaimed itself as "opposed to giving any time for such a clinic" because they were trying to find ways for "cutting down charity work."[66]

Systemic discrimination was not confined to Monongalia County. Lorena Hickok, a former newspaper reporter and close confidant of Eleanor Roosevelt, travelled the United States investigating the impact of Federal Employment Relief Administration programs on local communities. She reported to FERA director Harry L. Hopkins in 1933 that similar problems existed in the southern coalfields where she found the private hospitals "anything but cooperative," and federal relief workers had "a good deal of trouble with doctors" throughout the state. "Among our relief people, the profession has acquired most decidedly a black eye."[67]

Scotts Run, Monongalia County's most important coalfield, provides a laboratory for assessing the most severe problems confronted by immigrants, and also the most benevolent Americanization programs in the state of West Virginia. An exact calculation of the population on Scotts Run is not possible because it is a geographical rather than political subdivision of Cass District, and the census does not always indicate the exact location of residents. Also, the surge in population on Scotts Run which peaked during the mid-twenties at about four thousand was not recorded in the decennial census for either 1920 or 1930. Moreover, although the actual number of workers who commuted to jobs at Scotts Run mines is unknown, a significant proportion of the workforce fell into that category.[68] Nevertheless, the racially and ethnically diverse population on Scotts Run is revealed in a survey of families taken by the Presbyterian Church in 1927 (see charts 11.1 and 11.3).

The year 1923 was a momentous watershed in the Scotts Run coal industry. That year was the high-water mark when production reached 4.4 million tons. The boom lifted Scotts Run to prominence, but its phenomenal rise lasted only seven years before it began to disintegrate into the chaos of the mine wars in the late twenties, and the grinding poverty of the thirties when Scotts Run set a new standard for measuring human suffering. More than one-half of the miners' families stranded on Scotts Run were either foreign-born or African American. To what degree life was worse here than in other depression-era coal hollows is difficult to determine, but there was plenty of misery to go around, and the foreign born received the lion's share.

Had it not been for the personal attention of First Lady Eleanor Roosevelt, residents of Scotts Run would have suffered alone and outside of public attention. Lorena Hickok was sent into the Pennsylvania and West Virginia coalfields on a fact-finding mission in 1933, and was escorted by Morgantown relief workers to Scotts Run. There she "came upon a gutter along a village street filled with stagnant, filthy water used for drinking, cooking, washing, and everything else imaginable by the inhabitants of ramshackle cabins that most Americans would not have considered fit for pigs," and reported her findings to FERA director Hopkins. "Within these shacks, every night children went to sleep hungry, on piles of bug-infested rags spread on the floor."[69]

Lorena Hickok's alarming description prompted Eleanor Roosevelt to make her own personal examination of conditions in the mine camps near Morgantown, and she too was appalled by what she witnessed there. In her autobiography, Mrs. Roosevelt related a story similar to that reported by Hickok regarding the unsanitary condition of the water supply. "The Run in Jere, like all the others that ran down the gullies to the larger, main stream," she observed, "was the only sewage disposal system that existed. At the bottom of the hill there was a spigot from which everyone drew water. The children played in the stream and the filth was indescribable." Another experience which distressed her occurred at the kitchen table in a company house where a miner showed the First Lady his weekly pay slips. After the usual deductions for rent, and the company store, he was left with less than one dollar per week to feed his six children. "I noticed a bowl on the table filled with scraps, the kind that you or I might give to a dog," Mrs. Roosevelt wrote, "and I saw children, evidently looking for their noon-day meal, take a handful out of that bowl and go out munching. That was all they had to eat." Mrs. Roosevelt took many people to see Jere because it was "a good example of what absentee ownership could do as far as human beings were concerned."[70]

These interrelated themes of paralyzing poverty, debilitating hunger, unsanitary living conditions, absentee ownership, and corollary problems, such as poor education, were taken up during the thirties by reporters for national publications whose luridly detailed descriptions elevated Scotts Run as the very symbol of the depression in America's coalfields, and helped to indelibly link poverty and West Virginia in the public imagination. The most influential article was one published in 1935 in *Atlantic Monthly*, which quoted the famous radio commentator Lowell Thomas's description of Scotts Run as "the damnedest cesspool of human misery I have ever seen in America."[71] Some of America's greatest photographers, including Walker Evans, Lewis Hine, Marion Post Walcott, and Ben Shahn, documented the stories with powerful visual images.

Chart 11.1

Foreign-born Coal Miners in Monongalia County, 1923 (▦) and
Nationality of Families Surveyed on Scotts Run, 1927 (■)

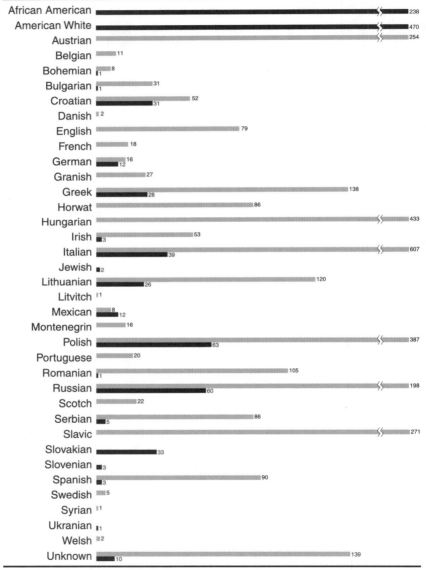

Sources: Compiled from the *West Virginia Department of Mines, Annual Report of Mines for the Fiscal Year Ending June 30, 1920* (Charleston: Tribune Printing Co. 1920), 259–260, and "Report of Missionary Survey in Scotts Run, W. Va.," Scotts Run Community Center, A&M 652, West Virginia and Regional History Collection, West Virginia University, Morgantown, West Virginia.

Chart 11.2
Foreign-born Coal Miners in Monongalia County, 1923

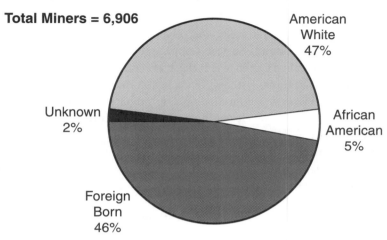

Total Miners = 6,906

American White 47%

Unknown 2%

African American 5%

Foreign Born 46%

Source: *West Virginia Department of Mines, Annual Report of Mines for the Fiscal Year Ending June 30, 1920* (Charleston: Tribune Printing Co. 1920), 259–260.

Chart 11.3
Nationality of Families Surveyed on Scotts Run, 1927

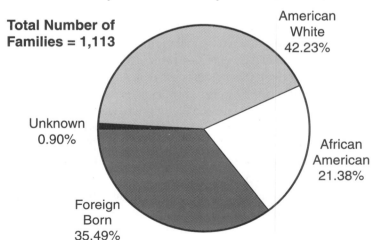

Total Number of Families = 1,113

American White 42.23%

Unknown 0.90%

African American 21.38%

Foreign Born 35.49%

Source: "Report of Missionary Survey in Scotts Run, W. Va.," Scotts Run Community Center, A&M 652, West Virginia and Regional History Collection, West Virginia University, Morgantown, West Virginia.

Long before the First Lady threw her influence into the struggle to improve living conditions on The Run, reformers had busied themselves in that effort. Indeed, because of the extended organizational campaign already in place, Mrs. Roosevelt probably regarded Scotts Run as a place that would respond immediately to experiments in relief and rehabilitation. The Coal Relief campaign of the American Friends Service Committee was already on the scene when Mrs. Roosevelt called Clarence E. Pickett, executive secretary of the AFSC, about inspecting conditions firsthand. Pickett and Alice O. Davis, an experienced relief worker who was coordinating the campaign in the Morgantown district, met with Mrs. Roosevelt and helped to establish the itinerary which brought her to the county and Scotts Run. With her came the inevitable corps of newspaper reporters and photographers who put a human face on the casualties of the Great Depression. They heightened the nation's consciousness about Scotts Run, which, in turn, facilitated the effort of social agencies to generate resources for relief.

The reformers and the relief organizations which descended on the coalfields were devoted to Americanizing the immigrants, but their programs were shaped by more benevolent influences and motivations than the 100 percenters. Benevolent Americanizers believed that, since immigrants arrived with no concept of self-government, it fell to native Americans to teach them the meaning of citizenship. Programs to socialize immigrants were intentionally sought to supplant old world cultures with American culture, but reformers were motivated by the desire to help them to move out of poverty and into mainstream America. One definition of Americanization widely adopted by the benevolent reformers indicated that neither rejection nor restriction was the answer, but rather the full assimilation of the immigrant population. In *Adult Immigrant Education: Its Scope, Content, and Methods*, published in 1925, William Sharlip and Albert Owens declared that Americanization "must include the native as well as the foreign born, must embrace the inculcation of American ideals and standards into the life of the newcomer, and must imply a willingness on the part of the native to accept the contributions of the foreigner, economic, political, social, cultural, and educational, that may promote the welfare of America."[72] The basic objectives of an Americanization program, therefore, were eliminating illiteracy, teaching the English language, good health practices, and civic and political responsibility, and at the same time encouraging foreigners to fully participate in American life. Taken together, such a program would teach immigrants to aspire to, and eventually achieve, "American standards." With its large concentration of immigrants trapped in poverty, therefore, Scotts Run was a prime proving ground for benevolent Americanizers in the late twenties.[73]

Initially, Americanization in Monongalia County became the responsibility of local churches and women's clubs. There was a difference between the Americanization programs in Morgantown and in the coal camps on the west side of the Monongahela River. Between 1900 and the take-off period of the coalfields during World War I, the immigrants who came to the city were better educated, were more conversant in English, and many prospered as businessmen. Those who came to work in the American Tin Plate Mill, which employed approximately eight hundred workers, lived in the company-planned community of Sturgiss City [later Sabraton]. With the assistance of the company, women's clubs, particularly the Women's Christian Temperance Union and the Daughters of the American Revolution, were active here as they were elsewhere in the city. Of course they had different emphases, one on prohibition of alcohol and the other on patriotic civics, but to achieve their aims both organizations hoped to teach immigrants to aspire to American standards. To this end, they organized mothers clubs, girls clubs, English and civics classes, established reading classes for children, and the DAR assisted in naturalization hearings. They focused their efforts on women because the men were exposed to American ideas at work, and the children were socialized at school, but the women generally worked at home isolated from broader community interaction.[74]

Immigrant workers who came to Morgantown or the planned community built by American Tin Plate lived under far different standards than their counterparts in the coalfields of the boom years. On Scotts Run temporary housing was thrown up, no sewer or running water lines were put in; it was all makeshift and, as the miners and their families crowded in, housing crumbled and health conditions deteriorated. The goal of Americanization had to give way to direct relief under these conditions which were magnified by the depression. The American Friends Service Committee, and the various federal relief agencies, brought a strong presence to Scotts Run, but local agencies, particularly the Council of Social Agencies and the County Welfare Board, had been struggling for years to improve conditions for the stranded mining families of Scotts Run. The burden had simply proven too great for local resources. A National Red Cross report for 1931 outlines the scale of the problem confronting local relief agencies in Monongalia County. Of the fifty thousand people in the county, sixteen thousand lived in Morgantown, fifteen thousand lived in the coal mining sections, and twenty thousand lived in the rural farm sections. According to the report, "a vast amount of miner's [sic] children are being fed by charitable organizations." A nutritional survey undertaken in the mining sections revealed that in "some instances as high as 40 percent of the children were found to be suffering from malnutrition with an average of 26 percent. Quite a few of the children are without sufficient clothing and shoes." Compounding the problem was the closure of every bank in the county. According to the 1931 Red Cross report, "the county funds have been tied up in the closed banks and it looks as if tax collections for the fiscal year are going to be considerably short."[75]

The problem of tax revenues became even worse in 1933 after passage of the Tax Limitation Amendment of 1932, which reduced and limited property taxes. This ill-advised measure left much of the relief effort to private agencies, such as the American Friends Service Committee which served 128,692 meals to children in the mine camps of Monongalia County between the Septembers of 1931 and 1932. One half of its twenty-four feeding stations in Monongalia County were located in the Scotts Run area, and by far the largest majority of meals were served there.[76]

The earliest, and most personalized, local relief efforts drew their inspiration from the Bible School Movement and the Settlement House Movement. The Bible School Movement depended on trained lay workers and volunteers to teach the principles of Christianity to the "religiously needy," but gave primary attention to the children. Most of the workers were young women who followed this avenue to leadership roles unavailable to them within the conventional structure of the church. Young women also played a major role in the Settlement House Movement, the best known example being Jane Addams's Hull House in Chicago. Settlement houses attempted to assist in the "Americanization" of newly arrived immigrants by promoting English literacy, citizenship, hygiene, and other basic adaptive social and life skills.[77]

The goals of both movements converged on Scotts Run during the 1920s when Methodist and Presbyterian churches in Morgantown undertook to extend their work among the immigrant families on The Run. The Scotts Run Settlement House opened in 1922 when the Women's Home Missionary Society of Wesley Methodist Church established a Bible school for children under the direction of Deaconess Edna L. Muir and Mrs. Frank Shriver. The hope inspiring these missionary projects was the desire to elevate the standard of life on Scotts Run which, according to one of the Christian ladies involved with the Settlement House, was infamous nationwide for its "wickedness and lawlessness." In addition to Bible school and Sunday school, the Settlement House gradually expanded its program to include classes on naturalization, cooking, motherhood, and other life skills. The DAR also assisted in the Settlement House work in 1924 and 1925, mostly with citizenship courses, but the Settlement House program quickly eclipsed the narrow patriotic mission of the DAR. A fire in the building, which some thought was deliberately set by residents who objected to the temperance teachings of the missionaries, temporarily halted classes in 1925. A permanent building for the Settlement House in Osage was completed in 1927, and continues to this day to offer assistance to those in need.[78]

Soon thereafter, the Presbyterian Board of National Missions decided its missionary campaign on Scotts Run should have a full-time director and hired Mary Behner, a recent Wooster College graduate. She began her work at Pursglove in 1928, and by 1931 was established in a donated mine building dubbed by locals as "The Shack." The name stuck.[79] The minutes of the 1929 Synod meeting reported that "a new work was opened up in the Grafton Presbytery on Scotts Run at Pursglove" by Mary Behner who "has put on a very rich and varied program, not only in getting a big work done, but also in securing the willing cooperation of university students at West Virginia University, together with the members of the Morgantown First [Presbyterian] Church."[80]

Ms. Behner set up Sunday schools, established a program of recreational activities for the children, launched a storytelling program, and began a loaning library because she found "very few books in the schools and practically none in the homes." Low education levels and the large number of foreign-born in Scotts Run accounted for the dearth of books, she concluded. "Many of the adults could speak virtually no English," so her mission activities concentrated on the children.[81]

In practice, Ms. Behner was less a missionary than a community organizer. This explains why a Presbyterian Church served by an ordained minister was not established at The Shack until nine years after her work began. She regarded it as fortuitous that the work was begun by a woman because a man probably would not have gained entrance into the homes as she did, and many of the services she made available appealed to the women. Like the Scotts Run Settlement House established by the Methodist church, The Shack also provided for the distribution of food, clothing, education, and a place for community organizing and meetings. By assuming the role of organizer and advocate for the powerless, both The Shack and the Settlement House assumed an active political agenda whether or not that was their intention. The local United Mine Workers of America met at The Shack, for example. The following activities reported for 1930 indicate the range of community projects undertaken at the Shack: Sunday School, Library Club, Daily Vacation Bible School, Community Sings, Charm School, Boy Scouts, directed recreation, parties, miscellaneous programs (such as Christmas and Easter), storytelling, Negro Girls Club, and Girls Chorus. Total attendance at these events was 12,089 people. In addition, Ms. Behner made 362 house calls during the year.[82]

The Roman Catholic church did not establish a presence on Scotts Run until 1932 when a mission church, St. Ursula's, was built at Liberty. Father Joseph Flynn began work there apparently in response to the efforts of the Protestant missionaries among the European immigrants, most of whom were Roman Catholics. The priest did not object to the Protestants organizing the

Catholic children into clubs, but he insisted that they avoid religion. Not wanting to cause a rift, Ms. Behner confined religious teaching to the Sunday schools. Father Flynn was not very cooperative with the Protestant missionaries. The Shack prepared a Christmas dinner and gifts for "single old men on Relief" in 1936. Father Flynn was invited, and surprised everybody when he actually came. As Ms. Behner remembered, "it was the first time Father Flynn had ever been inside The Shack. He is the catholic priest from [St. John's Chapel in] Morgantown who has started strong catholic work at Liberty in the last few years and who is so opposed to Protestantism and our work at The Shack."[83] In 1938 the Reverend Franklin Trubee became the first ordained Presbyterian minister to serve as director of The Shack. He also remembered Father Flynn as "uncooperative" with the Protestant missionaries, and also not very effective in his own relief work.[84] The Shack's activities need not have worried Father Flynn, for beyond Sunday school, it offered only a secular program provided by Protestant social workers.

Mr. Trubee built a new and larger Shack, and readily adopted the methods and philosophical approach of the American Friends Service Committee in developing local leadership, and promoting rehabilitation (helping people to help themselves) through cooperative exchanges of labor and goods. The unemployed needed no cash when they participated in the Scotts Run Reciprocal Economy, The Shack's cooperative. Most residents could not practice supplemental farming or extensive gardening as they did elsewhere in the coalfields because acrid fumes from the smoldering "gob" piles killed all the vegetation in the hollow, and congestion from overdevelopment precluded other uses of the land. However, through the co-op they exchanged their labor for produce raised in the hilltop community gardens, or for reconditioned clothing from the recycled clothing shop. Now in its third building, The Shack, like the Settlement House, has adapted to the circumstances of modern life and continues to serve people in need.[85]

The residents of Scotts Run survived the Great Depression through such imaginative coping strategies, and the help of many private and public relief agencies. The Presbyterian and Methodist missions on Scotts Run were initiated to provide Sunday schools for the children and Americanization programs for their immigrant parents. Confronted by the desperate conditions they found on Scotts Run, however, both missions transformed themselves into social work agencies to organize the dispossessed and alleviate starvation. Many other public and private agencies which became involved in the the campaign to save Scotts Run shifted focus from Americanization to direct relief. The WVU Extension Service helped residents with community gardens, and the Salvation Army distributed food and clothing. Individual citizens also organized themselves to help. In 1933, at least thirty-four garden clubs in the county raised, canned, and gave away food to the needy estimated at a value of $59,453.[86]

In the final analysis, saving people from starvation took precedence over turning immigrants into proper citizens. The one key federally directed project to have a direct impact on Scotts Run, the U.S. Department of Interior's Subsistence Homestead Project, provided the coup de grace for the immigrants who lived there. The purpose of resettlement communities was to help people escape an industrial area where employment was no longer viable by resettling them on farmsteads or in mixed industry-farming communities. The very first of approximately one hundred planned communities constructed during the New Deal was Arthurdale, established in Preston County, which neighbors Monongalia County. The idea for resettlement came to Mrs. Roosevelt on August 18, 1933, during the her first visit to the Monongalia County coalfields. Traveling incognito she was able to spend most of the day walking Scotts Run without being recognized. Conditions there convinced her that something had to be done. "This was only the first of many trips into the mining district [of Monongalia County] but it was the one that started the homestead idea," she wrote in her autobiography.[87]

The 1,018 acre Arthur farm in Preston County was soon purchased, and WVU Extension agent Bushrod Grimes, who had helped establish community farms on Scotts Run, was appointed project manager in November 1933. He immediately began taking applications from unemployed miners and was besieged with between six and seven hundred applicants for only two hundred houses planned for the project. But the project would be a deep disappointment to those Scotts Run residents most in need. According to Grimes, who was on the selection committee, African Americans and immigrants were excluded because African Americans "did not make much of an effort on their own count and the foreigners were even worse." Those finally selected were native-born whites.[88]

By the mid-thirties when the resettlement project determined to exclude the foreign born and blacks, the world had changed a great deal from the teens and twenties when the fear of "undigested" immigrants seemed to threaten the continued prosperity and moral fiber of America. They could not be blamed for an economic collapse that had come with the Great Depression. Scotts Run coalfield changed dramatically as well, and the thirties marks the beginning of a long slide into historical obscurity for this once teeming hollow. A number of explanations account for Scotts Run's short life and slow agonizing decline. Many left the area in search of a better life. As elsewhere in rural America, World War II took many of the young men from Scotts Run, and after the war they found little incentive to return.[89] The first generation aged and began to die off; many of them along with their children moved into town; the mines closed and their properties were purchased by Consolidation Coal Company; and the automobile freed miners from living at the work site. Americans lionize the winners so the second and third generations who finally assimilated, lost their ethnic identity, and achieved upward mobility are embraced as the "real Americans." But that first generation of immigrants who risked everything on the American Dream, who fought for a union that would look out for their interests and provide their first introduction to democratic organization, and were maligned or patronized by those who sought to mold them into proper Americans, laid the foundation on which succeeding generations built their world.

NOTES

1. John Higham, *Strangers in the Land: Patterns of American Nativism, 1860-1925* (New York: Athenaeum, 1971), 236-7.
2. Michael E. Workman, "Political Culture and the Coal Economy in the Upper Monongahela Region, 1776-1933" (Ph.D. diss., West Virginia University, 1995), 146.
3. Workman, "Political Culture," 147.
4. Workman, "Political Culture," 107, 265-6.
5. Earl L. Core, *The Monongalia Story: A Bicentennial History,* Vol. 4. *Industrialization* (Parsons, W.Va.: McClain Printing Co., 1982), 456, 492; "West Virginia Output Shows Decrease," *Black Diamond* 68 (28 January 1922): 85.
6. "Wonder Coal Field of West Virginia," *Black Diamond* 71 (11 August 1923): 180-1; "Sewickley Coal Is Premier Steam Fuel," *Black Diamond* 71 (11 August 1923): 185.
7. I. C. White, "Morgantown's Wealth of Fuel," Black Diamond 71 (11 August 1923): 178-9.
8. Howard N. Eavenson, *The First Century and a Quarter of the American Coal Industry* (Pittsburgh: By the Author, 1942), 418; West Virginia Geological Survey, *Characteristics of Minable Coals of West Virginia*, Vol. 8, ed. A. J. W. Headlee and J. P. Nolting (Morgantown: West Virginia Geological Survey, 1940), 9-10; Phil Ross, "The Scotts Run Coalfield from the Great War to the Great Depression: A Study in Overdevelopment," *West Virginia History* 53 (1994): 22; *Morgantown Post Chronicle*, 15 September 1910; Earl L. Core, *The Monongalia Story: A Bicentennial History*, Vol. 5, *Sophistication* (Parsons, W.Va.: McClain Printing Company, 1982), 386, 400-1.
9. *Dominion News*, 12 December 1971; *Morgantown Post*, 1 November 1921, 19 September 1972, 18 December 1972; Item, *Black Diamond* 72 (15 March 1924): 315.
10. White, "Morgantown's Wealth," 179.
11. Matthew Yeager, "Scotts Run: A Community in Transition," *West Virginia History* 53 (1994): 14; U. S. *Census of Population*. The quotation is from "Sewickley Coal Is Premier," *Black Diamond*, 185.
12. U. S. Bureau of Census, *Fourteenth Census of the United States, 1920. Population*, Vol. 3, Part 2: 1, 112; West Virginia, *Annual Report of the Department of Mines for Fiscal Year Ending June 30, 1920* (Charleston, W.Va.: Tribune Printing Co., 1920), 259, 260.
13. John Luchok, interview by the author, 9 Nov. 1993, Morgantown, W.Va. Charles died in 1958, age 81, and Anna lived to within two days of turning 102.
14. Cathy Pack, "Morgantown Churches: Serving Many Communities," in *Morgantown: A Bicentennial History* , ed. West Virginia University Public History Option (Morgantown: Monongalia County Historical Society, 1985), 56; Core, *Monongalia Story*, Vol. 4, 503-4; Dr. and Mrs. Gideon S. Dodds, "History of the Churches of Monongalia County," in *The 175th Anniversary of the Formation of Monongalia County, West Virginia and Other Relative Historical Data* (Morgantown: Monongalia Historical Society, 1954), 57.

15. Louis Birurakis, interview by the author, 15 Sept. 1993, Morgantown, W.Va.
16. Ibid.
17. Ruth Simkin, interview by Karin Lee, 1-2 March 1991, Tucson, Arizona, Oral History Interview No. 214, transcript page 6, Friends Archives, Philadelphia, Pa.
18. Louis Birurakis, interview.
19. John Luchok, interview.
20. Higham, *Strangers in the Land*, 205.
21. Ibid., 207.
22. Ibid., 242; quotation from Frank Julian Warne, *The Tide of Immigration* (New York: 1916), 358-9.
23. Higham, *Strangers in the Land*, 247.
24. My emphasis. Isaac B. Berkson, *Theories of Americanization: A Critical Study with Special References to the Jewish Group* (New York: Columbia University Press, 1920), 55.
25. Higham, *Strangers in the Land*, 249, quotation 255.
26. John C. Hennen, *The Americanization of West Virginia: Creating a Modern Industrial State, 1916-1925* (Lexington: University Press of Kentucky, 1996), 74.
27. West Virginia Coal Institute, *Addresses and Proceedings*, 25th Semi-Annual Session, June 3-4, 1919, 53-4; Hennen, *Americanization*, 77.
28. Hennen, *Americanization*, 78-9.
29. Workman,"Political Culture," 234. Workman based this conclusion on an examination of Consolidation Coal Company, the largest single employer of miners in the Fairmont District.
30. Rowland Tappan Berthoff, *British Immigrants in Industrial America* (Cambridge: Harvard University Press, 1953), 55-61.
31. See James P. Johnson, *The Politics of Soft Coal: The Bituminous Industry from World War I through the New Deal* (Urbana: University of Illinois Press, 1979).
32. Michael E. Workman, "The Fairmont Coal Field," in Michael E. Workman, Paul Salstrom, and Philip W. Ross, *Northern West Virginia Coal Fields: Historical Context*, Technical Report No. 10 (Morgantown: Institute for the History of Technology and Industrial Archaeology, 1994), 36; *Coal Age* 21 (29 June 1922): 1099.
33. Workman, "The Fairmont Coal Field," 36-7.
34. George E. Smith to Walter Davidson, 22 May 1931, Records of the American National Red Cross, 1917-1934, File 868, Box 701, RG 200, National Archives, Washington, D.C. Thanks to Sandra Barney for this item.
35. See Linda Nyden, "Black Miners in Western Pennsylvania, 1925-1931: The National Miners Union and the United Mine Workers of America," *Science and Society* 41 (Spring 1977): 96-9. For strike conditions and the NMU on Scotts Run, see also Stephen Edward Haid, "Arthurdale: An Experiment in Community Planning, 1933-1947" (Ph.D. diss., West Virginia University, 1975), chap. 1.
36. Howard B. Lee, *Bloodletting in Appalachia: The Story of West Virginia's Four Major Mine Wars and Other Thrilling Incidents of Its Coal Fields* (Parsons, W.Va.: McClain Printing Co., 1969), 150.
37. Ibid., 153, quotation 154.

38. Workman, "Political Culture," 369-70.
39. Ibid., 385; *Fairmont Times,* 17 July 1926.
40. Workman, "Political Culture," 385; Carl Bischoff to C. E. Smith, 2 April 1925, Box 4, Series 1, C. E. Smith Papers, West Virginia and Regional History Collection, West Virginia University, Morgantown, W.Va. (hereafter cited as WVRHC) See also the numerous "spy reports" in the Smith Papers.
41. Hennen, *Americanization,* 122.
42. Ibid., 123; Phil M. Conley, "The Man from West Virginia," *West Virginia Review* 1, no. 1 (October 1923): 19; Hays Brown, "Pure-Blooded Americans," *West Virginia Review* 1, no.5 (February 1924): 33.
43. Higham, *Strangers in the Land,* 267.
44. Ibid., 295.
45. Workman, "Political Culture," 394; Smith in "Good Morning!" *Fairmont Times,* 9 Sept 1925.
46. *Seventeenth Annual Convention of the West Virginia State Federation of Labor, Proceedings,* 8-13 September 1924, Wheeling, W.Va. (Charleston: Allied Printing Trades Council, 1924), 39-40.
47. Abram L. Harris, "Strike of 1925 in Northern West Virginia," in *The Negro In West Virginia* (Charleston: Bureau of Negro Welfare and Statistics of the State of West Virginina, 1925-26), 29. For African Americans and the Klan in Monongalia County see also, Connie Park Rice, *Our Monongalia: A History of African Americans in Monongalia County, West Virginia* (Terra Alta, W.Va.: Headline Books, Inc., for the Community Race Relations Forum Association, 1999), 141-2, 253.
48. *New Dominion,* 1 June 1926.
49. Morgantown *Post,* 1 June 1926.
50. Workman, "Political Culture," 240; quotation from "Feeling is High," *Fairmont Times,* 14 July 1911.
51. Morgantown *Post,* 11 March 1919. Numerous references to strike violence filled the Morgantown newspapers. See for example, *Post,* 24 Sept., 2 Oct., 8 Oct. 1924; 15 Nov., 21 Nov., 26 Nov. 1924.
52. Charles H. McCormick, "The Death of Constable Riggs: Ethnic Conflict in Marion County in the World War I Era," West Virginia History 52 (1993): 38, 40-8.
53. The prohibition amendment to the West Virginia constitution was submitted to the people in 1912, and was approved by a better than 2 to 1 margin. It was intended to close the saloons, rather than abolish the consumption of alcohol. The 1912 amendment was repealed in 1934 by a slim majority vote. Darrell E. Holmes, ed., *West Virginia Blue Book* (Charleston: Jerrett Printing Company, 1989), 526-7.
54. Frederick O. Blue, *When a State Goes Dry: A Brief Study in Law Enforcement* (Westerville, Ohio: American Issue Publishing Co., 1916), quotations are on 98, 103, and 105 respectively.
55. Ibid., 103-4.
56. Monongalia County Circuit Clerk's Office. Indictments. From Connie Rice, "Whose Prohibition Was It Anyway?" (seminar paper, Department of History, West Virginia University, 1996).

57. Marvin R. Weisbord, *Some Form of Peace: True Stories of the American Friends Service Committee at Home and Abroad* (New York: Viking Press, 1968), 85-6.

58. William E. Simkin, interview by Karin Lee, 1 March 1991, Tucson, Arizona, Oral History Interview No. 213, transcript pages 58-59, Friends Archives, Philadelphia, Pa.

59. Ruth Simkin, interview, transcript page 6.

60. Ibid., transcript page 29.

61. Ibid., transcript page 30.

62. Sandra Barney, "Health Services in a Stranded Coal Community: Scotts Run, 19. 20-47," *West Virginia History* 53 (1994): 43. See also Sandra Lee Barney, *Authorized to Heal: Gender, Class, and the Transformation of Medicine in Appalachia, 1880-1930* (Chapel Hill: University of North Carolina Press, 2000), 128-30.

63. Barney, "Health Services," 45. See also Nettie McGill, *The Welfare of Children in Bituminous Coal Mining Communities in West Virginia*, U.S. Department of Labor, Children's Bureau (Washington, D.C.: GPO, 1923), 14, 16, 47; and William Brooks, "The Proposed Upper Monongahela Valley Planning Board Report with Respect to Social Conditions and Problems," 1, Moreland Family Papers, WVRHC.

64. Barney, "Health Services," 47; Morgantown *New Dominion*, 1August 1929.

65. Barney, "Health Services," 48; Morgantown *New Dominion*, 2 August 1929.

66. Barney, "Health Services," 49.

67. Richard Lowitt and Maurine Beasley, *One Third a Nation: Lorena Hickok on the Great Depression* (Urbana: University of Illinois Press, 1981), 20-1.

68. Manuscript Census schedules, *Fourteenth Census of the U.S. 1920*, Cass District, Monongalia County, W.Va., available on microfilm in WVRHC; Core, *Monongalia Story*, Vol. 4, 509-10.

69. Doris Faber, *The Life of Lorena Hickok* (New York: William Morrow and Company, 1980), 143-4.

70. Eleanor Roosevelt, *This I Remember* (New York: Harper & Row Publishers, 1949), 126-9.

71. William E. Brooks, "Arthurdale: A New Chance," *Atlantic Monthly* 155 (February 1935): 199.

72. William Sharlip and Albert Owens, *Adult Immigrant Education: Its Scope, Content, and Methods* (New York: MacMillian Company, 1925), 17.

73. Ibid., 17-8.

74. Minutes, Womens Christian Temperance Union, 6 March 1918, and 1925, Womens Christian Temperance Union Records, WVRHC; Mary Behner Christopher Diaries, 16 November 1928, Mary Behner Christopher Collection, WVRHC; *Our Foreign Population*, 1916, Papers of the Elizabeth Luddington Hagan Chapter of the Daughters of the American Revolution, WVRHC.

75. Narrative Report, April-October 1931, Records of the American National Red Cross, 1917-1934, File 1310, Box 73, RG 90, National Archives, Washington, D.C. Thanks to Sandra Barney for this item.

76. Charles H. Ambler, *A History of Education in West Virginia from Early Colonial Times to 1949* (Huntington, W.Va.: Standard Printing & Publishing Co., 1951), 607-9; American Friends Service Committee, *Report of the Child Relief Work in the Bituminous Coal Fields, September 1, 1931-August 31, 1932* (Philadelphia: American Friends Service Committee, 1932), 27.

77. Marcia Clark Myers, "Presbyterian Home Mission in Appalachia: A Feminine Enterprise," *American Presbyterians* 71 (Winter 1993): 253-64. For the Bible School Movement, see Virginia Lieson Brereton, *Training God's Army: The American Bible School, 1880-1940* (Bloomington: Indiana University Press, 1990). For the best firsthand account of the urban settlement house movement, see Jane Addams, *Twenty Years at Hull-House* (New York: McMillan Company, 1910). For the best assessment of the movement, see Allen F. Davis, *Spearheads for Reform: The Social Settlements and the Progressive Movement, 1890-1914* (New York: Oxford University Press, 1967).

78. Edna Leona Muir, "Scotts Run Settlement Work," n.d., and Lena Brookover Barker, "The History of Scotts Run Settlement House," Autumn 1938, both in the Scotts Run Settlement House Collection, WVRHC. The Settlement House has suffered because its history has not been collected and told in the same way as The Shack.

79. Scotts Run Scrapbook, WVRHC; Bettijane Burger, *Missing Chapters II: West Virginia Women in History* (Charleston: West Virginia Women's Commission, 1986), 48. See also Christine M. Kreiser, "'I Wonder Whom God Will Hold Responsible?' Mary Behner and the Presbyterian Mission on Scotts Run," *West Virginia History* 53 (1994): 61-92.

80. "Work at Pursglove on Scotts Run." *Minutes of the Synod of West Virginia of the Presbyterian Church in the USA*, Vol 3, No. 3 (Sistersville, W.Va.: Review Publishing Co., 1929).

81. Mary Behner Christopher, interview by Lari Grubbs, Morgantown, W.Va., 23 March 1986 (in the author's possession).

82. Mary Behner Christopher, interview; "Second Year Expense Account of Scotts Run Mission, 1 Dec. 1929-30 Nov. 1930, Mary Behner Christopher Scrapbook, WVRHC. See also Bettijane Burger, "Mary Elizabeth Behner Christopher," in *Missing Chapters II: West Virginia Women in History,* ed. Frances S. Hensley (Charleston: West Virginia Women's Commission, 1986), 47-59.

83. Kreiser, "'I Wonder Whom God Will Hold Responsible,'" 86-7.

84. The Rev. Franklin Trubee, interview by the author, 1 April 1988, Minerva, Ohio.

85. Ronald L. Lewis, "'Why Don't You Bake Bread?' Franklin Trubee and the Scotts Run Reciprocal Economy," *Goldenseal* 15 (spring 1989): 34-41.

86. Clarence E. Pickett, *For More Than Bread: An Autobiographical Account of Twenty-Two Years' Work with the American Friends Service Committee* (Boston: Little, Brown and Company, 1953), 35.

87. Eleanor Roosevelt, *The Autobiography of Eleanor Roosevelt* (New York: Harper & Brothers, 1958), 177-8.

88. Haid, "Arthurdale," 78-9, quotation on 79.
89. For an example of this process, see the autobiography of former Osage, W.Va. resident Sidney D. Lee, *And the Trees* Cried (By the author, 1991), and the interview of John Luchok by Ronald Lewis. Both Mr. Lee and Mr. Luchok were from the first generation born in America, and both exceeded the general pattern by becoming prominent members of the local community.

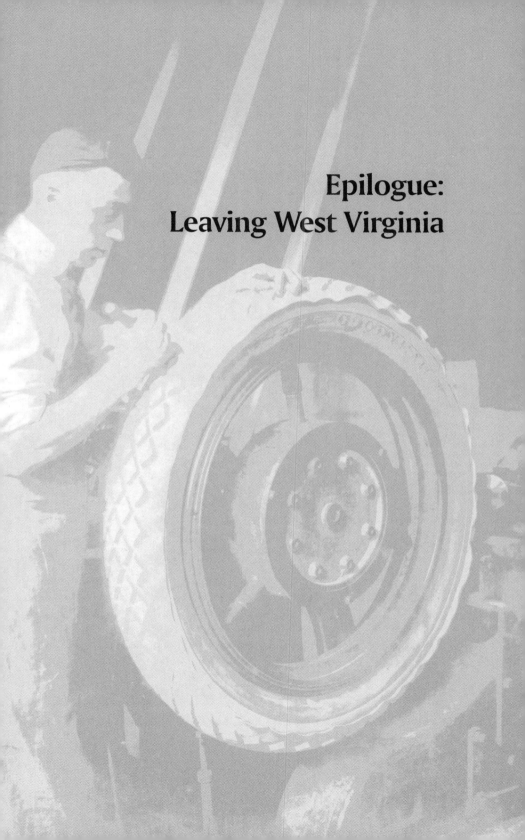

Epilogue:
Leaving West Virginia

A tirebuilder in the Goodyear Tire and Rubber factory, Akron, Ohio, in 1917. Photo courtesy University of Akron, Archival Services

West Virginia Rubber Workers in Akron

Susan Johnson

One of the most striking aspects of West Virginia's history is how many of its residents have found themselves living far from their home state. This departure was part of the larger exodus from economically troubled regions of Southern Appalachia. While the shifting of population from less rural to more urban areas was the pattern for much of the twentieth century, those who moved to growing industrial centers early in the century were encouraged to do so by the promise of new opportunities and experiences. By the middle of the twentieth century, however, soaring rates of unemployment in the coal-producing areas of Appalachia caused a mass exodus from the region that was decidedly less voluntary, as small communities faced economic crises that prompted many residents to leave, often with reluctance.

The outpouring from Appalachia was most noticeable in West Virginia as the sparsely populated state lost nearly 750,000 residents between 1940 and 1960 through interstate migration.[1] This migration has been lamented for both the drain of talented individuals and the underlying economic problems that prompted so many to seek opportunities elsewhere. The problem became so severe that, by the early 1970s, as high as 70 percent of youths in West Virginia left before the age of twenty-four.[2] Many who left reflected the ambivalent sentiments of one migrant about his family's decision to leave West Virginia. Years after their move, he still questioned his decision, but concluded, "In a city you can get some money; it may not be a lot of money, but back there we got *no* money. . . . I love the mountains, but look what goes with the mountains."[3]

Although the outpouring of population from Appalachian regions first attracted widespread notice in the 1950s, this was not simply a post-World War II phenomenon. During both world wars, the promise of better opportunities outside the state led thousands of West Virginians to move to neighboring regions; these early emigrants would subsequently encourage the migration of friends and family members. An estimated 50 percent of those who left West Virginia eventually settled in Ohio.[4]

This outpouring from West Virginia was nowhere more noticeable than in Akron, Ohio. The city became a popular destination point in the early twentieth century because its emergence as the center of the rubber tire industry produced bountiful job opportunities at comparably good wages. The rubber industry attracted thousands of West Virginians before the First World War. A photograph taken in 1909 depicts customers posing on the sidewalk outside the West Virginia Saloon on Main Street in Akron. The only vehicle in view is a horse-drawn carriage, but it was the incipient automotive boom and increased demand for rubber tires that soon cemented the relationship between Akron and communities in West Virginia.[5] The dramatic expansion of Akron's rubber tire industry during the first two decades of the twentieth century caused the city's population to increase nearly fivefold as the industry expanded and needed tens of thousands of additional workers. The influx of newcomers from West Virginia was critical to the industry's expansion and the city's development. This relationship proved so enduring that eventually half the city's population could trace their roots to Appalachia.[6]

Many of the early newcomers arrived from cities and towns in West Virginia. Although most of the early migrants could claim a family farm back home, most did not arrive in Akron directly from the farm. Rather, they had moved to larger towns within West Virginia and had been employed in non-agricultural fields—such as timber, oil, and coal—before heading to Akron.[7] The fact that so many migrants came from Parkersburg—the third-largest city in West Virginia and one on the Ohio border—is not surprising. The move to Akron was frequently the second or third in a series of moves for these migrants. By the early 1910s, it was common practice for the rubber manufacturers to recruit workers from all across the country, with the heaviest advertising in West Virginia and eastern Kentucky newspapers. Although thousands came in response to these recruitment efforts, the rubber industry's dramatic expansion required an ever-growing labor force. In addition to recruitment efforts by the rubber manufacturers, word-of-mouth news and family ties helped establish ties with the city that influenced the choice of destination of later migrants. Before the boom years of World War I prompted the first mass movement from rural areas to the industrial centers of the Midwest, Akron's sizable population of West Virginians had already earned the city the nickname, "the capital of West Virginia."

As the rubber industry expanded, tensions quickly emerged about the rubber companies' continual recruitment of new workers from outside the state. Reports of good jobs available in the city attracted newcomers even when jobs were in short supply. Local workers frequently complained that the rubber companies sought to have a ready surplus of labor in the city without regard for the hardships inflicted upon new arrivals or the competition for jobs created for existing workers when work became scarce. This problem arose because unsteady conditions of employment were common in the early rubber tire industry. In the early years of the automotive age, production levels and demand for labor in the tire industry were closely tied to the needs of automobile manufacturers, which varied considerably throughout the year. Peak months of production were frequently followed by slacker months during which employees were laid off until the manufacturer received new requisitions for tires. Thus, the seasonal needs of the manufacturers contributed greatly to the high level of labor turn-over that characterized the industry. The rubber company, admitted the president of Goodyear Tire & Rubber, Frank A. Seiberling, "employs these men for one season in the year to full capacity and then throws them out on the streets for a period of three to six months hunting a job."[8] In May and June of 1914, for example, the rubber factories laid off thousands of workers in Akron, with one factory alone discharging between 1,300 and 1,500 employees in a few weeks. During this period, the local YMCA reported that "scores of able-bodied men in Akron are actually on the verge of starvation because they cannot find work with which to earn food or money."[9] Yet, the rubber manufacturers continued to run advertisements in newspapers, and notices remained posted along high-ways that told of "the ideal conditions, easy work, and good wages of rubber workers." "I talked with one man who came here from West Virginia to get work in a rubber factory," reported a member of Akron's Central Labor Union. "He had only $4 when he arrived in Akron. He left a wife and two children at home. His money was gone and he could find no work and was becoming des-perate when I met him. He came here because he read an advertisement for men in the newspapers. The city is full of such men." For residents who already had concerns about the steady stream of newcomers arriving in Akron, the in-flux became more alarming when there was no work to be had, raising fears about the presence of so many unemployed young men who, unable to support themselves, might turn to crime.[10] During peak periods of production, how-ever, the rubber manufacturers depended on their ability to attract workers from neighboring states to fill their labor needs.

The practice of recruiting workers from West Virginia and elsewhere solved the manufacturers' problem of labor shortage, but created other problems. A high rate of labor turnover characterized the industry during peak periods, a pattern not unique to the rubber industry in the 1910s. Not only did many workers move from factory to factory looking for a more advantageous posi-tion, but many newcomers remained in the city for only a short while. Wages paid in the industry—which often exceeded Henry Ford's famous $5 a day—drew many to the city who had the intention of working only long enough to save some money before returning home. During World War I, Goodyear, B. F. Goodrich, and Firestone all averaged a loss of 6.5 percent of their labor force each week.[11] Although the rubber manufacturers often attributed this problem to an apparent fickleness among their employees, living conditions in a city grow-ing as quickly as Akron greatly contributed to the problem of labor turnover.

The industry's fluctuating demand for workers was but one of the uncer-tainties that confronted new arrivals. As a reporter observed in 1920, "Akron has grown so rapidly in the last few years that, although it lies in the heart of the Middle West, it bears some earmarks of a hurriedly set up mining camp—the excess of men, the preponderance of young men, the surging crowds in the streets, the plants in operation when times are good in three shifts of eight hours each, except on Sunday."[12] While the city's population grew by leaps and bounds, the available housing stock did not. Thus, in the winter of 1916-1917, an estimated 80 percent of the 6,670 men provided beds on a nightly basis by the Salvation Army were able to pay rent, but could not locate rooms available at a reasonable price.[13] Furthermore, as the cost of renting or purchasing a home soared, it became prohibitively expensive for many new arrivals to bring their families with them to the city. During the war, rents in Akron were 25 to 40 percent higher than rates in comparable cities, thus creating an additional diffi-culty for newcomers. By 1919, between eight thousand and ten thousand mar-ried men lived in Akron while supporting their families back home.[14] Company newsletters were filled with items about workers' visits back home, reporting for example, "Red Evans paid a visit to Wheeling a few days ago. He brought the news back that he was the father of a fine baby girl. The next time he visits his home we suspect that he will be wheeling the baby buggy."[15] This sort of com-muting arrangement put strains on families, but also meant workers had a place to return to during hard times.

As Akron became a magnet for job seekers from West Virginia and else-where, the city was unable to cope with its rapid population growth and living conditions deteriorated. As rents skyrocketed with increased demand, families who had once rented homes found themselves evicted by landlords who wished to convert single-family homes into boardinghouses. An investigation ordered by Harvey Firestone found many employees affected by this problem, including some members of management. When suitable family housing was unavailable, some employees sent their families to live temporarily with other relatives.[16] Furthermore, Akron developed alarmingly high rates of disease and infant mor-tality as conditions became overcrowded and municipal sanitation services failed to keep pace with the growth.[17] Business streets were unpaved in places and few residential ones were paved at all. In Akron's public schools, spending per pupil fell far below the national average for a city its size, and the "migratory" nature of the student population further undermined the educational system.[18]

Faced with such conditions, many newcomers to Akron found conditions less auspicious than anticipated. The city's own newspaper described living conditions in the city as "damnable . . . a menace to growth, prosperity, [and] sanity."[19] Many newcomers discovered that advertised wages did not translate into an improved quality of life. The growth of the industry created jobs that drew thousands to the city, but the soaring cost of living offset the promise of good wages. "The worker who comes here now finds that if he wants a house in which to locate his family he must be willing to part with not less than 40 per cent of his earnings as a rental for such a property," complained a reporter for the *People*. "If he wants to purchase, he must bind himself about the neck with a millstone and sink or swim as best he may."[20] Such disillusionment discouraged many from establishing permanent roots in the city. Many left to find work in other Akron factories, some returned to their home states, and others left Akron for opportunities elsewhere. Approximately two-thirds of all employees who quit neglected even to notify their foreman or supervisor that they were leaving.[21] Manufacturers experienced constant frustration that good wages were not sufficient to maintain employee loyalty and a stable workforce. Factory managers expressed their belief that the problem stemmed from the fact that many new recruits were simply too "green" and "thin-skinned" to stick it out. According to one factory superintendent:

> Out of seven men . . . I would lose two in the first forty hours. These men were thin-skinned strangers, who couldn't stand the good-natured kidding of their fellow-workers about the color of their hair or the cut of their clothes. They hadn't the stamina to stick. We give every new man special instruction for six days. At the end of the time his teacher has to back more or less away from him in order to pay some attention to somebody else who has come in meantime. And at this point two more men of the seven would go, thin-skinned ducks who hadn't followed the instruction or grasped the operation, and felt lost when the teacher let up on his attention a bit; a letter comes from home, or the room and board aren't just what they should be, whereupon these drop out. Then we have three left of the seven, and if we can hold two of these over a period of seven months and carry the third on indefinitely we think we are doing well.[22]

In an attempt to secure worker loyalty and diminish turnover rates, the rubber manufacturers offered new amenities for their workers and Goodyear and Firestone established home-building programs to alleviate the housing shortage. Nonetheless—even as wages paid by the rubber tire industry came to surpass wages paid by virtually every other industry—employee loyalty remained weak.[23]

High rates of labor turnover were certainly not unique to the rubber industry in the early twentieth century. Indeed, similar patterns of labor turnover characterized the mining industry in West Virginia, where five of the six coalfields in the nation with the highest rates of labor turnover were located.[24] At one

West Virginia mine, for example, out of fifty-eight men hired in November 1904, only twenty remained with the company ten months later; by March 1906, there remained but twelve of the original miners.[25] In his study of the southern West Virginia mines, historian David Alan Corbin examined why coal miners in the region were slow to embrace unionization. Corbin found that the native West Virginians, southern blacks, and European immigrants who went to work in the coalfields of southern West Virginia came predominately from nonunion backgrounds. Furthermore, many of them, particularly the native West Virginians, viewed mining as a temporary, or occasional, vocation.

> [The miners] cared little for making the coal fields a permanent home and a decent place in which to live and work. . . . The native miners were farmers and seemed intent on returning to their farms rather than making a career of mining coal. In fact, many of them kept their farms and returned to them during slack runs or strikes. . . . Bent on mining and earning their daily bread, or getting rich and moving on, or returning to their farms, the miners . . . were quick to accept both company promises and advice to stay away from the union.[26]

This tendency to regard mining as a part-time vocation became a source of vexation for mine operators and led to an increased reliance on immigrant labor. Investigating conditions in the coalfields in 1920, Mabel Brown Ellis reported:

> Alabama, West Virginia and Virginia have . . . seen the native white and negro labor in their mines largely, and in some cases wholly, displaced by foreign-born labor because, in the first place, the industry has expanded beyond the point where the native-born supply is large enough to fill the demand for workmen and, second, because both the negroes and the mountain born white men are universally considered by mine operators more inefficient and irregular employees than the foreign-born, and are replaced by them whenever possible.[27]

In addition, business "experts" noted that the independent nature of work in mining inculcated a spirit of resistance to the imposition of factory discipline. One author went so far as to list "those who have come from the coal mines, particularly the bituminous mines of our country" as among the "class of men to be avoided for industrial plants." The author specifically cited the impossibility of continuous supervision in mining where the foreman visits "once or twice a day . . . every approach heralded by the echoing foot-falls . . . and the flash from the lamp which adorns every head" as creating work habits ill-suited to factory work. "Transplant such a man into a factory where production is speeded and no imagination is required to picture what will happen. The ex-miner resents all suggestion as to his working methods, resents all effort to compel continuous application, and assumes in general a hostile attitude toward supervision."[28]

In many ways, the labor mobility patterns in the southern West Virginia mines paralleled those that vexed the Akron rubber manufacturers in the 1910s. As rubber workers would move between the various rubber factories in Akron, so southern West Virginia miners readily expressed to their employers any dissatisfaction with wages, facilities, or treatment by quitting and seeking out a different position. In addition, the family homestead—of relatively close proximity in both cases—presented a convenient alternative for many workers if they found their working situation unsatisfactory. Not only did the farm provide a refuge during harsh economic times when work became scarce, but also some West Virginia miners and rubber workers viewed their occupations as a source of temporary supplemental income, rather than a permanent career. Thus, many of them took employment on a short-term basis, with the expectation of returning home in a few months.

Despite their complaints about employees new to industry being too "green," when faced with the choice between an immigrant labor force and native-born workers, the rubber tire manufacturers had long preferred a native-born, English-speaking workforce. This preference only intensified in the wake of an abortive organizing effort, in 1913, by the Industrial Workers of the World— the embodiment of the dangerous foreign radical influence in the public mind— which, although a failure, paralyzed the industry for several weeks. The desire to hire only American workers was strongest at Goodyear, which regularly turned down applicants who could not read or speak English, even when the company needed more workers.[29] During World War I, Goodyear embraced the "100% Americanism" the war gave rise to and established a policy of hiring Americans whenever possible and requiring any employee who was not a citizen to become one.[30] At a time when immigrants composed the majority of America's industrial workers, 80 percent of Goodyear's employees were native-born.[31] Due to the company's heavy reliance on labor recruited from neighboring states, by the late 1920s the number of workers born in West Virginia and Kentucky nearly equaled the number of native Ohioans employed by Goodyear.[32]

Like most American industries, the rubber industry suffered a severe contraction in the aftermath of World War I. By early 1921, employment had dropped from its peak of approximately one hundred thousand workers, to around one-third that level.[33] For those who had come to Akron anticipating sustained employment, the depression hit hard and prompted many workers from West Virginia to return home. City relief offices made thirty-six thousand visits to the homes of families requesting assistance in the first half of 1921.[34] One West Virginia couple reported they had left home because of limited opportunities for work in their small farming community. The husband came from a large family and had left school after the sixth grade to help with the family farm. A staff member from Akron's Social Service Exchange visited their home in late 1921 after the couple requested assistance. They had both worked for Goodyear, but had been laid off and had already exhausted their limited savings. The husband had only two-months work since the previous autumn and the couple was living in an attic room, the only heat provided by a hot plate. Unlike many West Virginians who returned home during this period, the couple had no place to go. Both of their families struggled to make ends meet on their farms in West Virginia and could neither take them in nor offer any assistance.[35]

Such periods of economic distress exacerbated the unease felt by many locals about the flood of newcomers in the city and again raised protests against the rubber companies' recruitment practices. Indeed, the superintendent of Akron's State-City Employment Bureau regarded "the great number of men coming here from the south, from Tennessee, Kentucky and Alabama, every day" to be the major source of those applying for work during the recession. The city created a Special Committee on Unemployment in early 1922 to deal with the rising number of unemployed in Akron. The committee blamed the problem on "a story [that] had been sent from Akron that conditions were normal and industry booming."[36] As business revived during 1922, the industry again provoked ire when the Chamber of Commerce announced that one thousand men were to be recruited from outside the city to fill positions as tire builders. The rubber manufacturers claimed that although thirteen hundred men applied weekly at the State-City Free Labor Exchange, they lacked the necessary experience or were physically not qualified.[37] Protests came not only from rubber workers (employed and unemployed), who cited estimates that three thousand rubber workers in the city were currently unemployed and many of those fortunate to be working were reduced to three-day weeks.[38] Even the Akron *Beacon Journal* questioned: "Is this really the case or is it a method to insure a surplus of Labor? One does not know, but one suspects that this thing has been done rather freely in the past. . . . [I]t does seem strange when but a few weeks ago the papers were being importuned to aid in finding work for thousands that could not find it for themselves we should now begin to import labor."[39] As the 1920s progressed, the number of newcomers who reported coming to Akron in response to advertisements in out-of-town newspapers waned. Akron, however, remained a popular destination point and many West Virginians "came on their own initiative, thinking they could locate something anyway."[40]

Although the mid-1920s are popularly regarded as a prosperous period, Southern Appalachia did not share in the prosperity. Those employed in agriculture and coal mining struggled throughout the decade. Low agricultural prices had repeatedly provoked crises in farming communities, which was a major factor behind the city-ward movement from rural areas. A poor year in agriculture often left families with starkly limited chances for survival. For example, a year spent tending to his tobacco crop netted Garland Carl Parsons' father a profit of only twenty-three cents. After years of struggling to make ends meet, he decided to abandon his farm near Ripley, West Virginia, and moved his family to Akron where father, and later son, made their careers in the rubber industry.[41] The 1920s also witnessed the first great outpouring from the coal regions of Appalachia, as over two hundred thousand miners abandoned the coalfields between 1923 and 1927, as wages slipped steadily downward and fewer days of employment became the prevalent trend.[42] Such poor economic conditions helped to sustain the migration that began during World War I.

The rubber industry's reliance on workers from West Virginia meant thousands left the city to return home with the onset of the Great Depression. Nationwide, rural-to-urban migration abated and even reversed as unemployment rates rose dramatically in the early 1930s. In Akron, the number of workers employed by the rubber industry declined by approximately 43 percent in the first years of the depression.[43] Yet even during 1932, the depression's worst year, an estimated forty thousand natives of West Virginia remained in Akron.[44] The depression exacerbated underlying tensions in the city and provoked vocal criticisms about those "outsiders" competing for work when jobs were scarce. Gerald Udell recalled the antagonism toward West Virginians and other southern migrants:

> In my childhood, the terms *snakes* and *hillbillies* were used frequently by native Akronites about such persons. There was resentment especially during the depression days of the thirties, and the stories were widespread of West Virginians who collected relief money in Akron and lived handsomely from it in their mountain shacks. Their pronunciation was mocked. Their distinctive lexicon was made the butt of jokes. The association was massive and thorough in Akron between ignorance, shiftlessness, and illiteracy and the West Virginians, Tennesseeans, Georgians, etc.[45]

In addition to the strain of hard times, locals often blamed the southern newcomers for the labor upheaval and strikes that wracked the city in the 1930s. The struggle for union recognition in Akron was a protracted battle that witnessed the first organizing campaign to use the "sit-down" strike. Although the participation of so many West Virginians in the creation of the United Rubber Workers of America was simply a reflection of their strong presence in the factories, for those opposed to the movement, they made easy scapegoats.

Many of the rubber workers from West Virginia had memories of, and some actively participated in, the struggle to unionize mining in their home state. As future vice president of the United Rubber Workers Joe Childs recalled, one "glimpse of the conditions in the coal mines started [his] interest in the labor movement."[46] Experience organizing the United Mine Workers prepared many for the strong resistance by the rubber manufacturers to the recognition of any labor union. Frank Easterling, for example, was a member of the United Mine Workers before he moved his family to Akron and began working for B. F. Goodrich. During the organizing drive of 1936-1938, he was beaten one night by Pinkerton guards outside a pharmacy. He and his wife became involved in the effort to organize the United Rubber Workers, which provoked retribution from the rubber companies. The family lived in company housing, their daughter recalled, and "the company shut off our electricity because of my parents' union activism." [47] While the rubber manufacturers attempted to quash the United Rubber Workers, many residents singled out workers from West Virginia and Kentucky as the troublemakers behind all the strike agitation. "Akron citizens must we tolerate these pesky invaders?" questioned one resident. "Why don't we grab them by the seat of the pants and send them home to their mountains where they can start anything they want?"[48]

Although tensions became most acute during slack economic times, both native Akronites and newcomers in the city had long attempted to overcome divisions in the community. Concern first arose as Akron's booming wartime factories prompted heavy in-migration during World War I. Residents became increasingly concerned about how the city and its newcomers could adjust during Akron's rapid transformation. The war years attracted as many as seventy-seven thousand newcomers from West Virginia alone and the process of becoming integrated into the community was one problem facing new arrivals.[49] As in many boomtowns, taverns proliferated in Akron, but other avenues for social gatherings were limited. This situation was a concern for local ministers who noted that "young men had a social life among their own kind where they had lived. They come here and find no social life open to them . . . they are barred from the home life of the community."[50] Community leaders feared new arrivals were apt to fall prey to con artists and were more susceptible to the temptations available in the city. "Thousands of young married people, attracted here by spreading rumors of Akron's unlimited prosperity," noted Judge E. D. Fritch, "find temptation waiting for them and their easily earned money."[51] Akron's domestic relations court judge, H. C. Spicer, echoed this sentiment, noting that men "are prone to go wrong when they come to Akron to work and fail to find homes here to which to bring their families. They are very apt to become entangled in affairs with young girls or else take to gambling or drinking."[52]

Members of the Goodyear Industrial Assembly (akin to a company union) expressed similar concerns about the failure, or disinterest, of newcomers in becoming more involved in community activities. They especially noted that, "Too many people who come to Akron . . . fail to identify themselves with any church. . . . No matter how staunch church members they were in their home-towns, when they get here they forget all about their church connections."[53] Some local churches attempted to reach out to newcomers by inviting evange-lists from West Virginia to speak as guest preachers and designated certain evenings as "West Virginia night."[54] Yet, while there was much truth underlying the impression of a city teeming with newcomers and plagued by growing so-cial disorder, many of those who settled permanently in the city did establish new churches. Between 1910 and 1920 alone, the number of Baptist churches in the city rose from five to twenty-five and the number of Methodist churches increased from twelve to twenty-four.[55] Over time, religious life became one area of community life where the presence of so many natives of Southern Ap-palachia was most noticeable. The Akron Baptist Temple attendance regularly overflowed its seating capacity of twenty-six hundred at services when it opened in 1938. Its Sunday school was reportedly the largest in the world with over thirteen hundred children enrolled.[56] When the church's founder, Dallas Billington, arrived from Calloway County, Kentucky, in 1925, he was distressed to find "many people from the South who were not attending church. They had churches at home in the states from which they had come. They went to church at home regularly but, coming to Akron and away from the churches they were used to, they just did not attend anywhere. It was easy for them to drift from the teachings they had known back home."[57]

The large influx of West Virginians during World War I also inspired the formation of the West Virginia Society. On August 5, 1917, a gathering of eight hundred former residents of West Virginia established the organization with the goal of strengthening the bonds between West Virginians living in Akron and fostering friendly relations with local residents.[58] Initial membership drew heavily from new employees of the rubber factories, at times meeting at the Firestone Club House. The organization declared itself dedicated to promoting "the prosperity and general welfare of the rubber city."[59] Guests at meetings often included local politicians and business leaders, as well as special speakers from West Virginia. During its early years, the task of fostering more positive relations between West Virginians and Ohioans remained central to the organization's activities. Thus, "What West Virginia and Ohio Have in Common" was the theme of a speech given by a local judge at one outdoor meeting,[60]

Although residing in Akron, many West Virginia natives closely followed news and politics from their home state. Indeed, West Virginia's absentee vot-ing procedure was described as "one of the best, if not the best" in the nation and allowed many to cast votes from Akron.[61] Although the city's population more than tripled in the 1910s, the number of male citizens who voted increased only 87 percent between 1913 and 1919.[62] The large number of potential absentee voters in Akron thus facilitated the organization's ability to attract special visits from West Virginia politicians, including former Governor Howard Gore. Most speakers, however, encouraged West Virginians to become more fully involved in their new community. Appearing on behalf of Governor William Conley, his son-in-law and private secretary told an audience: "Now that you have made Ohio your home, you must take an active part in civic affairs, you must build your homes here and you must receive your education here, to better yourselves for the responsibility of becoming good citizens."[63]

Despite its sponsorship of special speakers, the organization was avowedly non-partisan and functioned primarily as a social club. The West Virginia Society was in its heyday in the 1930s, as it hosted social events throughout the year. The organization's most popular event was its annual picnic that attracted as many as 25,000 people—including some who came from West Virginia to enjoy the festivities and reunite with friends and family—and featured guest speakers and politicians from Ohio and West Virginia. The daylong event featured games as well as contests to choose a Miss West Virginia and bestow upon one man and woman the more dubious "honor" of "most homely."

Although West Virginians composed a sizable minority of the city's population from the beginning of the automotive age, antagonism toward them remained, emerging most vocally during tough economic times. Periodically, attacks on West Virginia and its citizens spilled over into the press. For example, the *Beacon Journal*—perhaps to be deliberately provocative or simply demonstrating poor judgment—reprinted this scathing assessment of West Virginia on its editorial page.

> Possessing the greatest natural resources of any state among the forty-eight, in timber, coal, oil, gas and waterpower, she has dissipated her natural resources and has not one city worthy of the name; no great buildings; no arts; no sciences. . . . A little while ago I met an aspirant for a place in the state legislative halls who was making a canvass with the slogan, "get a law passed to make compulsory the reading of the Bible in the public schools." He admitted he did not know how to draw up such a bill, but thought he could get some lawyer to do it. Do people really live in West Virginia? No they only exist, not knowing or caring how or why.[64]

Predictably, the story infuriated local West Virginians who, while resigned to some good-natured kidding about their home state, would not patiently abide such an outrageous attack. A torrent of outrage against the newspaper for printing the article and attacks on the author for his "ignorant" remarks followed its publication.[65] Dozens of letters defending the state and extolling its history and merits filled the paper for weeks. The blanket negative characterizations of the state infuriated West Virginians who had made their homes in Akron. In another instance, a newspaper reporter—attempting to put a humorous spin on a commonplace situation—wrote an account of a judge who ordered a man arrested for a minor offense in Akron to return to West Virginia and never return to the city. The story's headline announced the man had been "sentenced to life" in West Virginia. The story would be of no consequence, except that other newspapers picked it up and the resulting furor brought so much condemnation that it effectively doomed the judge's campaign for a seat on the appellate court.[66] Such widespread "Tobacco Road" characterizations of West Virginia were surprisingly enduring and the *Beacon Journal* helped to sustain this image. Front-page articles such as "West Virginia Mother, Sons Dazzled by Akron Sights"—which reported that "all the myriad complexities of modern civilization are all new to the family from the West Virginia hills"—served to perpetuate the stereotype of a state thoroughly permeated by ignorance and backwardness.[67]

Thus, long before post-World War II economic crises caused the great outpouring from West Virginia, its residents faced an uneasy reception in Akron and other Ohio cities. Fears that the influx of newcomers added to problems of unemployment and poor living conditions intensified in later decades when West Virginia's struggling economy prompted a mass exodus from the state. In Akron, job opportunities created by the rubber industry continued to act as a magnet for workers in the decades following the Great Depression, but on a less dramatic scale. World War II caused another wartime boom that motivated thousands to leave West Virginia, and Akron again experienced the influx of thousands of newcomers as employment in the city's rubber factories increased by 41 percent between 1940 and 1945.[68] Yet, out-migration from West Virginia only peaked during the 1950s, when mechanization of the coal industry caused soaring rates of unemployment in the coal-mining regions and spurred a mass exodus. By that time, other cities in Ohio offered better opportunities than Akron. The outpouring from West Virginia continued through the 1960s and into the 1970s, but fewer and fewer migrants would set their sights upon Akron.[69]

The rubber industry, which had encouraged the out-migration from West Virginia with its labor recruitment tactics and hiring policies, was no longer a magnet for job-seekers as the industry decentralized its operations and gradually closed its factories in the city. By the 1950s, the city was beginning to stagnate. Fewer individuals were moving to Akron and natives of Appalachia composed only one-fifth of all out-of-state newcomers arriving in the city.[70] The number of workers employed by Akron's rubber factories, which reached an all-time peak in 1920 at 73,000, declined to 30,000 in 1957, and to only 12,300 in

1977.[71] As a once-thriving industrial center in the process of decay, Akron was no longer a promising destination point for those who were leaving West Virginia for mainly economic reasons. Once touted as the "City of Opportunity," Akron was one of the most rapidly declining cities in America in the late twentieth century, with a declining population and sluggish per capita income growth.[72] While the city is still noted for its large population of West Virginians, the distinctions made based on origins have faded. Other Ohio cities, such as Cleveland and Cincinnati, experienced their heaviest influx of newcomers from West Virginia in later decades and saw the emergence of "little West Virginias" in inner-city neighborhoods. Akron's relationship with West Virginia, however, predates the heaviest period of out-migration from the state and, despite experiencing early difficulties, West Virginians became thoroughly integrated into the community.

NOTES

1, Data for years 1940-1950 taken from U.S. Bureau of the Census, *Census of Population: 1950, Vol. 4, Special Reports*, Part 4, Chapter A, Table 8. Data for 1950-1960 taken from U.S. Bureau of the Census, *Components of Population Change, 1950 to 1960*, Series P-23, No. 7.

2. James Branscome, "Annihilating the Hillbilly: The Appalachians' Struggle with America's Institutions," *Katallagete* (3): 29.

3. Quoted in Robert Coles, *The South Goes North*, vol. 3, *Children of Crisis* (Boston: Little, Brown and Co., 1967), 618-9.

4. Dan M. McKee and Phillip J. Obermiller, *From Mountain to Metropolis: Urban Appalachians in Ohio* (Cincinnati: Urban Appalachian Council, 1978), 1.

5. Kenneth Nichols, *Yesterday's Akron: The First 150 Years* (Miami: E. A. Seemann Publishing, Inc., 1976), 51.

6. McKee and Obermiller, *From Mountain to Metropolis*, 1.

7. Author's survey of Local History Collection, Akron-Summit Metropolitan Library, Akron, Ohio (hereafter cited as Akron-Summit).

8. Howard Wolf and Ralph Wolf, *Rubber: A Story of Glory and Greed* (New York: Covici Friede, 1936), 497.

9. Akron *Beacon Journal*, 6 May 1914.

10. Ibid., 3 June 1914.

11. Ibid., 15 October 1917.

12. Frederick M. Davenport, "Treating Men White in Akron Town," *The Outlook* 126 (3 November 1920): 407.

13. Akron *Beacon Journal*, 23 February 1917.

14. Harvey S. Firestone, *Men and Rubber: The Story of Business* (New York: Doubleday, Page, 1926), 245.

15. *Firestone Non-Skid*, 1 (April 1917).

16. Alfred Lief, *The Firestone Story: A History of the Firestone Tire & Rubber Company* (New York: McGraw-Hill, 1951), 95.

17. Theresa S. Halley, "Infant Mortality: Results of a Field Study in Akron, Ohio, Based on Births in One Year." U. S. Department of Labor, Children's Bureau No. 72. (Washington, D. C.: GPO, 1920), 58-65.

18. Horace L. Brittain, *Report on the Schools of Akron* (Akron: Educational Committee of the Chamber of Commerce, 1917), 33.

19. Akron *Beacon Journal*, 27 April 1920.

20. *The People*, 13 December 1918.

21. Alfred Winslow Jones, *Life, Liberty, and Property: A Story of Conflict and a Measurement of Conflicting Rights* (Philadelphia: J. B. Lippincott Company, 1941), 78

22. Davenport, "Treating Men White," 407.

23. U.S. Bureau of the Census, *Fourteenth Census of the United States, 1920, Volume 9: Census of Manufactures*, 1180.

24. David Alan Corbin, *Life, Work, and Rebellion in the Coal Fields: The Southern West Virginia Miners, 1880-1922* (Chicago: University of Illinois Press, 1981), 41.
25. Ibid., 40.
26. Ibid., 27.
27. Mabel Brown Ellis, "Children of the Kentucky Coal Fields," *The American Child* 1 (February 1920): 313.
28. H. A. Haring, "Three Classes of Labor to Avoid: Prejudices and Habits Displayed by Men in Certain Occupations," *Factory and Industrial Management* 62 (December 1921): 372.
29. Letter to Vincent S. Stevens, Secretary, Akron Chamber of Commerce, 7 March 1912, F. A. Seiberling Papers, MSS 347, Box 4, Ohio Historical Society, Columbus, Ohio.
30. Paul W. Litchfield, *Industrial Voyage: My Life as an Industrial Lieutenant* (New York: Doubleday, 1954), 175.
31. "Study of Methods of Americanization," David Saposs Papers, Box 21, folder 4, State Historical Society of Wisconsin, Madison.
32. Hugh Allen, *House of Goodyear* (Akron, Ohio: Superior Printing & Litho. Co., 1936), 294.
33. Akron *Beacon Journal*, 19 February 1921.
34. Ibid., 13 July 1921.
35. Daniel Nelson Papers, Box 6, University of Akron Archives, Akron, Ohio.
36. Akron *Beacon Journal*, 21 January 1922.

37. Ibid., 29 April 1922.
38. Ibid., 3 May 1922.
39. Ibid., 1 May 1922.
40. Ibid., 21 January 1925.
41. "Garland Carl Parsons," Local History Collection, Akron-Summit.
42. Ronald D Eller, *Miners, Millhands, and Mountaineers: Industrialization of the Appalachian South, 1880-1930* (Knoxville: University of Tennessee Press, 1982), 157.
43. Daniel Nelson, *American Rubber Workers and Organized Labor* (Princeton, N.J.: Princeton University Press, 1988), 113.
44. Akron *Beacon Journal*, 10 March 1932.
45. Gerald Udell, "The Speech of Akron, Ohio: The Segmental Phonology—A Study of the Effects of Rapid Industrialization on the Speech of a Community" (Ph.D. diss., University of Chicago, 1966), 78.
46. "Joseph William Childs," Local History Collection, Akron-Summit.
47. "Barbara Easterling," Local History Collection, Akron-Summit.
48. Akron *Beacon Journal*, 1 June 1938.
49. Jones, *Life, Liberty, and Property*, 61.
50 . Akron *Beacon Journal*, 11 April 1916.
51. Akron *Evening Times*, 9 July 1920.
52. Ibid., 11 April 1920.
53. *Goodyear Wingfoot Clan*, 7 June 1921.

54. Akron *Evening Times*, 28 February 1917.

55. Bob Downing, "Akron, West Virginia," *Mountain Review* 2 (May 1976): 5.

56. *Akron Baptist Temple: Fifty Golden Years, 1935-1985* (Akron, Ohio: Akron Baptist Temple, 1985), 16. Western Reserve Historical Society, Cleveland, Ohio.

57. Dallas Billington, *God Is Real: A Testament in the Form of an Autobiography* (New York: David McKay Co., Inc., [1962]), 28.

58. Akron *Beacon Journal*, 6 August 1917; 14 August 1917.

59. *Goodyear Wingfoot Clan*, 26 September 1917.

60. Akron *Evening Times, 13 July 1918.*

61. *Parkersburg News,* 8 August 1938.

62. *Goodyear Wingfoot Clan*, 1 October 1920.

63. Akron *Beacon Journal*, 4 August 1930.

64. Ibid., 9 March 1927.

65. Ibid., 23 March 1927.

66. Wolf and Wolf, *Rubber,* 436-7.

67. Akron *Beacon Journal*, 11 September 1936.

68. Charles A. Jeszeck, "Plant Dispersion and Collective Bargaining in the Rubber Tire Industry" (Ph.D. diss., University of California, Berkeley, 1982), 35.

69. Clyde B. McCoy and James S. Brown, "Appalachian Migrants to Midwestern Cities," in *The Invisible Minority: Urban Appalachians*, ed. William W. Philliber and Clyde B. McCoy (Lexington: University Press of Kentucky, 1981), 53-7.

70. U.S. Bureau of the Census, *Census of Population: 1960*, Final Report PC(2)-2E, *Subject Reports, Migration between State Economic Areas* (Washington, D.C.: GPO, 1967).

71. Nelson, *American Rubber Workers,* 78; Mansel G. Blackford and K. Austin Kerr, *BFGoodrich: Tradition and Transformation, 1870-1995* (Columbus: Ohio State University Press, 1996), 311.

72. Akron *Beacon Journal*, 4 March 1993.

About the Contributors

Kenneth R. Bailey retired as dean of the College of Business, Humanities, and Sciences at West Virginia University Institute of Technology, Montgomery, W.Va. He is an authority on West Virginia labor history and has been a frequent contributor to *West Virginia History*.

Frederick A. Barkey retired as professor of industial relations at Marshall University Graduate College, Institute, W.Va. He is an expert on West Virginia ethnic and labor history and has published in *West Virginia History*.

Elizabeth Cometti was a professor of history at West Virginia University. She published numerous articles on West Virginia history, and with Festus P. Summers coedited *The Thirty-Fifth State: A Documentary History of West Virginia* (1966). She is deceased.

Ken Fones-Wolf is associate professor of history at West Virginia University. In addition to numerous articles on labor history, he is the author of *Trade Union Gospel: Christianity and Labor in Industrial Philadelphia, 1865-1915* (1989). Currently, he is resn "Glass Towns: Labor, Capital, and Social Change in West Virginia, 1890-1940," which has received support from the West Virginia Humanities Council.

Susan Johnson is a Ph.D. candidate and lecturer at Ohio State University. Her doctoral dissertation, "The Southern Exodus: A Case Study," has received support from the Ohio Bicentennial Commission. She has published an article in the *Journal of Appalachian Studies*, and several encyclopedia articles and book reviews.

William B. Klaus is a Ph.D. candidate in history at West Virginia University where he is writing a dissertation on "Italians and Catholicism in West Virginia." Currently, he is teaching at Alderson-Broaddus College, Philippi, W.Va.

Anne Kelly Knowles is assistant professor of geography at Middlebury College, Middlebury, Vt. Among her numerous publications is *Calvinists Incorporated: Welsh Immigrants on Ohio's Industrial Frontier* (1997). She recently completed a study of the American iron industry to the Civil War.

Ronald L. Lewis is Stuart and Joyce Robbins Chair in History at West Virginia University. His most recent book is *Transforming the Appalachian Countryside: Railroads, Deforestation, and Social Change in West Virginia, 1880-1920* (1998). Currently, he is completing a book on the role of Welsh immigrants in the American coal industry.

Matthew Mason received his Ph.D. in history from the University of Maryland (2002). He has several publications including an article in *Labor History*. Currently, he is assistant professor of history at Eastern Michigan University, Ypsilanti, Mich.

Joe William Trotter Jr. is Mellon Bank Professor of History and chair of the history department at Carnegie Mellon University, Pittsburgh, Pa. Among his numerous books and articles is *Coal, Class, and Color: Blacks in Southern West Virginia, 1915-32* (1990).

Deborah R. Weiner received a Ph.D. in history at West Virginia University (2002) where she wrote a dissertation on "Jews in the Coalfields of Central Appalachia." She has published articles in several scholarly journals including the *Journal of Appalachian Studies*, *West Virginia History*, and *Journal of the Jewish Archives*.

Index

Addams, Jane 286

African-Americans xii–xiv, xvi–xvii, 21, 65, 122, 169, 243, 247, 262–63, 265, 270, 273–74, 278, 280, 289, 304; and Great Migration 137, 139; and United Mine Workers 144–45, 151–52, 169; as coal miners 137–53, 169, 248–49, 255; families and migration 142–44, 146; Great Depression and 149–51; Hawk's Nest tragedy 150, 153; recruitment of 141–43; voting rights 140, 152; women 143, 148–49; Akron, Ohio xviii, 299–303, 305–12

Alabama 139–43, 145, 304, 306

Alien Contract Labor Law (1903) 250, 253–54, 256

Alloy, W.Va. 162

Alpena 57–62, 65

Alsace 53, 56, 83

American Federation of Labor 128, 251, 366

American Friends Service Committee 278, 284–86, 288

American Window Glass Company 119, 123–24

Americanization xvii–xviii, 194, 204, 209–11, 261, 268–70, 272–74, 284–86, 305

Anglo-Saxons 262, 273

Arthurdale, W.Va. 289

Austria-Hungary 53, 74, 77, 80, 82–84, 86, 244, 248, 278

B&O (see Baltimore & Ohio Rail Road)

B.F. Goodrich Co. 301, 308

Baden, Germany 22, 24

Baldwin, George, 253–54

Baldwin-Felts detectives 142, 170, 173, 175, 244–45

Baltimore, Md. 9, 24, 53, 73, 92–93, 96–98, 116, 243–44

Baltimore & Ohio Rail Road x, xii, xv, 20–22, 25, 27, 53, 55, 92, 218, 220–21, 243, 262; Irish labor on, 3–13

Baltimore Bargain House 93–94

Basel-Stadt 51–52, 59

Bavaria 22, 24

Beckley, W.Va. 73–74, 85, 95–98, 178

Behner, Mary 287–88

Belgian Workers party 116–17

Belgians xiii–xiv, xvi, 113; communities and customs 113–17, 120–23; cooperative factories 119–21, 125; in mass production factories 126–29; influence in the Knights of Labor 116–21; insulation of 122–23; mobility of 117–18, 121–22, 127; politics of 119–20, 124–26; transnational labor markets of 114–18

Belgium 54, 113, 115–20, 123, 124–25, 183

Berger, Jacob 27, 32, 35, 37

Bern, Switzerland 59–60

Black Diamond 264–65

Bluefield, W.Va. 74, 149, 244

Bolshevism 392

Boomer, W.Va. xvi, 162–76, 178, 183–84

Boone County 146, 174–75, 251

British 9, 65, 231, 362, 265, 270

Buchanan, James 29

Buersner, John 26, 32, 64

Bulgarians 247

Burns, Robert 233–34

Cabin Creek, W.Va. 142, 167, 172–74, 176–78, 182–84

Calabria xvi, 165, 184, 193, 196–97, 199

Campania 165, 193, 197, 201

Campbell, Archibald 30–32, 36, 224, 226, 230

Cannelton, W.Va. 173

Cassville, W.Va. 265